Ronel Dorvil

Study Guide to accompany

Fundamentals of Nursing

CONCEPTS, PROCESS, AND PRACTICE

SECOND EDITION

KATHLEEN G. HOOVER, RN, MSN
Instructor
Barnes Hospital School of Nursing
St. Louis, Missouri

Printed in the United States of America

The C. V. Mosby Company

ST. LOUIS • BALTIMORE • PHILADELPHIA • TORONTO

Preface

Students are continually challenged to apply theoretical concepts to clinical practice. The volume and complexity of information that must be mastered in order to administer safe, competent care may often seem overwhelming. *A Study Guide to Fundamentals of Nursing* has been developed to provide students with strategies to assist in learning and to reinforce essential theoretical concepts, skills, and techniques basic to nursing practice.

This study guide consists of 49 chapters that correspond to the chapters in the text *Fundamentals of Nursing: Concepts, Process, and Practice*. Each study guide chapter includes prerequisite reading, learning objectives, review of key concepts from the text, activities for application of key concepts, and a brief annotated reference list. An answer key for self-study questions is given at the end of the text.

Before beginning the study guide activities in a chapter, it is strongly recommended that students complete the "Prerequisite Reading" of the corresponding chapter in the *Fundamentals* text and review the "Objectives." Each chapter includes a "Review of Key Concepts." This section explores major concepts presented in the *Fundamentals* text through the use of a variety of objective questions. Students have the opportunity to reinforce and validate their understanding of fundamental concepts of nursing practice through true-false, matching, multiple-choice, fill-in, listing, and short-answer questions. Students should use their own paper for all sections that need answers. The section entitled "Answers to Review of Key Concepts" at the end of the book provides students with immediate feedback regarding their attainment of the learning objectives.

The "Application of Key Concepts" provides guidance for independent or small group activities that may be employed to reinforce skills, techniques, or theoretical concepts presented in the corresponding chapter of the text. These learning activities have been structured to allow students to initiate activities independently or to be incorporated by instructors into their teaching plans. The activities to reinforce skills and techniques include suggestions for activities that facilitate student practice of the technical skills described in the text. The activities to reinforce theoretical concepts include experiential exercises and clinical situations that require students to apply the concepts to an actual or simulated practice situation. The nature of the activities in this section prohibits providing an answer key. Although the general information needed to complete segments of these exercises may be found in the *Fundamentals* text, optimal learning will occur through interaction with peers and feedback from instructors.

The "Additional Readings" identify selected references from the chapter that may be particularly useful to the beginning nursing student. The annotated format is intended to present information that may stimulate interest and provide direction for further reading and study.

Although students may engage in a variety of learning experiences, content mastery rarely occurs without dedicated independent study. It is hoped that the learning activities presented in this study guide will facilitate this process.

Kathleen G. Hoover

Contents

UNIT 1 The Nurse, Client, and Health Care Environment

Chapter 1
The Profession of Nursing

PREREQUISITE READING

Read Chapter 1, pp. 1 to 33.

OBJECTIVES

Mastery of content in this chapter will enable the student to:

1. Define selected terms related to the profession of nursing.
2. Discuss the historical development of professional nursing.
3. Discuss the modern definitions and philosophies of nursing.
4. Describe educational programs for becoming a registered nurse.
5. Describe practice settings and roles for nurses.
6. Describe at least three career roles for nurses.
7. List the five characteristics of a profession and discuss how nursing demonstrates these characteristics.
8. Discuss the influence of social and economic changes on nursing practice.
9. Discuss the influence of nursing on political issues and health care policy.

REVIEW OF KEY CONCEPTS

1. Define nursing.
2. The nursing profession was founded by Florence Nightingale. (true or false)
3. Throughout history, both men and women have practiced nursing. (true or false)
4. Entry of women into nursing was due to:
   a. Improved social position of Roman women.
   b. Christian teachings of equality of men and women.
   c. The Christian mandate to care for those in distress.
   d. All of the above.
5. Match the name of each person with the appropriate contribution to nursing practice and health care.
   a. Florence Nightingale ____
   b. Clara Barton ____
   c. Mary Adelaide Nutting ____
   d. Mary Agnes Snively ____
   e. Isabel Hampton Robb ____
   f. Mary Brewster/Lillian Ward ____

   1. Initiated affiliation of nursing education with universities
   2. Founded the Canadian National Association of Trained Nurses, later named the Canadian Nurses Association
   3. Founded the Nurses' Association of Alumni of the United States and Canada, later named the American Nurses' Association (ANA)
   4. Established the first organized program for nursing education
   5. Expanded the nursing role in the community setting
   6. Founded the American Red Cross
6. The survey of nursing education that advocated financial support to university schools of nursing is the ____________
7. The study that clarified nursing roles and responsibilities in relation to other health care professionals is the ____________.
8. List at least five common goals of theoretical nursing models.
   a.
   b.
   c.
   d.
   e.
9. Match the nurse theorist with the appropriate nursing model description.
   a. Levine ____
   b. Johnson ____
   c. Rogers ____
   d. Orem ____
   e. King ____
   f. Travelbee ____
   g. Neuman ____
   h. Roy ____

   1. An adaptation model that contends that the need for nursing care arises when the client cannot adapt to internal or external demands. Nursing care focuses on assisting the client to adapt.
   2. A model of nursing practice that views the person as an open system interacting with stressors. Nurses assist individuals, families, and groups to attain and maintain an optimal level of wellness.

3. A model based on the self-care deficit theory in which the need for nursing arises when the individual is unable to fulfill his or her needs. The goal of nursing is directed toward helping the client attain self-care.
4. A model that defines nursing as a dynamic interpersonal process between the nurse, the client, and the health care system. The goal of nursing is to use communication in helping the client to positively adapt to the environment.
5. An adaptation model that views the human as an integrated whole interacting with and adapting to the environment. Nursing focuses on conservation activities aimed at optimal use of client's resources.
6. The unitary man theory that views the client as continually changing and coexisting with the environment. The goal of nursing is to maintain and promote health, prevent illness, and care for and rehabilitate the sick and disabled through the "humanistic science of nursing."
7. A model that focuses on the client's adaptation to illness and the impact of stressors on this process. Adaptation is based on basic needs in terms of seven categories of behavior. The goal of nursing is to reduce stress so that the client can move more easily through the recovery process.
8. A model in which nursing is viewed as a human-to-human relationship formed during illness and suffering. The goal of nursing is to assist the individual or family to prevent or cope with the experience of illness and suffering.

10. In the table below, compare the three most common programs by which an individual can become a registered nurse.

	Length of program	Educational institution	Degree granted	Program focus
Associate degree program				
Diploma program				
Baccalaureate program				

11. Registered nurse licensure requires completion of a prescribed course of study from a state board (USA) or provincial board (Canada) approved program and satisfactory performance on a written licensure examination. (true or false)
12. According to the ANA, what is the purpose of graduate nursing education?
13. Define continuing education.
14. Identify at least three goals of continuing education in nursing.
    a.
    b.
    c.
15. Selected states require nurses to take continuing education courses for license renewal. (true or false)
16. Define in-service education.
17. A mechanism for career mobility that seeks to promote nurses based on their clinical competencies rather than education and seniority within an institution is called a ______.
18. Describe how each of the following influence the practice of nursing care:
    a. Health care agencies and institutions
    b. Professional nursing organizations
    c. State or provincial nurse practice acts
19. The majority of nurses are employed in hospital settings. (true or false)
20. What impact have the diagnostic related groups (DRGs) had on nursing practice in the United States?
21. Identify three factors that have contributed to rising hospital acuity rates.
    a.
    b.
    c.
22. Identify three factors that have contributed to the growth of long-term care facilities.
    a.
    b.
    c.
23. Identify four major health-related activities of community-based agencies.
    a.
    b.
    c.
    d.
24. Briefly describe the nursing role in each of the following community-based settings.
    a. Community health centers
    b. Schools
    c. Occupational health
    d. Home health care agencies
25. Identify the role or function that the nurse fulfills in each of the following situations:
    a. The nurse feeds a client breakfast. ______
    b. The nurse answers a client's question about his or her medication. ______
    c. The nurse writes out an organizational plan for the day. ______
    d. The nurse provides emotional support to a client who is crying. ______
    e. The nurse teaches a client how to walk with crutches. ______
    f. The nurse tests the temperature of a baby's bath water to prevent burns. ______
26. The nursing role that is central to all other nursing roles is that of ______.
27. Match the career role (employment position) with

the most appropriate description of its work-related activities.

Career role

a. Nurse educator ____
b. Clinical nurse specialist ____
c. Nurse practitioner ____
d. Certified nurse-midwife ____
e. Nurse anesthetist ____
f. Nurse administrator ____
g. Nurse researcher ____

Work-related activity

1. Manages client care and delivery of nursing services within a health care agency
2. Provides independent care for women during normal pregnancy, labor, and delivery, as well as some routine gynecological services
3. Teaches nursing students; provides in-service education or patient teaching
4. Provides primary health care to clients, usually in outpatient, ambulatory, and community-based settings
5. Administers surgical anesthesia under the supervision of a physician
6. Investigates problems to improve nursing care and to define and expand the scope of nursing practice
7. Functions as a clinician, educator, manager, consultant, and researcher within a specific practice area

28. Fill in the role of each health care team member based on the descriptions provided.
a. An individual licensed to make a medical diagnosis and treat clients is a ____________.
b. An individual trained in certain aspects of medical practice who provides support to physicians is a ____________.
c. An individual licensed to assist in the examination, testing, and treatment of physically disabled or handicapped people through use of exercise and other treatment modalities is a ____________.
d. An individual licensed or certified to develop and use adaptive devices that help chronically ill or handicapped clients carry out activities of daily living is an ____________.
e. An individual licensed to deliver treatments to improve clients' ventilatory function or oxygenation is a ____________.
f. An individual licensed to formulate and dispense medications is a ____________.
g. An individual trained to counsel clients and their families is a ____________.
h. An individual trained to offer spiritual support and guidance to clients and their families is a ____________.

29. List the five primary characteristics of a profession as described by Etzioni and briefly correlate these characteristics to nursing.
a.
b.
c.
d.
e.

30. Name the following professional organizations and identify the major objectives of each.
a. ANA
b. CNA
c. NLN
d. ICN
e. NSNA
f. CSNA

31. Identify four of six societal changes that influence current nursing practice.
a.
b.
c.
d.

32. Identify three ways in which nurses may become more politically influential.
a.
b.
c.

APPLICATION OF KEY CONCEPTS
Activities to reinforce theoretical concepts

1. Identify a period in history and discuss how nursing practice was influenced by events and societal characteristics of that time.
2. Review the conceptual model of your nursing curriculum. Identify the theorist or theorists whose goals of nursing and frameworks for practice most closely correlate with your nursing curriculum.
3. Select a nursing theorist. Review the nursing literature for an article that presents the selected conceptual model for practice in greater detail. Briefly summarize the information presented.
4. Formulate your personal definition of nursing. Compare your definition with the ICN definition of 1973 and the ANA definitions of 1965 and 1980.
5. Review and discuss the major points of the nurse practice act for your state or province.
6. Review the newspapers for advertisements of nursing positions. Identify the career roles and employment opportunities available, as well as recommended position requirements.
7. Review the daily (or weekend) newspaper. Identify issues presented that have a potential impact on nursing practice and those that may be influenced by professional nurses.
8. Contact the student nurses' association in your area to learn more about their activities and membership policies.
9. Experiential exercise: standards of practice
Observe nurses in actual clinical practice. Compare their activities to the ANA Standards of

Nursing Practice or the CNA Standards for Nursing Practice.

10. Experiential exercise: roles and functions of the nurse
Observe nurses in actual clinical practice. Identify their activities as they relate to roles and functions of the nurse.

11. Experiential exercise: roles of health team members
Care for, interview, or review the medical record of a client in a hospital. Identify the health care team members who come in contact with the client. Describe the role of the health care team member in the client's care.

ADDITIONAL READINGS

Donahue, MP: Nursing: the finest art, an illustrated history, St. Louis, 1985, The C.V. Mosby Co.

A richly illustrated, well-referenced historical compendium of the art and science of nursing.

Fawcett, J: Analysis and evaluation of conceptual model of nursing, Philadelphia, 1984, F.A. Davis Co.

Presents major conceptual models of nursing with analysis of their applicability to practice.

Huey, FL: Looking at ladders, Am J Nurs 82:1520, 1982.

Defines the concept of clinical ladders as a mechanism for recognition and reward of nurses electing to remain at the bedside. Identifies career ladder programs in the United States and examines their major characteristics.

Mason, D, and Talbott, S, editors: Political action handbook for nurses, Menlo Park, Calif., 1985, Addison-Wesley Publishing Co.

Examines the influence of nurses on health care via the political system. Demystifies politics in the workplace, government, organization, and community to encourage nurses to accept their professional role of political activism.

News: North Dakota's High Court frees nursing board to enforce its BSN requirement for RN licensure, Am J Nurs 87(3):372, 1987.

Discussion of a 1987 state supreme court decision that held that the state board of nursing could bar ADN and diploma graduates from the RN licensure examination.

Rogge, MM: Nursing and politics: a forgotten legacy, Nurs Res 36(1):26, 1987.

Discussion of the political activities of nurses through American history. Highlights nurses' impact on the political system resulting in health care policy changes.

Stevens, BJ: Nursing theory: analysis, application, evaluation, ed. 2, Boston, 1984, Little, Brown & Co., Inc.

An examination of popular nursing theories.

Walker, LO: Toward a clearer understanding of the concept of nursing theory, Nurs Res 20(5):428, 1971.

Analysis of the concept of nursing theory. Examines conflicting issues between practical and theoretical knowledge, as well as theory and practice.

Chapter 2
Health and Illness

PREREQUISITE READING

Read Chapter 2, pp. 34 to 59.

OBJECTIVES

Mastery of content in this chapter will enable the student to:

1. Define selected terms related to health and illness.
2. Discuss health definitions and concepts.
3. Discuss each of the following:
   a. Health-illness continuum model
   b. High-level wellness model
   c. Agent-host-environment model
   d. Health belief model
   e. Evolutionary-based model
   f. Health promotion model
4. Describe health promotion and illness prevention activities.
5. List and discuss the three levels of preventive care.
6. List and explain four kinds of risk factors.
7. Describe variables influencing a person's health beliefs and practices.
8. Describe variables influencing illness behavior.
9. State and discuss the stages of illness behavior.
10. Describe the impact of illness on the client and family.
11. Discuss the nurse's role for clients in health and illness.

REVIEW OF KEY CONCEPTS

1. Define health.
2. Define health beliefs.
3. List three positive health behaviors.
   a.
   b.
   c.
4. List three negative health behaviors.
   a.
   b.
   c.
5. Match the health model with the most accurate description.
   a. Health-illness continuum model _____
   b. Health promotion model _____
   c. Agent-host-environment model _____
   d. Health belief model _____
   e. Evolutionary-based model _____

   1. A model in which health outcomes are derived from a complex interaction of affective responses in combination with life events, personal adaptive strategies, perception of control over life circumstances, and the functional capacity to promote survival and well-being
   2. A model that views health as a dynamic state that continually changes as a person adapts to alterations in the internal and external environment, and illness as an abnormal process in which the person's ability to function is diminished or impaired in one or more dimensions when compared with the person's previous condition.
   3. A model that predicts how a person will behave in relation to his or her health and health care therapies by examining the individual's perception of three major factors: susceptibility to an illness, seriousness of the illness, and benefits of taking action
   4. A model that seeks to explain why individuals engage in health activities by examining cognitive-perceptual factors and other external variables that enhance or decrease participation in health promotion; health promotion viewed as increasing a client's level of well-being and self-actualization
   5. A model that originated in the community health setting and has been expanded as a model for describing the level of health or illness of an individual or group based on the dynamic relationship among three variables
6. For the past 5 years, Mrs. Jones has been taking medications and following a low-salt diet to control her blood pressure. During this time she has adhered to her prescribed therapy 90% of the time. Mrs. Jones says that she takes her medicines and stays on her diet because they make her "feel so much better." Which of the four models of health best explains Mrs. Jones' behavior?
   a. Health-illness continuum model
   b. Agent-host-environment model
   c. High-level wellness model
   d. Health belief model

7. Internal variables that influence health beliefs and practices would include:
   a. Family practices and cultural background.
   b. Socioeconomic factors and intellectual background.
   c. Spiritual factors and developmental stage.
   d. Cultural background and perception of functioning.
8. Actions that help a client maintain his or her present level of health, or enhance it in the future, are called ________________ activities.
9. Actions that protect a client from actual or potential threats to health are called ________________ activities.
10. Which of the following would constitute an active health promotion strategy?
    a. Fluoridating drinking water
    b. Fortifying milk with vitamin D
    c. Working in a smoke-free environment
    d. Beginning a weight reduction program
11. The primary goal of a total health program is to improve a person's physical health. (true or false)
12. List at least four habits that have been shown to promote total health, improve life expectancy, and help to prevent illness.
    a.
    b.
    c.
    d.
13. Match the level of prevention for each of the nursing activities listed.
    a. Bathing a client ____
    b. Assisting a client in adapting to an artificial limb ____
    c. Teaching children about the importance of exercise ____
    d. Administering medications ____
    e. Administering immunizations ____

    1. Primary prevention
    2. Secondary prevention
    3. Tertiary prevention
14. Any variable that increases the vulnerability of an individual or a group to illness or accident is a (an):
    a. Illness behavior.
    b. Risk factor.
    c. Negative health behavior.
    d. Life-style determinant.
15. For each of the following categories, identify at least two risk factors.
    a. Genetic and physiological factors
    b. Age
    c. Environment
    d. Life-style
16. Illness is synonymous with disease. (true or false)
17. Define illness.
18. All of the following would be characteristic of illness behavior *except:*
    a. Calling a physician.
    b. Ignoring physical symptoms.
    c. Interpreting physical symptoms.
    d. Withdrawing from work activities.
19. A client's perception of symptoms will influence illness behavior. (true or false)
20. Clients with chronic illness are more likely to seek health care and comply with therapy than clients with acute illness. (true or false)
21. List at least five determinants influencing illness behavior.
    a.
    b.
    c.
    d.
    e.
22. List and briefly describe the five stages of illness behavior.
    a.
    b.
    c.
    d.
    e.
23. All clients go through each of the five stages of illness behavior. (true or false)
24. Mr. Green entered a rehabilitation center to learn how to care for himself following an automobile accident that has left him partially paralyzed. Mr. Green is very quiet, stays in his room, and avoids interacting with other clients and staff. This behavior is characteristic of which emotional response to illness?
    a. Shock
    b. Anger
    c. Withdrawal
    d. Denial
25. A subjective concept of an individual's physical appearance is his or her ________________.
26. An individual's mental image of self, including all aspects of personality, is his or her ________________.
27. Identify the four factors that influence the reactions of a client and family to a change in body image.
    a.
    b.
    c.
    d.

APPLICATION OF KEY CONCEPTS

Activities to reinforce theoretical concepts

1. Experiential exercise: models of health and illness
   a. Identify the health model that most closely corresponds to your beliefs about health and health care.
   b. Discuss the reasons for your selection.
   c. Describe the ways in which this model influences nursing care.
2. Experiential exercise: risk factors and health promotion

Perform a self-assessment or interview a peer to elicit information concerning the presence of risk factors in each of the major categories. Formulate realistic actions that could be taken to prevent illness and promote health.

	Risk factors	Actions
Genetic and physiological		
Age		
Environment		
Life-style		

3. Experiential exercise: stress assessment
   Following a client care experience or interaction, use the Hospital Stress Rating Scale (Volicer, 1974) in your text to determine actual and potential stressors experienced by the client. Discuss your findings and propose ways that the nurse might assist in reducing the client's stress and its potential complications.
4. Experiential exercise: illness behavior
   During a client care experience or interaction, identify characteristic internal and external variables present in the client. Following the experience or interaction, analyze how these factors may influence the client's illness behavior.
   a. Internal variables
      (1) Perception of symptoms
      (2) Nature of illness
   b. External variables
      (1) Visibility of symptoms
      (2) Social group
      (3) Cultural background
      (4) Economic factors
      (5) Health care system accessibility
      (6) Social support
5. Experiential exercise: stages of illness behavior and reactions to illness
   Following a client care experience or interaction:
   a. Identify the client's stage of illness behavior.
   b. Describe client behaviors that reflect this stage of illness.
   c. Identify the client's or family's behavioral or emotional response to the illness.

ADDITIONAL READINGS

Edelman, C, and Mandle, CL: Health promotion throughout the life span, St. Louis, 1986, The C.V. Mosby Co.
Examines health promotion activities from a developmental perspective.

Lenz, ER: Information seeking: a component of client decisions and health behaviors, ANS 6:59, 1984.
Information seeking by clients is described as a subcomponent of the decision-making process. The six phases of information seeking are analyzed. Implications of the information-seeking process on nursing care and client decision making are also explored.

Muhlenkamp, AF, and Styles, JA: Self-esteem, social support and positive health practices, Nurs Res 35:334, 1986.
Attempts to identify relationships among perceived social support, self-esteem, and positive health practices in a small sample of adults.

Pender, NJ: A conceptual model for preventive health behavior, Nurs Outlook 23:385, 1975.
Describes the nature of personal, interpersonal, and situational factors in motivating persons toward preventive health actions. Discusses the nurse's role in influencing patient motivation.

Pender, NJ, and Pender, AR: Attitudes, subjective norms and intentions to engage in health behaviors, Nurs Res 35(1):15, 1986.
Explores how intent influences health behaviors in the areas of exercise, weight control, and avoidance of high levels of stress.

Pollock, SE: Human responses to chronic illness: physiologic and psychosocial adaptation, Nurs Res 35:90, 1986.
Attempts to identify factors promoting adaptation to chronic illness. Differentiates physiological and psychosocial adaptation of clients and the influence of "hardiness characteristics" in selected chronic illness states.

Volicer, BJ: Patient's perceptions of stressful events associated with hospitalization, Nurs Res 23:235, 1974.
Results of a survey of hospitalized patients to a questionnaire addressing stress-producing events associated with hospitalizations. Points out the high level of psychosocial stress experienced by hospitalized patients, and ranks events perceived as stressful.

Chapter 3
The Health Care Delivery System

PREREQUISITE READING

Read Chapter 3, pp. 60 to 73.

OBJECTIVES

Mastery of content in this chapter will enable the student to:

1. Define selected terms related to the health care delivery system.
2. Describe society's influence on the health care delivery system.
3. Discuss the client's entry into the system.
4. Discuss how a client can use the system.
5. Describe the six types of health care agencies.
6. Discuss the client's right to health care and describe client rights within the health care delivery system.
7. State various methods for financing health care.
8. Describe the problems of the system.

REVIEW OF KEY CONCEPTS

1. The primary impetus for current changes within the health care system is:
   a. consumer demand.
   ✓**b.** health care cost.
   c. third-party reimbursement.
   d. federal legislation.
2. The U.S. government program that provides medical and hospital insurance for persons who are over 65 years of age or disabled is called MEDICARE.
3. The U.S. government program that provides a joint federal and state health insurance program for low-income persons is called MEDICAID.
4. DRGs represent:
   a. the merger of national and private insurance programs.
   b. a method for controlling regional hospital expansion.
   ✓**c.** the basis for prospective reimbursement for hospital services.
   d. a plan for direct reimbursement for nursing care.
5. Health promotion activities are designed to help clients:
   a. reduce their risk of illness.
   b. maintain maximal function.
   c. promote habits related to good health.
   ✓**d.** all of the above.
6. Illness prevention activities are directed toward helping the client and family:
   ✓**a.** reduce risk factors.
   b. lower health insurance premiums.
   c. maintain maximal function.
   d. all of the above.
7. Define rehabilitation.
8. Rehabilitation services begin:
   ✓**a.** when the client enters the health care system.
   b. after the client has requested rehabilitation services.
   c. after the client's physical condition has stabilized.
   d. when the patient is discharged from the acute care setting.
9. Match the health care agency with the most appropriate description.
   a. Outpatient 5
   b. Community based 2
   c. Volunteer 6
   d. Institutional 1
   e. Hospice 4
   f. Governmental 3

   1. Settings where clients are admitted and remain at the agency for diagnosis, treatment, or rehabilitation
   2. Agencies providing health care to clients within their neighborhoods
   3. Clinics, hospitals, or other health services supported by local, state, provincial, or national taxes
   4. A system providing physical care and emotional support for the terminally ill client and family
   5. Settings that include physicians' offices, clinics, or other ambulatory care facilities
   6. National or community not-for-profit agencies established to meet a specific need such as the American Heart Association and the Canadian Heart Foundation
10. Describe the major type of services provided by each of the following health care agencies.
    a. Ambulatory care centers
    b. Day-care centers
    c. Crisis intervention centers
    d. Drug rehabilitation centers

   e. Extended care facilities
   f. Rehabilitation centers
   g. Psychiatric/mental health hospitals
11. Identify at least three changes in the health care system as a result of DRGs.
   a.
   b.
   c.
12. The Patient's Bill of Rights, developed by the American Hospital Association, is a legally binding document. (true or false)
13. The legal permission that must be obtained from the client before an invasive procedure, administration of experimental medication, or involvement in research is called ______.
14. Briefly describe the three major methods of financing health care services.
   a. Private health insurance plans
   b. Group health plans
   c. Governmental insurance plans
15. Briefly discuss the four major problems with the present health care delivery system.
   a.
   b.
   c.
   d.
16. Identify four ways that nursing can positively influence the health care system.
   a.
   b.
   c.
   d.

APPLICATION OF KEY CONCEPTS

Activities to reinforce theoretical concepts

1. Review local or national news publications for information about the health care delivery system. Discuss the immediate and long-term impact that the findings might have on health care delivery.
2. Contact your professional nursing organization for information concerning pending health care legislation and other health care issues.
3. Contact your government representative and request information concerning his or her position on pending health care legislation. Write to your government representative to give your position on pending health care legislation or other health care issues.
4. Experiential exercise: health care agencies
   a. Select a local geographical area or community.
   b. Survey the selected area to determine the agencies offering health care and the nature of their services.
   c. Talk with nurses employed by the various health care agencies to determine their role in providing care.
5. Review the Patient's Bill of Rights (see Chapter 18). Summarize the rights of clients in the health care system and identify ways in which nursing can actively assist in protecting the client's rights.
6. Examine the consent form utilized by your institution and compare it to the criteria described in your text.
7. Review your or your family's health insurance plan. Identify major benefits and limitations of the plan.
8. Contact the client accounts billing department of your institution to determine some of the typical costs incurred during hospitalization. Determine if nursing costs are separated out of the client's bill and the percentage of costs that are related to nursing care.
9. Talk with a staff nurse, head nurse, and nursing supervisor about ways in which nursing is attempting to control health care costs within your institution. Compare their perspectives.

ADDITIONAL READINGS

Curtin, L: Is there a right to health care, Am J Nurs 80:462, 1980.

Examines the ethical question of whether or not individuals have a right to health care. Explores the roles and responsibilities of health professionals in contemporary health care dilemmas.

Fagin, CM: Nursing as an alternative to high-cost care, Am J Nurs 82:56, 1982.

Discusses the impact of nursing on the quality of health care delivery and, ultimately, on health care costs. Emphasizes the importance of nurses challenging current constraints in order to legitimize the role of nurses and actualize the profession's potential.

Halloran, E, and Halloran, DC: Exploring the DRG/nursing equation, Am J Nurs 85:1093, 1985.

Examines data from retrospective analysis of patients' records. Contends that prospective payment for client care based on DRGs is insufficient because it only addresses the medical diagnosis. Proposes that care provided in a hospital is more accurately reflected in the patient's nursing diagnosis and that this would serve as a much more equitable basis for financial reimbursement.

Inglehart, JK: Federal health policies and the poor, N Engl J Med 307:836, 1982.

Examines the influence of current governmental health policies on the poor.

Chapter 4
Culture, Ethnicity, and Nursing

PREREQUISITE READING

Read Chapter 4, pp. 74 to 91.

OBJECTIVES

Mastery of content in this chapter will enable the student to:

1. Define selected terms related to culture, ethnicity, and nursing.
2. Describe the relationship of sociocultural background to health and illness beliefs and practices.
3. Explain the need for a nurse's self-evaluation when providing care to clients from other sociocultural backgrounds.
4. Compare concepts of traditional and modern health and illness beliefs and practices.
5. Describe heritage-consistent and heritage-inconsistent attributes.
6. Perform a cultural assessment using heritage consistency.
7. List traditional health and illness beliefs and practices of Asian Americans, black Americans, Native Americans, Americans of Spanish origin, and Americans of European origin.
8. Describe sociocultural barriers—communication and economic—to health care.
9. Discuss several ways nursing care may be adapted to a client's ethnicity.

REVIEW OF KEY CONCEPTS

1. Define intercultural communication.
2. Effective intercultural communication is facilitated by the nurse's identification of ________.
3. The rejuvenation of ethnic group identity within the United States has resulted in:
   a. strengthening of the melting pot theory.
   b. decreased ethnic group consciousness.
   c. increased awareness of heritage consistency.
   d. increased emphasis on heritage inconsistency.
4. The client's responses to health and illness are culture specific, based on experience and perception. (true or false)
5. Describe the theory of heritage consistency.
6. A person's life-style may simultaneously reflect heritage-consistent and heritage-inconsistent characteristics. (true or false)
7. Nonphysical traits, such as values, beliefs, attitudes, and customs shared by a group of people and passed from generation to generation, are that group's ________.
8. A cultural group's sense of identification associated with common social and cultural heritage is called ________.
9. A belief in a divine or superhuman power (or powers) to be obeyed and worshiped as the creator and ruler of the universe is a ________.
10. Compare heritage-consistent attributes with heritage-inconsistent attributes in each of the designated areas.

	Heritage consistent	Heritage inconsistent
a. Location of childhood development		
b. Visits to a country or neighborhood of origin		
c. Location of family home		
d. Extended family relationships		
e. Name		
f. Education		
g. Knowledge of culture and language		
h. Participation in traditional religious or cultural activities		
i. Individual's present philosophy		

11. Define traditional epidemiology.
12. Compare the traditional healer with the modern physician.
13. Match the general characteristic with the most appropriate ethnic group.
    a. View health as a result of good luck; reward from God; balance of hot and cold, wet and dry ____
    b. Traditional remedies include Sloan's liniment and Father John's Medicine ____
    c. View illness as an imbalance between yin and yang ____

d. Health reflects the ability to live in total harmony with nature and the ability to survive under extreme difficulty ____

e. Traditional remedies include bangles, talismans, and asafoetida (incense of the devil) ____

f. Define health as the ability to do activities of daily living or a state of physical and emotional well-being ____

g. Illness prevention may include wearing Thunderbird amulets or masks to hide from the devil or evil spirits ____

h. Traditional remedies include burning novena candles, manzanilla tea, anise seeds, and amulets ____

i. Illness may be attributed to demons and evil spirits that may be controlled by voodoo ____

j. Traditional remedies include acupuncture, moxibustion, and ginseng root ____

1. Native Americans
2. Asian Americans
3. Spanish-origin Americans
4. Blacks
5. Whites

14. The most important factor in providing nursing care to ethnic group clients is:
a. language.
b. time orientation.
c. personal space.
d. territoriality.

15. An attitude toward an area a person has claimed and defends or reacts emotionally about when it is encroached upon is:
a. ethnocentrism.
b. acculturation.
c. personal space
d. territoriality.

16. Identify and describe the four zones that make up an individual's personal space.
a.
b.
c.
d.

17. The most critical economic barrier preventing people from entering the health care system is:
a. underemployment.
b. unemployment.
c. poverty.
d. lack of health insurance.

18. Before a nurse from the dominant cultural group can effectively care for a Filipino client she must first:
a. study the Filipino culture.
b. determine her own cultural beliefs and values.
c. work with a Filipino folk healer.
d. minimize intercultural communication.

APPLICATION OF KEY CONCEPTS

Activities to reinforce theoretical concepts

1. Clinical situation: heritage consistency

Mrs. Antonio and Mrs. Totino are both of Italian descent. Mrs. Antonio, a recent immigrant, is a 62-year-old widow. She is living with her daughter, son-in-law, and their three school-age children. Mrs. Antonio speaks little English because all of her family members and close relatives can speak Italian. She lives in an area of the city almost entirely populated by families of the same ethnic origin. Mrs. Antonio attends the local church, which continues to include a weekly Mass in Italian.

Mrs. Totino is 50 years old. She and her husband have three children. Two are attending the university and living at home. The eldest is married, has three small children, and lives in a different part of the same city. Mrs. Totino speaks fluent English and Italian. She is active in a local church group and is a volunteer at a local nursing home.

Both women are admitted to the hospital with arthritic-related problems.

a. Would you expect these two individuals to react in the same way to hospitalization? Support your answer by considering each of the variables influencing heritage consistency.

2. Clinical situation: ethnic and cultural factors affecting health care

Mrs. Sanchez, 38 years old, is admitted to the hospital with the diagnosis of menorrhagia (excessive bleeding during menstruation). She is scheduled for several diagnostic tests and possible surgery to remove her uterus. Mrs. Sanchez speaks little English. Mr. Sanchez's work takes him away from home for several weeks at a time, so he is not able to visit his wife at this time. Mrs. Sanchez seems very tense. This is the first time she has even been hospitalized.

a. Discuss how Mrs. Sanchez's cultural background may influence her perception of her current illness and cooperation with her hospital care.
b. Discuss ways in which the language barrier may be bridged.
c. Identify ways in which the nurse can provide individualized care to Mrs. Sanchez in the context of her culture and ethnicity.

3. Experiential exercise: cultural aspects of health and illness

Care for or interview a client in any health care setting.

a. Identify the cultural group to which the individual belongs.
b. Describe the traditional definitions of health and illness, beliefs about the causes of illness, methods of prevention, and illness remedies associated with the identified cultural group.
c. Determine the client's beliefs and practices as compared to traditional cultural beliefs and practices.

d. Identify specific nursing actions to promote individualized, culturally based care to the client.

ADDITIONAL READINGS

Abril, IF: Mexican American folk beliefs: how they affect health care, MCN 1977:168, 1977.

Presents traditional cultural ideas about health and illness held by Mexican Americans. Describes how these culturally derived perceptions affect health care. Offers suggestions for planning and implementing health care to this particular population.

Campbell, T, and Chang, B: Health care of the Chinese in America, Nurs Outlook 21:245, 1973.

Presents traditional cultural beliefs held by Chinese Americans. Fundamental concepts of the culture and beliefs related to health and illness are explored. Characteristic responses to illness and hospitalization are described, and suggestions for integrating cultural practices into health care are offered.

Muecke, MA: Overcoming the language barrier, Nurs Outlook 18(4):53, 1970.

Gives overview of situations in which barriers exist in nurse-client verbal communications. Offers concrete methods for transcending language barriers to more effectively interact with clients.

Spector, RE: Cultural diversity in health and illness, ed. 2, Norwalk, Conn., 1985, Appleton-Century-Crofts.

Explores various traditional and modern health care practices and addresses issues relating to health care for Asian, black, Hispanic, and Native Americans. Challenges readers to become aware of their own beliefs about health and illness.

Chapter 5
Home Health Care

PREREQUISITE READING

Read Chapter 5, pp. 92 to 99.

OBJECTIVES

Mastery of content in this chapter will enable the student to:

1. Define selected terms related to home health care.
2. Identify the types of home health care agencies and reimbursement mechanisms.
3. Identify recent social, economic, technological, and governmental forces that have influenced the development of home health nursing.
4. Describe roles and responsibilities of nurses in home health care.
5. Describe the way regulatory standards and quality assurance guidelines affect the clinical practice of home health nursing.
6. Identify at least two areas of specialized nursing care in the home setting.
7. Identify future trends in home health care and the way they affect clinical practice.

REVIEW OF KEY CONCEPTS

1. Define home health care.
2. Identify at least four purposes of home health care.
   a.
   b.
   c.
   d.
3. What is the primary focus of home health care?
4. Briefly describe each of the following types of home health care services in terms of assistance offered and mechanisms for reimbursement.
   a. Home health agencies
   b. Private duty agencies
   c. Durable medical equipment companies
5. Identify at least four conditions creating an increased demand for home health care.
   a.
   b.
   c.
   d.
6. Nurses can evaluate the client's need for home health care services without a medical order. (true or false)
7. Identify the three factors that must be examined to determine client eligibility for home health services.
   a.
   b.
   c.
8. Identify at least five areas that must be assessed before planning home health care.
   a.
   b.
   c.
   d.
   e.
9. It is important for the nurse to maintain control over the home environment in order to provide optimal home health care. (true or false)
10. Governmental and private insurers will pay for home visits only until the client or family has had time to learn procedures. (true or false)
11. The most important action to ensure accreditation and reimbursement for home health care services is to:
    a. provide highly technical, innovative nursing care.
    b. carefully document nursing assessments, plans, actions, and patient response.
    c. identify all professional and nonprofessional services that the patient requests or requires.
    d. document the agency need for specialty nursing teams and implement continuing-education programs for staff.
12. Briefly describe at least four projected developments in the home health care field.
    a.
    b.
    c.
    d.

APPLICATION OF KEY CONCEPTS

Activities to reinforce theoretical concepts

1. Experiential exercise: home health care needs
   After providing nursing care (or performing a nursing assessment) for a hospitalized client:
   a. Identify the current professional, paraprofessional, and health care equipment services being utilized by the client.

b. Determine those services that the client will require at the time of discharge.
c. Consult with your instructor or your institution's home health coordinator or discharge planner to determine the client's eligibility for home health care.

2. Experiential exercise: hospital discharge planning
   a. Identify the individuals within your institution who are responsible for discharge planning or coordinating home health care.
   b. Determine if your institution has any formal protocols for planning a client's discharge and home care.
   c. Talk with staff nurses on a nursing division to determine their role and responsibilities concerning discharge planning.
3. Experiential exercise: home health care agencies
   a. Survey a designated geographical area within your community to identify home health care agencies.
   b. Contact local home health care agencies to determine the nature of services that they offer and their primary sources of reimbursement for services.
4. Experiential exercise: role of the nurse
   Interview nurses employed by a home health agency. Determine their level of academic preparation, area of clinical specialization or primary interest, experiences before employment by the agency, and job responsibilities.

ADDITIONAL READINGS

American Nurses' Association: Standards of nursing care for home health care practice, Kansas City, Mo., 1986, The Association.

Stewart, JE: Home health care, St. Louis, 1979, The C.V. Mosby Co.

Describes the nature and role of home care in the health care delivery system. Provides guidelines for nursing care in the home. Explores major professional and economic influences on current home health care practice.

Stuart-Siddall, S, editor: Home health care nursing: administrative and clinical perspectives, Rockville, Md., 1986, Aspen Publishers, Inc.

Comprehensive, highly readable text that presents information about current issues in management and delivery of home health care. Presents both administrative and clinical practice perspectives of home health. Discusses trends in this health care approach.

Walsh, J, Perrsons, CB, and Wieck, L: Manual of home health care nursing, Philadelphia, 1987, J.B. Lippincott Co.

Adapts acute care nursing techniques to the home setting. Each technique is presented utilizing a nursing process framework with emphasis placed on family teaching.

UNIT 2 The Nursing Process

Chapter 6

Assessment

PREREQUISITE READING

Read Chapter 6, pp. 102 to 121.

OBJECTIVES

Mastery of content in this chapter will enable the student to:

1. Define selected terms related to assessment.
2. State the five components of the nursing process.
3. Describe the three components of the nursing assessment.
4. Discuss the purpose of nursing assessment.
5. Differentiate between objective and subjective data.
6. State the sources of data for a nursing assessment.
7. Describe the interviewing techniques that may be utilized during a nursing assessment.
8. State the purpose of a nursing history.
9. State the purpose of a physical examination.
10. Describe the four skills of physical examination.
11. Conduct and record a nursing history.

REVIEW OF KEY CONCEPTS

1. Define nursing process.
2. List the five components of the nursing process in their appropriate sequence.
   - a.
   - b.
   - c.
   - d.
   - e.
3. Fill in the component of the nursing process that most accurately matches its purpose described below.
   - a. ______ To identify client's goals, determine priorities, design nursing strategies, and determine outcome criteria
   - b. ______ To gather, verify, and communicate data about client in order to establish a data base
   - c. ______ To determine the extent to which goals of care have been achieved
   - d. ______ To complete nursing actions necessary for accomplishing the plan of care
   - e. ______ To identify health care needs of the client
4. Define objective data.
5. Define subjective data.
6. Which of the following assessment data is subjective?
   - a. Temperature of 102.2° F (39° C)
   - b. Heart rate of 96 beats per minute
   - c. Weight loss of 22 pounds (10 kg)
   - d. Sharp leg pain lasting 2 hours
7. Identify five sources of data for a nursing assessment.
   - a.
   - b.
   - c.
   - d.
   - e.
8. In most circumstances, the best source of information for the nursing assessment of the adult client is the:
   - a. client.
   - b. physician.
   - c. nursing literature.
   - d. medical record.
9. Identify the four methods of data collection that the nurse uses to establish a data base.
   - a.
   - b.
   - c.
   - d.
10. The interviewing technique that is most effective in strengthening the nurse-client relationship because it demonstrates the nurse's willingness to hear the client's thoughts is:
    - a. open-ended question.
    - b. direct question.
    - c. problem solving.
    - d. problem seeking.
11. While obtaining a health history, the nurse asks Mr. Jones if he has noted any change in his activity tolerance. This is an example of which interview technique?
    - a. Problem seeking
    - b. Problem solving
    - c. Direct question
    - d. Open-ended question
12. Mr. Davis tells the nurse that he has been experiencing more frequent episodes of indigestion. The

nurse asks him if the indigestion is associated with meals or a reclining position, and what relieves the indigestion. This is an example of which interview technique?
a. Problem seeking
b. Problem solving
c. Direct question
d. Open-ended question

13. Identify and briefly describe the three phases of the interview.
a.
b.
c.

14. Match the communication strategy with the most accurate description or definition.
a. Silence ____
b. Attentive listening ____
c. Conveying acceptance ____
d. Planning related questions ____
e. Paraphrasing ____
f. Clarifying ____
g. Focusing ____
h. Stating observations ____
i. Offering information ____
j. Summarizing ____

1. Demonstrates willingness to listen to the client without being judgmental
2. Condenses data into an organized review; validates data
3. Asking the client to restate information or provide an example
4. Provides time for nurse to make observations and for client to organize thoughts
5. Provides client with feedback about how nurse sees his or her behavior or actions
6. Activity facilitated by maintaining eye contact, remaining relaxed, and using appropriate touch techniques
7. Allows nurse to clarify health-related issues, initiate teaching, and identify and correct misconceptions
8. Formulation of client's statement by nurse, in more specific words, without changing its meaning
9. Use of words and word patterns in client's normal sociocultural context
10. Limits area of discussion; helps nurse to direct attention to pertinent aspects of client's message

15. Identify the four purposes (objectives) for obtaining a nursing health history.
a.
b.
c.
d.

16. The reason the client is seeking health care will consistently correspond with the medical diagnosis. (true or false)

17. A client is admitted with pain in the right shoulder. What specific information should the nurse obtain concerning this symptom?

18. During an admission interview a client reports an allergy to aspirin. What additional information should be elicited by the nurse?

19. Why is it important to explore life-style patterns and habits such as the use of alcohol, drugs or medications, caffeine, or tobacco?

20. Why is it important to assess the client's patterns of sleep, exercise, and nutrition?

21. The information obtained in a review of systems is:
a. objective.
b. subjective.
c. based on physical examination findings.
d. based on the nurse's perspective.

22. What is the purpose of a physical examination?

23. Fill in the technique of physical examination with the description provided.
a. ____ The process of listening to sounds produced by the body
b. ____ Use of the hands and sense of touch to gather data
c. ____ Observation of responses, behaviors, and physical appearance
d. ____ Tapping the body's surface to produce vibration and sound

24. Identify at least two contributions that laboratory data make to the nursing assessment.
a.
b.

APPLICATION OF KEY CONCEPTS

Activities to reinforce skills and techniques

1. Interviewing technique
   a. Interview an individual (peer, family member, client) on a topic of your choice.
   b. Videotape or audio tape the interview—with the individual's permission (if recording is not possible, write out the conversation as you recall it took place).
   c. Analyze the interview, including type of technique, phases of the interview, and communication strategies employed.
   d. Formulate alternative techniques or strategies that you might have used in the interview.
   e. Submit your analysis to your instructor for feedback.
2. Nursing health history
   a. Obtain a nursing health history form (the one provided in your text or perhaps one currently being utilized by your institution).
   b. Elicit a nursing health history from a peer, friend, or family member.
   c. If feasible, tape record or videotape the interview. (If this is not possible, ask another peer to observe the interview and critique your performance.)
   d. Record the data obtained in the interview on the health history form.

e. Analyze your techniques and communication skills utilized in obtaining the health history.
f. Submit the health history form and analysis of interviewing skills to your instructor for feedback.

Activities to reinforce theoretical concepts

1. Outline the historical development of the nursing process from its inception in 1955.
2. Experiential exercise: nursing process
   a. Observe a nurse in any practice setting.
   b. Identify components of the nursing process that you see operationalized.
   c. Discuss your findings with your instructor.
3. Experiential exercise: nursing health history
   a. Review a completed nursing health history form found in a client's medical record or in your text. (Design your own nursing health history form.)
   b. Analyze the health history in each of the following areas:
      (1) Are each of the basic components for a nursing health history included in the health history form or tool?
      (2) What other data, if any, are present that are not identified in the basic components described in your text? Is this additional information important? Why or why not?
      (3) What sources were consulted in obtaining the needed data?
      (4) Identify data present in the health history as objective or subjective.
4. Experiential exercise: nursing interview
   a. Observe a peer, nurse, or faculty member conduct a nursing interview.
   b. Analyze the interview by responding to each of the following:
      (1) Were the objectives of the nursing interview met?
      (2) Did you observe the three phases of the interview? Describe their effectiveness.
      (3) What type of interview techniques were utilized?
      (4) What communication strategies were employed?
   c. Formulate alternative interview techniques and communication strategies to improve the nursing interview.
5. Experiential exercise: laboratory data
   Review the medical record of a client. From the list presented in your text, search for common laboratory and diagnostic tests that appear in the record. Identify the institutional norms for the data. Determine if the client has any abnormal laboratory or diagnostic test results.
6. Clinical situation: data collection
   Mary Anne Robinson, 29 years old, is admitted to the hospital with severe abdominal pain. She is alert, oriented, and able to describe her signs and symptoms. Mrs. Robinson's husband and mother have accompanied her to the hospital.
   a. List five sources for data collection about Mrs. Robinson.
   b. Formulate one or two sentences you might utilize while obtaining the nursing health history that reflect the nature of each of the three phases of an interview (orientation, working, and termination).
   c. Formulate at least four questions you would ask Mrs. Robinson about her abdominal pain.
   d. Is the information obtained from Mrs. Robinson considered objective or subjective data? Why?

ADDITIONAL READINGS

Bermost, LS: Interviewing: a key to therapeutic communication in nursing practice, Nurs Clin North Am 1:205, 1966.
Discusses principles of interviewing clients. Includes examples to clarify major points. Briefly analyzes examples of nurse-client interaction for learner to gain further insight into techniques.

Malasanos, L, et al: Health assessment, ed. 3, St. Louis, 1986, The C.V. Mosby Co.
A comprehensive reference addressing the theoretical concepts and techniques needed to elicit a comprehensive health history and perform a physical examination. Liberally illustrated with pictures and drawings to assist the student in understanding techniques of physical assessment. Discusses normal findings and describes abnormal conditions that the examiner may identify during assessment. Includes adult and pediatric assessment.

Mengel, A: Getting the most from patient interviews, Nurs 82 12(11):46, 1982.
Presents a systematic, personalized approach to interviewing clients. An excellent resource for the beginning practitioner.

Norris, L: Coaching the questions, Nurs 86 16(5):100, 1986.
Outlines 10 simple steps that the nurse may follow in assisting clients to obtain information needed for health care providers about their health status and plan of care.

Perry, AG: Analysis of the components of the nursing process. In Carlson, JH, Craft, CA, and McGuire, AD, editors: Nursing diagnosis, Philadelphia, 1982, W.B. Saunders Co.
Concise overview of the nursing process. Defines and explains each of the five components and discusses their interrelationships.

Chapter 7
Nursing Diagnosis

PREREQUISITE READING

Read Chapter 7, pp. 122 to 133.

OBJECTIVES

Mastery of content in this chapter will enable the student to:

1. Define selected terms related to nursing diagnoses.
2. Describe the way defining characteristics and the etiological process individualize a nursing diagnosis.
3. List and discuss the steps of the nursing diagnostic process.
4. Demonstrate the nursing diagnostic process.
5. Differentiate between a nursing diagnosis and a medical diagnosis.
6. Explain what makes a nursing diagnosis correct.
7. Discuss the advantages of nursing diagnoses for the client.
8. Discuss the advantages of nursing diagnoses for the profession of nursing.
9. Discuss the limitations of nursing diagnoses.
10. Formulate nursing diagnoses from a nursing assessment.

REVIEW OF KEY CONCEPTS

1. Define nursing diagnosis.
2. List the three steps of the nursing diagnostic process in the appropriate sequence.
   a.
   b.
   c.
3. The process of grouping related data in order to form a picture of the client's health needs is called ______.
4. List three ways to validate information obtained during a nursing health history.
   a.
   b.
   c.
5. The presence of one sign or symptom is adequate support for a nursing diagnostic label. (true or false)
6. Define defining characteristics.
7. Identify and briefly describe the two components of the nursing diagnosis.
8. Which component of the nursing diagnostic statement assists in individualization of the diagnosis and gives direction to planning client care?
9. It is acceptable to use the medical diagnosis as the etiology of the nursing diagnosis. (true or false)
10. Compare characteristics of medical and nursing diagnoses in each of the following areas:

	Medical diagnosis	Nursing diagnosis
Nature of the diagnosis		
Goal		
Objective		

11. Identify three advantages of nursing diagnoses.
    a.
    b.
    c.
12. Mrs. French is a 45-year-old mother of two who is 50 pounds overweight. She has a smoking history of two packs per day for 20 years. She is to have a hysterectomy tomorrow. Which of the following nursing diagnoses should appear on Mrs. French's nursing care plan?
    a. Social isolation
    b. Potential uterine cancer
    c. Potential ineffective airway clearance related to obesity and smoking
    d. Altered urinary elimination related to incisional pain
13. Mr. Margaux, a 52-year-old business executive, has been admitted to the coronary care unit during the last hour. He states he has no chest pain or shortness of breath. His pulse and blood pressure are normal. He appears tense and does not want the nurse to leave the bedside. When questioned he states that he is very nervous. At this moment, which nursing diagnosis is most appropriate?
    a. Alteration in comfort, chest pain
    b. Alteration in bowel elimination related to restricted mobility
    c. Potential altered cardiac output related to heart attack
    d. Anxiety related to intensive care admission
14. If a nurse stated the client's nursing diagnosis as "potential malnutrition," it would be incorrect because it is:

a. an error of omission.
b. an error of commission.
c. stated as a medical diagnosis.
d. stated as a nursing intervention.

15. If a nurse stated the client's nursing diagnosis as "encourage client to verbalize fear," it would be incorrect because it is:
a. an error of omission.
b. an error of commission.
c. stated as a medical diagnosis.
d. stated as a nursing intervention.

APPLICATION OF KEY CONCEPTS
Activities to reinforce theoretical concepts

1. Divide a small group of peers into two groups (pro and con) to debate the use of nursing diagnoses.
2. Experiential exercise: NANDA classification system
Visit your nursing library and find a text that addresses the topic of nursing diagnoses utilizing the NANDA classification system.
   a. Select one nursing diagnosis.
   b. Find the defining characteristics for that diagnosis.
   c. Find common etiologies for the diagnosis.
   d. Discuss how nursing care might be different for individuals with the same diagnosis but with different etiologies.
   e. Share your conclusions with your instructor.
3. Experiential exercise: nursing diagnoses
Review the medical record of a client in your institution.
   a. Identify the nursing diagnoses for your client.
   b. Identify the medical diagnoses for your client.
   c. Discuss the differences between these diagnoses.
   d. Select one of the nursing diagnoses.
      (1) List all the data present in the medical record that support this diagnosis.
      (2) Identify the etiology of the nursing diagnosis.
      (3) Compare the data with the defining characteristics and etiologies as outlined in the NANDA classification system.
4. Experiential exercise: nursing diagnoses
   a. Obtain a nursing health history from a peer or a client (or review a completed nursing health history provided by your instructor).
   b. Validate the data utilizing other sources.
   c. Cluster the data.
   d. Identify general health care needs.
   e. Formulate nursing diagnoses.
   f. Submit your work to your instructor for feedback.
5. Clinical situation: nursing diagnoses
Working independently or in a small peer group, implement the steps of the diagnostic process (analysis and interpretation—validation and clustering, identification of general health problems, formulation of nursing diagnoses) with the case studies provided. Present information in each section to your instructor for feedback.

Situation A: Jennifer Shampeon is a 16-year-old high school student who has experienced intermittent nausea and vomiting over the past 2 weeks. She has been admitted for diagnostic studies to determine the source of her physical problem.

During the nursing interview, Jennifer states that she hasn't had an appetite for the last 2 weeks and has only eaten toast or crackers with jelly, soda, jello, and tea. She tells the nurse she is worried about what is wrong, feels "tense" and "jittery" most of the time, and has difficulty getting to sleep at night.

Jennifer's mother tells the nurse that her daughter "is just bored and sleeps only 3 to 4 hours each night because she doesn't do anything all day long." Jennifer responds that she is bored and misses her friends and involvement in school and social activities. She says the only thing to do at home and in the hospital is to "watch the soaps."

During the initial part of the physical examination, the following information is obtained:

Height: 5 feet, 2 inches
Current weight: 86 pounds
Usual weight: 92 pounds
Vital signs
  Temperature: 37° C (98.6° F)
  Pulse: 80
  Respirations: 16
  Blood pressure: 100/60
Pale skin color
Restless, frequently shifting positions in bed
Voice quivers when discussing hospitalization
Hands shake when picking up water glass or performing other self-care activities
Vomited 200 ml of greenish-colored emesis during the admission interview

Situation B: Mrs. Anderson, a 32-year-old single parent of two preschoolers, has been admitted to the hospital following a motor vehicle accident.

Mrs. Anderson sustained a fractured right arm, multiple cuts and bruises to her face, and a whiplash injury to her neck. Surgery was required to repair the right arm fracture. She returned from the operating room with a cast on her injured arm from above her elbow to her fingertips. She also must wear a cervical collar around her neck to help reduce muscle spasm.

Mrs. Anderson is right-handed. She is employed as a secretary. She states: "I don't know how I'm going to look after my children with this cast on my arm and my neck hurting so much. Right now my friend is looking after them, but she and her husband are leaving for Hawaii in 2 days. Also, I'm not sure what will happen with my job. I won't be able to type for at least 2 months. What if my boss lays me off! Look, I can't even cut the meat on my plate, so how can I help my kids?

ADDITIONAL READINGS

Carpenito, LJ: Nursing diagnoses: application to clinical practice, ed. 2, Philadelphia, 1987, J.B. Lippincott Co.
A comprehensive text that provides clear methods for application of nursing diagnosis and care planning to clinical

situations. Discusses the basic theoretical concepts underlying nursing diagnosis. Includes an analysis of each of the currently accepted diagnostic categories in terms of definition, defining characteristics, contributing and risk factors, assessment criteria, principles and rationale for nursing care, interventions, and outcome criteria.

Edel, MK: Noncompliance: an appropriate nursing diagnosis? Nurs Outlook 33:183, 1985.

Discusses the concept of client compliance and factors that influence compliant behavior. Proposes elimination of noncompliance as a nursing diagnosis in order to direct interventions toward the cause of the behavior, thus more appropriately meeting the client's real needs. Upholds the client's need for independent decision making, informed choice, and responsibility for personal behaviors.

Gebbie, KM, and Lavin, MA: Classifying nursing diagnoses, Am J Nurs 74:250, 1974.

Describes the original work of Gebbie and Lavin associated with the First National Conference on Classification of Nursing Diagnoses. Briefly discusses the proceedings and the development of the classification system currently in use.

Iyer, PW, Taptich, BJ, and Bernocchi-Losey, D: Nursing process and nursing diagnosis, Philadelphia, 1986, W.B. Saunders Co.

Comprehensive text designed for nursing students and practitioners. Emphasizes the diagnostic phase of the nursing process. Straightforward approach to the care-planning process. Includes multiple examples, self-tests, and sample case studies to enhance reader understanding of concepts presented.

Martens, K: Let's diagnose strengths, not just problems, Am J Nurs 86:192, 1986.

Proposes that nurses direct care toward maintaining health by reinforcing wellness behaviors. Emphasizes that nurses must build on client strengths in overcoming health-related problems. Supports use of diagnostic statements of strengths in order to provide the nurse with a more accurate picture of the client and enhance the quality and continuity of care. Includes methodology for formulation of diagnostic statements of client strength.

Rantz, M, and Maas, M, editors: Nursing diagnoses: implementation, Nurs Clin North Am 22(4):873, 1987.

Series of articles addressing the advancement of nursing diagnosis in a variety of nursing practice settings.

Chapter 8
Planning

PREREQUISITE READING

Read Chapter 8, pp. 134 to 146.

OBJECTIVES

Mastery of content in this chapter will enable the student to:

1. Define selected terms related to the planning step of the nursing process.
2. List the purposes of the nursing care plan.
3. Discuss differences between institutional, standardized, and student care plans.
4. Describe the differences between care plans used in hospital and community health settings.
5. Identify correct nursing interventions developed during the planning component.
6. Develop a nursing care plan for a nursing assessment.
7. List the six steps involved in obtaining a consultation.
8. Discuss the consultation process.

REVIEW OF KEY CONCEPTS

1. List the four activities that are involved in the planning process.
   a.
   b.
   c.
   d.
2. Mrs. Marks is a 45-year-old homemaker who had a cholecystectomy (removal of the gallbladder) 2 days ago. She complains of severe incisional pain that interferes with her ability to ambulate, cough, and deep breathe. She is extremely fearful and states that her best friend died following gallbladder surgery. Her nursing history reveals a 30-year-history of smoking, chronic obstructive lung disease (COPD), and obesity. She is the primary care giver for her 15-year-old mentally retarded son. Her husband, a businessman, travels frequently. According to Mrs. Marks, her husband has not had the opportunity to spend much time with their son. Based on the information provided, prioritize Mrs. Marks' nursing diagnoses that follow as high (1), intermediate (2), or low (3).
   a. ____ Alteration in nutrition: more than body requirements related to excessive intake in relationship to metabolic need
   b. ____ Alteration in comfort: acute pain related to abdominal incision
   c. ____ Potential for infection related to invasive procedures (surgery, intravenous therapy), COPD
   d. ____ Coping, family: potential for growth
   e. ____ Fear related to perceived threat of death associated with surgical procedure
   f. ____ Ineffective airway clearance related to pain, history of smoking, and COPD
3. Under what circumstance would the nurse or nursing team independently develop the client-centered goals?
   a. When directed to do so by the physician
   b. When the hospital uses standardized care plans
   c. If the client is unable to participate in goal setting
   d. If the client is unable to read or write
4. Describe the difference between short-term and long-term goals.
5. List three functions achieved by formulation of projected outcomes.
   a.
   b.
   c.
6. The following statement appears on a nursing care plan for a client who is immunosuppressed: the client will remain free from infection throughout hospitalization. This statement is an example of a:
   a. nursing diagnosis.
   b. short-term goal.
   c. long-term goal.
   d. projected outcome.
7. The following statements appear on a nursing care plan for a client following a mastectomy: incision site approximated, absence of drainage or prolonged erythema at incision site, client remains afebrile. These statements are examples of:
   a. nursing interventions.
   b. short-term goals.
   c. long-term goals.
   d. projected outcomes.
8. The following statement appears on a nursing care plan for a client following a stroke: client performs self-care activities independently within 6 months. This statement is an example of a:

a. nursing diagnosis.
b. short-term goal.
c. long-term goal.
d. projected outcome.

9. List four purposes of a nursing care plan.
   a.
   b.
   c.
   d.
10. Briefly describe the differences between institutional, standardized, and student care plans.
    a. Institutional
    b. Standardized
    c. Student
11. A scientific rationale is:
    a. a projected outcome for client care derived from supporting literature.
    b. the reason, based on supporting literature, a specific nursing action was taken
    c. the reason that a nursing diagnosis poses a risk to the client.
    d. a scientific reason that nursing care is required by the client.
12. What four questions may be asked to determine if nursing interventions are appropriately stated?
    a.
    b.
    c.
    d.
13. Which of the following nursing interventions is correctly stated?
    a. Ambulate the client once each shift.
    b. Student nurse will provide oral hygiene 30 minutes before breakfast.
    c. Primary nurse will observe the client cough and deep breathe at 10 AM, 2 PM, 6 PM, 10 PM, 2 AM.
    d. Client will request pain medication before physical therapy exercise program.
14. Under what two circumstances would a nurse initiate a consultation?
    a.
    b.
15. List the six steps that the nurse follows in obtaining consultation.
    a.
    b.
    c.
    d.
    e.
    f.

APPLICATION OF KEY CONCEPTS

Activities to reinforce theoretical concepts

1. Experiential exercise: review of nursing care plans
   Review the nursing care plan for a selected client in any health care setting.
   a. Is it an institutional, a standardized, or a student care plan?
   b. What components of the nursing process can be seen in the care plan format?
   c. Are the goals, projected outcomes, and nursing interventions correctly stated?
   d. Are the goals, projected outcomes, and nursing interventions appropriate to the identified nursing diagnosis?
   e. How are the care plans used in the health care setting?
   f. If other care plans are available, compare characteristics of ones utilized for clients in different health care settings: hospitals, clinics, and home health settings.
   g. If other care plans are available, compare characteristics of care plans utilized for a client during hospitalization and in preparation for discharge.
2. Experiential exercise: designing a nursing care plan
   a. Develop a nursing care plan, based on a nursing history, for an assigned (or simulated) client. Unless directed otherwise, include in your care plan two nursing diagnoses, one goal for each diagnosis, at least two projected outcomes for each goal, and at least two interventions (with rationale) for each goal. (Keep in mind that this is a practice exercise. In any care planning situation, the number of diagnoses, goals, projected outcomes, and interventions is specific to that particular client.)
   b. Discuss your care plan with a peer to determine if your plan is clearly stated and replicable without additional information. Make any necessary revisions.
   c. Submit your care plan to your instructor for feedback.
3. Experiential exercise: consultation
   a. Identify nursing specialists and other health team members in your institution who are available for consultation in planning and implementing client care.
   b. Determine the appropriate method for obtaining consultation in your institution.
   c. Explore the role of the primary nurse (student nurse) in the consultation process.
   d. Care for, or review the nursing assessment of, a client. Identify the areas in which consultation might promote improved client care. List those individuals who would be available for consultation. With your instructor's assistance, initiate the consultation process.
4. Clinical situation: consultation
   Mr. Laine is a 29-year-old single parent whose only son, Jimmy (9 years old), was diagnosed with insulin-dependent diabetes mellitus 8 months ago. The medical treatment to control Jimmy's diabetes was a diabetic diet with low dose insulin. During the last 6 months, Jimmy has been hospitalized three times with his diabetes out of control. Jimmy refuses to adhere to his diet because he can't eat what his friends eat. In addition, Mr. Laine states that he "doesn't think the diet is important" and wants the physician to in-

crease Jimmy's insulin dose to control his disease.

a. Identify two problems that may require Jimmy's primary nurse to seek consultation.

b. From the following list, select the most appropriate consultants.

(1) Medical-surgical clinical nurse specialist
(2) Psychiatric clinical nurse specialist
(3) Social worker
(4) Diabetic clinical nurse specialist
(5) Pediatric nurse practitioner
(6) Nutritionist (dietitian)

c. List three pieces of pertinent information that would need to be provided to the consultants.

ADDITIONAL READINGS

Please refer to readings cited in Chapters 6 and 7, which include several sources to assist in care plan development. Texts cited in those chapters have not been repeated here.

Hendrix, MJ, and LaGodna, GE: Consultation: a political process aimed at change. In Lancaster, J, and Lancaster, W, editors: Concepts for advanced clinical nursing practice, St. Louis, 1982, The C.V. Mosby Co.

Explores the consultation process in the context of nursing practice. Describes the roles and functions of the consultant. Emphasizes the interaction model of consultation. Provides in-depth descriptions of the nursing role in each phase of the consultation process.

Pilcher, MW: Post discharge care: how to follow up, Nurs 86 16:50, 1986.

Describes postdischarge care program developed for clients on a neurosurgical unit. Includes client examples to reinforce the importance of planning home care as an element to ensure true continuity of care.

Sanborn, CW, and Blount, M: Standard plans for care and discharge, Am J Nurs 84:1394, 1984.

Discussion of care plan and discharge standardization project at the University of Virginia hospitals. Project outcomes discussed include reduction in time required for documentation, establishment of standards of care, and enhancement of staff resources and education, as well as individualization of client care.

Chapter 9
Implementation

PREREQUISITE READING

Read Chapter 9, pp. 148 to 161.

OBJECTIVES

Mastery of content in this chapter will enable the student to:

1. Define selected terms related to the implementation component of the nursing process.
2. Discuss the differences between dependent, independent, and interdependent interventions.
3. List and discuss the five steps of the implementation process.
4. Describe the five different implementation methods.
5. Select appropriate implementation methods for an assigned client.

REVIEW OF KEY CONCEPTS

1. Implementation is a continuous activity performed throughout the nursing process. (true or false)
2. An example of an independent nursing intervention is:
   - **a.** administering a prescribed pain medication.
   - **b.** administering a laxative according to a protocol.
   - **c.** turning a client every 2 hours to prevent skin breakdown.
   - **d.** ambulating a client according to a therapist's recommendation.
3. An example of a dependent nursing intervention is:
   - **a.** administering oral hygiene to a disabled client.
   - **b.** contacting a psychiatric nurse specialist about a depressed client.
   - **c.** teaching a client about relaxation techniques.
   - **d.** giving an enema to a client before x-ray studies.
4. An example of an interdependent nursing intervention is:
   - **a.** following admission protocol during an initial client interview.
   - **b.** assessing a client for side effects of medications.
   - **c.** administering a prescribed laxative.
   - **d.** providing counseling to a client having difficulty adjusting to an unplanned pregnancy.
5. Match the following terms to the most appropriate description or definition.
   - **a.** Protocol ___
   - **b.** Standing order ___
   - **c.** ADL ___
   - **d.** Counseling ___
   - **e.** Teaching ___
   - **f.** Adverse reaction ___
   - **g.** Preventive nursing action ___
   - **h.** Lifesaving ___

   1. Promotes intellectual growth or acquisition of new knowledge or psychomotor skills
   2. Written plan that specifies procedures to be followed
   3. Activity directed toward promoting health and reducing risk of illness
   4. Written document containing rules, policies, procedures, or orders to be followed in client care
   5. A harmful or unintended effect of any nursing action
   6. Activity to restore client's physiological or psychological equilibrium
   7. Promotes development of new attitudes and feelings
   8. Tasks of eating, dressing, bathing, brushing teeth, or grooming
6. A nurse performing a dependent intervention that was incorrectly ordered by the physician is not liable for any complications that might occur. (true or false)
7. List and briefly describe the five steps of the implementation component of the nursing process.
   - **a.**
   - **b.**
   - **c.**
   - **d.**
   - **e.**
8. Identify the three areas in which the nurse may require assistance in implementing the nursing care plan.
   - **a.**
   - **b.**
   - **c.**
9. List and briefly describe four methods of implementing nursing strategies.
   - **a.**
   - **b.**
   - **c.**
   - **d.**

10. When delegating a client's nursing care to another staff member, the nurse is responsible for ensuring that the interventions were completed correctly. (true or false) T

APPLICATION OF KEY CONCEPTS

Activities to reinforce theoretical concepts

1. Experiential exercise: independent, interdependent, and dependent interventions
   - **a.** Review or design a nursing care plan for a selected client, or observe a nurse caring for clients in any health care setting.
   - **b.** Identify and describe at least three nursing actions for each type of nursing intervention: dependent, independent, and interdependent.
   - **c.** Compare your findings with those of your peers.
   - **d.** Discuss your findings with your instructor.
2. Experiential exercise: methods of implementation
   - **a.** Review or design a nursing care plan for a selected client, or observe a nurse caring for clients in any health care setting.
   - **b.** Identify and describe at least one example of each of the five methods for implementing nursing strategies.
   - **c.** Compare your findings with those of your peers.
   - **d.** Discuss your findings with your instructor.
3. Experiential exercise: implementation process
   - **a.** Design a nursing care plan for a selected client.
   - **b.** Perform the five steps of the implementation component of the nursing process
   - **c.** Describe and evaluate your activities in each of the five implementation steps; for example, what actions did you take, what worked well, what didn't work well, how would you modify your activities in the future.
   - **d.** Discuss your activities and self-evaluation with your instructor.
4. Experiential exercise: communication of nursing strategies
   - **a.** Review your institution's protocol for communication of nursing strategies in the nursing care plan and medical record.
   - **b.** Observe communications utilized by the nursing staff in any health care setting to communicate information concerning nursing care strategies. Describe the type of information presented. What facilitated or inhibited the communication process? Discuss your findings with your instructor.
   - **c.** Based on an actual (or simulated) client care situation, practice verbal and written communication of nursing strategies in a small peer group.
   - **d.** Provide an opportunity for critique of your written and verbal communication by your instructor.
5. Experiential exercise: protocols and standing orders
   - **a.** Examine your institution's policies concerning protocols and standing orders
   - **b.** Obtain a copy of a protocol and standing order or orders for a specific clinical setting. Compare these two documents. What do they describe? How are they similar? How are they different? What responsibility or authority is given to the nurse? Discuss your conclusions with your instructor.
   - **c.** Discuss protocols and standing orders with a staff nurse in a specified health care setting. What are the common protocols and standing orders used in the clinical setting? What are the advantages and disadvantages of protocols and standing orders on this nurse's practice? Discuss your findings with your instructor.
   - **d.** Discuss with your instructor or head nurse the specific responsibilities of student nurses in relation to institutional protocols and standing orders.

ADDITIONAL READINGS

Please refer to readings cited in Chapters 6 and 7, which include several sources to assist in care plan development and implementation. Texts cited in those chapters have not been repeated here.

Marriner, A: The nursing process: a scientific approach to nursing care, ed. 4, St. Louis, 1987, The C.V. Mosby Co.

A thorough discussion of the nursing process. Presents various theoretical concepts relating to the components of the nursing process. Includes practical examples to enhance application of the nursing process to client care planning.

Redman, BK: The process of patient education, ed. 6, St. Louis, 1988, The C.V. Mosby Co.

A comprehensive text addressing theoretical and practical issues associated with client education. A valuable resource for students and experienced nurses.

Chapter 10
Evaluation

PREREQUISITE READING

Read Chapter 10, pp. 162 to 169.

OBJECTIVES

Mastery of content in this chapter will enable the student to:

1. Define selected terms related to the evaluation component of the nursing process.
2. State and discuss the four steps of the evaluation process.
3. Describe interactions between the components of the nursing process.
4. Evaluate the nursing actions selected for an assigned client.

REVIEW OF KEY CONCEPTS

1. Define evaluation as it relates to the nursing process.
2. The evaluation component of the nursing process is oriented toward the client receiving care and the institution providing care. (true or false)
3. The criteria for determining the effectiveness of nursing action are based on:
   a. nursing diagnoses.
   b. projected outcomes.
   c. client satisfaction.
   d. nursing interventions.
4. The evaluation process determines the quality of care in relation to:
   a. accepted standards.
   b. institutional resources.
   c. patient recovery.
   d. staff availability.
5. List and briefly describe the four steps of the evaluation component of the nursing process.
   a.
   b.
   c.
   d.
6. The ongoing, systematic, comprehensive evaluation of health care services and the impact of those services on the health care consumer are known as:
   a. quality assurance.
   b. concurrent audit.
   c. nursing audit.
   d. nursing process evaluation.
7. Once an individualized nursing care plan has been developed, it rarely needs modification. (true or false)
8. Quality of nursing care may be measured by:
   a. concurrent nursing audit.
   b. the evaluation component of the nursing process.
   c. ANA standards of practice.
   d. all of the above.
9. Identify three major benefits of the nursing process evaluation.
   a.
   b.
   c.
10. Complete the table below, outlining the purpose and steps of each component of the nursing process.

	Assess-ment	Diag-nosis	Planning	Imple-men-tation	Evalu-ation
Purpose					
Steps	1.	1.	1.	1.	1.
	2.	2.	2.	2.	2.
	3.	3.	3.	3.	3.
			4.	4.	4.
				5.	

APPLICATION OF KEY CONCEPTS
Activities to reinforce theoretical concepts

1. Experiential exercise: quality assurance.
   Meet with a member of your institution's quality assurance committee. Use the following questions as a guide for your discussion.
   a. What are the components of the quality assurance program for your institution? How does the quality assurance program meet the JCAHO's (Joint Commission on Accreditation of Healthcare Organizations') seven requirements for quality assurance?
   b. What type of nursing audit is carried out in your institution?
   c. Who conducts the nursing audit?
   d. How are the audit findings shared with nurses?
   e. How are the audit findings utilized to implement change?
2. Experiential exercise: peer review
   Meet with staff nurses in any health care setting. Utilize the following questions as a guide for discussion.

a. Are nursing peer reviews used in your employment setting?
b. What is the purpose of the review?
c. How is the review conducted?
d. How are the review findings shared with the staff member?
e. What are the advantages and limitations of the peer review process?

3. Experiential exercise: ANA standards of practice
   a. Review a client's nursing assessment, notes, and care plan.
   b. Utilizing the ANA standards of practice, analyze the care that the client has received. Which standards have been met? What nursing activities could be modified in order to better meet the prescribed standard of practice?
   c. Discuss your findings with your instructor.
4. Clinical situation: projected outcomes
   Using the following case study, develop nursing diagnoses, goals, and evaluation criteria (projected outcomes) you would use to measure Mr. Reynold's response to nursing care and his progress toward achieving his health care goals. Submit your written work to your instructor for feedback.

   Mr. Reynolds, a 48-year-old business executive, was admitted to the hospital with a medical diagnosis of a myocardial infarction (heart attack). His height is 6 feet (182.8 cm), weight 230 pounds (104.33 kg). His life-style is sedentary. He is recently divorced.

   He smokes 1½ packs of cigarettes per day and has one or two cocktails per day, usually more on weekends. He has been in the intensive care unit for 5 days and has just been transferred to a cardiac rehabilitation unit in preparation for discharge. He has no complaints of pain on transfer but states: "I'm dying for a cigarette." His physician has ordered a low-calorie, low-salt, reducing diet, smoking cessation, and a progressive aerobic exercise program. Mr. Reynolds angrily demands a telephone in his room because he is behind at work and has deadlines to meet. He also wants to talk to his teenage son about his recent decision to drop out of high school.
5. Experiential exercise: evaluating nursing care
   a. Design and implement a nursing care plan for an assigned client.
   b. Compare the client's response to the projected outcomes.
   c. Analyze the reasons for the client's ability to meet or not meet the desired outcomes and goals. (For example, Was the nursing diagnosis accurate? Were the goals realistic? Were the outcomes appropriate? Were the interventions performed correctly? Were the interventions appropriate and inclusive enough to assist the client in goal achievement?)
   d. Modify the care plan, providing rationale for your changes.
   e. Submit your work to your instructor for feedback.

ADDITIONAL READINGS

Anderson, PA, and Davis, SE: Nursing peer review: a developmental process, Nurs Management 18(1):46, 1987.

Describes a process-focused peer review model developed and implemented as part of a quality assurance program at a midwest Veteran's Administration hospital.

Crockett, D, and Sutcliffe, S: Staff participation in nursing quality assurance, Nurs Management 17(19):41, 1986.

Describes one institution's unique plan for implementing a nursing quality assurance program involving all levels of staff nurses.

Davis-Martin, S: Outcome and accountability: getting into the consumer dimension, Nurs Management 17(10):25, 1986.

Describes the increasing need for consumer satisfaction with health care delivery systems. Emphasizes that sensitivity to the client's satisfaction is important to professional development. Presents a consumer tool used for nursing student evaluation. Proposes that similar tools could be developed for utilization by staff nurses and nurse managers.

Maciorowski, LF, Larson, E, and Keane, A: Quality assurance, evaluate thyself, J Nurs Admin 15(6):38, 1985.

Proposes that quality assurance programs must be evaluated for effectiveness. Describes a tool designed and tested for this purpose.

More, KR: What nurses learn from nursing audit, Nurs Outlook 27(4):254, 1979.

Describes the benefits to nurses that may be derived from well-developed quality assurance programs.

Chapter 11
Research in Nursing Care

PREREQUISITE READING

Read Chapter 11, pp. 170 to 187.

OBJECTIVES

Mastery of content in this chapter will enable the student to:

1. Define selected terms related to nursing research.
2. Compare the various ways to acquire knowledge.
3. List the characteristics of scientific investigation.
4. Compare methods for developing new knowledge in nursing.
5. Define scientific and nursing research.
6. Compare the research process with the nursing process.
7. List the ANA priorities for nursing research.
8. Explain the rights of human research subjects.
9. Explain the rights of others who assist in the conduct of human research studies.
10. Describe a typical research report.
11. Discuss methods of locating research reports in nursing and related areas.
12. Explain how to organize information from a research report.
13. List the characteristics of a clinical nursing problem that can be researched.
14. List the criteria for using research findings in nursing practice.

REVIEW OF KEY CONCEPTS

1. Match the method of knowledge acquisition with the examples provided.
   - **a.** For the last 3 years the nurses have always used povidone-iodine (Betadine) to clean intravenous dressing sites. It seems to work best. ____
   - **b.** The nursing staff is uncertain about what type of flotation mattress will work best for Mr. Thomas' bedsore. They call a nurse specialist for advice. ____
   - **c.** Mrs. Theros has worked in critical care for 5 years. After working with many clients she believes her technique for suctioning is most effective. ____
   - **d.** Lynn is concerned about controlling pain in clients who have nasogastric tubes. She and the nurse specialist have read about various therapies. They plan to study the effects of applying cold compresses to the necks of clients with tubes inserted over 24 hours. ____
   - **e.** Jan is frustrated in caring for Mr. Wilm's bedsore. It does not seem to be healing. One day, the physician orders heat lamp treatments. Two days later the nurses use povidone-iodine (Betadine) to clean the bedsore. Of all the treatments, thorough cleansing and keeping the client off the sore seem to work best. ____

   1. Trial and error
   2. Tradition
   3. Experience
   4. Scientific method
   5. Using experts

2. List the five characteristics of scientific investigation.
   - **a.**
   - **b.**
   - **c.**
   - **d.**
   - **e.**
3. Define scientific research.
4. Define nursing research.
5. Biomedical research is concerned with:
   - **a.** how clients and families cope with health problems.
   - **b.** the psychological implications of health and illness.
   - **c.** the study of health promotion behaviors.
   - **d.** identifying the course of specific diseases.
6. In an experimental study:
   - **a.** subjects are randomly assigned to the experimental and control groups.
   - **b.** the control group receives the therapy being studied.
   - **c.** conditions affecting the subjects are left uncontrolled in order to allow generalization of findings.
   - **d.** clients most likely to perform the best are assigned to the experimental group.
7. Match the description of the phase of nursing research with the component of the nursing process to which it most closely compares.

a. Nurse publishes results of a research study so other nurses might use the study's finding. ___
b. Nurse uses a new treatment method on an experimental group and records results. ___
c. Nurse identifies the anticipated response of clients to the experimental treatment. ___
d. Nurse identifies the factors that should be measured in determining effects of new treatment. ___
e. Nurse determines the type of statistical tests that will be used to measure results of study. ___

1. Assessment
2. Diagnosis
3. Planning
4. Implementation
5. Evaluation

8. The purpose of the ANA's priorities for nursing research is:
a. to review nurse researchers' ethical standards.
b. to identify areas of nursing practice needing further knowledge to improve client care.
c. to assess the quality of nursing research proposals.
d. to identify the educational preparation required of nurse researchers.

9. List at least five of the eleven ANA priorities for nursing research.
a.
b.
c.
d.
e.

10. The responsibility of an institutional review board is to:
a. conduct research that benefits the general public.
b. select nurse researchers capable of conducting research.
c. determine the risk status of research projects.
d. establish ethical standards for nursing organizations.

11. The Canadian Nurses Association's "Ethics of Nursing Research" state that:
a. subjects in a research study must understand the purpose of the research.
b. once clients are informed, they should feel obliged to participate.
c. the ultimate decision of a client's participation in research rests with the researchers.
d. researchers can use a hidden coding system to identify participants in a study.

12. Under what circumstance does a student or nurse have the right to refuse to carry out a research procedure?

13. Identification of research studies can best be done by:
a. looking for the word "research" in the title of the report.
b. looking only in research journals.
c. examining the contents of the report.
d. reading the first paragraphs of the report.

14. Which statement concerning research reports is accurate?
a. Nursing textbooks are primary sources of information.
b. Primary sources are those written by one of the researchers in the study.
c. The fact that a report is a primary source guarantees its accuracy.
d. Secondary sources are the best source of information about the research study.

15. To find articles on a particular subject, one first checks:
a. the citation list at the end of the article.
b. through pages of other related journals.
c. other articles written by the same author.
d. the subject headings in a cumulative index.

16. A computerized search for research articles is obtained through:
a. MEDLINE.
b. the *Cumulative Index to Nursing.*
c. the *Index Medicus.*
d. the *Annual Review of Nursing Research.*

17. A research report includes all of the following except:
a. a summary of literature used to identify the research problem.
b. the researcher's interpretation of the study results.
c. a summary of other research studies with the same results.
d. a description of methods used to conduct the study.

18. Identify at least three characteristics of a clinical nursing problem that has the potential to be researched.
a.
b.
c.

19. List four criteria for determining if research findings can or should be applied to nursing practice.
a.
b.
c.
d.

20. Explain the meaning of the following statement and its relevance to nursing practice: "Some people estimate that the half-life of knowledge in the health care field is 5 years."

APPLICATION OF KEY CONCEPTS
Activities to reinforce theoretical concepts

1. Clinical situation: rights of human subjects
A nursing student, Robert Maury, enters his client's room to find a physician attempting to persuade the client to try an experimental drug. The client appears anxious, and his questions reveal he is confused. The

physician leaves the room. The client states, "I don't know what to do, but I'm afraid my doctor will be upset if I don't agree to take the drug."

a. Review the case study independently or with a peer group.

b. Answer the following questions:

(1) What are the client's rights in this situation?

(2) What are the physician's responsibilities?

(3) What must the physician explain about the drug?

(4) What are the nursing student's role and responsibility to the client?

(5) Assuming that the student is qualified to pass medications, what rights does he have in this situation?

c. Share your answers with your instructor.

2. Clinical situation: nursing research process

Cathy O'Malley is a professional nurse interested in studying the effects of environmental factors on the visitors in an intensive care unit (ICU). While working in the cardiac care unit for 6 years, Cathy has seen visitors become anxious when they enter the unit. Whenever a client is surrounded by equipment or numerous staff members, family members seem hesitant to touch their loved one.

a. Review the case study independently or in a small peer group.

b. Answer the following questions:

(1) Which method for acquiring knowledge has influenced Cathy's impressions about the effects of the ICU environment on family members?

(2) What methods could be used to study the problems faced by ICU visitors? Which of these methods would be considered the most reliable?

(3) Cathy is not knowledgeable about all the studies previously conducted involving family members of ICU clients. What steps should she take before planning a formal study? Cathy decides to study 75 family members by giving them a questionnaire measuring their feelings and perceptions about events in an ICU. Three different ICUs will be used.

(4) How will Cathy maintain confidentiality of the subjects?

(5) What specific actions must be taken to ensure that ethical principles of informed consent are followed?

(6) Cathy must form a hypothesis before conducting a study. What will the hypothesis describe?

(7) Why is it important for Cathy to include a description of the setting when reporting the study?

c. Share your answers with a peer. Discuss the rationale for your responses.

d. Discuss your answers with your instructor.

3. Experiential exercise: clinical nursing problems

a. Working independently or in a small peer group, formulate a list of clinical nursing problems that you believe would be interesting to study.

b. Identify some important questions to ask about the relevance of each problem.

c. Share this information with your instructor.

4. Experiential exercise: organizing information from a research study

a. Select any topic of interest related to clinical nursing practice.

b. Using the *Cumulative Index to Nursing* (or other appropriate cumulative index) select a research article (primary source article) from a nursing journal of your choice.

c. Locate the article in your nursing library.

d. Read the article.

e. Write an index card for the article using the sample bibliography card illustrated in the text as a guide.

f. Submit your card to your instuctor for feedback.

5. Experiential exercise: application of research findings

a. Review a primary source research article addressing a clinical nursing problem.

b. Identify whether the research report includes all the pertinent sections and components of a typical research report based on the information presented in your text.

c. Analyze the applicability of the research findings to clinical practice based on the criteria presented in your text.

d. Share your analysis with your instructor.

6. Meet with a nurse who is researching a clinical nursing problem to discuss the activities involved in the nursing research process.

ADDITIONAL READINGS

Armiger, B: Ethics of nursing research: profile, principles, perspective, Nurs Res 26:330, 1977.

Discusses ethical considerations related to nursing research from 1952 to 1977. Includes implications of nursing research for the individual nurse as well as society at large. Examines ethical perspectives of various aspects of the research process.

Brown, JJ, Fanner, CA, and Padrick, KP: Nursing's search for scientific knowledge, Nurs Res 33:26, 1984.

Analysis of characteristics of current nursing research through examination of trends and changes over the past 30 years. Makes recommendations for the future research based on the presented analysis.

Castles, MR: Primer of nursing research, Philadelphia, 1987, W.B. Saunders Co.

Presents the language and process of nursing research in simple terms in order for individuals to better understand research and more readily apply findings to clinical practice.

Fox, DA: Fundamentals of research in nursing, ed. 4, Norwalk, Conn., 1982, Appleton-Century-Crofts.

Textbook that presents information for consumers of nursing research as well as the beginning nurse researcher. Describes each step of the research process in detail. Chapters include additional references to direct student reading and enhance independent learning.

Seaman, CH, and Verhonick PJ: Research methods for undergraduate students in nursing, ed. 2, Norwalk, Conn., 1982, Appleton-Century-Crofts.

A text specifically developed for the undergraduate student to assist in understanding research well enough to critique, propose, and implement a limited research project. Organizes the research process into an understandable, step-by-step approach.

Stetler, CB, and Marram G: Evaluating research findings for applicability in practice, Nurs Outlook 24:559, 1976.

Proposes that the utility of research study findings must be based on more than evaluation of the project design. Presents other criteria that research consumers should apply in determining the usefulness of study findings.

Chapter 12
Vital Signs

PREREQUISITE READING

Read Chapter 12, pp. 190 to 231.

OBJECTIVES

Mastery of content in this chapter will enable the student to:

1. Define selected terms associated with vital sign measurement.
2. Explain the principles and mechanisms of thermoregulation.
3. Discuss the rationale for a nursing care plan for a client with a fever.
4. Identify steps used to assess a client's oral, rectal, and axillary temperature.
5. Explain the physiology for the normal regulation of blood pressure, pulse, and respirations.
6. Describe the types of factors that normally cause variations in body temperature, pulse, respirations, and blood pressure.
7. Identify steps used to assess a client's pulse, respirations, and blood pressure.
8. Identify normal vital sign values for an adult.
9. Explain variations in technique used to assess an infant's and child's vital signs.
10. Describe the benefits and precautions involving self-measurement of blood pressure.
11. Accurately record and report vital sign measurements.

REVIEW OF KEY CONCEPTS

1. A person's normal body temperature may vary above or below 37° C (98.6° F). (true or false)
2. The part of the brain that is responsible for controlling body temperature is the ______________.
3. The skin plays a role in temperature regulation by:
   a. insulating the body.
   b. constricting blood vessels.
   c. sensing external temperature variations.
   d. all of the above.
4. List the four sources of mechanisms for heat production.
   a.
   b.
   c.
   d.
5. Match the mechanisms for body heat loss with the example provided.
   a. Conduction ____
   b. Convection ____
   c. Radiation ____
   d. Evaporation ____

   1. Bathing the client in tepid water
   2. Placing a cooling blanket over a febrile client
   3. Release of sweat in response to temperature elevation
   4. Wearing lightweight, light-colored clothing
6. Identify three groups of clients who may experience difficulty in maintaining body temperature and briefly explain why this may occur.
   a.
   b.
   c.
7. In the absence of fever, the nurse expects that a client's body temperature will peak between:
   a. 1 and 4 AM.
   b. 6 and 10 AM.
   c. 10 AM and 2 PM.
   d. 4 and 7 PM.
8. Define fever.
9. Which statement concerning fever is incorrect?
   a. Chilling occurs as the body's attempt to increase heat loss.
   b. Fever results from an alteration in the hypothalamic set point.
   c. Metabolism and oxygen consumption increase during fever.
   d. Fevers may be caused by conditions other than infection.
10. Health care providers generally believe that all fever should be treated. (true or false)
11. High temperatures in young children may result in ______________.
12. List at least five areas to assess in the febrile client.
    a.
    b.
    c.
    d.
    e.
13. How do antipyretic medications act to reduce a fever?

14. Mr. Silverman is experiencing a fever of 39° C (102.2° F). Which nursing measure would be appropriate during the course of the fever?
    a. Bathe the client in cold water.
    b. Raise the room temperature to avoid chills.
    c. Encourage activity to maintain energy levels.
    d. Provide at least 3000 ml of fluid per day.
15. Which route provides the most reliable measure of body temperature?
    a. Oral
    b. Rectal
    c. Axillary
    d. Skin
16. In the examples given, indicate the best method for measuring the client's temperature: O—oral, R—rectal, A—axillary.
    a. _____ A young infant who is restless, irritable, and crying
    b. _____ An adult following surgical repair of a fractured mandible
    c. _____ An adult receiving continuous oxygen therapy
    d. _____ An adolescent who is confused and has traction applied to the lower extremities
    e. _____ An adult who is alert and ambulatory
17. Disposable gloves should be worn when taking an oral or rectal temperature. (true or false)
18. Compare and contrast the three methods for assessing temperature of adults and children by completing the table below.

Site	Type of glass thermometer	Time left in place	Client's position	Special precautions
Oral				
Rectal				
Axillary				

19. Convert the following temperature readings:
    a. 100.4° F TO C
    b. 38.8° C to F
    c. 98° F to C
    d. 39.4° C to F
20. Which of the following statements concerning pulse regulation is inaccurate?
    a. The medulla regulates heart rate through sympathetic and parasympathetic stimulation.
    b. The heart maintains a relatively constant blood flow despite heart rate variations.
    c. Mechanical, neural, and chemical factors influence heart contractions.
    d. The pulse rate provides a direct measurement of cardiac output.
21. With each ventricular contraction the heart pumps 80 ml of blood. Assessment of the heart rate for 15 seconds reveals a value of 18.
    a. What is the pulse rate?
    b. What is the cardiac output?
    c. Is the cardiac output normal?
22. When a client's condition suddenly deteriorates, where is the best site for finding a pulse quickly?
    a. Radial
    b. Apical
    c. Carotid
    d. Femoral
23. Identify three situations when it is preferable to assess the apical pulse.
    a.
    b.
    c.
24. Which site is best for assessing an infant's or young child's pulse?
25. List the five characteristics to evaluate when assessing a peripheral pulse. Circle the two characteristics that are evaluated when assessing an apical pulse.
    a.
    b.
    c.
    d.
    e.
26. To accurately assess pulse rate, the nurse should:
    a. know that the pulse typically increases with age.
    b. know that postural changes will not alter the pulse.
    c. recognize that anxiety lowers the heart rate.
    d. measure the pulse when a client is at rest.
27. Match the terms associated with pulse assessment with the most accurate description or definition.
    a. Tachycardia _____
    b. Bradycardia _____
    c. Dysrhythmia _____
    d. Pulse deficit _____
    e. Doppler _____
    f. Diaphragm _____
    g. Bell _____

    1. Electronic stethoscope that magnifies sounds
    2. Abnormal, irregular heart beat
    3. Stethoscope chest piece that best amplifies heart and vascular sounds
    4. Adult heart rate greater than 100 beats per minute
    5. Concurrent pulses: apical 100, radial 90
    6. Adult heart rate less than 60 beats per minute
    7. Stethoscope chest piece that best amplifies bowel and lung sounds
28. Compare and contrast the three methods for pulse assessment by completing the table below.

Site	Equipment needed	Length of time	Indications	Special techniques or precautions
Radial				
Apical				
Apical-radial				

29. Match the terms associated with respiration with the definitions provided.
    a. External respiration _____
    b. Internal respiration _____
    c. Ventilation _____

d. Conduction ____
e. Diffusion ____
f. Perfusion ____

1. Distribution of blood through pulmonary capillaries
2. Mechanical movement of air to and from the lungs
3. Movement of air between the environment and lungs
4. Movement of oxygen and carbon dioxide between alveoli and red blood cells
5. Movement of oxygen between hemoglobin and single cells
6. Movement of air through lung airways

30. The most important factor in control of ventilation in the typical adult is the arterial blood:
a. O_2.
b. CO_2.
c. pH.
d. hemoglobin.

31. **a.** What is the breathing stimulus for a client with chronic lung disease?
b. Why does this occur?

32. Describe how each of the following conditions may affect ventilatory movements.
a. Chest wall pain
b. Anemia
c. Pneumothorax
d. Emphysema

33. List the three objective measurements making up assessment of respirations.
a.
b.
c.

34. Which of the following can lower respiratory rate?
a. Fever
b. Exercise
c. Pain
d. Narcotics

35. Fill in the blank with the most appropriate term associated with respiratory assessment.
a. Difficulty in breathing ________________
b. A harsh, crowing sound associated with airway obstruction ________________
c. Regular, but abnormally rapid breathing ________________
d. Temporary cessation of respirations ________________
e. Inability to breathe comfortably while lying down ________________

36. Label the following alterations in respirations by comparing each with the normal respiratory pattern included.

a. ________________

b. ________________

c. ________________

37. The normal respiratory rate for an adult is ________________ .

38. List four criteria used to assess respirations other than rate, depth, and rhythm.
a.
b.
c.
d.

39. Define:
a. Blood pressure
b. Systolic
c. Diastolic

40. The client's blood pressure is 116/50.
a. What is the diastolic pressure?
b. What is the systolic pressure?
c. What is the pulse pressure?

41. Indicate the effect of each of the variables on blood pressure by writing "IBP" for increased blood pressure or "DBP" for decreased blood pressure.
a. Diuretic medication ____
b. Decreased cardiac output ____
c. Acute pain ____
d. Increased blood volume ____
e. Increased blood viscosity ____
f. Anxiety ____
g. Hemorrhage ____
h. Advancing age ____
i. Increased peripheral vascular resistance ____

42. What are the criteria for diagnosis of hypertension in an adult?

43. When a nurse assesses a client's blood pressure for the first time it is especially important to:
a. compare blood pressures in both arms.
b. have the client lie down for the first reading.
c. have the client perform light exercise before measurement.
d. use the bell of the stethoscope for auscultation.

44. Which sphygmomanometer is most accurate?
a. Aneroid
b. Mercury

45. The nurse is auscultating Mrs. McKinnon's blood pressure. The nurse inflates the cuff to 180 mm Hg. At 156 mm Hg the nurse hears the onset of a tapping sound. At 130 mm Hg the sound changes to a murmur or swishing. At 100 mm Hg the sound momentarily becomes sharper and then becomes muffled at 92 mm Hg. At 88 mm Hg the sound disappears. What is Mrs. McKinnon's blood pressure?

46. Place the following steps for auscultating blood pressure in their proper sequence.
a. ____ Palpate radial pulse and inflate cuff 30 mm Hg above point pulsation disappears.

b. _____ Slowly release valve at a rate of 2 to 3 mm Hg per second.
c. _____ Palpate brachial artery and place cuff 2.5 cm (1 inch) above pulsation site.
d. _____ Place stethoscope's diaphragm over brachial artery.
e. _____ Note point on manometer when sound disappears.
f. _____ Inflate cuff 30 mm Hg above client's normal systolic value.
g. _____ Deflate cuff rapidly and wait 30 seconds.
h. _____ Note point on manometer when first sound is heard.

47. Which of the following statements concerning blood pressure assessment is accurate?
   a. Systolic pressure in the legs is usually lower than in the brachial artery.
   b. Blood pressure should be measured in the arm with the lower pressure.
   c. Two minutes should elapse before repeating measurements in the same arm.
   d. A difference of 12 mm Hg in readings between arms is considered normal.
48. Describe auscultatory gap.
49. List two methods the nurse may use to assess blood pressure when Korotkoff sounds are not audible with the standard stethoscope.
   a.
   b.
50. Clients should be advised that stationary automated blood pressure machines found in public places are often unreliable. (true or false)

APPLICATION OF KEY CONCEPTS

Activities to reinforce skills and techniques

1. Temperature assessment
   a. Examine your institution's policy and procedures for temperature assessment.
   b. Examine the variety of thermometers available within your institution. Practice handling the thermometer that you will be using in the clinical setting.
   c. Practice the proper procedure for taking an oral temperature while a peer observes and critiques your performance.
   d. Using a mannequin in your nursing laboratory, practice the proper procedure for taking a rectal and an axillary temperature while a peer observes and critiques your performance.
   e. Obtain several mercury-in-glass thermometers. In a small group, have each member assess and record his or her own temperature. Clean the thermometers with alcohol, but do not "shake down" the thermometers. Exchange thermometers and read the registered temperature. Compare results.
   f. Elicit an instructor's evaluation of your temperature assessment technique, including validation of the temperature reading.
2. Pulse assessment
   a. With a partner, locate the following sites for pulse assessment: temporal, carotid, brachial, radial, femoral, popliteal, posterior tibial, dorsalis pedis, apical.
   b. Practice the technique for obtaining radial and apical pulses. Ask a peer to critique your performance.
   c. In groups of three, practice obtaining a radial-apical pulse rate.
   d. Elicit an instructor's evaluation of your pulse assessment technique, including validation of the pulse rate.
3. Respiration assessment
   a. Practice the technique for measuring respirations. Ask a peer to critique your performance.
   b. Elicit an instructor's evaluation of your respiration assessment technique, including validation of the respiratory rate.
4. Blood pressure assessment
   a. Examine aneroid and mercury sphygmomanometers. Practice handling the pieces of each type with particular attention to reading the scale, and opening and closing the bulb with one hand.
   b. Practice the technique for blood pressure assessment. Ask a peer to critique your performance.
   c. If a teaching stethoscope (one chest piece, two sets of ear pieces) is available, obtain one. Practice assessing blood pressure with an instructor or experienced student listening with you.
   d. Elicit an instructor's evaluation of your blood pressure assessment technique, including validation of the blood pressure reading.
5. Vital sign assessment
   a. Practice obtaining temperature, radial pulse, respirations, and blood pressure in an organized fashion. Ask a peer to critique your performance.
   b. Set up a blood pressure screening session with other students at your school. Be sure to involve a nursing faculty member who can serve as a consultant.
   c. As your confidence and skill increase, participate in a blood pressure screening program in your community.
6. Recording vital signs
   a. Obtain and examine vital sign graphic sheets or charts used at your institution.
   b. Obtain a set of vital signs on a partner (or create a set of vital signs) and record these on the forms supplied by your institution (or on the forms provided on pp. 41 and 42).
   c. Submit your vital sign charting to your instructor to confirm the accuracy of your recordings.

Activities to reinforce theoretical concepts

1. Clinical situation: vital sign assessment
   Mr. West is admitted to the hospital with the complaint of chest pain and feeling dizzy for the last 24 hours.

BARNES HOSPITAL
BLOOD PRESSURE CHART

STAMP ADDRESSOGRAPH PLATE HERE

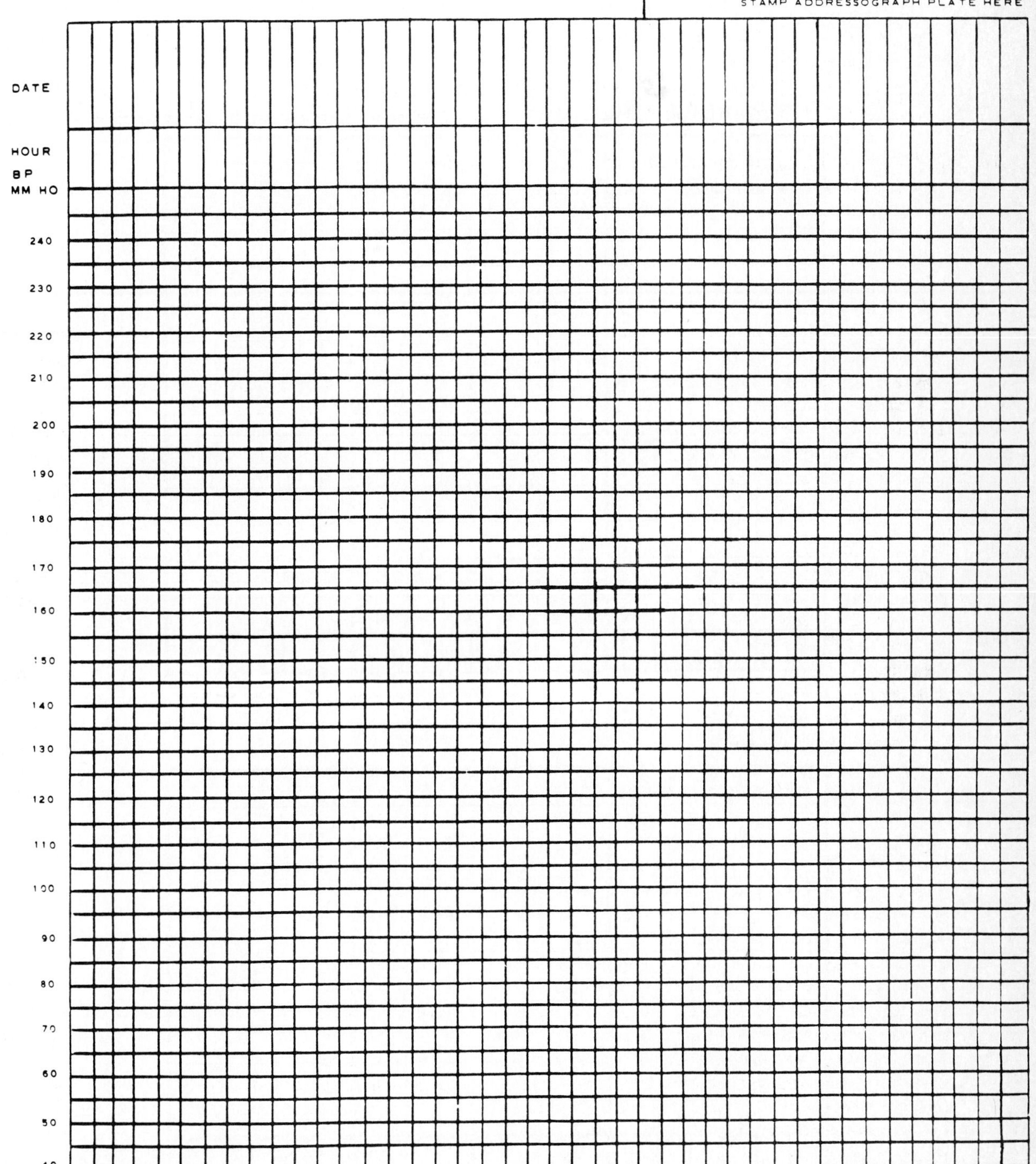

● *blood pressure*
x *pulse*

BARNES HOSPITAL
GRAPHIC SHEET

B - 1

STAMP ADDRESSOGRAPH PLATE HERE

TEMPERATURE

	DATE:	DATE:	DATE:
	HOSP DAY # O.R. DAY #	HOSP DAY # O.R. DAY #	HOSP DAY # O.R. DAY #
TIME	02 04 06 08 10 12 14 16 18 20 22 24	02 04 06 08 10 12 14 16 18 20 22 24	02 04 06 08 10 12 14 16 18 20 22 24
41°			
40°			
39°			
38°			
37°			
36°			
↓35.5°			

Centigrade

O = Oral
R = Rectal
A = Axilliary

PULSE

TIME	02 04 06 08 10 12 14 16 18 20 22 24	02 04 06 08 10 12 14 16 18 20 22 24	02 04 06 08 10 12 14 16 18 20 22 24
140			
130			
120			
110			
100			
90			
80			
70			
↓50			
RESPIRATIONS			
WEIGHT			

X = Pulse
a = Apical

a. To assess Mr. West's vital signs accurately, the nurse should obtain what three categories of information from a previous medical record?
(1)
(2)
(3)

b. The physician examines Mr. West and orders oxygen therapy. Blood samples are also ordered. Propranolol, a medication to improve heart function, is prescribed. Mr. West is also to undergo a cardiac catheterization to diagnose the extent of any heart disease. In relation to this information, when would the nurse need to assess Mr. West's vital signs?

c. At 8 AM Mr. West's radial pulse is 88 and regular. At 12 PM, the nurse notes the radial pulse rate to be 102 and irregular. What actions should the nurse take at this time?

d. Mr. West is very anxious about this hospitalization. He has received heart medication before, but Inderal is a new drug. Even though he is feeling better, the chest pain occasionally recurs. The physician has discussed the plan of therapy with Mr. West and orders a fat-free diet. Which of the situations just described could potentially affect Mr. West's pulse rate?

e. Late one evening, the nurse enters Mr. West's room to find him in respiratory distress. The client states, "I can't get my breath." His respiratory rate is approximately 32 per minute. Respirations are shallow with evidence of increased chest wall movement. The rhythm of respirations is regular.
(1) How would these respirations be described?
(2) What changes might you expect in Mr. West's other vital signs?

f. During this episode, Mr. West's nurse assesses a blood pressure of 90/70. A second nurse checks the blood pressure again and gets a reading of 100/60. Assuming the second reading is correct, what factors might have caused an inaccurate reading by the first nurse?

2. Experiential exercise: the client with fever
Care for, or review the medical record of, a client who has a fever.
a. Assess the client and identify defining characteristics associated with fever.
b. Trace the fever pattern manifested by the client. Determine if the pattern is characteristic of those described in your text.
c. Formulate nursing diagnoses that relate to the problem of the client's fever. For each diagnosis, identify at least one goal and describe at least two pertinent nursing interventions and their rationale.
d. Compare the medical therapies prescribed for the client with those described in your text.

3. Clinical situation: client education, heat stroke
A group of Boy Scouts (10 to 12 years old) has invited you to talk to their group about the hazards of heat in preparation for their 10-mile hike. Devise a teaching program for the scouts including prevention, symptoms, and treatment.

4. Clinical situation: client education, hypertension
Mr. Williams is a 50-year-old black man recently diagnosed with hypertension. His history indicates that he is 20% above his ideal body weight, smokes about 10 cigarettes per day, and enjoys a glass of wine before dinner. He reports that his work is extremely stressful, and often requires him to travel two or three times per month. His physician has prescribed antihypertensive drugs, home blood pressure monitoring, and life-style changes. Mr. Williams is concerned that his children (10 and 24 years old) are at risk. He repeatedly states that his blood pressure is "back to normal" and he feels fine. He tells you, "You know, lots of people have high blood pressure, it's no big thing."
a. How would you explain hypertension and its effects on the body to Mr. Williams?
b. What are the risks for Mr. Williams' children? What factors may increase their risk for development of hypertension?
c. Mr. Williams is uncomfortable with the idea of checking his own blood pressure with the mercury sphygmomanometer and asks about using the electronic digital readout devices or the automated machines he sees at airports and drug stores. How would you advise Mr. Williams concerning these different types of blood pressure monitoring equipment?
d. Devise a teaching plan for Mr. Williams designed to promote compliance with his medical regimen and successful control of his blood pressure.

ADDITIONAL READINGS

Adelman, ED: When patient's blood pressure falls, what does it mean? What should you do? Nurs 80 10(2):26, 1980.

Presents mechanisms and physiological response to acute hypotension. Describes errors in technique that may produce abnormally low readings. Summarizes questions to consider in evaluating client hypotension. Nursing care is prescribed; however, the student is advised to consult more recent references for appropriate supportive care.

Birdsall, C: How accurate are your blood pressures? Am J Nurs 84(11):1414, 1984.

Summarizes four critical components of blood pressure measurement techniques. Places emphasis on ways to increase accuracy of blood pressure assessment.

Birdsall, C: How do you interpret pulses? Am J Nurs 85(7):786, 1985.

Brief overview of characteristics to evaluate during pulse assessment. Includes descriptions of a variety of diagnostic pulses.

Griffin, JP: Fever: when to leave it alone, Nurs 86, 16:58, 1986.

Discusses development and physiological effects of fever. Gives brief overview of selected nursing interventions.

McCarron, K: Fever: the cardinal vital sign, Crit Care Q, 9(1), 1986.

Brief overview of thermoregulation, fever mechanisms, and current research addressing fever management.

Sample, JF, et al: Circadian rhythms: basis for screening for fever, Nurs Res 34:377, November-December 1985.

Examines routine temperature assessment dictated by convenience or policy. Proposes, based on circadian rhythm studies, that temperatures measured at the peak of circadian thermal rhythm are an adequate screen for fever.

Thomas, DO: Fever in children, RN 48:18, 1985.

Brief discussion of fever in children. Describes unique problems associated with fever in children. Discusses treatment from a pediatric perspective.

Working Group on Hypertension in the Elderly: Statement on hypertension in the elderly, JAMA 256:70, 1986.

Addresses prevalence of hypertension in the elderly. Discusses current research related to hypertension management in this population.

Chapter 13
Physical Examination and Health Assessment

PREREQUISITE READING

Read Chapter 13, pp. 232 to 327.

OBJECTIVES

Mastery of content in this chapter will enable the student to:

1. Define selected terms related to physical assessment.
2. Discuss the purposes of physical assessment.
3. Describe the techniques used with each of the physical assessment skills.
4. Describe the proper position for the client during each phase of the examination.
5. List techniques used to promote the client's physical and psychological comfort during an examination.
6. Make environmental preparations before an examination.
7. Use physical assessment skills during the performance of routine nursing care measures.
8. Conduct physical assessments in an organized and proper fashion.
9. Identify information to collect from the nursing history before an examination.
10. Discuss normal physical findings in a young and middle-aged adult compared with an elderly client.
11. Discuss ways to incorporate health teaching into the examination process.
12. Described physical measurements made in assessment of each body system.
13. Summarize assessment findings on a physical examination form.

REVIEW OF KEY CONCEPTS

1. The nurse should perform a comprehensive physical assessment on all acutely ill clients. (true or false)
2. List four purposes of physical assessment.
   a.
   b.
   c.
   d.
3. Baseline data refer to the normal values or findings expected during physical examination. (true or false)
4. Identify four principles to facilitate accurate inspection of body parts.
   a.
   b.
   c.
   d.
5. Which statement describing the technique of palpation is accurate?
   a. Tender areas should be palpated first to reduce client apprehension.
   b. Light palpation requires that tissues be depressed approximately 2 cm (1 inch).
   c. Student nurses should only attempt deep palpation with an instructor's assistance.
   d. The client should be encouraged to hold his or her breath to minimize abdominal wall movement.
6. Identify the parts of the hand used to assess each of the following:
   a. Temperature
   b. Pulsations
   c. Vibrations
   d. Turgor
7. Describe the bimanual palpation technique.
8. What information is obtained through the use of percussion?
9. To perform indirect percussion correctly, the nurse does all of the following except:
   a. keep the wrist extended and tensed when striking the finger.
   b. place the middle finger of the nondominant hand over the body's surface.
   c. deliver a sharp quick stroke to the finger placed against the body's surface.
   d. use the middle finger of the dominant hand to deliver the blow.
10. Match the type of sound expected to be produced by percussion of the anatomical area described.
    a. Middle of the anterior part of thigh _____
    b. Left lower anterior aspect of rib cage _____

c. Posterior aspect of thorax _____
d. Right seventh intercostal space _____

1. Tympany
2. Dullness
3. Resonance
4. Flatness

11. To auscultate body parts correctly, the nurse:
a. stretches the tubing the full length before placing the chest piece.
b. learns the normal characteristics for each type of sound auscultated.
c. places earpieces so that they turn out from the ear canal.
d. holds the bell firmly against the skin's surface.

12. The sense of smell may help the nurse detect abnormalities that cannot be recognized by any other means. (true or false)

13. List at least three environmental factors that the nurse should attempt to control before performing a physical examination.
a.
b.
c.

14. The component that should receive highest priority before a physical examination is the:
a. preparation of the environment.
b. preparation of the equipment.
c. physical preparation of the client.
d. psychological preparation of the client.

15. Match the client position or positions with the body part to be examined. (There may be more than one correct position for selected body parts.)
a. Heart _____
b. Abdomen _____
c. Posterior aspect of thorax _____
d. Female genitalia _____
e. Prostate _____

1. Supine
2. Lithotomy
3. Dorsal recumbent
4. Sims'
5. Sitting

16. The purpose of having a third person of the client's sex in the room during the physical examination is to:
a. observe the client's emotional responses and inform the examiner.
b. assure the client that the examiner will behave in an ethical manner.
c. respond to the client's questions so that the examiner may work without interruption.
d. validate any abnormal findings that the examiner elicits.

17. Identify at least one variation in the nurse's interview style appropriate for an individual from each of the specified age groups.
a. Infants and younger children
b. Older children
c. Adolescents
d. Aging clients

18. Identify four assessment areas that make up the general survey.
a.
b.
c.
d.

19. List eight specific observations that the nurse makes when evaluating the client's general appearance and behavior.
a.
b.
c.
d.
e.
f.
g.
h.

20. Before measurement of height and weight the nurse should:
a. ask the client his or her height and weight.
b. ask if there has been a recent change in weight.
c. calibrate the scale by setting the weight at zero.
d. all of the above.

21. What three actions should be taken to ensure accurate measurement of a hospitalized client's weight?
a.
b.
c.

22. How would the nurse measure the height of a client who is unable to stand?

23. For each of the skin color variations listed in the table below, identify the mechanism that produces the color change, common causes of the variation, and optimal sites for assessment.

Skin color	Mechanisms	Causes	Assessment sites
Cyanosis			
Pallor			
Jaundice			
Erythema			

24. Increased skin color in certain body areas is known as ____________________.

25. Which skin assessment parameter is essential for a client at risk for impaired peripheral circulation?
a. Temperature
b. Turgor
c. Moisture
d. Texture

26. Describe normal skin turgor.

27. Tiny, pinpoint-sized, red or purple spots on the skin caused by small hemorrhages in the skin layers are called ____________________.

28. List at least five criteria the nurse uses to assess a lesion
    a.
    b.
    c.
    d.
    e.
29. Supply the correct term for each of the following skin conditions from the following list.

macule	papule	nodule	atrophy
wheal	vesicle	pustule	ulcer

    a. Deep loss of the skin surface ____________
    b. Thinning of the skin with loss of normal appearance ________________
    c. Flat, nonpalpable change in skin color, such as a freckle ________________
    d. Circumscribed elevation of skin filled with pus, such as acne ________________
    e. Circumscribed elevation of skin filled with serous fluid, such as a blister ____________
    f. Irregularly shaped, elevated area, such as a hive ________________
    g. Palpable, circumscribed, solid skin elevation ________________
    h. Elevated solid mass, deeper and firmer than a papule, such as a wart ________________
30. a. How does the nurse assess a client for pitting edema?
    b. Describe what is meant by the assessment finding: "2+ pitting edema."
31. Identify at least two teaching points to include when instructing a client on skin cancer prevention.
    a.
    b.
32. What type of abnormality might the nurse expect in a client with unusual distribution and growth of body hair?
33. An absence of hair growth over the lower extremities may indicate:
    a. genetic abnormality.
    b. circulatory insufficiency.
    c. febrile illness.
    d. poor nutrition.
34. Define alopecia.
35. During inspection of the hair follicles on the scalp and pubic areas, the nurse is more likely to observe the eggs from lice than the lice themselves. (true or false)
36. Nail clubbing is characterized by:
    a. red or brown linear streaks in the nail bed.
    b. transverse depressions in the nail bed.
    c. approximately a 160° angle between nail plate and nail base.
    d. softened nail bed, nail flattening, and enlarged fingertips.
37. A disorder caused by excessive growth hormone resulting in enlarged jaw and facial bones is ________________.
38. Identify the components of the eye examination described below:
    a. ___________ Reading the letters on the Snellen chart
    b. ___________ Asking the client to follow movement of the nurse's finger along eight directions of gaze
    c. ___________ Instructing a client to state when the nurse's finger enters the field of vision
    d. ___________ Moving a penlight from the side of the client's face, shining the light on the pupil
39. Match the name of the common visual problem with the most accurate description.
    a. Abnormal elevation of pressure within the eye ____
    b. Impaired near vision in middle-aged and elderly adults ____
    c. Ability to see distant objects, but not close objects ____
    d. Loss of transparency of the lens ____
    e. Lack of coordination of muscles controlling eye movement ____
    f. Ability to see close objects, but not distant objects ____

    1. Hyperopia
    2. Myopia
    3. Presbyopia
    4. Strabismus
    5. Cataract
    6. Glaucoma
40. What is the easiest way to assess a client's visual acuity?
41. What does the following assessment finding mean: vision 20/60 s̄c?
42. Warning signs of eye disease include all of the following except:
    a. diplopia.
    b. halos around lights.
    c. floaters.
    d. consensual constriction.
43. Supply the correct term for the descriptions associated with examination of the eye from the list provided.

arcus senilis	conjunctivitis	exophthalmos
nystagmus	photophobia	ptosis
red reflex		

    a. Fine, rhythmical oscillation of the eyes ________________
    b. Bulging or protrusion of the eyes ________________
    c. Abnormal drooping of the eyelid over the pupil ________________
    d. Inflammation of the membrane covering the surface of the eyeball and the lining of the eyelids ________________

e. Thin, white ring along the margin of the iris ________________
f. Bright orange glow in response to light on the pupil ________________
g. Sensitivity to light ________________

44. Define, PERRLA.
45. Normally the pupils dilate when focusing on a near object. (true or false)
46. Identify three normal findings expected during an ophthalmoscopic examination.
a.
b.
c.
47. Annual eye examinations are recommended for:
a. all clients over 15 years old.
b. all clients after 30 years old.
c. all clients after 40 years old.
d. all clients after 65 years old.
48. List three risks for hearing problems that may be identified during a nursing history.
a.
b.
c.
49. Place the mechanisms for sound transmission in their appropriate sequence.
a. _____ The cochlea receives the sound vibration.
b. _____ The sound waves reach the tympanic membrane, causing it to vibrate.
c. _____ Sound waves in the air enter the external ear, passing through the outer ear canal.
d. _____ Nerve impulses from the cochlea travel to the auditory nerve and the cerebral cortex.
e. _____ Vibrations are transmitted through the middle ear by way of the bony ossicular chain to the oval window at the opening of the inner ear.
50. If palpation of the auricle and tragus causes a client no pain, the nurse may rule out the possibility of ear infection. (true or false)
51. Which assessment finding during examination of the ears would be considered abnormal?
a. Presence of cerumen
b. Upper point of ear attachment to head slightly below the lateral canthus
c. Pearly gray or translucent eardrum
d. Cone-shaped light reflection in ear canal
52. To insert the speculum correctly when examining the ear of an adult the nurse:
a. pulls the auricle back and down.
b. pulls the auricle up and back.
53. List and briefly describe the three types of hearing loss.
a.
b.
c.
54. Normally sound can be heard longer through air than through bone conduction. (true or false)
55. What is the meaning of a negative Rinne test?
56. A pale nasal mucosa with clear discharge is a sign of infection. (true or false)
57. Describe the normal characteristics of the following mouth structures:
a. Soft palate
b. Tongue
c. Teeth
d. Gingiva
58. Identify three early warning signs of oral cancer.
a.
b.
c.
59. Which statement concerning lymph node assessment is accurate?
a. Small, mobile, nontender nodes are uncommon.
b. Normally nodes are easily palpable.
c. Malignant nodes are usually tender.
d. Infections can cause permanent node enlargement.
60. Which statement concerning thyroid gland assessment is accurate?
a. Masses or nodules can be signs of malignant disease.
b. Enlargement is a normal finding.
c. Normally the thyroid gland is easily visualized.
d. Normally the thyroid gland descends during swallowing.
61. Complete the table below describing assessment findings of the thorax.

Assessment finding	Assessment skill used	Explanation or possible cause
Bulging		
Reduced tactile fremitus		
Reduced excursion		
Resonance over posterior aspect of thorax		
Retraction		
Anteroposterior diameter 1:1		

62. Which of the following statements concerning normal breath sounds is correct?
a. Bronchial sounds are audible over the posterior part of the thorax.
b. Inspiratory and expiratory phases of vesicular sounds are equal.
c. Vesicular sounds are audible over the peripheral area of the lung.
d. Bronchovesicular sounds are audible over the trachea.
63. Complete the following table describing adventitious breath sounds.

Sound	Site of auscultation	Cause	Character
Pleural friction rub			Grating quality heard on inspiration; does not clear with cough
Rhonchi	Primarily over trachea and bronchi; if loud, over both lung fields		Low-pitched, continuous, musical; loudest on expiration; may clear with cough
Wheezes		Severely narrowed bronchus	
Crackles	Most common in dependent lobes, right and left bases		

64. **a.** What is the PMI?
b. Where is the PMI normally located in the infant and young child?
c. Where is the PMI normally located in the older child and adult?
d. What techniques may be used to locate the PMI in an adult?

65. From the list provided, label the diagram below describing each of the cardiac assessment areas and the sites at which each of the four sounds would be most clearly audible.

aortic area pulmonic area S_1 S_2
mitral area tricuspid area S_3 S_4

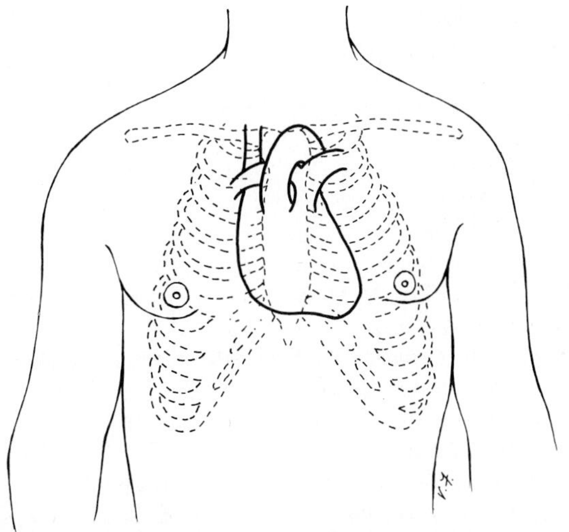

66. Which statement concerning assessment of extra heart sounds and murmurs is correct?
a. S_3 and S_4 are normal in children.
b. Abnormal heart sounds are best heard with the client on the right side.
c. Murmurs are best heard with the diaphragm of the stethoscope.
d. Abnormal heart sounds are best heard over the aortic area.

67. List the six factors to be assessed when a murmur is detected.
a.
b.
c.
d.
e.
f.

68. A continuous palpable sensation like the purring of a cat that may accompany a murmur is called a __________________.

69. The blowing or swishing sound that is created by blood flow through a narrowed vessel is called a __________________.

70. Identify and state the rationale for two precautions the nurse must take to avoid client injury when palpating the carotid artery.
a.
b.

71. A bruit is a normal assessment finding when auscultating the carotid arteries. (true or false)

72. When the client is lying flat, bilateral jugular vein distention is considered abnormal. (true or false)

73. The rating assigned to a peripheral pulse that is easy to palpate and not easily obliterated is:
a. 0.
b. 1^+.
c. 3^+.
d. 4^+.

74. Match the circulatory alteration with the assessment finding described.
a. Decreased or absent pulse _____
b. Cyanotic skin color _____
c. Dusky red color of dependent extremity _____
d. Normal skin temperature _____
e. Marked edema _____
f. Shiny skin with thickened nails _____

1. Arterial insufficiency
2. Venous insufficiency

75. Describe the inspection and palpation techniques, and expected findings, when assessing a client for phlebitis.
a. Inspection
b. Palpation

76. Breast examination is a necessary component of the physical assessment of a male client. (true or false)

77. When palpating breast tissue, the proper technique involves:
a. using the palm of the hand to compress underlying tissue.
b. palpating each quadrant and tail of the breast slowly and methodically.

c. palpating only the tail when lymph node enlargement is present.
d. palpating the breast with a mass before proceeding to the unaffected breast.

78. Write "N" for normal or "A" for abnormal to describe the assessment findings from breast examinations described below.
a. _____ A 26-year-old pregnant woman with a yellowish fluid draining from her nipples
b. _____ A 35-year-old woman with tissue retraction noted in the right breast when raising her arms above her head
c. _____ A 20-year-old woman with breasts that are nontender and without masses, but the right breast is larger than the left with nipple asymmetry
d. _____ A 30-year-old woman with palpable lymph nodes in the right axilla
e. _____ A 24-year-old man with a small, hard, fixed, nontender mass in the lower outer quadrant
f. _____ A 78-year-old woman with breast tissue that feels stringy and nodular

79. List five characteristics that should be included when describing an abnormal breast mass.
a.
b.
c.
d.
e.

80. In the diagram below, use one of the two systems of landmarks to map out and label the abdominal region.

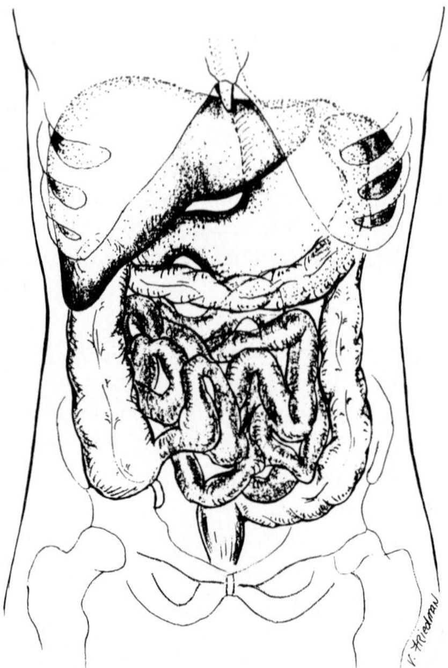

81. The anatomical landmark used for kidney assessment is the ____________________.

82. Describe four techniques the nurse may use to help the client relax during the abdominal assessment.
a.
b.
c.
d.

83. What is the correct sequence for abdominal assessment?
a. Inspection, palpation, percussion, auscultation
b. Auscultation, inspection, palpation, percussion
c. Palpation, auscultation, percussion, inspection
d. Inspection, auscultation, percussion, palpation

84. The position that a client with abdominal pain assumes may be a clue to the source of the pain. (true or false)

85. Match the physical finding of abdominal assessment with the most appropriate description.
a. Abdominal skin taut, flanks do not bulge _____
b. Symmetrical abdomen appears to sink into muscular wall _____
c. Large, protruding abdomen with rolls of adipose tissue along flanks _____
d. Abdominal skin taut, dependent protuberance in side-lying position _____

1. Gaseous distention
2. Fluid distention
3. Obesity
4. Concave abdomen

86. As the nurse inspects the client's abdomen, all of the following findings would be considered normal except:
a. The shape of the abdomen is symmetrically flat or rounded.
b. Venous patterns are prominent and distinct.
c. The umbilicus is flat or concave.
d. In a thin client, regular pulsations are present along the midline of the umbilicus.

87. When assessing bowel sounds the nurse should know:
a. Normal sounds are loud and "growling" in character.
b. If no sounds are heard within 1 minute, the client has no gastric motility.
c. Bowel sounds are normally soft, gurgling, and irregular in frequency.
d. An inflamed bowel usually causes reduced motility.

88. What action should the nurse take to assure accurate auscultation of bowel sounds in a client with a nasogastric tube connected to suction?

89. How long is it necessary to listen for bowel sounds before determining that they are absent?

90. Loud, "growling" bowel sounds that indicate increased gastrointestinal motility are called ____________________.

91. Tenderness in response to percussion over the costovertebral angle indicates:

a. liver enlargement.
b. bowel inflammation.
c. kidney inflammation.
d. spinal cord injury.

92. A voluntary tightening of underlying abdominal muscles in response to palpation of a sensitive area is known as ________________.

93. **a.** Describe the correct technique for assessing rebound tenderness.
b. What does a positive rebound tenderness test indicate?

94. What would a smooth, dome-shaped elevation over the symphysis pubis indicate?

95. Identify three warning signs of colorectal cancer.
a.
b.
c.

96. Complete the table below, describing assessment findings of the female and male genitalia.

Assessment finding	Normal or abnormal	Assessment technique	Possible cause (if abnormal)
Bulging at inguinal ring			
Smooth, round, firm prostate			
Yellow drainage at cervical os			
Labia minora thin and darker in color than surrounding skin			
Left testicle lower than right			
Small, pea-sized lump on front of testicle			

97. The nurse uses a wooden spatula to collect cells from the endocervical area. (true or false)

98. In the elderly man the testicles shrink and become softer. (true or false)

99. A hernia is the protrusion of the spermatic cord through the inguinal canal. (true or false)

100. Fill in the blank with the musculoskeletal condition described.
a. Lateral spinal curvature ________________
b. Muscle that feels flabby, position determined by gravity ________________
c. "Hunchback," or an exaggeration of the thoracic spine curvature ________________
d. Crackling sound associated with joint movement ________________
e. "Swayback," or an increased lumbar curvature ________________
f. Considerable resistance of a muscle to passive movement ________________

101. The nurse might use a goniometer to measure:
a. a client's muscle strength.
b. joint range of motion before and after exercise.
c. vibration sense.
d. a client's balance.

102. Describe two maneuvers to assess muscle strength and identify the muscle group that is being tested.

103. A client must be aroused to maximal alertness before level of consciousness can be assessed. (true or false)

104. Describe the correct technique for application of painful stimuli during neurological assessment.

105. A client who understands written and verbal speech but cannot write or speak appropriately is said to have:
a. sensory aphasia.
b. receptive aphasia.
c. motor aphasia.
d. mental retardation.

106. Match the nurse's assessment questions with the mental or emotional area being tested.
a. _____ "Mr. Mays, tell me what the phrase 'A rolling stone gathers no moss' means."
b. _____ "Who visited you this morning, Ms. Klein?"
c. _____ "Tell me what you know about the new medication you are taking."
d. _____ "What is the year? . . . What is the name of this place?"

1. Knowledge
2. Orientation
3. Abstract thinking
4. Memory

107. Match the cranial nerve with the most appropriate method of assessment described.
a. _____ Ask client to identify sour, salty, or sweet tastes.
b. _____ Ask client to shrug shoulders.
c. _____ Ask client to clench teeth.
d. _____ Ask client to read Snellen chart.
e. _____ Ask client to smile, raise and lower eyebrows.
f. _____ Ask client to identify aroma of coffee.
g. _____ Elicit a gag reflex.
h. _____ Check pupil constriction in response to light.

1. Olfactory
2. Optic
3. Oculomotor
4. Trochlear
5. Trigeminal
6. Abducens
7. Facial
8. Auditory
9. Glossopharyngeal
10. Vagus
11. Spinal accessory
12. Hypoglossal

108. All sensory testing is performed with the client's eyes closed. (true or false)

109. Coordination of muscle activity and maintenance of balance and equilibrium occur in the ___________________.

110. Describe one maneuver to evaluate:
   a. Coordination
   b. Balance

111. To correctly assess reflexes the nurse:
   a. asks the client to flex the extremity to be tested.
   b. holds the reflex hammer firmly and strikes it lightly against the tendon.
   c. ask the client to relax the limb to be tested and then applies a slight stretch to the muscle.
   d. compares the speed of all reflexes on one side of the body.

112. A deep tendon reflex that is described as 2+ is:
   a. diminished.
   b. normal.
   c. brisker than normal but not necesarily indicative of disease.
   d. hyperactive and often associated with spinal cord disorders.

APPLICATION OF KEY CONCEPTS

Activities to reinforce skills and techniques

1. Physical examination techniques
   a. Check with your instructor or nursing library personnel to find available audiovisual materials that demonstrate techniques or illustrate common findings of physical assessment. Review these materials in preparation for laboratory practice sessions and client assessment. Contact your instructor to clarify any questions.
   b. Check with your instructor or nursing laboratory personnel to find models or mannequins that may be used to practice assessment techniques and evaluate specific physical findings. Practice your skills using these models. Contact your instructor for additional guidance or direct assistance.
   c. Using a nursing assessment form as a guide, write a list of all the equipment needed to conduct a physical assessment on a client. Find and prepare all the necessary equipment on your assigned clinical division or in your nursing arts laboratory.
   d. With a partner, practice using the techniques of light palpation and direct and indirect percussion.
   e. With a partner, practice using your stethoscope to evaluate breath, heart, and bowel sounds.
   f. With a partner and the assistance of an instructor, practice use of the otoscope, ophthalmoscope, percussion hammer, tuning fork, or other special pieces of equipment required to perform physical assessment.
   g. Audiotape a recording of the explanations you would give clients in preparation for the physical examination. Include as your clients a toddler, an adolescent, and an adult. Perform a self-evaluation, or submit your tape to a peer or instructor for feedback.
   h. Practice assisting a partner into the various positions for examination. Be sure to identify the name of the position, and provide your simulated client with appropriate physical and psychological support while assuming the selected position.
   i. Using a nursing assessment form or a self-developed assessment tool, perform a general survey of a partner. Record your findings on the form or tool. Formulate nursing diagnoses based on your findings. Submit your work to your instructor for feedback.
   j. Using a nursing assessment form or a self-developed assessment tool, perform a complete or partial head-to-toe or systems assessment of a partner. Record your findings on the form or tool. Formulate nursing diagnoses based on your findings. Submit your work to your instructor for feedback.
   k. Perform a complete or partial physical assessment of a partner. Elicit an instructor's feedback of your performance and validate your physical findings.
2. Testicular self-examination
   a. For male students: Compare your testicular self-examination techniques with those presented in the text. Modify your personal technique to comply with the guidelines of the American Cancer Society. Clarify questions concerning technique with an instructor or clinical specialist.
   b. For all students: Audiotape a teaching session in which you provide instruction to a simulated client concerning the technique of testicular self-examination (or present the information to a peer for critique).
3. Breast self-examination
   a. For female students: Compare your breast self-examination techniques with those presented in the text. Modify your personal technique to comply with the guidelines of the American Cancer Society. Clarify questions concerning technique with an instructor or clinical specialist.
   b. For all students: Audiotape a teaching session in which you provide instruction to a simulated client concerning the technique of breast self-examination (or present the information to a peer for critique).
4. Glasgow Coma Scale
   Provide care for or observe a client with an altered level of consciousness.
   a. Assess the client using the Glasgow Coma Scale.
   b. Compare your assessment with that of an experienced staff nurse or your instructor.
   c. Identify factors that are contributing to the client's level of consciousness.
   d. Based on your findings, identify nursing diagnoses and related nursing care that would be required.
   e. Submit your written work to your instructor for feedback.

Activities to reinforce theoretical concepts

1. Experiential exercise: physical assessment
Following an observation or after providing routine client care:
 a. Observe an experienced nurse perform a physical assessment of a client in any health care setting.
 b. Note modifications that the nurse makes in techniques and determine the rationale for such modifications.
 c. Compare your observations with students who have observed in other settings. Share your impressions with your instructor.

2. Experiential exercise: integration of physical assessment with nursing care
 a. Independently or in a small peer group determine the specific components of the physical examination that may be assessed during each of the following routine client care activities.
  (1) Bathing a client
  (2) Assisting with oral care
  (3) Assisting with breakfast
  (4) Walking a client to the bathroom

3. Experiential exercise: disease prevention education
Working in a small group, have each member select an area for client education from the list provided (or independently develop a list of teaching points for each area listed). Present the major points to be included in a client teaching plan addressing the selected topic. Critique peer performance, or elicit instructor evaluation of written or verbal presentations.
 a. Early warning signs of cancer
 b. Skin cancer prevention
 c. Lung disease prevention
 d. Heart disease prevention
 e. American Cancer Society guidelines for detection of breast cancer
 f. American Cancer Society guidelines for detection of testicular cancer
 g. Colon cancer prevention

4. Clinical situation: preparation for physical examination
Mr. Clancy is a 69-year-old client who has a long history of serious lung disease and a recent onset of chest pain. He is short of breath with a respiratory rate of 28 per minute and complains of a dull, aching sensation in the center of his chest. He is diaphoretic and appears anxious as he watches every move the nurse makes.
 a. What is the best position for examination of Mr. Clancy?
 b. What positions should be avoided during the examination?
 c. How might the nurse organize the assessment?
 d. What examination elements are essential and which may be deferred?
 e. What should be done to prepare Mr. Clancy psychologically?

ADDITIONAL READINGS

Bates, B: A guide to physical examination, ed. 4, Philadelphia, 1987, J.B. Lippincott Co.
Comprehensive, clearly written, extensively illustrated text describing techniques for obtaining a health history and performing a physical examination. Illustrates normal and abnormal findings. Includes adult and pediatric assessment.

Berliner, H: Aging skin. I, Am J Nurs 86:1138, 1986.
Presents common skin conditions associated with pruritus in the elderly client. Content highlighted by colored photographs illustrating skin conditions described. Treatment modalities are also briefly discussed.

Berliner, H: Aging Skin. II, Am J Nurs 86:1259, 1986.
Presents common skin conditions associated with lesions of unusual shape, color, or consistency in the elderly client. Content highlighted by colored photographs illustrating skin conditions described. Treatment modalities are also briefly discussed.

Burger, D: Breast self-examination, Am J Nurs 79:1088, 1979.
Although statistics cited are outdated, author describes step-by-step process of breast self-examination. Explanations of the purpose of each step and guidelines for evaluating findings are also included.

Burggraf, V, and Donlon, B: Assessing the elderly, system by system, Am J Nurs 85:974, 1985.
One of a two-part continuing education program on assessment of the elderly client. Identifies, by system, specific client problems, age-related factors, and other possible etiologies for assessment findings. Client and family teaching points related to problems identified during assessment are also presented.

Dennison, R: Cardiopulmonary assessment, Nurs 86 16(4):34, 1986.
Presents 15 practical tips to improve the quality of cardiopulmonary assessment.

Erickson, BA: Detecting abnormal heart sounds, Nurs 86 16(1):58, 1986.
Clearly describes the techniques required to accurately identify abnormal heart sounds. Includes a table summarizing etiology, auscultatory findings, and related assessment data associated with common cardiac conditions.

Fraser, MC, and McGuire, DB: Skin cancer's early warning system, Am J Nurs 84:1232, 1984.
Colored photographs clearly illustrate malignant and premalignant conditions associated with malignant melanoma. Includes overview of melanoma, prevention guides, and client education. Heavily referenced to guide the learner to additional information.

Malasanos, L, et al.: Health assessment, ed. 3, St. Louis, 1986, The C.V. Mosby Co.
Comprehensive reference presents concepts and techniques needed to elicit a health history and perform a physical examination. Liberally illustrated with pictures and drawings to assist the student in correctly performing physical assessment. Illustrates normal and abnormal findings. Includes adult and pediatric assessment.

Rutledge, DN: Factors related to womens' practice of breast self-examination, Nurs Res 36:117, 1987.
Identifies variables influencing breast self-examination in a selected client population. Data presented may be applied when developing a plan for client education.

Whaley, LF, and Wong, DL: Nursing care of infants and children, ed. 3, St. Louis, 1987, The C.V. Mosby Co.
A comprehensive pediatric nursing text. Includes developmental approach to assessment. An excellent resource to assist in identification of normal and abnormal assessment findings based on disease states of infants and children.

Chapter 14
Recording and Reporting

PREREQUISITE READING

Read Chapter 14, pp. 328 to 357.

OBJECTIVES

Mastery of content in this chapter will enable the student to:

1. Define selected terms associated with reporting and recording.
2. Describe guidelines for effectively communicating thorough reporting and recording.
3. Discuss the relationship between documentation and health care financial reimbursement.
4. Identify ways to maintain confidentiality of records and reports.
5. Describe the purpose of a change-of-shift report.
6. Explain how to verify telephone reports.
7. Identify six purposes of a health care record.
8. Discuss legal guidelines for recording.
9. Differentiate between a source record and a problem-oriented record.
10. Discuss the advantages and disadvantages of standardized documentation forms.
11. Identify computerized applications for documentation.

REVIEW OF KEY CONCEPTS

1. Documentation and reporting are less important nursing activities than providing client care. (true or false)
2. List six guidelines that must be followed to ensure quality documentation and reporting.
   - **a.**
   - **b.**
   - **c.**
   - **d.**
   - **e.**
   - **f.**
3. Record your signature as you would for an entry in the client's record.
4. Which of the following nursing activities need not be recorded immediately?
   - **a.** Administering a medication
   - **b.** Providing a back rub
   - **c.** Applying a pressure dressing for bleeding
   - **d.** Transporting a client to the x-ray department
5. What is the military time that corresponds to 10:05 PM civilian time?
6. Which statement concerning confidentiality is inaccurate?
   - **a.** A legal suit can be brought against any nurse who discloses information about clients without their consent.
   - **b.** Nurses are responsible for protecting their clients' records from unauthorized readers.
   - **c.** Nurses may only use a client's records for activities directly related to the client's health care management.
   - **d.** Nurses are legally and ethically obligated to keep information about a client confidential.
7. The major purpose of a change-of-shift report is to:
   - **a.** communicate actual care delivered.
   - **b.** provide an opportunity for nurses to share concerns.
   - **c.** inform the physician of a client's progress.
   - **d.** provide continuity of client care.
8. The basis for a change-of-shift report is the communication of:
   - **a.** the client's health problems.
   - **b.** routine nursing orders.
   - **c.** information on the Kardex.
   - **d.** prescribed medical care.
9. All of the following are examples of information to include in a verbal report except:
   - **a.** Mr. Jones has been started on ampicillin, 500 mg every 6 hours.
   - **b.** Mrs. Smith stated that the heating pad decreased her leg pain.
   - **c.** Ms. Carter has been uncooperative most of the morning.
   - **d.** Mr. Boylan's pulse was 80 at 0800 and 102 at 1200.
10. **a.** Why is it particularly important that information communicated in a telephone report is clear, accurate, and concise?
    b. How does the nurse ensure that information conveyed in a telephone report is accurate?
11. When a physician gives a verbal order over the telephone, the only way for the order to be legal is:
    - **a.** a registered nurse must accept the order.
    - **b.** the physician gives his or her name over the phone.

c. the physician signs the order within a prescribed time.
d. the nurse records the order in the medical record.

12. Define incident.
13. All information documented in an incident report is duplicated in the client's medical record. (true or false)
14. What is the purpose of an incident report?
15. Match the purposes of health care records with the best example provided.
    a. _____ Client's records are reviewed to determine if the standards of care have been met.
    b. _____ Student reviews client's chart to assist in planning care.
    c. _____ Nurse reviews charts of 10 clients to examine the effects of a preoperative teaching class.
    d. _____ Nurse describes client's response to a medication given in error.
    e. _____ Client's record is available to all health team members caring for the client.
    f. _____ Student reviews the records of two clients with the same nursing diagnosis as a class assignment.

    1. Assessment
    2. Education
    3. Legal documentation
    4. Auditing
    5. Research
    6. Communication
16. Briefly discuss the relationship between accurate documentation and health care financial reimbursement.
17. Clients have the right to review their medical records. (true or false)
18. The client's record is confidential and cannot be used in a court of law. (true or false)
19. Which of the following is a recording error?
    a. Refusing to chart someone else's assessment data.
    b. Erasing any errors completely.
    c. Beginning each entry with the time.
    d. Ending each entry with your signature and title.
20. The medical record that is organized into separate sections for data from each discipline is known as a:
    a. source record.
    b. problem-oriented record.
    c. modified problem-oriented record.
    d. SOAP record.
21. Identify one advantage and one disadvantage of a source record:
    Advantage:
    Disadvantage:
22. List three advantages of the POMR charting method.
    a.
    b.
    c.
23. Briefly describe the information to be included in each of the sections of the SOAP note.
    S:
    O:
    A:
    P:
24. Briefly describe the information to be included in each of the sections of the PIE note.
    P:
    I:
    E:
25. a. What is a standardized care plan?
    b. Identify three advantages of a standardized care plan.
    c. What nursing responsibilities are related to the use of standardized care plans?

APPLICATION OF KEY CONCEPTS

Activities to reinforce skills and techniques

1. Change of shift report
   a. Observe or listen to an audiotape of a change-of-shift report. Analyze the report based on the guidelines discussed in your text. Identify positive characteristics of the report. Determine strategies that may be used to improve the report.
   b. Before a client care experience, or in a simulated situation, practice receiving and presenting an intershift report with a group of peers. Identify areas where additional information may be required and formulate appropriate questions. Critique personal and peer performance.
   c. Following a client care experience, formulate an intershift report on your client. Practice presenting this report to a peer, or audiotape it for self-evaluation or instructor feedback. Request feedback on your report from the staff nurse to whom you have reported.
2. Kardex forms
   a. Review the Kardex form used in your institution.
   b. Review the Kardex information on an assigned client. Compare the information that appears with data from the medical record.
   c. Complete the Kardex form used in your institution (or the one provided at the end of this chapter) with the information from the following hypothetical postoperative situation.

   Ms. Gina Ross
   Date of birth: June 12, 1963
   Graduate student
   Attending physician: Dr. Wilbur
   Medical diagnosis: appendicitis, appendectomy 12/6/88
   Condition: fair
   Allergies: A.S.A. (aspirin), adhesive tape
   Fluids as tolerated
   IV fluids—1000cc D5NS q8′
   Change abdominal dressing prn
   Up in chair qid
   I & O

Vital signs q4h × 48 hours
Obtain CBC 12/7/88
Portable chest film 12/7/88
Turn, cough, and deep breaths q2h while awake

3. Charting
   a. Review your institution's policies concerning nurses' charting. Clarify the responsibilities of nursing students in charting nurse's notes with your instructor or head nurse.
   b. Review the charting forms used by nurses in your institution.
   c. Locate the list of approved charting abbreviations for your institution. With the assistance of your instructor or head nurse, identify the most frequently used abbreviations and write these on a file card for reference when reviewing charts, or memorize the list to facilitate chart review.
   d. During a client care experience, complete all appropriate flow sheets and formulate a nurse's note. Submit your written work to your instructor for review before entering it in the medical record.
4. Alternative nurse's note formats
   a. SOAP notes: rewrite the following nurse's note in a SOAP note format.
      Client's skin over the sacral area has a 4 cm reddened area, without breakdown, tender to palpation. Client states, "I can't seem to stay off my back." Client's immobility increases risk of skin breakdown. Sacral area massaged and lotion applied. Continue turning every 1 to 2 hours.
   b. Narrative notes: rewrite the following SOAP note in a narrative format.
      S— Client states: "The pain is unbearable when I cough."
      O—Abdominal incision well approximated, without drainage, tender on palpation. Morphine sulfate, 10 mg, given at 10:40 AM for incisional pain, with moderate relief after 30 minutes. Client grimaces during turning. Coughing is shallow and nonproductive.
      A—Alteration in comfort related to abdominal incision
      P— Instruct client on method for splinting incision during coughing. Assist with turning by log rolling. Offer pain medication 30 minutes before ambulation or breathing exercises.
   c. PIE notes: rewrite the above SOAP note in a PIE format.

Activities to reinforce theoretical concepts

1. Clinical situation: criteria for reporting and recording
   Mr. Knowles enters the hospital with nausea and abdominal pain. His abdomen is distended, tense, slightly tender to touch, with hypoactive bowel sounds in all four quadrants. Mr. Knowles states that he feels jittery and becomes lightheaded when rising to a sitting position. The physician orders codeine, 30 mg IM, for abdominal pain, which the nurse administered at 1425. An endoscopy has been scheduled for the following day, and the primary nurse has provided the client with the standardized endoscopy teaching plan information.
   a. Identify Mr. Knowles' signs and symptoms that should be described in the medical record.
   b. For each of the signs and symptoms you have identified, give examples of at least four criteria that the nurse might use to describe Mr. Knowles' sign or symptom.
   c. Identify four criteria that the nurse should use to describe the administration of codeine to Mr. Knowles.
   d. Identify three criteria that may be used by the nurse to describe the client teaching that occurred.
2. Clinical situation: confidentiality
   You have been caring for Mrs. Clark, a 39-year-old woman with terminal cancer, for several days. While Mrs. Clark is visiting with her family in the lounge and you are straightening the room, Ms. Olsen, her roommate, begins talking with you. Ms. Olsen tells you that it is so sad to see such a nice young woman (Mrs. Clark) so sick and that it must be hard for you too. She asks you about the nature of Mrs. Clark's diagnosis and her prognosis.
   a. How would you handle this situation?
   b. Specifically, what could you say to Mrs. Olsen?
3. Experiential exercise: medical records
   Review a client's medical record.
   a. Locate each of the major pieces of information:
      (1) Demographic data
      (2) Consent forms
      (3) Admission nursing histories
      (4) Medical history
      (5) Reports of physical examinations
      (6) Reports of diagnostic studies
      (7) Medical diagnosis (diagnoses)
      (8) Therapeutic orders
      (9) Progress notes
      (10) Nursing care plans
      (11) Record of care and treatment
      (12) Discharge plan and summary
   b. Determine if your client's medical record is a source, problem-oriented, or modified problem-oriented record.
   c. Identify the characteristics that led you to reach this determination.
4. Experiential exercise: standards of practice
   Review a copy of your institution's standards of nursing practice. Compare these with the examples of the JCAHO nursing service standards cited in your text on p. 339.
5. Experiential exercise: standardized care plans
   a. Review the nursing assessment and medical record of an assigned client.
   b. Identify the priority nursing diagnosis.

   c. Obtain a standardized care plan for the identified diagnosis from those available in your institution or from a textbook of nursing care plans.
   d. Individualize the standardized care plan to meet the unique needs of your client.
   e. What are the advantages of using the standardized care plan for your client?
   f. What are the limitations of using the standardized care plan for your client?
6. Experiential exercise: computerized communication systems
   Arrange for an orientation to the computer system at your institution. Identify specific computer applications that directly impact client care.
7. Clinical situation: incident reports
   Mr. Neal is an 88-year-old client who underwent surgery for repair of a fractured femur. He returned to the nursing division after surgery and is in stable condition. During the night, he becomes confused. While attempting to crawl out of bed, over the side rails, he falls to the floor.
   a. What actions should the nurse take?
   b. Using your institution's incident policies as a guide, identify the information needed to complete the incident report form. (Or, if feasible, complete a sample incident report form using the information from the simulated clinical situation.)
   c. What information should appear in the client's medical record?

ADDITIONAL READINGS

Blake, P: Incident investigation: a complete guide, Nurs Management 15(11):37, 1984.
Comprehensive discussion of the nurse's role and responsibilities when incidents occur.

Donaghue, AM, and Reiley, PJ: Some do's and don'ts for giving report: sometimes knowing what not to say is as important as knowing what to say, Nurs '81 11:117, 1981.
Presents recommendations for giving an organized, effective intershift report using an organizational framework based on client problems.

Gamber, D, et al: Outcome charting, Nurs Management 12(10):36, 1981.
Identifies elements necessary for outcome charting. Illustrates the charting process through a case study.

Harkins, B: Keep your eye on the patient's problems, RN 49(12):30, 1986.
A step-by-step guide to charting using the POMR system.

Hoke, JL: Charting for dollars, Am J Nurs 85:658, 1985.
Emphasizes the importance of documentation in financial reimbursement via the prospective payment system (DRGs). Illustrates how nursing documentation can affect reimbursement through a case study of a client with peripheral vascular disease.

Reigel, B: A method of giving intershift report based on a conceptual model, Focus Crit Care 12:12, 1985.
Review of the literature concerning intershift report which suggests that there is little research addressing methods for systematic intershift report. Proposes a model for intershift report based on Roy's adaptation model. Illustrates efficacy of the model with sample reports.

Sanborn, CW, and Blount, M: Standard plans for care and discharge, Am J Nurs 84:1394, 1984.
Discussion of care plan and discharge standardization project at the University of Virginia hospitals. Project outcomes discussed include reduction in time required for documentation, establishment of standards of care, enhancement of staff resources, and education, as well as individualization of client care.

Medical Diagnosis and other pertinent medical information:

Condition

Allergies (Drugs, food, other)

Adm. Date	Age	Religion	Mode of Travel

Service	Doctor	Resident	Intern

Stamp Addressograph Plate Here

FREQUENTLY ORDERED ITEMS

Temp.
Pulse & Resp.
BP
I & O
Weights
Spot Checks
Chest P.T.
Incentive Spirometer
P.T.

ACTIVITIES	NUTRITION
Ad lib	Diet
Ambulate	
Chair	
BRP	
Bedrest	
Bath	Feedings
Self	
Tub	Assist c̄ meals
Shower	**FLUID BALANCE**
Bed	Force
Assist.	D E N
	Restrict
	D E N
Orderlies Needed	

Family:

Date	Specimens/Daily Lab	Date	Treatments

Date	Diagnostic Procedures

NURSING CARE PLAN

Date	Nursing Diagnosis	Expected Outcomes	Nursing Plan/Orders

Discharge Planning: Destination: Transportation: Probable Date: Referral Agencies: Appointment:

Supplies:

Patient Name

Chapter 15 WEEK # 6

Administration of Medications

PREREQUISITE READING

Read Chapter 15, pp. 358 to 429.

OBJECTIVES

Mastery of content in this chapter will enable the student to:

1. Define selected terms related to medication administration.
2. Discuss the nurse's legal responsibilities in drug prescription and administration.
3. Describe the physiological mechanisms of drug action, including absorption, distribution, metabolism, and excretion of medications.
4. Differentiate between toxic, idiosyncratic, allergic, and side effects of drugs.
5. Discuss developmental factors that influence drug pharmacokinetics.
6. Discuss factors that influence drug actions.
7. Discuss methods to improve compliance with drug regimens.
8. Describe and differentiate the roles of the pharmacist, physician, and nurse in drug administration.
9. Describe factors to consider in choosing routes of drug administration.
10. Correctly calculate a prescribed drug dose.
11. Discuss factors to include in assessing needs for and response to drug therapy.
12. List the "five rights" of drug administration.
13. Correctly prepare and administer subcutaneous, intramuscular, and intradermal injections; oral medications; topical skin preparations; eye, ear, and nose drops; vaginal instillations; rectal suppositories; and inhalants.
14. Correctly prepare an insulin injection.
15. Discuss the purposes of irrigations.

REVIEW OF KEY CONCEPTS

1. Match the drug name with the correct description.
   - **a.** __4__ Name under which drug is listed in official publications
   - **b.** __1__ Name the drug manufacturer uses to market a drug
   - **c.** __2__ Name that describes the drug's composition
   - **d.** __3__ Name given to a drug by the manufacturer who develops the drug

   1. Brand name
   2. Chemical name
   3. Generic name
   4. Official name
2. A drug classification indicates:
   - **a.** the effect on a body system.
   - **b.** the symptoms relieved.
   - **c.** the desired effect.
   - **d.** all of the above.
3. Fill in the form of medication described below.
   - **a.** __Suspension__ Oral medication of finely divided drug particles dispersed in a liquid medium
   - **b.** __TROCHE (LOZENGE)__ Flat, round dosage form dissolved in the mouth to release the drug
   - **c.** __Capsule__ Medication encased by a gelatin shell
   - **d.** __ointment__ Semisolid, externally applied preparation, usually containing one or more drugs
   - **e.** __Syrup__ Medication dissolved in a concentrated sugar solution
   - **f.** __ENTERIC-COATED__ Oral tablet coated with materials that dissolve in the intestines
   - **g.** __LOTION__ Drug in liquid suspension, applied externally to protect the skin
   - **h.** __TABLET__ Powdered medication compressed into hard disks or cylinders
   - **i.** __PASTE__ Semisolid preparation, thicker and stiffer than ointment, absorbed more slowly than an ointment
   - **j.** __ELIXIR__ Oral medication of clear fluid containing water and alcohol
4. What actions may be taken against a nurse who fails to follow legal provisions when administering controlled substances?
5. Define pharmacokinetics.
6. Dispersal of a drug to body tissues, organs, and specific action sites is referred to as:

a. absorption.
b. metabolism.
c. distribution.
d. excretion.

7. Which statement concerning drug absorption is correct?
   a. Most drugs must enter systemic circulation to exert their therapeutic effect.
   b. Skin and mucous membranes are relatively impermeable to chemicals, making absorption slow.
   c. Oral medications are absorbed more easily when administered with meals.
   d. Drugs administered subcutaneously are absorbed more quickly than those injected intramuscularly.
8. Which of the following factors would increase drug distribution?
   a. Vasoconstriction
   b. Decreased serum albumin
   c. Application of cold over injection site
   d. Increased protein binding
9. Most drug biotransformation occurs in the:
   a. kidneys.
   b. blood.
   c. intestines.
   d. liver.
10. Most drug excretion occurs through the:
   a. kidneys.
   b. intestines.
   c. liver.
   d. lung.
11. Define therapeutic drug effect.
12. Match the unpredicted or unintended effect of a drug with the best definition or description.
   a. 5 Severe reaction characterized by wheezing, shortness of breath, and hypotension
   b. 4 Reaction characterized by urticaria, eczema, pruritus, or rhinitis
   c. 2 Response to excess amounts of drug within the body
   d. 3 Reaction to a drug that is different from normal or expected response
   e. 1 Unintended, secondary effects of a drug

   1. Side effect
   2. Toxic effect
   3. Idiosyncratic reactions
   4. Allergic reaction
   5. Anaphylactic reaction
13. Describe synergistic drug interaction.
14. Drug interactions are typically undesirable and nontherapeutic (true or false)
15. Define serum half-life.
16. Fill in the correct drug action time interval described.
   a. PLATEAU Blood serum concentration that is maintained after repeated, fixed doses
   b. PEAK Time it takes for a drug to reach its highest effective concentration
   c. DURATION Length of time drug is present in concentration sufficient to produce a response
   d. ONSET Time required for a drug to produce a response after administration
17. List three physiological variables that influence drug metabolism.
   a.
   b.
   c.
18. A client's response to a medication may be influenced by environmental conditions at the time the drug is administered (true or false)
19. The nurse's behavior when administering a medication can significantly impact the client's response to the drug. (true or false)
20. The nurse's judgment is essential for safe medication administration. Which of the following can the nurse not determine?
   a. The injection site
   b. The form of the drug preparation to administer
   c. The drug to be administered
   d. The need to hold a medication
21. Mrs. Carr is ordered to receive an antibiotic intramuscularly. Which factor might influence the nurse's method of administration?
   a. Client's level of alertness
   b. Presence of renal disease
   c. Condition of muscle tissue
   d. Permeability of skin's surface
22. The route of choice for medicating clients with poor peripheral perfusion is:
   a. oral.
   b. rectal.
   c. subcutaneous.
   d. intravenous.
23. Local medications, such as those applied to the skin, may cause systemic effects. (true or false)
24. List two instructions to be given to a client before administering sublingual or buccal medications.
   a.
   b.
25. List four major sites for administration of parenteral injections by the nurse.
   a.
   b.
   c.
   d.
26. Why it is necessary to maintain strict sterile technique when preparing medications for parenteral injection?
27. Identify the corresponding basic units of metric measurement (and the abbreviation) for each of the following:

a. Length
b. Weight
c. Volume

28. In which direction is the decimal point moved for the following mathematical calculations in the metric system?
a. Division
b. Multiplication

29. Write in the correct term and the value relative to the basic unit of measurement for each of the following subdivisions or multiples of the metric system.
a. dl ____________________ = _____ L
b. mg ____________________ = _____ G
c. cm ____________________ = _____ M
d. kl ____________________ = _____ L

30. Fill in the apothecary measurement units for each of the abbreviations or symbols listed below.
a. gr ____________________
b. ℥ ____________________
c. f℥ ____________________
d. m ____________________
e. ʒ ____________________

31. Write the appropriate abbreviation for 4 grains.

32. Complete the table of measurement equivalents below.

Metric	Apothecary	Household
1 ml	_____ minims	_____ drops
_____ ml	_____ fluidrams	1 tablespoon
30 ml	_____ fluid ounce	_____ tablespoons
_____ ml	_____ fluid ounces	1 cup
_____ ml	1 pint	_____ pint
_____ ml	_____ quart	1 quart

33. Describe what is meant by the following descriptions of a solution concentration.
a. 5% dextrose in water
b. 1:1000
c. 250 mg/ml

34. Complete the following conversions:
a. 100 mg = _____ g
b. 2.5 L = _____ ml
c. 500 ml = _____ L
d. 60 ml = _____ f℥
e. 15 mg = _____ gr
f. 30 gtt = _____ ml
g. gr 1/6 = _____ mg

35. Write out the formula that is applied to determine the correct dose when preparing solid or liquid forms of medications.

36. Write out the formula that is applied to most accurately calculate pediatric dosages.

37. The physician's order reads: digoxin, 0.125 mg PO qAM. The drug available is digoxin, 0.25 mg tablets.
a. What would the nurse administer?
b. How would this be prepared?

38. The physician's order reads: morphine sulfate, gr 1/8 IM q4h p.r.n. pain. The drug available is morphine sulfate, 10 mg/ml.
a. What would the nurse administer?
b. How would this be prepared?

39. The physician's order reads: erythromycin suspension, 200 mg PO q6h. The drug available is erythromycin suspension, 400 mg/5 ml.
a. What would the nurse administer?
b. How would this be prepared?

40. A 3-year-old is to receive the antibiotic cephalothin (Keflex). The normal single adult dosage is 500 mg. The child's body surface area according to the standard chart is 0.40 M^2. How many milligrams of cephalothin should the child receive?

41. Match the common type of medication order with the examples provided.
a. _____ Colace, 1 capsule PO qAM
b. _____ NPH insulin, 12 units SC at 0800, 5/7
c. _____ Morphine sulfate, 10 mg IM now
d. _____ Tylenol gr × PO q4h for headache

1. Stat order
2. p.r.n. order
3. Onetime order
4. Standing order

42. Identify the primary responsibilities of each of the following health team members in giving medications to clients.
a. Physician
b. Pharmacist
c. Nurse

43. The medication distribution system that most effectively reduces the number of medication errors and reduces dispensing time is the:
a. stock supply.
b. individual client supply.
c. unit-dose system.

44. Identify at least seven areas for nursing assessment and the rationale for obtaining this information before medication administration.
a.
b.
c.
d.
e.
f.
g.

45. A nurse who administers an incorrect drug or dose because of a secretary's transcription error is legally responsible for the medication error. (true or false)

46. The appropriate time to record routine drug administration is:
a. before administering it to the client.
b. immediately after administering it to the client.
c. within 30 minutes of administering it to the client.
d. anytime before the end of the shift.

47. List five guidelines that should be taught to a client to ensure proper use and storage of drugs in the home.

a.
b.
c.
d.
e.

48. Mr. Williams is very unhappy about the medications he is receiving to prevent seizures. Each time he takes the medications he states that he feels "different and very uneasy." Mr. Williams has all of the following rights except:
a. to be informed of the drug's action and potential undesired effects.
b. to request that the nurse reduce the prescribed dose to decrease side effects.
c. to request that the physician assess for drug allergies.
d. to refuse to take the medications that are preventing seizures.

49. List the "five rights" of medication delivery.
a.
b.
c.
d.
e.

50. Describe the three checks that the nurse performs to ensure that the client receives the right drug.
a.
b.
c.

51. In which situation may the nurse correctly administer a medication?
a. When the drug is prepared by another nurse
b. When the drug label is not clear but confirmed by another nurse
c. When a scored tablet is broken unevenly, but administered for two successive doses
d. When a second nurse validates the dose prepared in the syringe

52. What two steps must be taken by the nurse to ensure that the client is correctly identified before receiving the prescribed medication?
a.
b.

53. A routine medication is ordered for 9:00 AM. The medication may be administered:
a. between 8:00 AM and 9:00 AM.
b. between 8:30 AM and 9:30 AM.
c. only between 8:45 AM and 9:15 AM.
d. only at 9:00 AM.

54. Which nursing action would be considered appropriate in administering medications to an infant or child?
a. Allowing the parent to give the medication to the child with the nurse's supervision
b. Providing detailed explanations to the child before administering the medication
c. Giving the child the option of taking or refusing the medication
d. Avoiding any explanation that might increase the child's anxiety before administering injections

55. Which of the following would be an acceptable guideline to follow for administration of medications through a nasogastric tube?
a. Crush sustained-release and enteric-coated tablets into a fine powder.
b. Dissolve powder in 20 to 30 ml of cold water.
c. Administer medications over 30 to 60 minutes.
d. Follow medications with at least 60 ml of water.

56. Number the following steps for preparation of an oral medication in their proper order.
a. _____ Assist the client to a sitting position.
b. _____ Pour or place unit dose medication into a medicine cup.
c. _____ Chart medications in the medicine record.
d. _____ Check accuracy and completeness of information on medication ticket or record with physician's order.
e. _____ Compare medication ticket or record with the prepared drug and its container.
f. _____ Check client identification band and ask client's name.
g. _____ Calculate correct dosage.
h. _____ Offer preferred or recommended liquids with drugs to be swallowed.

57. When preparing unit dose tablets or capsules, the package or wrapper should be removed before placing the medication into the medicine cup. (true or false)

58. Powdered liquids and effervescent powders or tablets should be prepared with the appropriate liquid at the bedside. (true or false)

59. Label the parts of the syringe shown in the diagram at the bottom of the page.
a.
b.
c.
d.
e.

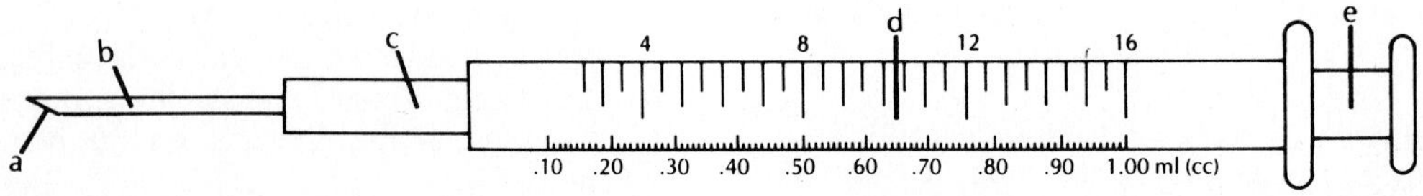

60. What three factors must be considered in selecting the needle for an injection?
a.
b.
c.

61. When preparing small amounts of potent medication for injection (less than 1 ml) the nurse would select which type of syringe?
a. 5 ml syringe
b. 3 ml syringe
c. insulin syringe
d. TB syringe

62. What does it mean when an insulin bottle is labeled U-100?

63. From the list provided, select the needle most appropriate for the specified injection.
a. _____ Intramuscular injection
b. _____ Subcutaneous injection
c. _____ Intravenous injection
d. _____ Intradermal injection

1. 26 gauge, ¼ in.
2. 21 gauge, 1½ in.
3. 18 gauge, 1 in.
4. 25 gauge, ⅝ in.

64. A glass container that must be broken in order to remove medication for injection is called a (an): ________________.

65. A glass container that has a rubber seal at the top to maintain a closed system for medication storage is called a (an): ________________.

66. When a nurse mixes diluent with a powder in a multiple dose vial, what two pieces of information must be placed on the label?
a.
b.

67. The nurse is preparing a medication from a multidose vial.
a. Which key step is missing from the following actions?
(1) Wipe top of vial with alcohol swab.
(2) Pull back on plunger to draw air into syringe equivalent to drug volume.
(3) Insert needle tip into the vial.
(4) Invert vial.
(5) Withdraw medication from vial.
b. Where should the missing step be inserted into the process described above?

68. Briefly describe how the nurse would avoid contamination of one medication with another when mixing medications from one single dose vial (vial A) and one multidose vial (vial B).

69. What technique will prevent medication contamination when mixing medications from two multidose vials (vial A and vial B)?

70. When mixing medications from an ampule and a vial, which medication should be prepared first?
a. Medication in the vial
b. Medication in the ampule
c. Either may be prepared first

71. Which statement about insulin preparations is correct?
a. An insulin vial must be shaken to properly distribute particles.
b. Insulin must be kept refrigerated at all times.
c. The only insulin for IV use is regular (short acting).
d. Slower-acting, modified insulins appear clear.

72. When preparing insulin from two vials, the nurse:
a. shakes each vial to properly distribute the particles.
b. injects air into the clear, unmodified (regular) vial first.
c. uses separate syringes to draw up the dose from each vial.
d. withdraws the cloudy (modified) insulin last.

73. List six techniques to minimize client discomfort associated with injections.
a.
b.
c.
d.
e.
f.

74. Using the diagrams below, shade in the areas of the body that are suitable for subcutaneous injections.

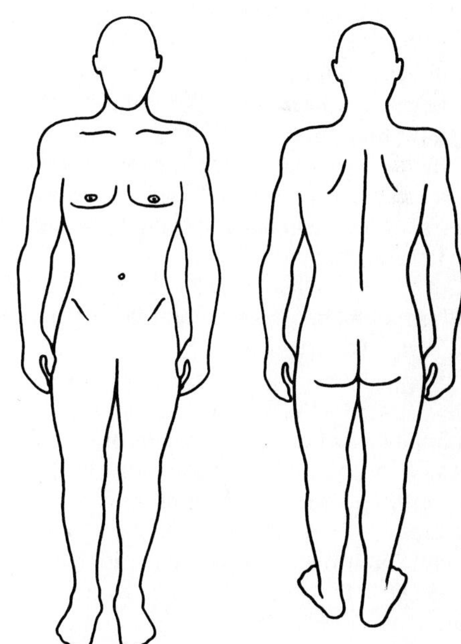

75. The site most frequently recommended for subcutaneous heparin injection is the ________________.

76. The maximal volume of water-soluble medication that may be administered to an adult by the subcutaneous route is:
a. 0.5 ml.
b. 1.0 ml.

c. 1.5 ml.
d. 2.0 ml.

77. State the rule that may be followed to determine whether a subcutaneous injection should be given at a 90-degree or a 45-degree angle.

78. The angle of needle insertion for an intramuscular injection is:
a. 15 degrees.
b. 45 degrees.
c. 60 degrees.
d. 90 degrees.

79. Indicate the maximal volume of medication for intramuscular injection in each of the following situations.
a. Well-developed adult
b. Older children, elderly or thin adult
c. Older infants and small children

80. The preferred sites for intramuscular injections in the adult or child are the:
a. vastus lateralis and ventrogluteal.
b. dorsogluteal and deltoid.
c. ventrogluteal and dorsogluteal.
d. vastus lateralis and deltoid.

81. The injection site that poses the greatest risk of contamination and potential client injury is the:
a. vastus lateralis.
b. ventrogluteal.
c. dorsogluteal.
d. deltoid.

82. The deltoid injection site:
a. is an acceptable injection site for infants and children.
b. has well-developed muscle tissue for injection in most adults.
c. lacks major nerves and blood vessels.
d. is acceptable only for small volumes of drugs.

83. Describe the method for accurately locating the following injection sites.
a. Deltoid
b. Ventrogluteal
c. Vastus lateralis
d. Dorsogluteal

84. The Z-track technique for administering an intramuscular injection is used when the:
a. amount injected is greater than 3 ml of fluid.
b. drug is extremely irritating to subcutaneous tissue.
c. drug is extremely potent or has many side effects.
d. client is incontinent or cachexic.

85. Describe the procedure used in administering an intramuscular injection using the Z-track technique.

86. Number the following steps for preparing and administering an intramuscular injection in the correct sequence.
a. _____ Aspirate medication by pulling back on the plunger.
b. _____ Discard needle and syringe into appropriate receptacle.
c. _____ Cleanse injection site with alcohol swab.
d. _____ Quickly inject needle at a 90-degree angle.
e. _____ Explain procedure to client, assist to proper position.
f. _____ Massage injection site slowly.
g. _____ Inspect and palpate injection site for proper landmarks, masses, or tenderness.
h. _____ Spread skin tightly across injection site.
i. _____ Withdraw needle quickly from site.
j. _____ Inject medication slowly.

87. A skin test will not be valid if a bleb does not appear at the injection site. (true or false)

88. When should an intradermal injection site be "read"?
a. Within 24 hours
b. 24 to 48 hours
c. 48 to 72 hours
d. After 72 hours

89. All of the following actions are appropriate to medication administration. Which is specific to the nurse giving intravenous drugs?
a. Know the five rights of safe drug administration.
b. Have the antidote available during administration.
c. Monitor the client's vital signs.
d. Observe the client for adverse reactions.

90. The most dangerous method of drug administration is:
a. dorsogluteal intramuscular injection.
b. large-volume IV infusions.
c. IV bolus injections.
d. piggyback infusions.

91. When no specific rate of administration is recommended for an IV bolus medication, what is the recommended injection rate?
a. 1 mg/min
b. 1 ml/min
c. 10 mg/min
d. 100 ml/min

92. After administering an injection, the nurse carefully recaps the needle before discarding it in the designated container. (true or false)

93. What precaution should the nurse take when administering locally applied medications such as lotions or ointments?

94. As long as the tip of the applicator remains clean, it is acceptable for a person to use another individual's eye drops. (true or false)

95. Which action is appropriate when administering eye medications?
a. Cleanse away any crusts or drainage by wiping from outer to inner canthus.
b. Instill eye drops onto the cornea from a distance of approximately 1 to 2 cm.
c. Apply gentle pressure to the nasolacrimal duct for 30 to 60 seconds after medication administration.
d. Instruct the client to squeeze the eyelids closed after instilling eye drops.

96. Lisa is a 4-year-old client with an infection of the right ear. The nurse observes a collection of cerumen in the ear canal. Which of the following measures would the nurse not use while administering ear drops to Lisa?
   a. Pull the pinna upward and backward.
   b. Assist Lisa to lie on her left side.
   c. Remove ear wax gently with an applicator.
   d. Instill drops at least 1 cm above ear canal.
97. Which statement concerning instillation of vaginal medications is correct?
   a. The client should be instructed to remain on her back at least 10 minutes after administration.
   b. The pointed end of the vaginal suppository should be inserted into the vagina.
   c. Disposable gloves need not be worn if an applicator is used.
   d. Suppositories need to be inserted approximately 2.5 to 5 cm.
98. Which statement concerning administration of rectal suppositories is correct?
   a. Suppositories should reach room temperature before insertion.
   b. Suppositories must pass the anus and internal sphincter.
   c. The client should be placed in the prone position.
   d. Asking the client to bear down assists in relaxing the sphincters.
99. To maximize the effect of metered dose inhaler medications, the nurse advises the client to:
   a. depress the medication canister fully, immediately after exhalation.
   b. hold his or her breath for approximately 10 seconds after delivering the aerosol spray.
   c. exhale through an open mouth to minimize the risk of side effects.
   d. wait 1 to 2 minutes between inhalations to maximize therapeutic effect.

APPLICATION OF KEY CONCEPTS

Activities to reinforce skills and techniques

1. Dosage calculations
   Answer each of the following medication administration problems. Submit your answers to your instructor for validation.
   a. Pronestyl, 500 mg, is ordered q.i.d. for Mrs. Adams. The drug is dispensed in 250 mg tablets. Mrs. Adams is going home on a weekend pass, leaving the hospital at 9:00 AM Saturday and returning at 8:00 PM Sunday. How many tablets will Mrs. Adams require at home?
   b. Dr. Rose has ordered codeine gr ½ for Wendy Smith. The stock on the unit is codeine gr ⅙. How many tablets would you use?
   c. Convert 250 mg to grams.
   d. 1½ f℥ = _____ ml.
   e. Mr. Cox has Demerol (meperidine), 35 mg, ordered. The supply on the unit is meperidine, 50 mg/ml.
      (1) How many milliliters would you administer?
      (2) How many minims would that be using a 3 ml syringe?
   f. What is the estimated child's dose of morphine sulfate for a 5-year-old weighing 20 kg (45 pounds) who is 109 cm (43 inches) tall? The adult dose is 10 mg. (Refer to the West nomogram, Fig. 15-2, p. 375, in your text.)
   g. The physician's order reads: ampicillin, 50 mg IM q6h. Stock available is a 125 mg vial of ampicillin that requires reconstitution. When 1.2 ml of normal saline is added, the resulting solution strength is 125 mg/ml. How many milliliters would you administer?
   h. The physician's order reads: 5000 U heparin SC q12h. Stock available is 10,000 u/ml or 1000 U/ml. Both strengths come in a 5 ml multidose vial.
      (1) Which strength would you use and why?
      (2) How many milliliters would you administer?
   i. Joe Williams has a preoperative sedation order as follows:
      Meperidine, 100 mg } IM on call
      Atropine, 0.2 mg }
      Stock available is meperidine, 50 mg/ml; meperidine, 75 mg/ml; meperidine, 100 mg/ml; and atropine, 0.4 g/ml. (Meperidine and atropine are compatible.)
      (1) Which strength of meperidine would you use and why?
      (2) How many milliliters of meperidine would you draw up in the syringe?
      (3) How many milliliters of atropine would you draw up in the syringe?
      (4) How many milliliters (total) would be in the syringe when both medications have been drawn up?
2. Oral medication administration
   In a laboratory setting practice each of the following techniques:
   a. Prepare tablets or capsules (any over-the-counter medication such as aspirin or acetaminophen or a simulated medication provided by your instructor) from a bottle by pouring into bottle cap and transferring to a medication cup without touching the tablet or capsule with your fingers.
   b. If available, prepare tablets or capsules dispensed in a unit dose package. Over-the-counter medications, such as cold capsules, are available in this form.
   c. Prepare 650 mg of aspirin for administration through a nasogastric tube.
   d. Prepare 10 ml of a liquid medication from a bottle.
   e. Prepare 1/2 teaspoon of a liquid medication from a bottle. (Be sure that this dose is accurately measured using equipment available in the hospital setting.)
3. Preparing injections
   In a laboratory setting, with the materials and equip-

ment provided by your instructor or laboratory assistant:

a. Examine the various types of disposable syringes and needles available in your institution.
b. Identify the following parts of a syringe: bevel, barrel, needle shaft, plunger, hub, milliliter scale, minim scale.
c. Identify the syringe and most appropriate needle size for each of the following activities:
   (1) Insulin injection in an obese adult
   (2) Intramuscular injection of 2.5 ml in a well-developed adult
   (3) Intramuscular injection of 0.5 ml in an infant
   (4) Subcutaneous injection of 1.0 ml in an emaciated adult
   (5) Intradermal skin testing with 0.1 ml of prescribed solution
d. Practice handling the syringes, capping and recapping the needle, and changing needles while maintaining aseptic technique. (Remember that once a needle has been used for injection, it is *never recapped but discarded immediately into the appropriate receptable.*)
e. Examine a Tubex or Carpuject syringe and cartridge system. Practice loading, handling, and unloading the cartridge.
f. Examine ampules and vials.
g. If available, practice drawing up each of the following volumes. Have a peer or instructor critique your performance and validate the accuracy of your measurement.
   (1) 1.5 ml from a multidose vial
   (2) 1.8 ml from an ampule
   (3) Mixing 1 ml from an ampule and 0.5 ml from a vial
   (4) Mixing 0.75 ml from one vial and 0.5 ml from another vial

4. Locating injection sites
   With a partner, practice locating each of the following injection sites. Have an instructor validate the accuracy of your site identification.

   IM sites

   Right and left ventrogluteal
   Vastus lateralis
   Dorsogluteal
   Deltoid

   SQ sites

   Arms
   Legs
   Abdomen
   Scapular area

   Intradermal sites

   Arms
   Scapular area

5. Administering injections
   In the laboratory setting using an injection pad, grapefruit, injection hip, or mannequin designed for injection practice, perform each of the designated tasks. Have a peer or instructor critique your performance based on the steps presented in your text.
   a. Prepare and administer 0.5 ml of sterile saline for subcutaneous injection.
   b. Prepare and administer 1.0 ml of sterile saline for intramuscular injection.
   c. Prepare and administer 1.5 ml of sterile saline using the Z-track technique.
6. Eye applications
   In the laboratory setting, using a mannequin, practice administering eye drops. Have a peer or instructor critique your performance using the steps presented in your text.
7. Ear instillations
   In the laboratory setting, using a mannequin, practice administering ear drops to an adult and a child. Have a peer or instructor critique your performance using the steps presented in your text.
8. Insulin injections
   In the laboratory setting:
   a. Examine the variety of insulin syringes available for clients in your institution.
   b. If available, examine a variety of insulin preparations. Practice preparation of insulin for injection including:
      (1) 8 units of regular insulin
      (2) 13 units of NPH insulin
      (3) 15 units of NPH and 7 units of regular insulin

Activities to reinforce theoretical concepts

1. Experiential exercise: drug names and forms
   Using a nursing pharmacology text, look up the drug Prostaphlin.
   a. Is this a trade name, a proprietary name, an official name, or a generic name?
   b. What is the drug's generic name?
   c. What is the drug's classification?
   d. What are the general characteristics of medications in this classification?
   e. What are the nursing implications of administering medications in this classification?
   f. What forms of this medication are available?
2. Legislation and drug control
   a. Review your state nurse-practice act as it pertains to the nurse's role and responsibilities in medication administration.
   b. Review your institution's policies and procedures concerning drug administration.
   c. In a small group, invite a hospital pharmacist to discuss narcotic control in your institution.
   d. Compare the guidelines for safe narcotic administration and control listed in your text on p. 363 with your institution's policies and procedure for narcotic administration and control.
   e. Observe a nurse's procedure for signing out narcotics and counting narcotics at the change of shift.
3. Clinical situation: narcotic administration

Mr. Towns is a 50-year-old client who suffered a traumatic injury to his right leg. His physician ordered codeine, 60 mg PO q4h prn, for pain.

a. What procedure must the nurse adhere to when administering the controlled drug to Mr. Towns?

b. While the nurse is assisting Mr. Towns to sit up on the side of the bed, the medicine cup is overturned and the codeine tablets fall onto the floor. What responsibilities are involved with the proper disposal of the contaminated codeine?

c. When the nurse returns to Mr. Towns' room with the codeine tablets, he requests that the nurse only give him half of the dose (30 mg instead of the 60 mg that is ordered). What should the nurse do?

4. Clinical situation: nature of drug actions

Mrs. Post is a 32-year-old mother of three with metastatic breast cancer. She is requesting pain medication for intense pain. The physician has ordered morphine, 8 mg Sq q3-4h.

a. You review the medication record and find that Mrs. Post received her last morphine injection 1 hour ago. What would you do at this time?

b. Discuss the differences between the mechanism of action of morphine and its pharmacokinetics (absorption, distribution, metabolism, and excretion). Which factors associated with drug action might be contributing to Mrs. Post's lack of response to her most recent morphine injection?

c. The physician changes the route of morphine administration to IV.

(1) Why would a different route make the same dose of morphine more effective?

(2) What risks are associated with the use of the IV route for morphine administration?

(3) What nursing actions should be taken before, during, and after IV administration of morphine?

(4) Describe each of the following effects of morphine that might be expected.

(a) Therapeutic effect
(b) Side effects
(c) Toxic effects
(d) Idiosyncratic reactions
(e) Allergic reactions

d. In addition to the IV morphine p.r.n., the physician orders enteric-coated aspirin, 650 mg po qid, for Mrs. Post. Why would the physician prescribe two different medications for pain?

e. What could the nurse do to maximize the pain-relieving action of Mrs. Post's analgesic medications?

5. Clinical situation: IV medications

Mr. Martin has an IV line infusing.

a. List three methods that can be used to administer a drug intravenously to Mr. Martin

b. Discuss your responsibilities as a nurse when administering Mr. Martin's drug intravenously.

c. Mr. Martin has 500 mg of ampicillin ordered q6h IV. Describe how you would add this drug to a 100 ml bag of IV solution. What supplies and equipment do you need? Would this 100 ml bag be considered a primary or secondary IV infusion? Why?

d. Mr. Martin's physician has ordered the continuous IV infusion to be discontinued and a heparin lock inserted. What nursing implications are involved when administering drugs through a heparin lock? What nursing responsibilities are involved when caring for Mr. Martin while this heparin lock is in place?

6. Clincal situation: topical medications

Mr. White has a draining abdominal wound. The physician orders a steroid ointment to be applied to the surrounding skin.

a. What does the nurse do before preparing the medication?

b. How does the nurse apply the medication?

7. Experiential exercise: medication orders

In any client care setting, examine the physician's orders for a specific client.

a. Identify each of the following types of orders in the client's record.

(1) Standing orders
(2) p.r.n. orders
(3) Single (onetime) orders
(4) Stat orders

b. Examine one medication order and identify each of the seven essential parts.

(1) Client's full name
(2) Date of order
(3) Drug name
(4) Dosage
(5) Route of administration
(6) Time and frequency of administration
(7) Signature of physician or nurse

c. Examine the medication record for the specified client. Compare the medication orders to the information recorded on the medication record.

8. Experiential exercise: medication assessment

Perform a medication assessment on an assigned client or a peer. Formulate nursing diagnoses and interventions related to medication administration based on the information obtained in each of the designated areas. Submit your written work to your instructor for feedback.

a. Pertinent medical history
b. History of allergies
c. Client's current condition
d. Diet history
e. Client's perceptual and coordination abilities or limitations
f. Client's knowledge and understanding of drug therapy
g. Client's attitude about the use of drugs

9. Experiential exercise: drug data

Review a client's medication record. Identify at least two drugs the client is receiving routinely. Prepare a drug card or sheet that includes the following information. Submit your written work to your instructor for feedback.

a. Generic and trade names
b. Classification
c. Action
d. Purpose
e. Normal dosages
f. Routes
g. Side effects
h. Toxic effects
i. Nursing implications for administration and monitoring

(There are medication cards that may be purchased, summarizing this information. Your instructor can best advise you about use of published cards as a quick reference.)

10. Clinical situation: medication errors
A student is caring for two clients, Mr. Roth and Mr. Evans, who are roommates. The student is to administer Mr. Roth's 10 PM medications, which have already been checked in the medicine room by the student's clinical instructor. The student enters the room and administers the medication to Mr. Evans.
a. What should the student do?
b. Which of the five rights have been violated in this situation?
c. How could this error have been prevented?
d. Using your institution's guide, determine what information should be included on the incident report.
e. What information should be charted in Mr. Evans' medication record and chart?

11. Clinical situation: care planning
Ms. Owens is a 32-year-old client who lives at home with her parents. She has diabetes that is complicated by renal disease and blindness. Ms. Owens requires regular insulin injections, an antihypertensive medication given four times per day, and a daily iron supplement. Develop a care plan that will enable Ms. Owens to maintain her independence and ensure that she takes her prescribed medications at the right time each day.

12. Clinical situation: medications and the elderly client
Mr. Win is an 84-year-old client admitted to your nursing division. The physician has ordered three different oral medications for Mr. Win. Considering the physiological changes that accompany aging, identify those factors that should be assessed to determine the likelihood that the drugs can be administered effectively.

13. Bryan is an 18-month-old toddler who is hospitalized for croup. His medications include an oral antibiotic suspension to be taken every 6 hours and an intramuscular injection twice daily.
a. What resources would you consult before attempting to administer Bryan's medications?
b. What psychological preparation would be appropriate for Bryan:
(1) before giving his antibiotic?
(2) before giving his injection?
c. What techniques would you use in administering the antibiotic?
d. What techniques would you use in administering the injection?

ADDITIONAL READINGS

Allen, MD: Drug therapy in the elderly, Am J Nurs 80:1474, 1980.
Brief discussion of physiological changes associated with aging and their impact on medication efficacy in the elderly.

Birdsall, C, and Uretsky, S: How do I administer medication by NG? Am J Nurs 84:1259, 1984.
Question-and-answer format used to present basic techniques of medication administration via nasogastric tubes.

Chaplin, G, Shull, H, and Welk, PC: How safe is the air-bubble technique of I.M. injections? Nurs 85 15(9):59, 1985.
Presents information that refutes the use of the air-bubble technique in preparing intramuscular injections. Proposes that the air-bubble [air-lock] technique increases the risk of medication error and should not be routinely used for intramuscular injection.

Clayton, M: The right way to prevent medication errors, RN 50(6):30, 1987.
Explores the five "rights" of medication administration. Presents several helpful hints and examples to assist in maintaining the client's safety.

Davis, NM, and Cohen, MR: Learning from mistakes: 20 tips for avoiding medication errors, Nurs 82 12(3):63, 1982.
Presents 20 common medication errors. Conditions that could contribute to the error are described and actions to prevent the error are discussed.

Keithley, JK, and O'Donnell, J: Look out for those drug-nutrient interactions, Nurs 86 16(2):42, 1986.
A table of common drug-nutrient interactions that place clients at risk.

LeSage, J, editor: Symposium on drugs and the older adult, Nurs Clin North Am 17(2):251, 1982.
Series of articles addressing drug therapy in the older adult. Includes issues of pharmacokinetics and pharmacodynamics, compliance and self-care, and drug abuse. Articles addressing cardiovascular and psychotropic drugs are included.

McConnell, EA: The subtle art of really good injections, RN 45(2):24, 1982.
Detailed continuing-education program that discusses injection techniques. Includes illustrations and tables to summarize major teaching points. Injection techniques presented are supported by scientific rationale.

Miyares, MV: Medication aids your elderly patient will love, RN 48(11):44, 1985.
Pictoral presentation of devices that can increase medication compliance in clients with motor or sensory impairments.

Moree, NA: Nurses speak out on patients and drug regimens, Am J Nurs 85:51, 1985.
Explores factors associated with noncompliance to drug regimens. Presents guidelines to be followed in diagnosing, analyzing, and treating noncompliance.

Perez, S: Reducing injection pain, Am J Nurs 84:645, 1984.
Abstract of study revealing that slower injection time was associated with significantly lower pain intensity

during injection and a shorter duration of pain after injection.

Shepherd, MJ, and Swearington, P: Z-track injections, Am J Nurs 84:746, 1984.

Detailed explanation of the Z-track injection technique. Photographs illustrating each step of the process correlate with the text.

Statz, E: Hand strength and metered dose inhalers, Am J Nurs 84:800, 1984.

Presents research findings of study measuring hand strength associated with 2-point and 3-point position using metered dose inhalers. Recommends evaluation of hand strength as a critical element in determining the efficacy of metered dose inhalers. Suggests presenting most appropriate method to clients based on hand strength.

Thatcher, G: Insulin injections, the case against random rotation, Am J Nurs 85:690, 1985.

Cites findings that suggest that random injection site rotation may produce erratic insulin levels. Presents teaching plan that recommends using all available sites in one area before moving to an alternate site.

Thompson, DA: Teaching the client about anticoagulants, Am J Nurs 82:278, 1982.

Detailed discussion of teaching program presented to clients requiring anticoagulant therapy. Teaching principles and information presented may also be useful in formulating a plan for client medication teaching for drugs other than anticoagulants.

Todd, B: Drugs and the elderly: using eye drops and ointments safely, Geriatr Nurs 4(1):53, 1983.

Brief overview of prescription eye medications. Offers administration guidelines for both nurse and client. Includes major client teaching points.

Wong, DL: Significance of dead space in syringes, Am J Nurs 82:1237, 1982.

Discussion of the nature of syringe dead space with particular attention to its effect on insulin administration. Makes recommendations to promote client safety and therapeutic action of injectable medications.

UNIT 4 Professional Nursing Concepts

Chapter 16
Values

PREREQUISITE READING

Read Chapter 16, pp. 432 to 447.

OBJECTIVES

Mastery of content in this chapter will enable the student to:

1. Define selected terms associated with personal and professional values.
2. Describe how values influence behavior and attitudes.
3. Discuss the ways in which values are learned.
4. Contrast and compare modes of value transmission.
5. Compare how values are formed at different stages of development.
6. Discuss the influence of ethnicity on value formation.
7. Explain the relationship between nurse's values and clinical decision making.
8. Describe the process of values clarification.
9. Discuss the advantages of values clarification in nursing.
10. Use a values clarification strategy to examine personal values.
11. Discuss the techniques used to help clients clarify values.
12. Analyze personal values as a student of nursing.

REVIEW OF KEY CONCEPTS

1. Define value.
2. Which statement concerning values is correct?
   - **a.** Most individuals possess a great number of personal values.
   - **b.** A person's values about health will determine personal health care decisions.
   - **c.** Extrinsic values are related to the maintenance of life.
   - **d.** Personal values rarely influence an individual's perception of others.
3. The type of care a nurse administers to a client is influenced by the nurse's personal and professional values. (true or false)
4. Define attitude.
5. Identify two ways in which values are learned.
   - **a.**
   - **b.**
6. Identify and briefly describe the four traditional modes of value transmission.
   - **a.**
   - **b.**
   - **c.**
   - **d.**
7. The mode of value transmission that is viewed as one that promotes greater understanding of an individual's personal values is known as ________.
8. A nursing instructor is comforting a grieving parent. By actions, the instructor may be transmitting a value through the mode of:
   - **a.** modeling.
   - **b.** moralizing.
   - **c.** laissez-faire.
   - **d.** responsible choice.
9. The developmental stage in which parents may actively begin directing the child toward behaviors they value is:
   - **a.** infancy.
   - **b.** school age.
   - **c.** preschool age.
   - **d.** adolescence.
10. An adult's established values may be threatened with advancing age. (true or false)
11. A process through which an individual gains clearer insight into his or her values is called ________.
12. Identify the three major phases of values clarification.
    - **a.**
    - **b.**
    - **c.**
13. Identify and briefly describe a strategy that the nurse may use in helping an individual clarify values.
14. By clarifying personal and professional values, the nurse:
    - **a.** establishes more effective relationships with clients.
    - **b.** increases personal growth and professional satisfaction.
    - **c.** facilitates decision making and problem solving.
    - **d.** all of the above.
15. List four examples of client behaviors that may suggest the need for values clarification.

a.
b.
c.
d.

16. List three characteristics of a clarifying response.
   a.
   b.
   c.

17. Match the steps in the values clarification process with the supportive nursing measures described.
   a. The nurse shows acceptance of a client's views and encourages verbalization of what the client values. ____
   b. The nurse assesses the client's ability to make decisions. ____
   c. The nurse assists the client in identifying ways to act on personal values. ____
   d. The nurse evaluates behaviors the client has initiated that reflect an identified value. ____

   1. Choosing from alternative beliefs
   2. Prizing a choice
   3. Making a choice part of one's behavior
   4. Acting consistently

18. In the first step of the values clarification process, which of the following behaviors might the nurse use to support the client?
   a. Encouraging the client to state personal values
   b. Assisting the client in examining alternative values
   c. Helping the client plan ways to translate values into behaviors
   d. Offering a set of values from which the client may choose those preferred

APPLICATION OF KEY CONCEPTS

Activities to reinforce theoretical concepts

1. Identify three of your own personal values and discuss how each may influence your professional practice. Determine the factors that you believe contributed to your acquiring these values. Share this information with other nursing students during a small group discussion.
2. Describe the similarities and differences between attitudes and values. Cite examples of each to support your answer.
3. Compare and contrast the traditional modes of value transmission in the table below. Note ways parents use each mode, and cite examples of potentially desirable and undesirable outcomes of each mode.

Modes of value transmission	Parent's behavior	Desirable effect	Undesirable effect
Modeling			
Moralizing			
Laissez-faire			
Responsible choice			

4. Describe and give an example of how values are formed in each of the developmental stages.
   a. Infancy
   b. Toddlerhood
   c. Preschool childhood
   d. School-age childhood
   e. Adolescence
   f. Adulthood
      (1) Young adult
      (2) Middle-aged adult
      (3) Older adult
5. Experiential exercise: personal values clarification
   a. Independently, or in a small group, complete the health value scale found on p. 442 in your text. Identify factors that you feel have contributed to your acquiring these specific values. Discuss your ranking of the values with other group members.
   b. In a small group, independently complete the rank ordering tool found on p. 441 in your text. If possible, include an experienced student nurse, staff nurse, head nurse, or instructor in your group. Identify factors that you feel have contributed to your acquiring these values. Discuss your ranking of the values with the group members.
   c. File the values clarification exercises that you have just completed. Review your value ranking when you have completed the first year of your nursing program to determine if professional growth has altered your value system. (If possible, review these exercises when you complete the entire nursing program.)
6. Experiential exercise: values clarification with clients
   a. Following a clinical experience, identify a client (or nurse) who may be a candidate for values clarification.
   b. Describe the client's (nurse's) behaviors that indicate the potential need for values clarification.
   c. Discuss how values clarification might benefit the client (nurse).
   d. Describe the strategies that might assist the client in the process of values clarification.
7. Clinical situation: values clarification
   Mr. Barnes is a 26-year-old client who entered the hospital following a gunshot wound to the spinal cord. The injury has left him with a complete paralysis of his legs and a partial paralysis of his arms. You learn that Mr. Barnes was shot during a police raid on his home, where a large supply of illegal drugs was found. Mr. Barnes has made frequent requests for pain medication.
   a. Discuss how strategies for values clarification might assist you in caring for this client.
   b. Identify resources in your nursing program and health care setting that might be available to assist you in the values clarification process.
8. Clinical situation: clarifying responses
   Mr. Watkins enters the hospital with severe cardiac failure. The physician has informed Mr. Watkins that his condition will not improve with medication and

he will be severely limited in his ability to carry out activities of daily living for the remainder of his life.

The physician tells Mr. Watkins that the only other treatment available to him is open heart surgery, which may improve his condition, but the risk of death associated with the procedure is extremely high. Mr. Watkins tells the student nurse, "I just don't know what to do. I want to do what's right. What do you think?"

a. What behaviors indicate that values clarification may be helpful in this situation?

b. In a small group, role-play this situation with one student as Mr. Watkins and another as the student. Be sure to structure your responses according to the five characteristics described in your text. Attempt to work through the situation using the seven steps of the values clarification process.

c. Evaluate the role-playing situation. Identify what strategies were most successful and those that were least successful. Determine how your own values influenced role playing as the student nurse and as Mr. Watkins. Discuss your conclusions.

ADDITIONAL READINGS

Bernal, EW: Values clarification: a critique, J Nurs Educ 24:174, 1985.

Describes the concept of values clarification. Points out the limitations of values clarification in resolution of ethical dilemmas. Emphasizes the need for nurses to become skillful in ethical reasoning.

Coletta, SS: Values clarification in nursing: why? Am J Nurs 78:2057, 1978.

Briefly reviews the seven steps of the values clarification process. Explains the importance of values clarification in nursing practice.

McNally, JM: Values. II, Superv Nurs 11:52, 1980.

Describes the impact of economics on values in nursing practice.

McNally, JM: Values. III, Superv Nurs 11:40, 1980.

Examines values influencing nursing practice in the context of the law, rights, and responsibilities.

Uustal, DB: Values clarification in nursing: application to practice, Am J Nurs 78:2058, 1978.

Discusses the theoretical concepts that guide values clarification. Presents 10 strategies that may be used in personal or professional values clarification exercises.

Chapter 17
Ethics in Nursing

PREREQUISITE READING

Read Chapter 17, pp. 448 to 463.

OBJECTIVES

Mastery of content in this chapter will enable the student to:

1. Define terms associated with ethics in nursing practice.
2. Describe the influence of ethics on nursing practice.
3. Differentiate ethical issues from moral and legal issues.
4. Explain the influence of historical changes in health care on nursing ethics.
5. Describe the influence of personal and professional values on ethical decisions.
6. Contrast and compare responsibility and accountability.
7. Explain the relationship between accountability and ethics.
8. Identify the purposes of a professional code of ethics.
9. Explain the ethical implications of client advocacy.
10. Discuss the type of ethical conflicts confronted by nurses.
11. Discuss the process used to resolve ethical problems.

REVIEW OF KEY CONCEPTS

1. Define ethics.
2. What is an ethical dilemma?
3. Ethics provide standards that assist the nurse in making decisions and implementing appropriate actions. (true or false)
4. A health care issue often becomes an ethical dilemma because:
   a. a client's legal rights coexist with a health professional's obligations.
   b. decisions must be made quickly, under stressful conditions.
   c. decisions must be made based on value systems.
   d. the choices involved do not appear to be clearly right or wrong.
5. The personal conviction that something is absolutely right or wrong in all situations is a (an):
   a. legal obligation.
   b. personal value.
   c. moral belief.
   d. ethical issue.
6. Ethical issues are usually easily translated into law. (true or false)
7. The field of ethics that addresses complex issues faced by health care professionals is known as ______________.
8. Which statement concerning an ethical code for a profession is false?
   a. An ethical code describes duties and responsibilities of professional practice.
   b. An ethical code identifies a standard of behavior for members of a professional group.
   c. Ethical codes allow a profession to discipline its members.
   d. Ethical codes provide a foundation for development of professional curricula.
9. Match the term associated with professional practice with the most accurate definition or description.
   a. ______ That which provides standards for a professional nurse's conduct
   b. ______ To be willing to answer for one's own actions
   c. ______ The scope of functions and duties associated with the nurse's role
   d. ______ A structure against which competent care may be measured
   e. ______ A process of providing clients with information and supporting decisions
   1. Responsibility
   2. Code of ethics
   3. Standard of care
   4. Advocacy
   5. Accountability
10. List three purposes of professional accountability.
    a.
    b.
    c.
11. Identify the two primary functions of advocacy.
    a.
    b.
12. The nurse enters Mrs. Wilson's room and finds her crying. Mrs. Wilson states, "My doctor just told me I need surgery for the tumor in my neck. What should I do?"

As a client advocate the nurse's best reply would be:

- **a.** "It may be helpful for you to ask for another physician's opinion."
- **b.** "It seems that your physician was giving you an honest opinion based on your test results."
- **c.** "I know that it must be a difficult time for you to talk. I will come back to discuss any question you have."
- **d.** "You seem very upset now, and I understand, but you should know that your doctor is very experienced in this procedure."

13. Which of the following does not describe the nurse's actions as a client advocate?
- **a.** To assist a client in clarifying personal values
- **b.** To properly inform a client about health care needs
- **c.** To recognize that advocacy is required by all clients
- **d.** To offer information that allows a client to make his or her own decisions

14. Identify four factors that influence a nurse's ability to make ethical decisions within an institutional setting.
- **a.**
- **b.**
- **c.**
- **d.**

15. Identify two characteristics of a problem that indicate that an ethical dilemma (as opposed to a legal problem) exists.
- **a.**
- **b.**

16. List the six steps to be followed in resolving ethical dilemmas.
- **a.**
- **b.**
- **c.**
- **d.**
- **e.**
- **f.**

APPLICATION OF KEY CONCEPTS

Activities to reinforce theoretical concepts

1. Compare and contrast a legal right and an ethical right. Provide examples to support your discussion.

2. Compare and contrast ethical and moral issues. Provide examples to support your discussion.

3. Discuss how the evolution of nursing practice has influenced professional ethics.

4. Discuss the ANA or ICN code of ethics as it relates to each of the following:
- **a.** Standards of nursing care
- **b.** Responsibility to clients
- **c.** Role in society

5. Compare and contrast the ANA or ICN code of ethics to the nurse practice act of your state or province in each of the following areas:
- **a.** Professional responsibility
- **b.** Professional accountability
- **c.** Client advocacy
- **d.** Legal obligations

6. Describe at least two ways in which student nurses are able to maintain professional accountability to each of the following individuals or groups:
- **a.** Personal (self)
- **b.** Client
- **c.** Profession
- **d.** Educational institution or health care institution
- **e.** Society

7. Clinical situation: resolution of ethical problems
Independently, or in a small group, apply the process for resolving ethical problems to the following hypothetical situations. For each step, identify the information that you would gather and describe the actions that you would take in resolving the dilemma.

Situation A: You are employed as a staff nurse on a busy surgical unit. You have noticed that the narcotic drug count for meperidine (Demerol) is inaccurate every time Ms. Green, another nurse, is working. One day you see Ms. Green take something from the narcotic cupboard and put it in her pocket.

Situation B: You are performing a head-to-toe assessment on an assigned client. You think that you hear crackles during auscultation of the lungs, but the co-assigned staff member charts that the client has rhonchi. The client tells you that you are the only person who has listened to his chest that morning.

8. Experiential exercise: ethical problems in nursing
- **a.** Independently, or as a small group exercise, contact nurses practicing in different areas in your institution or community. Ask them to identify at least three ethical issues they have encountered in their particular practice setting.
- **b.** Following an observational experience, or after providing nursing care to a client in any health care setting, identify ethical issues that would be considered unique to the practice setting or your particular client situation. Support your identification of the issue as an ethical problem based on the characteristics of ethical problems described in your text.
- **c.** Invite an experienced staff nurse to discuss an ethical dilemma encountered in clinical practice. Compare the method employed by the nurse to resolve the dilemma with the process outlined in your text.

ADDITIONAL READINGS

American Nurse's Association: Code for nurses, Am J Nurs 50:196, 392, 1950.

Original publication of principles guiding professional nursing practice developed by the ANA Committee on Ethics.

Aroskar, MA: Anatomy of an ethical dilemma: the theory, Am J Nurs 80:658, 1980.

Discussion of the nature of an ethical dilemma. Gives

overview of ethical theories and strategies that may be used in clarifying ethical dilemmas.

Aroskar, MA: Anatomy of an ethical dilemma: the practice, Am J Nurs 80:661, 1980.

Detailed discussion relating ethical principles and resolution strategies to a nursing practice situation.

Aroskar, MA: Nurses as decision makers: ethical dimensions, Imprint 32:29, 1985.

Detailed discussion of ethical problems, principles, and the ethical decision-making process.

Chinn, P, editor: Ethical issues in nursing, Rockville, MD., 1986, Aspen Publishers, Inc.

Selected articles from two nursing journals (Advances in Nursing Science and Topics in Clinical Nursing) addressing ethical issues associated with nursing practice.

French, DG: Ethics: nurse, am I going to live? Nurs Management 15(11):43, 1984.

Describes the ethical dilemma posed by a terminally ill client's right to know. Proposes that the disclosure of information to a client is not a medical question, but a moral question to which the nurse is obligated to respond.

Scott, RS: When it isn't life or death, Am J Nurs 85:19, 1985.

Examines a common ethical dilemma encountered by middle-aged children and their chronically ill parents. Presents a four-step framework for ethical decision making as it applies to this ethical problem.

Smith, SJ, and Davis, AJ: Ethical dilemmas: conflicts among rights, duties and obligations, Am J Nurs 80:1463, 1980.

Examines ethical dilemmas in the context of daily nursing practice. Clarifies and contrasts legal and ethical rights, duties, and obligations.

Chapter 18

Legal Issues in Nursing

PREREQUISITE READING

Read Chapter 18, pp. 464 to 489.

OBJECTIVES

Mastery of content in this chapter will enable the student to:

1. Define selected legal terms associated with nursing practice.
2. Discuss legal concepts that apply to nursing practice.
3. Describe legal responsibilities, obligations, parameters of nursing practice.
4. List sources for standards of nursing care.
5. Identify areas of potential legal liability.
6. Define legal aspects of professional relationships.

REVIEW OF KEY CONCEPTS

1. Match the sources and categories of contemporary law with the most accurate description.
   - **a.** ____ Laws created by elected legislative bodies
   - **b.** ____ Laws created by judicial decision
   - **c.** ____ Laws concerned with protection of persons' rights
   - **d.** ____ Laws concerned with acts that threaten society

   1. Civil law
   2. Criminal law
   3. Statutory law
   4. Common law
2. List three sources for nursing standards of care.
   - **a.**
   - **b.**
   - **c.**
3. Nurses in the intensive care unit or operating room are held to the same standards of care and skill as the general duty nurse. (true or false)
4. The state or provincial board of nursing has the authority to suspend or revoke a nurse's license. (true or false)
5. Which statement regarding legal liability for a nursing student is correct?
   - **a.** A nursing student who has safely administered oral medications may perform this task when employed as a nurse's aide.
   - **b.** Student nurses are expected to perform at the level of a professional nurse.
   - **c.** A student's instructor may share liability when a student's action or lack of action injures a client.
   - **d.** A student nurse cannot be held liable for performing tasks that are being learned.
6. A civil wrong committed against a person or property is called a ____________.
7. Define negligence.
8. List four major types of action for which the nurse could be found legally liable.
   - **a.**
   - **b.**
   - **c.**
   - **d.**
9. Mr. Nelson, a student nurse, tells his peers that he is caring for Sam Jones, an AIDS victim. Mr. Jones is the president of a large business organization. Mr. Nelson could be charged with:
   - **a.** libel.
   - **b.** negligence.
   - **c.** malpractice.
   - **d.** invasion of privacy.
10. Identify the four criteria that must be established in a malpractice lawsuit against a nurse.
    - **a.**
    - **b.**
    - **c.**
    - **d.**
11. The RN accidentally leaves a crib side down. The child falls out of bed and sustains a skull fracture. The nurse could be charged with:
    - **a.** assault.
    - **b.** battery.
    - **c.** an intentional tort.
    - **d.** malpractice.
12. The physician orders an injectable tranquilizer for an uncooperative client in the emergency room. The nurse asks the student to hold the client's arm so she can safely give the injection. The student could be accused of:
    - **a.** assault.
    - **b.** battery.
    - **c.** negligence.
    - **d.** malpractice.

13. Identify two ways for the nurse to avoid being named in a lawsuit.
    a.
    b.
14. An institution's liability insurance usually offers adequate protection for professional nursing employees. (true or false)
15. The Patient's Bill of Rights:
    a. is a formal legal document.
    b. is a statement of guidelines for interactions with clients.
    c. provides a written standard of care for clients.
    d. is only applicable to hospitalized clients.
16. List the four conditions that must be present for informed consent to be valid.
    a.
    b.
    c.
    d.
17. A signed consent form is required for:
    a. surgical procedures or treatments that place the client at risk.
    b. diagnostic tests that are potentially hazardous.
    c. any research involving clients.
    d. all of the above.
18. It is a nurse's responsibility to obtain client consent for medical or surgical procedures. (true or false)
19. Mr. Trent is scheduled for a cholecystectomy and has already signed the consent form. As the nurse enters the room to administer the preoperative injection, Mr. Trent says he just isn't sure if he wants to have the surgery. Which nursing action would be appropriate?
    a. Give Mr. Trent his preoperative injection because it will help him to relax.
    b. Remind Mr. Trent that he consented to the surgery the evening before, and his doctor is waiting for him.
    c. Withhold the injection and notify the physician that Mr. Trent is having second thoughts about the surgery.
    d. Encourage Mr. Trent to have the surgery, since it will ultimately make him feel better.
20. What factor has been identified as the most important issue in legally determining death?
21. Nurses are legally obligated to treat a corpse with dignity and care. (true or false)
22. A nurse who follows an inaccurate physician's order would be legally responsible for any harm suffered by the client. (true or false)
23. Ms. Watson, an experienced pediatric nurse, has been assigned charge nurse responsibilities on the evening shift. Because of a staffing shortage and a high pediatric census, she is told that she must be in charge and provide primary care for six children. Which action by Ms. Watson would place her at greatest risk of legal liability?
    a. Informing the supervisor that she is not qualified for the assignment
    b. Attempting to reject the assignment
    c. Submitting a written protest to nursing administration
    d. Informing the supervisor that she is leaving the hospital
24. What is the purpose of a Good Samaritan law?
25. An oral contract with a client is as legally binding as a written contract. (true or false)
26. Mrs. Taylor, RN, has been offered a job in the operating rooms. In this particular institution three or four therapeutic abortions are done each working day. Mrs. Taylor is strongly opposed to abortions but likes all the other aspects of the job. Mrs. Taylor should:
    a. assist with the procedure, remembering that her personal values should not influence her professional actions.
    b. contact the local pro-life group to discuss her rights in assisting with abortions.
    c. ask if the employer has a "conscience clause" that would allow her to refuse assisting with abortions.
    d. reject the job offer and seek employment elsewhere.

APPLICATION OF KEY CONCEPTS

Activities to reinforce theoretical concepts

1. Talk with a hospital attorney about the procedure involved in a malpractice lawsuit that involves nursing employees. What recommendations does the attorney have concerning liability insurance for professional nurses and nursing students?
2. Review the contract that your education institution has with your assigned clinical agency. Identify the areas of responsibility for students, instructors, and nursing staff.
3. Review the nursing licensure statutes for your state or province.
    a. Identify the licensure requirements.
    b. What circumstances are cited as grounds for license suspension or revocation?
4. Determine the status of required request laws for organ donation in your state or province.
5. Invite a hospital representative who is responsible for obtaining consents for autopsy and organ donation to discuss legal and ethical responsibilities to the institution and the client.
6. Experiential exercise: legal issues in practice areas
    a. Independently or in a small group, survey nurses practicing in a variety of clinical areas or settings.
    b. Ask each nurse the legal issues encountered in clinical practice.
    c. What actions does the nurse take in order to limit the legal liabilities encountered?
    d. Identify common legal issues described by the nurses surveyed.
    e. Identify unique legal issues associated with specialty areas.

7. Experiential exercise: the Patient's Bill of Rights
Following a client care or observational experience, review the Patient's Bill of Rights.
   a. Which of the client's rights were preserved? What actions did you observe that preserved these client's rights?
   b. Were any of the rights violated or not met? What measures might be taken in future situations to ensure that these rights are preserved?
8. Clinical situation: malpractice and incident reports
Mr. Thompson has been caring for Mrs. Adams for the past week. Mr. Thompson enters Mrs. Adam's room to administer her 10:00 medications. This is the third time he has given medications to Mrs. Adams today, so he does not check her identification band before administering the pills. Just before administering medications to his second client, Mrs. Peters, he realizes he has mixed up the drugs and given the wrong ones to Mrs. Adams.
   a. What is the nature of Mr. Thompson's legal liability in this situation?
   b. What actions should Mr. Thompson take at this time?
   c. What documentation should be made concerning this incident? (If possible, obtain a sample of the form that your institution uses for documentation of incidents and complete it as part of the exercise.)
   d. How might Mr. Thompson approach Mrs. Adams concerning what has occurred? What should he say?
   e. What actions could be taken to avoid this situation in the future?
9. Clinical situation: informed consent
Mr. Barnes is scheduled for a bone marrow biopsy. The physician explained the procedure and obtained informed consent yesterday. Mrs. Barnes was present during the physician's explanation, and the consent was witnessed by the assistant head nurse.

   You are assigned to care for Mr. Barnes and will remain with him during the biopsy. The physician enters the room and begins the procedure. Mr. Barnes is extremely anxious and cries out in pain. He states, "Please stop, I'm just not sure if I want to go through with this." The physician tells Mr. Barnes to relax, he is almost finished. Describe the actions you would take and provide the rationale for your interventions.
10. Clinical situation: patient rights
Mr. James is admitted with acute gastrointestinal bleeding and hypotension. The physician has ordered packed red blood cells to be transfused immediately. The admitting nurse is aware that Mr. James' religious beliefs prohibit any form of blood or blood product transfusion. She is also aware that Mr. James' condition is rapidly deteriorating and that the transfusion may prevent him from going into shock.
   a. What are the patient's rights in this situation?
   b. What are the nurse's responsibilities to the client?
   c. Who should be involved or consulted in this situation?
   d. What documentation must be made concerning this situation?

ADDITIONAL READINGS

Creighton, H: Law every nurse should know, ed. 5, Philadelphia, 1986, W.B. Saunders Co.
Comprehensive presentation of legal facts associated with nursing practice. Information presented in clear, nontechnical manner; applicable to both student and experienced practitioner.

Cushing, M: Verbal no-code orders, Am J Nurs 81:1215, 1981.
Legal examination of verbal orders to not resuscitate clients.

Feutz, SA: Professional liability insurance. In Nothrup, CE, and Kelly, ME: Legal issues in nursing, St. Louis, 1987, The C.V. Mosby Co.
Discussion of issues associated with liability insurance for the professional nurse.

Horsley, JE: Short-staffing means increased liability for you, RN 44:73, 1981.
Lawyer responds to questions concerning liability arising from the nursing shortage. Provides guidelines for professional protection when encountering reduced staffing.

Kreitzer, M: Legal aspects of child abuse: guidelines for the nurse, Nurs Clin North Am 16(1):149, 1981.
Discusses legal aspects of child abuse and neglect in the context of nursing practice. Describes critical information needed in reporting and record keeping. Provides guidelines for the nurse to increase awareness of, and ability to participate in, the judicial process.

Northrop, C: Student nurses and legal accountability, Imprint 32:16, 1985.
Summarizes student nurse's legal accountability for actions during clinical practicums.

Northrop, CE, and Kelly, ME: Legal issues in nursing, St. Louis, 1987, The C.V. Mosby Co.
Comprehensive resource addressing legal issues influencing nursing practice. Written in a clear, nontechnical manner; applicable to student or experienced practitioner.

Regan, WA: Nursing malpractice: a giant leap in damages, RN 44:69, 1981.
Discusses Wyoming nursing malpractice suit in which a significant amount of money was awarded for damages. Proposes that this sets precedent for future cases in which nursing negligence causes permanent injury to a minor.

Chapter 19
Communication Skills in Nursing

PREREQUISITE READING

Read Chapter 19, pp. 490 to 517.

OBJECTIVES

Mastery of content in this chapter will enable the student to:

1. Define selected terms associated with communication in nursing practice.
2. Describe differences between the three levels of communication.
3. Identify characteristics of verbal and nonverbal communication.
4. Discuss the importance communication skills play in the nurse-client relationship.
5. Describe each element of the communication process.
6. Identify factors that influence communication.
7. Give examples of techniques that promote therapeutic communication.
8. List and discuss the phases of a therapeutic helping relationship.
9. Explain the dimensions of a helping relationship.
10. Discuss nursing care measures for clients with communication alterations.

REVIEW OF KEY CONCEPTS

1. Define communication.
2. List and briefly describe the three levels of communication.
   a.
   b.
   c.
3. The nurse enters Mr. Ford's room and notes the client's facial expression of discomfort. The nurse considers the factors that may be causing Mr. Ford's pain. This level of communication is best described as:
   a. public.
   b. private.
   c. interpersonal.
   d. intrapersonal.
4. Fill in the element of the communication process with the description provided.
   a. ______ The person to whom the message is sent
   b. ______ Factors that influence communications such as values, cultural background, and perceptions
   c. ______ The information that is sent
   d. ______ Methods for conveying information
   e. ______ The person who initiates the interpersonal communication
   f. ______ The factor that motivates a person to communicate
5. In demonstrating the method for deep breathing exercises, the nurse places his or her hands on the client's chest to explain diaphragmatic movement. This technique involves the use of the communication element known as:
   a. feedback.
   b. the tactile channel.
   c. the referent.
   d. interpersonal variables.
6. Match the verbal communication technique with the appropriate description or example.
   a. ______ Describing the client's illness without using medical terminology
   b. ______ Waiting until a client's pain is relieved before discussing the importance of exercise
   c. ______ Avoiding prolonged pauses or rapid shifts to other subjects
   d. ______ Providing examples and repeating important parts of a message

   1. Pacing
   2. Timing
   3. Clarity
   4. Vocabulary
7. Briefly compare and contrast the major characteristics of verbal and nonverbal communication.
8. Which of the following statements concerning nonverbal communication is correct?
   a. It is easy for nurses to judge the meaning of a client's facial expressions.
   b. The nurse's verbal messages should be reinforced by nonverbal cues.
   c. The physical appearance of the nurse rarely influences the nurse-client interaction.

d. Words convey meanings that are usually more significant than nonverbal communication.

9. Identify and define five factors that influence interpersonal communications.
a.
b.
c.
d.
e.

10. To establish a therapeutic relationship, it is important for the nurse to discuss his or her personal emotions with the client. (true or false)

11. Communication is more effective when the participants remain aware of their role in a relationship. (true or false)

12. A client's personal space:
a. is clearly visible to others.
b. is the same as the client's territoriality.
c. can be separated from the client.
d. is highly mobile.

13. List the three dimensions of an individual's personal space, including the actual distance characteristic of each dimension.
a.
b.
c.

14. Interpersonal communication is least threatening at a:
a. social distance.
b. personal distance.
c. intimate distance.

15. Social interaction with a client is inappropriate when attempting to establish a therapeutic relationship. (true and false)

16. Describe four skills that facilitate active listening.
a.
b.
c.
d.

17. Identify two nursing actions that convey that the nurse accepts what the client has to say.
a.
b.

18. When a nurse conveys acceptance of a client, it means that the nurse agrees with the client. (true or false)

19. Which communication technique would be most effective in eliciting detailed information from a client?
a. Maintaining silence
b. Open-ended question
c. Stating observations
d. Summarizing

20. Identify the communication technique illustrated in each of the sample interactions below.

a. ____ *Client:* The medication always seems to upset my stomach.
Nurse: That may be because you are not taking it with meals. The drug can cause stomach irritation.

b. ____ *Client:* This test tomorrow—the doctor says it's painless, but I've heard differently from my friends. I'm not sure I want it.
Nurse: It sounds as if you are frightened about the test.

c. ____ *Client:* Well, whenever I seem to move wrong the pain gets worse.
Nurse: Tell me what you mean by "move wrong."

d. ____ *Nurse:* Tell me what medications you are currently taking.
Client: I take Inderal and occasionally Valium.
Nurse: How long have you taken each drug?
Client: About 2 years for each.
Nurse: What dose do you take of each drug?

1. Paraphrasing
2. Asking related questions
3. Focusing
4. Offering information

21. Identify four nontherapeutic communication techniques and briefly describe the reason that each inhibits communication.
a.
b.
c.
d.

22. Which of the following statements by the nurse could be considered false reassurance to the client?
a. "I understand your concern about the surgery, but at your age, there is nothing to worry about."
b. "I know that it must be frightening to be in the hospital, but you will receive the care you need."
c. "It is a difficult time for you, but be assured that I am willing to listen to anything you have to say."
d. "No, I've never lost a close relative to cancer, but I can understand how difficult it must be for you."

23. Define therapeutic relationship.

24. Identify and briefly describe the five characteristics of any helping relationship.
a.
b.
c.
d.
e.

25. Describe the difference between sympathy and empathy.

26. Match the phase of a helping relationship with the characteristic behaviors or goals described.

a. ____ The nurse chooses the location and setting for the interaction.

b. ______ The nurse helps the client adjust to changes of illness.
c. ______ The nurse's initial goal is to direct the conversation to help the client feel at ease.
d. ______ The client tests the nurse's genuineness in wanting to help.
e. ______ The nurse and client evaluate goals and their outcomes.
f. ______ The nurse uses communication skills in performing routine care measures.
g. ______ The nurse and client identify mutual goals.

1. Preorientation phase
2. Orientation phase
3. Working phase
4. Termination phase

27. The client should be informed about the termination of a relationship during which phase of the working relationship?
a. Preorientation
b. Orientation
c. Working
d. Termination

28. Identify and briefly describe two communication skills that promote client self-understanding.
a.
b.

29. The following interaction occurs between Ms. Russ, a 70-year-old client with heart disease, and her nurse.

Ms. Russ: I'm afraid I won't be able to do the things I enjoy any more.
Nurse: I'd like to understand your concern. Tell me more, and perhaps I can explain how your condition might affect you.
Ms. Russ: It's important to me to be able to visit my friends.
Nurse: I believe we can find ways that will allow you to continue your visits.

This interaction is an example of:
a. clarifying roles.
b. separation.
c. testing.
d. building trust.

30. Mr. Towns has a rare blood disorder and is in the hospital for tests to adjust his medications. The nurse enters the room.

Nurse: Mr. Towns, I'm Ms. Long. I'll be caring for you today.
Mr. Towns: You are a different nurse than the one I had yesterday.
Nurse: Yes, but I am aware of the test you had yesterday and thought you might want to talk about what is planned for today.
Mr. Towns: Are you sure you can explain what I need to know?

This interaction is an example of:
a. asking related questions.
b. testing.
c. contract formation.
d. identifying problems.

31. Communication skills are of importance only in low-visibility tasks associated with psychological, spiritual, and socioeconomic needs of the client. (true or false)

32. Client communication may be impaired by:
a. physical changes associated with disease states or therapies.
b. psychological alterations associated with coping or social interaction.
c. environmental conditions.
d. all of the above.

33. List five alternate methods for communicating with clients who have physical conditions that create barriers to interactions.
a.
b.
c.
d.
e.

34. Identify three methods of environmental control that can facilitate interpersonal communication.
a.
b.
c.

35. All of the following are important factors when communicating with clients. Which is the most important in establishing effective communication with a child?
a. Meeting the child at eye level
b. Providing a quiet, comfortable environment
c. Informing the child about any discomfort associated with a procedure
d. Understanding the influence of development on language and thought processes

36. Identify three interventions to facilitate communication with a client who is hearing impaired.
a.
b.
c.

37. The nurse maximizes communication with the aphasic client by:
a. speaking very loudly.
b. avoiding the use of visual cues.
c. asking "yes" or "no" questions.
d. interrupting to provide appropriate words.

38. Identify two goals to be achieved with a client who has an alteration in communications.
a.
b.

APPLICATION OF KEY CONCEPTS

Activities to reinforce skills and techniques

1. During interactions with peers or friends, practice using each of the 11 therapeutic communication skills

described in your text. (It may be helpful to focus on one skill at a time.)
   a. Identify those skills with which you feel most comfortable.
   b. Identify and continue to practice those skills with which you feel less comfortable.
2. Record on an audio or video tape, a role-playing situation or interaction with a peer or friend. Attempt to use the therapeutic techniques described in your text. Play back the tape and critique your performance in each of the following areas:
   a. Factors that influenced the communication
   b. Therapeutic communication techniques used
   c. Nontherapeutic communication techniques used
   d. Alternative approaches to communication
3. Transcribe a segment of an interaction with an assigned client. (While this will not be an exact recording, try to recall the points discussed and the techniques employed.) Analyze your interaction, including:
   a. Factors that influenced the communication
   b. Nonverbal communication that you observed in the client or transmitted yourself
   c. Therapeutic communication skills that you used
   d. Barriers to communication and techniques that may have been used to minimize them
   e. Nontherapeutic communication skills that you used and alternative responses that are more therapeutic

Activities to reinforce theoretical concepts

1. Experiential exercise: elements of the communication process
   a. Conduct a 5-minute observation of two people interacting (nurse-client, student-instructor, student-student, two family members).
   b. Identify and give examples of the modes of communication that you observed.
      (1) Verbal
      (2) Nonverbal
   c. Identify and give examples of the elements of the communication process that you observed.
      (1) Referent
      (2) Sender
      (3) Message
      (4) Channels
      (5) Receiver
      (6) Intrapersonal variables
2. Clinical situation: therapeutic communication
   Read the hypothetical interaction between a nurse and client.
   a. Identify therapeutic communication techniques.
   b. Identify techniques that inhibit communication, and explain why communication was disrupted.
   c. Formulate an alternative approach to the nontherapeutic techniques identified.

Client: You see, Ms. Williams, I am 68 years old and now my doctor has told me that I have cancer. I've always felt I could live forever. I guess that was foolish.

Nurse: I want to understand how you feel, please go on.

Client: How can you understand—you are so young?

Nurse: Oh, that's silly, I'm not that young.

Client: Well, of course you are. Anyway it seems as though I will either have to take chemotherapy or choose surgery.

Nurse: I think you should look for another doctor.

Client: Oh? I've always liked Dr. Rose. He has taken care of most of my family and has always done a good job when we needed him.

Nurse: You're saying that you trust him?

Client: Yes, I do. He has suggested I try chemotherapy.

Nurse: By the way, have you been taking any pain medications recently?

Client: What? Oh yes, but only before I go to bed so I can sleep.

3. Experiential exercise: communication in the nursing process
   Following an observational experience, or after administering care to an assigned client, identify the communication skills that were used in each step of the nursing process.
   a. Assessment
   b. Diagnosis
   c. Planning
   d. Implementation
   e. Evaluation

ADDITIONAL READINGS

Bradley, J, and Edenberg, MA: Communication in the nursing context, New York, 1982, Appleton-Century-Crofts.
Presents theories and techniques of communication. Focuses on communication skills as they apply to clinical practice. Highlights discussion with practice exercises.

Egan, G: The skilled helper, Monterey, Calif., 1975, Brooks/Cole Publishing Co.
Presents an easy-to-understand, three-stage approach to effective interactions and counseling. Emphasizes application of techniques rather than cognitive learning. Includes numerous practice exercises.

Knowles, RD: Building rapport through neuro-linguistic programming, Am J Nurs 83:1011, 1983.
Examines the impact of visual, auditory, and kinesthetic messages on the communication process. Proposes that most individuals' communications reflect a perference for one of these transmission methods. Recommends techniques that may assist in enhancing interactions when implementing these neurolinguistic modes.

Murray, RB: Therapeutic communication for emotional care. In Murray, RB, and Huelskoetter, MM: Psychiatric mental health nursing: giving emotional care, Englewood Cliffs, N.J., 1983, Prentice-Hall, Inc.

Clear presentation of principles of communication and techniques to facilitate interviewing process. Addresses techniques appropriate for specific client behaviors frequently encountered by the nurse. Also describes techniques appropriate for each developmental level.

Purtilo, R: Health professionals-patient interaction, ed. 2, Philadelphia, 1978, W.B. Saunders Co.

Discusses the basis for achieving effective client interactions. Describes methods that foster therapeutic relationships.

Raudseff, E: 7 ways to cure communication breakdowns, Nurs Life, p. 51, January/February 1984.

Identifies common blocks to communication. Describes seven active listening skills that may enhance communication.

Chapter 20

Teaching-Learning Process

PREREQUISITE READING

Read Chapter 20, pp. 518 to 543.

OBJECTIVES

Mastery of content in this chapter will enable the student to:

1. Define selected terms associated with teaching and learning.
2. Describe the similarities and differences between teaching and learning.
3. Identify the purposes of client teaching.
4. Compare the communication process with the teaching process.
5. Describe the domains of learning.
6. Differentiate factors that determine readiness to learn from those that determine ability to learn.
7. Explain the importance of learner participation in teaching and learning.
8. Discuss factors that contribute to a positive learning environment.
9. Develop a client's teaching plan.
10. Write a learning objective.
11. Describe ways to incorporate teaching with routine nursing care.
12. Identify methods for evaluating learning.
13. Identify principles of effective teaching.

REVIEW OF KEY CONCEPTS

1. Define teaching.
2. Define learning.
3. Agencies responsible for accrediting health care institutions require that clients receive health care education. (true or false)
4. List the three major purposes for client teaching.
   a.
   b.
   c.
5. Learning is most effective when a single sensory channel is used. (true or false)
6. Match the element of the communication process with the corresponding activity in the teaching process.
   a. _____ Referent
   b. _____ Sender
   c. _____ Intrapersonal variables of the sender
   d. _____ Message
   e. _____ Channels
   f. _____ Receiver
   g. _____ Intrapersonal variables of the receiver
   h. _____ Feedback

   1. Content or information taught
   2. Perceived need to provide information
   3. Teacher's knowledge, approach, values, emotions
   4. Determining achievement of learning objectives
   5. The learner
   6. The teacher
   7. Teaching methods
   8. Willingness and capability to learn
7. Fill in the name of each learning domain described below.
   a. ___________ Learning that deals with expression of feelings and acceptance of attitudes, opinions, or values
   b. ___________ Learning that involves acquisition of skills requiring integration of mental and muscular activity
   c. ___________ Learning that involves development of intellectual behaviors
8. Identify and briefly describe the three conditions necessary for learning to occur.
   a.
   b.
   c.
9. Learning readiness is influenced by all of the following except:
   a. the ability to concentrate on information to be learned.
   b. internal impulses that cause a person to take action.
   c. the individual's intellectual level of development.
   d. the individual's psychosocial adaptation to illness.
10. Which level of anxiety is most likely to motivate an individual to learn?
    a. An absence of anxiety
    b. Mild level of anxiety
    c. Moderate level of anxiety
    d. High level of anxiety

11. Use of appropriate teaching techniques will result in learning, even when the client does not want to learn. (true or false)
12. Identify three beliefs the client must have in order to initiate a health action.
    a.
    b.
    c.
13. Mr. Miller was involved in an automobile accident that resulted in the loss of his right leg. Which comment by Mr. Miller indicates that he is ready for teaching related to self-care on discharge?
    a. "If those ambulance people would have done their job right, this never would have happened."
    b. "You know, they said my leg is gone, but I still feel it. I'll be ready to get up and walk in a few days."
    c. "Nothing in my life will need to change, so long as I do everything you and the doctor tell me."
    d. "Without my leg, I'm not sure how I'll be able to work. I feel helpless."
14. A plan for client teaching is best introduced during which stage of the grieving process?
    a. Acceptance
    b. Bargaining
    c. Denial
    d. Anger
15. Identify the three major factors that influence an individual's ability to learn.
    a.
    b.
    c.
16. The use of role playing would be an effective teaching method for which developmental level?
    a. Toddler
    b. Preschooler
    c. Adolescent
    d. Older adult
17. Mr. Dennis, a newly diagnosed diabetic, must learn self-injection of insulin. Which physical attribute would not relate to his physical capability to perform this psychomotor task?
    a. Size
    b. Strength
    c. Coordination
    d. Sensory acuity
18. List five principles to promote teacher effectiveness (basic teaching principles).
    a.
    b.
    c.
    d.
    e.
19. Which statement concerning teaching methodology is accurate?
    a. More difficult, complex content should be presented first.
    b. Repetition should be avoided to prevent client boredom.
    c. Frequent sessions of 20 to 30 minutes are most beneficial.
    d. The most essential information should be presented last.
20. A client's interest in learning may be lost if the nurse begins the teaching session with familiar information. (true or false)
21. Mr. Jones has difficulty performing breathing exercises correctly. He argues with the nurse, who silently leaves the room. When the nurse returns, Mr. Jones is performing the exercises properly. Mr. Jones' behavioral change is a result of:
    a. material reinforcement.
    b. positive reinforcement.
    c. negative reinforcement.
    d. activity reinforcement.
22. Match the teaching activity with the corresponding step of the nursing process.
    a. _____ Writing learning objectives
    b. _____ Determining available teaching resources
    c. _____ Organizing group discussions
    d. _____ Identifying learning needs
    e. _____ Determining the client's ability to perform a new skill independently

    1. Assessment
    2. Diagnosis
    3. Planning
    4. Implementation
    5. Evaluation
23. List the five major areas requiring assessment in the teaching process.
    a.
    b.
    c.
    d.
    e.
24. Ms. Derring, a 21-year-old college student, has come to the campus clinic for a routine health check. During the physical examination, the nurse determines that Ms. Derring is unaware of the need for regular breast self-examination. Which nursing diagnosis would be most appropriate for this client situation?
    a. Knowledge deficit: affective
    b. Knowledge deficit: psychomotor
    c. Knowledge deficit: cognitive
    d. Health maintenance, altered
25. Identify and briefly describe the three components of a learning objective.
    a.
    b.
    c.
26. Which of the following is the most accurately stated behavioral objective?
    a. Will know how to change abdominal dressing
    b. Will demonstrate how to change abdominal dressing

   c. Will demonstrate how to change abdominal dressing before being discharged
   d. Will know how to change abdominal dressing before discharge
27. Which of the following verbs should the nurse avoid when writing a behavioral learning objective?
   a. To explain
   b. To understand
   c. To identify
   d. To state
28. Mr. Browner needs to learn how to perform back-strengthening exercises. The best teaching method for his need is:
   a. group discussion.
   b. demonstration.
   c. formal lecture.
   d. watching a slide program.
29. Which teaching method would be most appropriate in stimulating affective learning?
   a. Discussion
   b. Lecture
   c. Teaching booklets
   d. Demonstrations
30. Why is it important to develop a written teaching plan for clients?
31. How is the approach to teaching different from teaching methodology?
32. List three guidelines to follow when explaining an unfamiliar procedure or treatment to client.
   a.
   b.
   c.
33. Identify the three topics to be included when documenting client teaching.
   a.
   b.
   c.

APPLICATION OF KEY CONCEPTS

Activities to reinforce skills and techniques

1. Identify a specific target audience. Select any topic of interest and organize a 5- to 10-minute teaching presentation. Attempt to use more than one teaching technique. Audio tape, videotape, or present the teaching session to a peer or small group. Play back the tape for self-evaluation and elicit peer or instructor review of the presentation.
2. Select a health-maintenance topic such as breast self-examination, testicular self-examination, cancer warning signs, cancer risk factors, heart disease risk factors, or prudent heart living. Organize a 10-minute teaching session that could be used for client education. Practice presenting the session to a peer group. Elicit peer and instructor feedback.
3. Conduct an assessment of an assigned client (or role-play with a peer) to determine learning needs, readiness to learn, ability to learn, teaching environment, and resources for learning. Formulate diagnoses related to learning needs.
4. Following client assessment and diagnosis of a knowledge deficit, formulate learning objectives, specific teaching interventions, and outcome criteria. Submit your plan for teaching to your instructor for feedback before implementation. Evaluate the teaching session based on the stated outcome criteria and learning objectives.

Activities to reinforce theoretical concepts

1. Clinical situation: communications and the teaching process
   Using the information provided in the situation that follows, fill in the data appropriate to the teaching process as it relates to the elements of communication identified in the chart on p. 94.
   Ms. Loomis has rheumatoid arthritis and is unaware of the types of exercises to perform to maintain joint motion. Ms. Loomis lives with her sister and is anxious to remain as independent as possible. Her vision is reduced but she can read the large print in the newspapers and magazines. Mr. Rosen, her nurse, plans to teach Ms. Loomis exercises by explaining their purpose and directing Ms. Loomis through each exercise. Mr. Rosen has worked with arthritic clients in the past and has been able to adjust exercises to the client's abilities. After the teaching session, Ms. Loomis will demonstrate each exercise.
2. Experiential exercise: teaching process in nursing
   Identify the opportunities and potential topics for client education during routine morning care.
3. Clinical situation: domains of learning
   Mr. Gasen is a 48-year-old man who has had a heart attack. His physician has prescribed a new medication, an exercise program, and a diet for him. Mrs. Gasen is anxious about her husband's return home since she is unfamiliar with his restrictions.
   Identify at least two examples of knowledge or skills that the client or his wife will need to acquire in each of the learning domains.
   a. Cognitive
   b. Affective
   c. Psychomotor
4. Experiential exercise: learning environment
   After an observational experience in any health care setting:
   a. Identify factors in the environment that would be conducive to client education.
   b. Identify factors in the environment that could create barriers to client education.
   c. Identify actions that could be taken by the nurse to overcome or control environmental factors that could inhibit client education.
5. Experiential exercise: learning objectives
   Formulate a behavioral learning objective for each of the following situations:
   a. Your client needs to know how to take her radial pulse before she goes home from the hospital.
   b. A client at home is unfamiliar with the side effects of new medications.

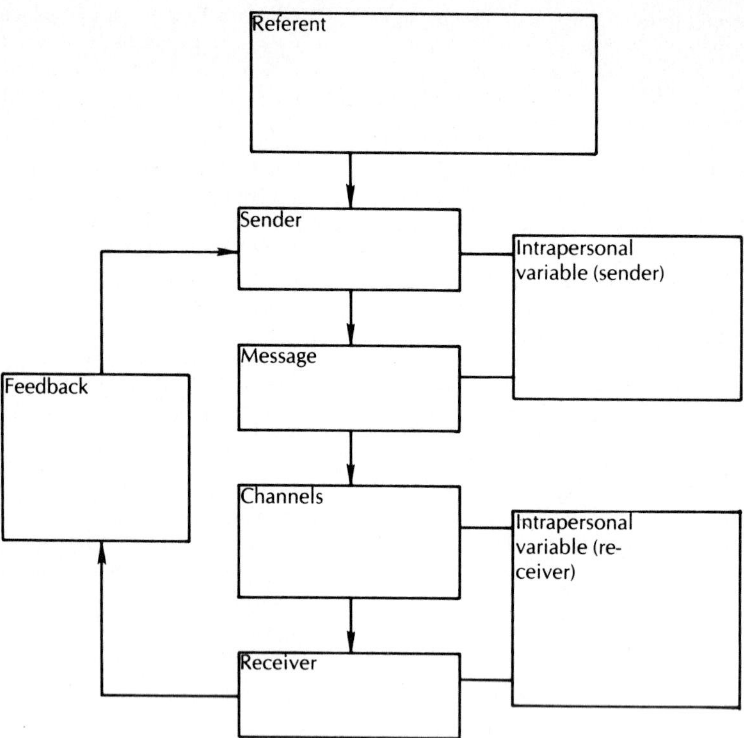

c. Your client needs to develop a daily menu for a weight reduction program she has joined.
d. Your client is expected to report any signs of visual loss to his physician.

6. Clinical situation: the teaching process
Ms. Jeffries has had arthritis for several years. She lives in a six-room home with her husband, who is semiretired and works 3 days each week. Ms. Jeffries has considerable pain in her joints and takes an analgesic every 6 hours. She is limited in her ability to perform any activity for very long because of her discomfort and fatigue. Ms. Jeffries tells her nurse, "I wish I knew why this arthritis affects me like it does." A nurse who previously worked with Ms. Jeffries began to teach her pain control methods, but Ms. Jeffries was admitted to the hospital for a week before the teaching had been completed. Now you are responsible for Ms. Jeffries' home care. Develop a teaching plan for Ms. Jeffries, including:
   a. Three factors you would assess to determine her ability to learn
   b. Three factors you would assess to determine her readiness to learn
   c. Two diagnoses of learning needs
   d. Three learning objectives
   e. A specific discussion of proposed teaching methods
   f. Potential methods of reinforcement
   g. A description of evaluation techniques used to measure achievement of objectives
7. For each developmental level listed, describe the teaching method or methods and the approach you would use to instruct the client about oral hygiene.
   a. Infant
   b. Toddler
   c. Preschooler
   d. School-age child
   e. Adolescent
   f. Young and middle adult
   g. Older adult

ADDITIONAL READINGS

Barron, S: Documentation of patient education, Patient Educ Counseling 9:81, 1987.
Identifies major trends that require improved documentation of client education. Describes three specific standards to be incorporated in all documentation of client teaching. Discusses the process of chart audit and development of a form for documentation of client education.

Bennett, HL: Why patients don't follow instructions, RN 49:45, March 1986.
Identifies use of negotiation and communication to promote client understanding and compliance with instructions.

Cunningham, MA, and Baker, D: How to teach patients better and faster, RN 50:52, September 1986.
Identifies major principles to promote client education in the acute care setting.

Cushing, M: Legal lessons on patient teaching, Am J Nurs 84:721, 1984.
Cites cases that emphasize the nurse's legal responsibility to teach and document instruction. The importance of written instructions as a supplement to verbal explanations is emphasized.

Fox, V: Patient teaching: understanding the needs of the adult learner, AORN J 44:234, 1986.
Contrasts pedogogical (teacher-directed) and androgogical (self-directed) teaching-learning styles. Briefly explores androgogical teaching strategies for the adult learner.

Leff, EW: Ethics and patient teaching, MCN 11:375, 1986.
Examines ethical and legal dimensions of the nurse's teaching role, and the dilemma that occurs when benefits perceived by the nurse conflict with the client's desire to know. Emphasizes the nurse's responsibility to respect the client's autonomy in structuring a teaching program.

McHugh, NG, Christman, NJ, and Johnson, JE: Preparatory information: What helps and why, Am J Nurs 82:780, 1982.
Discusses study which revealed that sensory information was most useful in preparing clients for health care procedures. Guidelines for structuring preparatory information are presented.

Miller, A: When is the time ripe for teaching? Am J Nurs 85:801, 1985.
One in a series of articles in a continuing-education self-study program. Offers recommendations for assessing clients before initiating teaching. Presents methods for determining readability of materials and other suggestions to enhance teaching techniques.

Moss, RC: Overcoming fear: a review of research on patient, family instruction, AORN J 43:1107, 1986.
Well-referenced discussion of current research addressing client preoperative instruction.

Redman, BK: The process of patient education, ed. 6, St. Louis, 1988, The C.V. Mosby Co.
A comprehensive text addressing theoretical and practical issues associated with client education. A valuable resource for students and experienced nurses.

Ward, DB: Why patient teaching fails, RN 49:45, January 1986.
Identifies and describes six common obstacles that prevent clients from learning. Discusses nursing approaches to remove barriers and facilitate client learning.

Chapter 21
The Family

PREREQUISITE READING

Read Chapter 21, pp. 546 to 559.

OBJECTIVES

Mastery of content in this chapter will enable the student to:

1. Define selected terms used to describe families.
2. Discuss the way family members influence one another's health.
3. Describe current trends in the American family.
4. Define the family in terms applicable to all family forms.
5. Describe five common family forms and discuss the relevant health concerns of each.
6. Explain the way family structure and patterns of functioning affect the health of family members and the family as a whole.
7. Compare family as environment to family as client, and explain the way these perspectives influence nursing practice.
8. Describe the family nursing process in terms of assessment, nursing diagnosis, planning, intervention, and evaluation.
9. Describe the attributes of effective and ineffective families.

REVIEW OF KEY CONCEPTS

1. Define family.
2. Which of the following statements concerning current family trends is inaccurate?
   - **a.** The majority of women are in the work force.
   - **b.** Most elderly live in nursing homes.
   - **c.** There are fewer men than women in the prime marrying ages.
   - **d.** Marriage remains a valued institution.
3. Joan's parents, Ed and Sue, were killed in an automobile accident.
   - **a.** The family, which consisted of Joan, Ed and Sue would be called a ________________ family.
   - **b.** For Joan, this family would be referred to as her family of ________________.
   - **c.** For Ed and Sue, this family would be referred to as the family of ________________.
4. The nuclear family is the dominant family form in North America. (true or false)
5. Divorce constitutes a major cause of poverty among women and children. (true or false)
6. The adjustment period experienced by members of a blended family may take as long as:
   - **a.** 6 to 8 weeks.
   - **b.** 6 to 12 months.
   - **c.** 2 years.
   - **d.** 5 years.
7. Match the family form with the characteristic described.
   - **a.** _____ Family members may often be geographically separated.
   - **b.** _____ Presence or absence of children has strong impact on the family's health concerns.
   - **c.** _____ The female family members typically provide the majority of child care.
   - **d.** _____ Availability of child care when a parent becomes ill is a major family concern.
   - **e.** _____ The family often has a concern over the speed with which all members must initially adapt to their new living arrangement.

   1. Blended
   2. Nuclear
   3. Extended
   4. Single-parent
   5. Communal
8. The key to healthy stepfamily functioning is establishment of:
   - **a.** very flexible structures within the family.
   - **b.** traditional roles within the family unit.
   - **c.** friendly sibling relationships.
   - **d.** a strong couple bond.
9. Identify five support functions of the family.
   - **a.**
   - **b.**
   - **c.**
   - **d.**
   - **e.**
10. Match the family developmental stage with the task described.
    - **a.** _____ Between families: the unattached young adult

b. _____ The newly married couple
c. _____ The family with young children
d. _____ The family with adolescents
e. _____ Launching children and moving on
f. _____ The family in later life

1. Development of adult-to-adult relationships
2. Life review and integration
3. Refocus on marital and career issues
4. Development of intimate peer relationships
5. Taking on parenting roles
6. Realignment of relationships with extended family and friends

11. Behaviors within a family influence the health of each family member. (true or false)
12. Identify three activities that are characteristic of healthy or effective families.
    a.
    b.
    c.
13. Briefly describe the similarities and differences between the family as environment and the family as client.
14. When only one family member is available for nursing care, the nurse must view the family as:
    a. dysfunctional.
    b. the environment.
    c. the client.
    d. a one-person household.
15. When working with families, the nurse attempts to change the structure in order to best meet the needs of the client requiring care. (true or false)
16. When formulating a plan of care for a family as client, it is imperative that all members understand and agree to the plan. (true or false)
17. List three characteristics considered family strengths that the nurse could use when formulating a plan for family care.
    a.
    b.
    c.

APPLICATION OF KEY CONCEPTS
Activities to reinforce theoretical concepts

1. Family forms and health concerns
   Compare the types of health concerns or problems typically faced by each of the following family forms.
   a. Single-parent
   b. Blended
   c. Communal
2. The concept of family
   a. Describe your concept of family.
   b. Identify how your perception and values may positively influence your care of families.
   c. Identify how your perception and values might create potential conflict in caring for families. Discuss how you might address this dilemma to ensure quality client care.
3. Clinical situation: family assessment
   Mrs. Godinez is a 40-year-old Hispanic woman who has recently divorced. She has a 3-year-old son, a 5-year-old daughter, and a 16-year-old-daughter. A referral has been made to a community health nurse from the school nurse because of increased absenteeism of the 16-year-old girl.
   a. What type of family form is this unit?
   b. What three major areas of functioning should the nurse evaluate in this type of family form?
   c. What resources could the nurse and client pursue to address these three areas of concern?
   d. In addition, Mrs. Godinez's 70-year-old mother has now moved into the household. What type of family form is this unit now called?
   e. Mrs. Godinez's mother has a chronic respiratory condition that requires frequent medical treatment. How will this influence the health of the family members and the family as a whole?
   f. What is the developmental stage of this family, and what are the tasks of this family stage?
   g. When you visit the home, you note that Mrs. Godinez, her mother, and her 16-year-old daughter are obese. Would you intervene in this situation with the family as client or as environment? How would you approach this problem?
4. Experiential exercise: family nursing process
   a. Review the sample family assessment form in your text on p. 555. Consider any additional data you feel are important for a complete data base, and modify the form accordingly.
   b. Using the sample assessment form in your text, with or without modifications, conduct a family assessment of your own or an assigned client's family.
   c. Formulate nursing diagnoses that address the needs of the family.
   d. Based on your assessment and diagnoses, determine if you will intervene with family as client or environment.
   e. Develop a nursing care plan to address the priority nursing diagnosis.

ADDITIONAL READINGS

Engelbretson, JC: Stepmothers as first time parents: their needs and problems, Pediatr Nurs 8:387, 1982.
Identifies prevalent myths affecting stepmothers. Describes structural differences between reconstituted and nuclear families. Discusses common expectations of stepmothers. Presents, in detail, interventions to assist in adaptation of stepmothers and promotion of successful family relationships.

Friedman, M: Family nursing: theory and assessment, New York, 1981, Appleton-Century-Crofts.
Discusses dynamics of family structure and functions. Includes family case study and analysis to reinforce theoretical concepts.

Knafl, KA, and Grace, HK: Families across the life cycle, Boston, 1978, Little, Brown & Co.
Selection of articles about families in each stage of de-

velopment based on interview of family members. Appendices include interview guides that may be adapted for use in any practice setting.

Leavitt, M, editor: Symposium on family nursing in acute care, Nurs Clin North Am 19(1):83, 1984.

Series of articles that focus on care of the family unit. Although articles address a variety of acute care situations, principles are applicable to any practice setting. Includes topics related to family needs associated with areas of specialized nursing practice including psych–mental health, maternal-child, pediatrics, oncology, and cardiology.

Romanzuk, A: Helping the stepparent parent, Matern Child Nurs J 12:1096, 1987.

Attempts to dispel myths associated with stepparenting. Discusses assessment and care planning to facilitate family adjustment. Includes helpful annotated bibliography of books and audiovisual media for parents and children in reconstituted or blended families.

Sund, K, and Ostwald, SK: Dual-earner families' stress levels and personal and life-style-related variables, Nurs Res 34(6):357, 1985.

Identifies stressors and stress levels experienced by dual-earner families in the preschool stage of family development. Information presented may be helpful in counseling dual-earner families from other developmental stages.

Chapter 22
Conception Through Preschool

PREREQUISITE READING

Read Chapter 22, pp. 560 to 589.

OBJECTIVES

Mastery of content in this chapter will enable the student to:

1. Define selected terms relevant to human growth and development.
2. Describe three commonalities in human development and the six related principles of growth and development.
3. Discuss the major factors influencing growth and development.
4. Compare the theories of development and discuss their relationship to nursing practice.
5. Discuss teratogenic agents and ways in which the nurse can promote fetal health through prenatal education.
6. Describe ways in which the nurse can provide support to the woman during pregnancy.
7. Describe the physical growth characteristics of the unborn child, infant, toddler, and preschooler.
8. Discuss physiological and psychosocial health concerns during the transition from intrauterine to extrauterine life.
9. Identify factors important for normal cognitive development through infancy, toddlerhood, and the preschool years.
10. Explain the importance of parent-child attachment and list factors that may impede the attachment process.
11. Describe variables influencing how a child learns about and perceives health status.
12. Discuss ways the nurse can assist parents in promoting the child's health in all dimensions.
13. Discuss the nursing process for the hospitalized child.

REVIEW OF KEY CONCEPTS

1. Which statement concerning human growth and development is inaccurate?
   a. Growth and development are orderly and predictable processes.
   b. Growth and development begin with conception and continue until death.
   c. All individuals progress through the same phases of growth and development.
   d. All individuals accomplish developmental tasks at the same pace.
2. An individual's health may be influenced by ability to progress through each developmental phase. (true or false)
3. The process of becoming fully developed and grown through physical and behavioral change is called ________________.
4. Behavioral change that promotes progressive adaptation to the environment is called ____________.
5. The quantitative changes reflecting an increase in physical measurements are called ____________.
6. Identify the three commonalities of growth and development that are true of all people.
   a.
   b.
   c.
7. List the six basic principles of growth and development.
   a.
   b.
   c.
   d.
   e.
   f.
8. In the table below, identify the age span and at least one physical and one psychosocial milestone for each developmental stage.

Stage	Age span	Physical milestone	Psychosocial milestone
Prenatal			
Neonatal			
Infancy			
Toddlerhood			
Preschool			
School age			
Adolescence			
Young and middle adulthood			
Older adulthood			

9. The use of a developmental framework for nursing care is necessary only when working with infants and children. (true or false)

10. Match the theorist with the appropriate human development theory focus.
    a. _____ Piaget
    b. _____ Erikson
    c. _____ Havighurst
    d. _____ Maslow
    e. _____ Freud
    f. _____ Kohlberg

    1. Psychoanalytical theory
    2. Psychosocial development
    3. Human needs
    4. Cognitive development
    5. Learning to develop
    6. Moral development
11. What is the cause of most intrauterine health problems?
12. Define teratogen.
13. List three teratogens.
    a.
    b.
    c.
14. What is meant by the phrase: the fetus is viable?
15. The cheeselike protective substance covering the skin of the fetus is ________________.
16. The fine hair covering most of the body of the fetus is ________________.
17. When is the mother most likely to become aware of fetal movement?
    a. First trimester
    b. Second trimester
    c. Third trimester
18. The two most common causes of damage to the fetal central nervous system during the third trimester are:
    a. viral infection and maternal stress.
    b. noxious agents and poor maternal nutrition.
    c. bacterial infection and maternal drug abuse.
    d. maternal tobacco and alcohol abuse.
19. It is believed that the biochemical environment of the uterus and postbirth emotional status of the mother can influence the psychosocial development of the child. (true or false)
20. Identify the three major physical health needs of the neonate.
    a.
    b.
    c.
21. Immediately after birth, the neonate receives an instillation of antibiotic or silver nitrate solution into the eyes to prevent ________________.
22. List the five physiological characteristics evaluated through the Apgar assessment.
    a.
    b.
    c.
    d.
    e.
23. A neonate receives an Apgar score of 4 one minute after birth and a score of 6 five minutes after birth. These Apgar scores indicate that the neonate:
    a. is adjusting well to extrauterine life.
    b. is experiencing little difficulty adjusting to extrauterine life.
    c. is experiencing moderate difficulty adjusting to extrauterine life.
    d. is experiencing severe distress.
24. What two factors are most important in promoting closeness of the parents and the neonate?
25. The most important action by the nurse to promote parental and neonate acquaintance is placing the family unit together. (true or false)
26. Describe what is meant by parent and neonate attachment.
27. Which of the following would be considered an abnormal physical finding in a neonatal assessment?
    a. Cyanosis of the hands and feet during activity.
    b. Palpable anterior and posterior fontanels
    c. Soft protuberant abdomen
    d. Sporadic, asymmetrical limb movements
28. Baby Jones weighs 3200 grams at birth and 2900 grams 3 days later. Mrs. Jones has elected to breast feed her baby. The nurse advises Baby Jones' mother that:
    a. she must discontinue breast feeding since the baby is not receiving enough milk.
    b. her baby is underweight and will require supplemental feedings.
    c. her baby's weight is normal and weight loss is expected in the first few days of life.
    d. her baby is overweight and the weight loss will reduce the risk of obesity later in life.
29. The newborn's response to the environment is primarily mediated through reflexes. (true or false)
30. Which statement concerning guidelines for infant feeding is accurate?
    a. There is a standard diet plan appropriate for all infants.
    b. Solid foods are usually introduced before the sixth month.
    c. The nurse should encourage all mothers to breast feed.
    d. Fluoride supplements are necessary for breast-fed infants.
31. Cow's milk may be substituted for breast milk or formula in infants over 6 months old. (true or false)
32. Which statement concerning the cognitive development of the infant is inaccurate?
    a. Sensory stimuli are as important as food for healthy development.
    b. Hospitalized infants require continuous stimuli to enhance cognitive development.
    c. By 12 months, the infant begins to name familiar objects in the environment.
    d. By 12 months the infant knows the meaning of several different sounds.
33. To promote optimal stimulation, it is appropriate to

assign several nurses to provide daily care for a hospitalized infant. (true or false)

34. What is the cause of temper tantrums in the toddler?

35. One of the most identifying cognitive characteristics of the toddler is:
- **a.** the differentiation of self as a separate being.
- **b.** an egocentric thought pattern.
- **c.** the ability to play with other children.
- **d.** the ability to understand right from wrong.

36. Which dietary guideline is appropriate to teach the parents of a toddler?
- **a.** Encourage at least 28 ounces of milk per day.
- **b.** Mealtime has psychosocial significance.
- **c.** When intake falls, the parent should attempt to feed the toddler.
- **d.** Serving sizes for the toddler are comparable to other age groups.

37. Describe the meaning of "refueling" as it applies to the toddler's psychosocial development.

38. Fill in the expected age of children and the behaviors characteristic of the following types of play patterns.

Play pattern	Age span	Characteristic behaviors
Cooperative		
Parallel		
Associative		

39. The preschool years are characterized by:
- **a.** the development of autonomy.
- **b.** rapid physical development.
- **c.** slowed psychosocial development.
- **d.** the beginning of intuitive thought.

40. The preschooler tends to think concretely and interpret words literally. (true or false)

41. Indicate the age span and average heart and respiratory rate for each of the following age groups.

Stage	Age span	Average heart rate	Average respiratory rate
Fetus			
Neonate			
Infant			
Toddler			
Preschooler			

42. Define regression.

43. Regression is a normal coping behavior for children experiencing physical or emotional stress. (true or false)

44. Hospitalization and illness are stressful experiences for children because of:
- **a.** separation from their normal environment.
- **b.** separation from significant others.
- **c.** a limited number of learned coping behaviors.
- **d.** all of the above.

45. Identify four factors that influence a child's reaction to illness and hospitalization.
- **a.**
- **b.**
- **c.**
- **d.**

46. What standardized test may the nurse use in determining a child's developmental level?

47. Fear of body injury and pain reactions occur in all children, including newborns. (true or false)

48. State four goals to include when planning care for a hospitalized child.
- **a.**
- **b.**
- **c.**
- **d.**

49. Who may appropriately implement nursing interventions for the hospitalized child?

APPLICATION OF KEY CONCEPTS

Activities to reinforce theoretical concepts

1. Experiential exercise: stages of growth and development
- **a.** Observe children in any setting (home, hospital, day care center, school). Identify physical and psychosocial behaviors of the children and match these to the milestones expected at each stage of growth and development. When possible, attempt to confirm the actual chronological ages of the children with the individual supervising the activity.
- **b.** Conduct a developmental assessment of an assigned client, friend, or relative. Identify the individual's stage of growth and development and determine the developmental tasks that have been accomplished. Formulate nursing interventions that would promote the individual's developmental task achievement.
- **c.** Observe a skilled nurse perform a Denver Developmental Screening Test (or examine the materials in a DDST kit). Attempt to perform the DDST on a healthy child and plot out the development levels on a DDST graph. Identify play activities for the child appropriate to the developmental level displayed.

2. Clinical situation: developmental theories, factors influencing growth and development

Timmy Johnson is a 24-month-old child who has had a recurrent history of ear infections (otitis media and serous otitis). He lives with his mother (21 years old), his stepfather (35 years old), and his stepbrother (14 years old). He and his mother have a well-child appointment with the pediatric nurse practitioner.
- **a.** What physical developmental milestones should the nurse evaluate for someone Timmy's age? (Name at least five.)
- **b.** According to Freud, what is Timmy's developmental stage, and what developmental skills are affected by this stage?
- **c.** According to Erikson, what conflict is commonly experienced by children Timmy's age, and what anticipatory guidance can the nurse offer?
- **d.** According to Erikson, what are the psychosocial tasks for the other members of Timmy's family

and what anticipatory guidance can the nurse offer?

   e. According to Maslow, what category or stage would Timmy be in? What needs must Timmy and his family meet in order to progress?

   f. Identify the major external forces that present opportunities for Timmy's growth and development. What are the relevant influences of each of these forces?

3. Discuss why it is important to select a developmental framework for providing nursing care. (Be sure to include advantages for nurse, client, and family members.)

4. Experiential exercise: promoting fetal growth and development
Structure a teaching plan for a pregnant woman that is directed toward maintenance of fetal health in each of the following areas.
   a. Physical development
   b. Cognitive development
   c. Psychosocial development

5. Experiential exercise: transition from intrauterine to extrauterine life
   a. Arrange to talk with a nurse or clinical specialist who works in the area of maternal-child care. Ask the nurse to discuss how the staff promotes the neonate's physical and psychosocial health and facilitates family acquaintance and attachment.
   b. Ask your instructor to arrange for an observational experience in any setting in which prenatal, intrapartal, or postpartal care is provided. Identify actions by the nurse that promote physical health and psychosocial development of the mother, father, and child as individuals and as a family unit.

6. Clinical situation: nursing care of the hospitalized child
Thomas Matthews is a 4-year-old boy admitted to the hospital for a tonsillectomy. He is accompanied by his mother who will remain with him throughout the entire hospitalization. His father is out of town on business and will not be available to the family except by telephone. Thomas' paternal grandparents live nearby and will be caring for his 8-year-old brother, Brian.
   a. Identify the factors that should be assessed during the admission interview with Thomas and his mother. Describe why each of these factors will be important in planning care.
   b. Formulate at least four nursing diagnoses that might be applicable to Thomas.
   c. State four goals for care during Thomas' hospitalization.
   d. Identify at least one outcome criterion and three interventions to achieve each of the stated goals. Be sure that your interventions are appropriate to the developmental level of the typical 4-year-old child.

ADDITIONAL READINGS

Behrman, RE, and Vaughan, VC, editors: Nelson textbook of pediatrics, ed. 13, Philadelphia, 1987, W.B. Saunders Co.
A comprehensive pediatric textbook. Includes detailed discussion of growth and development from the prenatal period through adolescence. A superior reference for information related to physical and psychological disorders found in neonates, infants, children, and adolescents. Describes, in detail, the pathology, diagnostic tests, symptomatology, and usual medical treatment of pediatric disorders.

Craft, MJ, and Wyatt, N: Effect of visitation of siblings on hospitalized children, Matern Child Nurs J 15(1):47, 1986.
Describes a study to evaluate effect of sibling visitation on the hospitalized child. Findings suggest visitation produces age-related change in sibling feelings and behaviors. Identifies needs of siblings of hospitalized children. Well referenced to assist in accessing related readings.

Dole, JC: A multidimensional study of infant's response to painful stimuli, Pediatr Nurs 12(1):27, 1986.
Study to identify common behaviors of infants in response to acute pain. Points to the need for multisystem assessment for accurate pain assessment.

Garot, PA: Therapeutic play: work of both child and nurse, J Pediatr Nurs 1(2):111, 1986.
Discusses therapeutic play as a valuable nursing intervention.

LaMontagne, LL: Children's locus of control beliefs as predictors of preoperative coping behaviors, Nurs Res 33(2):76, 1984.
Examines children's locus of control and response to preoperative care. Identifies differences in coping styles based on locus of control. Suggests approaches to preoperative care based on coping strategies and locus of control.

Moore, ML, and Galloway, K: Newborn family and nurse, ed. 2, Philadelphia, 1981, W.B. Saunders Co.
Describes fetal development. Discusses the influence of environment and genetics on development. Describes care of the normal and high-risk newborn and the family.

Scipien, G, et al: Comprehensive pediatric nursing ed. 3, New York, 1986, McGraw-Hill Book Co.
A comprehensive pediatric nursing text. Discusses childhood health and illness from a developmental approach. Integrates nursing process in discussion of pediatric care. Includes discussion of special problems encountered by children and their families. Describes common disease states and related nursing care of pediatric clients and their families.

Whaley, LF, and Wong, DL: Nursing care of infants and children, ed. 3, 1987, The C.V. Mosby Co.
A comprehensive pediatric nursing text. Detailed description of normal growth and development, physical and developmental assessment, and common and unusual health problems [and related treatment] from infancy through adolescence. Describes the nurse's role in pediatric care from the perspective of traditional as well as expanded practice roles.

Chapter 23
School-Age Child to Adolescent

PREREQUISITE READING

Read Chapter 23, pp. 590 to 607.

OBJECTIVES

Mastery of content in this chapter will enable the student to:

1. Define selected terms relevant to growth and development.
2. Describe the influence of the school environment on the cognitive psychosocial development of the school-age child and adolescent.
3. Discuss ways in which the nurse can help parents adjust to their child's developmental needs.
4. Describe the normal physical changes that occur during the school-age years and adolescence.
5. Discuss behavior reflecting cognitive development of the school-age child and adolescent.
6. List nursing interventions for health concerns specific to the school-age child and adolescent.
7. Compare and contrast the ways by which a school-age child and an adolescent develop moral values.
8. Discuss ways in which an adolescent gains a sexual, group, and personal identity.

REVIEW OF KEY CONCEPTS

1. Match the developmental behavior with the typical age group.
   - **a.** _____ Establishes a moral code
   - **b.** _____ Talkative
   - **c.** _____ Values group conformity
   - **d.** _____ Worries about loss of identity
   - **e.** _____ Has a strict literal conscience
   - **f.** _____ Sees self as others see him or her
   - **g.** _____ Has completed major gross and fine motor development
   - **h.** _____ Returns to parents for companionship and comfort

   1. School-age
   2. Adolescent
2. It is generally accepted that optimal learning occurs before 6 years of age. (true or false)
3. Which statement concerning physical development in the school-age child is inaccurate?
   - **a.** Continued evaluation of height and weight on a growth chart is unnecessary.
   - **b.** Alterations in growth provide a clue to the onset of many disease processes.
   - **c.** Neuromuscular refinement is a major accomplishment during the school-age years.
   - **d.** Skeletal growth alters the eye shape and improves visual acuity.
4. The prepubertal physical changes and growth spurts occur between:
   - **a.** 10 and 14 years for girls.
   - **b.** 10 and 14 years for boys.
   - **c.** 12 and 16 years for girls.
   - **d.** 14 and 18 years for boys.
5. Identify the average heart rate, respiratory rate, and blood pressure for the typical school-age child.
   - **a.** Heart rate
   - **b.** Respiratory rate
   - **c.** Blood pressure
6. What is the best way to ensure adequate nutritional intake for the school-age child?
7. Define metacognition.
8. Match the cognitive, moral, and psychosocial developmental behavior with the appropriate age group.
   - **a.** _____ Uses abstract thinking
   - **b.** _____ Refines understanding of spatial relationships
   - **c.** _____ Experiences conflict between group and personal values
   - **d.** _____ Seeks sense of identity
   - **e.** _____ Develops sense of right and wrong
   - **f.** _____ Develops inductive reasoning skills
   - **g.** _____ Has good language development but lacks communication skills

   1. School-age
   2. Adolescent
9. It is appropriate for the nurse to involve the child in any decisions about changes and actions for implementing changes in activities of daily living. (true or false)
10. The leading cause of death for school-age children is:
    - **a.** cancer.
    - **b.** infectious diseases.

c. accidents.
d. suicide.

11. The standard by which the school-age child judges personal health and the health of others is:
    a. physical comfort.
    b. ability to socialize.
    c. functional ability.
    d. body image.
12. The period of psychological maturation of the individual is known as ________________.
13. The period of an individual's biological maturation, making reproduction possible, is known as ________________.
14. Describe the differences between primary and secondary sex characteristics.
15. Identify the four major physical changes associated with sexual maturation.
    a.
    b.
    c.
    d.
16. The prepubertal growth spurt generally precedes adult physical maturity by:
    a. 6 to 12 months.
    b. 1 to 2 years.
    c. 2 to 3 years.
    d. 4 years.
17. The time of the onset of pubertal changes may have an effect on psychosocial development. (true or false)
18. Which statement concerning pubertal growth changes is correct?
    a. The timing of pubertal growth changes is the same in most females.
    b. The time when sexual changes begin is more significant than their pattern of onset.
    c. The sequence of pubertal growth changes is the same in most individuals.
    d. Growth changes result from the pituitary gland secreting gonadotropin-releasing hormones.
19. Adolescents have mastered age-appropriate sexuality when they feel comfortable with their sexual:
    a. behaviors.
    b. choices.
    c. relationships.
    d. all of the above.
20. The strong need for group identity often conflicts with the adolescent's quest for personal identity. (true or false)
21. The leading cause of death in adolescence is:
    a. motor vehicle accidents.
    b. suicide.
    c. cancer.
    d. infectious diseases.
22. The most common communicable diseases among adolescents are ________________.
23. List the five areas for nursing assessment of the school-age child and adolescent.
    a.
    b.
    c.
    d.
    e.
24. Briefly describe the differences between a child's internal and external support system.

APPLICATION OF KEY CONCEPTS
Activities to reinforce theoretical concepts

1. Experiential exercise: stages of growth and development
    a. Observe school-age children and adolescents in any setting. Identify physical and psychosocial behaviors and match these to expected characteristics of the designated stage of growth and development.
    b. Conduct a developmental assessment of a school-age child or adolescent. Determine the developmental tasks that have been accomplished. Formulate nursing interventions that would promote the individual's developmental task achievement.
2. Clinical situation: developmental theories, factors influencing growth and development

   Chip Brown is a 7-year-old child who has fractured his right arm in a fall while climbing a tree. He lives with his parents and brother (4 years old). The pediatric nurse practitioner is responsible for Chip's follow-up care.
    a. What physical characteristics should be evaluated for someone Chip's age?
    b. According to Freud, what is Chip's developmental stage and what developmental skills are affected by this stage?
    c. According to Erikson, what conflict is commonly experienced by children Chip's age, and what anticipatory guidance can the nurse offer?
    d. According to Erikson, what are the psychosocial tasks for other members of Chip's family and what anticipatory guidance can the nurse offer?
    e. According to Maslow, what category or stage would Chip be in? What needs must Chip and his family meet in order to progress?
    f. Identify the major positive and negative forces influencing Chip's growth and development at this time. What actions can the nurse take to promote his normal growth and development?
3. Experiential exercise: school-related stresses

   For each of the designated age groups, identify at least two school-related stresses and an appropriate nursing intervention to assist the child in preventing or reducing each stressor identified.

Age	Stressor	Nursing intervention
5-8 yr		
8-10 yr		
10-12 yr		

4. Experiential exercise: developmental health concerns
    a. Identify the major health problem for the school-

age child. Identify the target audience and develop a teaching plan to address this issue.

b. Identify the major health problem for the adolescent. Identify the target audience and develop a teaching plan to address this issue.

5. Clinical situation: nursing care of the hospitalized adolescent

Barry Dobbs is a 15-year-old who is being treated for a fractured jaw resulting from an automobile accident. He has had surgery and is experiencing postoperative pain and swelling. He is very concerned about his appearance. His jaw is wired, impairing his ability to speak clearly. At the present time he is receiving his meals in a semiliquid form through a small feeding tube.

a. Identify the factors that should be assessed before planning care for Barry.

b. What major task would concern Barry during the adolescent stage of development? What areas of developmental adjustment should the nurse consider when formulating a plan of care?

c. Formulate at least four nursing diagnoses that might apply to Barry.

d. State four goals for care during Barry's hospitalization.

e. Identify at least one criterion and three interventions to achieve each of the stated goals. Be sure that your interventions are appropriate to the adolescent developmental level.

ADDITIONAL READINGS

Please refer to readings cited in Chapter 22, which include several sources pertinent to the school-age child and adolescent. References cited in that chapter have not been repeated here.

Blaesing, S, and Brockhaus, J: The development of body image in the child, Nurs Clin North Am 7(4):597, 1972.

Discusses the process of body image development in children. Information presented may be used in care planning to promote positive self-concept development in children.

Dempsey, M: The development of body image in the adolescent, Nurs Clin North Am 7(4):609, 1972.

Discusses the process of body image development in the adolescent. Information presented may be used in care planning to promote positive self-concept development in adolescents.

Giuffra, M: Demystifying adolescent behavior, Am J Nurs 75(10):1725, 1975.

Correlates "typical" adolescent behavior with the developmental process. Describes approaches to more effectively meet needs of the adolescent client.

Oldaker, S: Identity confusion: nursing diagnosis for adolescents, Nurs Clin North Am 20(4):763, 1985.

Describes research investigating developmental health and psychological symptoms among high school adolescents. Explores potential causes of identity confusion, as well as diagnostic criteria. Correlates etiology and diagnostic criteria with developmental tasks.

Chapter 24
Young and Middle Adult

PREREQUISITE READING

Read Chapter 24, pp. 608 to 630.

OBJECTIVES

Mastery of content in this chapter will enable the student to:

1. Define selected terms relevant to the young and middle adult years.
2. Discuss developmental theories of the young and middle adult.
3. List and discuss major life events of the young and middle adult and the childbearing family.
4. Describe developmental tasks of the young adult, the childbearing family, and the middle adult.
5. Discuss the significance of family in the life of the adult.
6. Describe normal physiological changes in young and middle adulthood and in pregnancy.
7. Discuss cognitive and psychosocial changes occurring during the adult years.
8. Describe health concerns of the young adult, the childbearing family, and the middle adult.
9. List nursing diagnoses appropriate for the young and middle adult.
10. Use the nursing process to administer care to young- and middle-adult clients.

REVIEW OF KEY CONCEPTS

1. Define maturity.
2. List the four phases of young adult development described by Levinson.
   a.
   b.
   c.
   d.
3. Describe the five developmental tasks of the young adult proposed by Diekelmann.
   a.
   b.
   c.
   d.
   e.
4. Match the age span with the personal or social task most often addressed.
   a. _____ 23-28 years
   b. _____ 29-34 years
   c. _____ 35-43 years

   1. Examining life goals and relationships
   2. Refining self-perception and ability for intimacy
   3. Achieving goals and mastering the surrounding world
5. At what stage of development is an individual usually able to initiate mature sexual relationships?
   a. Puberty
   b. Adolescence
   c. Young adult years
   d. Middle adult years
6. List the four major phases of the childbearing cycle in their appropriate sequence.
   a.
   b.
   c.
   d.
7. Describe four tasks that should ideally be completed by a couple before marriage.
   a.
   b.
   c.
   d.
8. Describe four tasks to be accomplished by the married couple establishing a household and family.
   a.
   b.
   c.
   d.
9. Briefly describe the parental responsibilities associated with each of the following phases or roles of parenthood.
   a. Departure phase
   b. Nurturing role
   c. Initial phase
   d. Authoritative role
   e. Integrative role
10. Identify six hallmarks of emotional health indicating that the young adult has successfully mastered this developmental stage.
    a.
    b.

c.
d.
e.
f.

11. Life-style patterns during the young adult years may place the individual at risk for development of illnesses or disabilities during middle or older adult years. (true or false)
12. List the five categories of health risk factors for the young adult.
    a.
    b.
    c.
    d.
    e.
13. Define infertility.
14. Pregnancy produces cognitive and psychosocial changes that affect the husband, siblings, and grandparents. (true or false)
15. An overweight woman who is attempting to become pregnant should be advised to begin a weight reduction diet. (true or false)
16. Match the physiological changes of pregnancy with the trimester in which they most commonly occur.
    a. _____ Increased colostrum
    b. _____ Fatigue
    c. _____ Quickening
    d. _____ Hypertrophy of gums
    e. _____ Waddling gait
    f. _____ Chadwick's sign
    g. _____ Nausea or vomiting
    h. _____ Dyspnea

    1. First trimester
    2 Second trimester
    3. Third trimester
17. Define puerperium.
18. Fill in the type of lochia discharge described below.
    a. ___________ White to yellow discharge
    b. ___________ Bright red to pink discharge
    c. ___________ Pink to brownish discharge
19. Which statement concerning breast feeding is accurate?
    a. Breast milk is available for the infant on the second postpartum day.
    b. Lochia discharge decreases when the infant is nursing.
    c. The woman should be advised to begin each nursing period with the same breast.
    d. The quantity of breast milk is directly proportional to the amount consumed.
20. Psychosocial changes of pregnancy commonly involve all of the following areas except:
    a. body image.
    b. anxiety and depression.
    c. role changes.
    d. sexuality.
21. Define prenatal care.
22. What is usually considered the ideal weight gain during pregnancy?
23. The theorist who proposes that the primary developmental task of the middle years is to develop the willingness to care for and guide others is:
    a. Havighurst.
    b. Diekelmann.
    c. Erikson.
    d. Buhler.
24. Identify four developmental tasks for the middle adult described by Havighurst.
    a.
    b.
    c.
    d.
25. Which physiological change would be an expected finding during physical assessment of the middle adult?
    a. Increased breast size
    b. Abdominal tenderness and organomegaly
    c. Increased anteroposterior diameter of thorax
    d. Reduced auditory acuity
26. Define menopause.
27. Define climacteric.
28. A male is capable of fathering a child after andropause. (true or false)
29. Identify and briefly describe four risk factors for depression in the middle adult.
    a.
    b.
    c.
    d.
30. State three goals, directed toward health maintenance, that would be appropriate for the young or middle-aged adult.
    a.
    b.
    c.

APPLICATION OF KEY CONCEPTS

Activities to reinforce theoretical concepts

1. Experiential exercise: stages of marriage
    a. Interview at least one married couple from each of the following stages of a marriage: establishment stage, family orientation stage, postparental family stage.
    b. For each couple interviewed, attempt to have them identify the primary focus of their work as a couple, the major stressors that they encounter, and coping mechanisms that they employ to deal with stressors.
    c. Compare the information elicited with the tasks and goals of married couples described in your text.
2. Experiential exercise: psychosocial assessment
    a. Develop a questionnaire, or structure interview questions that may be used to evaluate the emotional health of a young adult. Be sure to refer to

the ten hallmarks of emotional health described in your text as a guide.

b. Interview a young adult based on the questionnaire or interview questions developed (or use the personal life-style assessment tool in Chapter 2, p. 44)

c. Analyze the data obtained to determine if the young adult has successfully matured in this developmental stage. Identify specific behaviors that reflect the individual's ability or inability to meet the developmental tasks.

d. Formulate goals and related nursing interventions that support or promote successful maturation for the individual at this developmental stage.

3. Experiential exercise: life-style habits and illness risk

a. Develop a 10- to 20-minute teaching session that identifies common life-style habits that increase the risk of illness in the young and middle adult. Be sure to include a brief overview of methods of illness prevention related to each life-style habit.

b. Present the teaching session to a group of peers or submit the plan to your instructor, and request feedback.

c. If feasible, identify a target audience in your community and, with your instructor as a resource, present this information in a formal or informal teaching session.

4. Clinical situation: marriage and family development
Jim and Juanita Hammer (both 35 years old) have been married for 2 years and have been struggling with the decision to begin a family. They describe their marriage as "good" and frequently state that "our biological clock is running out." They have requested an appointment with the nurse at the neighborhood family-planning clinic to discuss their concerns and questions.

a. What behaviors would indicate that Jim and Juanita have successfully worked through the establishment stage of their marriage? (Identify at least five factors.)

b. Several factors influence the decision to start a family. Identify and briefly describe the factors that the nurse would explore with the Hammers.

c. If the Hammers elect to begin a family, what advice should the nurse give to Mrs. Hammer concerning her health practices before conception?

5. Experiential exercise: assessment of the middle adult

a. Conduct an assessment of a middle adult using any comprehensive assessment tool (sample tool in your text, tool used in your institution, or tool you have developed or revised).

b. Identify the developmental tasks for the middle adult, and determine if the individual is working toward or has achieved the tasks identified.

c. Identify assessment findings that reflect the expected physiological changes occurring in the middle adult years.

d. Describe positive and negative health behaviors identified in the assessment.

e. Identify the presence of risk factors for:
(1) Cancer
(2) Cardiovascular disease: hypertension, heart attack, stroke
(3) Depression

6. Clinical situation: nursing process for the middle adult
Grace Charis is a 53-year-old woman admitted to the hospital for a hysterectomy for cervical cancer. Mrs. Charis has been married for 30 years and has three children, 17 to 24 years old. She describes her husband as her "best friend" and tells the nurse she is preparing to send her youngest child to college this fall. Mrs. Charis has smoked approximately five cigarettes per day for the past 35 years.

a. What major tasks would concern Mrs. Charis as an individual in the middle years? What impact could her current status have on task achievement?

b. What stage of family development are the Charises experiencing? What feelings might be experienced by parents during this stage? What behaviors or activities are characteristic during this stage? What influence could Mrs. Charis' status have on this stage of family development?

c. Formulate at least four nursing diagnoses that might be applicable to Mrs. Charis.

d. State four goals for Mrs. Charis' care during hospitalization.

e. Identify at least one outcome criterion and three interventions to achieve each of the stated goals. Be sure your interventions are appropriate to the middle adult developmental tasks.

ADDITIONAL READINGS

Please refer to reading cited in Chapter 21, which include several sources pertinent to the young and middle adult. References cited in that chapter have not been repeated here.

Beck, CM, Rawlins, RR, and Williams, SR: Mental health—psychiatric nursing: a holistic life-cycle approach, St. Louis, 1984, The C.V. Mosby Co.

A comprehensive text that explores psychosocial development and mental health throughout the life span. Presents a detailed discussion of theoretical foundations for practice. Physical, emotional, intellectual, social, and spiritual dimensions of mental health and illness are used as an organizational framework for the study of normal development, behavior, and psychopathology. Presents nursing care using the nursing process format.

Brown, MA: Social support, stress, and health: a comparison of expectant mothers and fathers, Nurs Res 35:72, 1986.

Examines the influence of social support and stress on the health of expectant mothers and fathers. Identifies differences in social supports valued by mothers and fathers.

Dickelmann, JL: The young adult: the choice is health or illness, Am J Nurs 76:1272, 1976.

Discusses the importance of health maintenance for adults between ages 20 and 35 years. Emphasizes the need for attention to emotional development, diet, exercise, and sleep in preventing health problems in later years. Identifies preventive activities that could be incorporated in a health maintenance plan.

Laffrey, SC: Normal and overweight adults: perceived weight and health behavior characteristics, Nurs Res 35:173, 1986.

Concludes that there is no difference in perception of health in comparative groups of normal and overweight adults. Emphasizes the importance of understanding client's perception of health and individual approaches to health practices.

Walker, LO, Crain, H, and Thompson, E: Maternal role attachment and identity in the postpartum period: stability and change, Nurs Res 35:68, 1986.

Describes study focusing on maternal role and perceptions during the postpartum period. Indicates increased maternal self-confidence and positive attitudes toward self from birth to 4 to 6 weeks later. Findings suggest that mothers viewed their babies less positively at the end of the postpartum period.

Chapter 25
Older Adult

PREREQUISITE READING

Read Chapter 25, pp. 632 to 659.

OBJECTIVES

Mastery of content in this chapter will enable the student to:

1. Define selected terms relevant to the older adult and the aging process.
2. Describe common myths and stereotypes about older adults.
3. Discuss nurses' attitudes toward older adults.
4. Discuss the three physiological theories of aging.
5. Discuss the three psychosocial theories of aging.
6. State and discuss developmental tasks of the older adult.
7. Describe physiological changes of aging.
8. Describe cognitive changes of dementia and delirium found in some older adults.
9. Describe common causes of dementia and delirium.
10. Discuss psychosocial changes of retirement, social isolation, sexuality, housing, and death to which older adults must adjust.
11. Discuss physical and psychosocial health concerns of older adults and describe related nursing interventions.
12. Describe community and institutional health care services available to older adults.

REVIEW OF KEY CONCEPTS

1. Define geriatrics.
2. Define gerontology.
3. Which statement concerning older adults is accurate?
   - **a.** Most elderly persons are institutionalized.
   - **b.** Most older people live on a fixed income.
   - **c.** Most older clients cannot learn to care for themselves.
   - **d.** Most older adults have no sexual desire.
4. Define ageism.
5. It is important to incorporate routines or rituals of the older adult into the plan of care. (true or false)
6. Match the theory of aging with the most accurate description.
   - **a.** _____ Chemical reactions cause collagen to become rigid and less permeable with age.
   - **b.** _____ Aging people withdraw from customary roles and engage in introspective, self-focused activities.
   - **c.** _____ Extracellular changes create a reaction altering the structure or function of the cell membrane.
   - **d.** _____ Older adults need to maintain physical, mental, and social activities.
   - **e.** _____ Life-style, personality, and environmental factors influence aging.
   - **f.** _____ Erratic cellular mechanisms attack body tissues through autoaggression or immunodeficiency.

   1. Free radical theory
   2. Cross-link theory
   3. Immunological theory
   4. Psychosocial theory
   5. Disengagement theory
   6. Activity theory
7. Identify five developmental tasks of the older adult.
   - **a.**
   - **b.**
   - **c.**
   - **d.**
   - **e.**
8. Indicate whether the following physical assessment findings are normal (N) or abnormal (A) in the older adult.
   - **a.** _____ Melanoma
   - **b.** _____ Presbyopia
   - **c.** _____ Increased bowel sounds
   - **d.** _____ Decreased lung expansion
   - **e.** _____ Diminished light reflex on tympanic membrane
   - **f.** _____ Enlarged prostate
   - **g.** _____ Decreased pedal pulses
   - **h.** _____ Positive ankle clonus
   - **i.** _____ Positive guaiac stools
   - **j.** _____ Stress incontinence in women
9. Structural and physiological changes in the brain during the aging process will affect adaptive and functional abilities of the older adult. (true or false)
10. Preexisting behavioral tendencies tend to be magnified as a person ages. (true or false)

11. Define dementia.
12. What is the most frequent cause of irreversible dementia?
13. List three common causes of reversible dementia in the older adult.
    a.
    b.
    c.
14. Which statement describing delirium is correct?
    a. Illusions and hallucinations may be experienced by persons with delirium.
    b. The onset of delirium is slow and insidious.
    c. Symptoms of delirium are stable and unchanging.
    d. Symptoms of delirium are irreversible.
15. Cognitive changes in the older adults are normal, expected outcomes of aging. (true or false)
16. List three signs characteristic of the early stages of Alzheimer's disease.
    a.
    b.
    c.
17. Jack Waycome is a 56-year-old business executive who has evidenced behavioral changes over the past few years. Mr. Waycome is hesitant in responding to questions posed by his coworkers. He misses regularly scheduled weekly meetings. His secretary must constantly remind him about scheduled appointments and find his reading glasses, pens, papers, and briefcase. Lately he has come to work without showering, shaving, or changing clothes from the previous day. Mr. Waycome's behaviors are characteristic of which stage of irreversible dementia (Alzheimer's disease)?
    a. Final or terminal
    b. Early
    c. Advanced
    d. Later
18. Multi-infarct dementia is primarily associated with:
    a. substance abuse.
    b. vascular disorders.
    c. cardiac disorders.
    d. infectious processes.
19. Long-term abuse of alcohol and drugs can produce permanent damage to the nervous system. (true or false)
20. Individuals who plan retirement activities generally make a better adjustment during the older adult years. (true or false)
21. Identify four issues to be addressed when counseling an older adult for retirement.
    a.
    b.
    c.
    d.
22. Briefly describe the four types of social isolation experienced by older adults.
    a. Attitudinal isolation
    b. Presentation isolation
    c. Behavioral isolation
    d. Geographical isolation
23. List four factors to be assessed when assisting older adults with housing needs.
    a.
    b.
    c.
    d.
24. By the time adults reach old age, they are emotionally prepared to die. (true or false)
25. Identify the four major causes of death in older adults.
    a.
    b.
    c.
    d.
26. Confusion regularly occurring during the evening or night is referred to as ____________________.
27. Nutritional needs of the older adult:
    a. are exactly the same as those of young and middle adults.
    b. require greater amounts of vitamin C and vitamin A.
    c. require increased calories to support decreased metabolism.
    d. require less calcium to prevent bone demineralization.
28. Identify and briefly describe the six techniques used in maintaining the psychosocial health of the older adult.
    a.
    b.
    c.
    d.
    e.
    f.
29. The following are examples of nursing interventions appropriate for reality orientation. Label each example with the characteristic principle that it illustrates.
    a. ____________ Give directions in clear, simple, short statements.
    b. ____________ Encourage client to perform tasks and make decisions without assistance from others.
    c. ____________ Reward correct behavior with verbal praise, touch, or smiles.
    d. ____________ Use time, date, place, and name in conversations.
    e. ____________ Maintain continuity of care by assigning the same personnel to care for the client.
    f. ____________ Repeat information, directions, statements, and questions when necessary.
    g. ____________ Allow client to keep familiar treasures and objects.
30. List four guidelines for conducting discussion sessions with older adults.

a.
b.
c.
d.

31. Identify the type of community or institutional care facility appropriate for the older adult based on the primary health care service described below.
   a. ____________ Services focusing on self-care and maintenance of activities of daily living
   b. ____________ Services to meet the needs of the terminally ill client and family
   c. ____________ Health services for a client who is able to remain home during the evening
   d. ____________ Service that enables the caretaker of a dependent adult to be away from home for a few days
   e. ____________ Extended residential, intermediate, or specialized health care

32. List three factors to be considered when establishing goals of care for the older adult client.
   a.
   b.
   c.

APPLICATION OF KEY CONCEPTS
Activities to reinforce theoretical concepts

1. Describe your attitudes toward older adults and your feelings about aging. Discuss the importance of clarifying personal values related to aging before caring for older clients.
2. Experiential exercise: developmental assessment
   a. Conduct an interview of an older adult using the personal life-style assessment tool found in Chapter 2, p. 44.
   b. Analyze the data obtained to determine if the older adult has successfully achieved the tasks of this developmental stage. Identify specific behaviors that reflect the individual's ability or inability to meet the developmental tasks.
   c. Formulate goals and related nursing interventions that support or promote successful maturation for the individual at this developmental stage.
3. Experiential exercise: assessment of the older adult
   a. Conduct an assessment of an older adult using any comprehensive assessment tool (sample tool in your text, tool used in your institution, or tool you have developed or revised).
   b. Identify the developmental tasks for the older adult, and determine if the individual is working toward or has achieved the tasks identified.
   c. Identify assessment findings that reflect expected physiological changes occurring in the older adult years.
   d. Formulate a list of nursing diagnoses based on your assessment finding.
   e. Identify the priority nursing diagnosis, and formulate a plan of care. Be sure that interventions reflect the developmental stage of the client.
4. Clinical situation: client with SDAT (senile dementia, Alzheimer's type)
   Anna Mueller is a 58-year-old housewife in the advanced stages of Alzheimer's disease. Her husband continues to work outside the home, but is increasingly concerned about leaving Mrs. Mueller alone at home during the day. Although the Muellers have two adult children living in the area, they both work full-time and have their own families.
   a. What symptoms would Mrs. Mueller most likely display during this stage of irreversible dementia?
   b. Identify at least four nursing objectives that would be particularly important for Mrs. Mueller at this time. Formulate at least three interventions for each nursing objective.
   c. What health care services might be appropriate for the Muellers at this time? (community based or institutional)
5. Clinical situation: retirement
   Mr. and Mrs. Jones have been married for over 40 years. Mr. Jones works with a company that has an employee health nurse. Before his annual physical, Mr. Jones tells the nurse that he plans to retire after his next birthday.
   a. What six issues should the nurse and Mr. Jones discuss?
   b. Mr. Jones tells the nurse that he and his wife anticipate that Mrs. Jones' mother, who recently suffered a stroke, will be brought into their household. Assuming that the Joneses are living in your community, what community services would be available to assist them in adapting to this change? (Include at least five different services or agencies.)
   c. What formal or informal contacts could Mr. and Mrs. Jones utilize to increase their social network after retirement? (Include at least five formal and five informal contacts.)
6. Clinical situation: reversible dementia
   Margaret Hutchinson is an elderly client who has been independently caring for herself at home. Recently hospitalized for congestive heart failure, Miss Hutchinson has become confused almost every night during her hospital stay.
   a. What factors may be contributing to Miss Hutchinson's confusion?
   b. What is the name given to the episodes of confusion Miss Hutchinson has been experiencing?
   c. Identify at least five nursing interventions that could be initiated to reduce the incidence of Miss Hutchinson's nighttime confusion.

ADDITIONAL READINGS

Please refer to readings cited in Chapters 21 and 24, which include several sources pertinent to the older adult. References cited in those chapters have not been repeated here.

Abraham, IL, Buckwalter, KC, and Neundorfer, M, editors: Alzheimer's disease, Nurs Clin North Am 23(1), 1988.

Series of articles addressing issues and comprehensive approaches to care of the client and family encountering Alzheimer's disease.

Bartol, M: Dialogue with dementia: non-verbal communication in patients with Alzheimer's disease, J Gerontol Nurs 5(4):21, 1979.

Presents clear, detailed guidelines for nurse-client communications in the presence of dementia. Emphasizes use of nonverbal techniques. Analyzes interaction between nurses and clients with dementia via sample case studies.

Chang, BL, et al: Adherence to health care regimens among elderly women, Nurs Res 34:27, 1985.

Report of a study to determine factors that contributed to the intent of elderly women to adhere to a plan of care. Findings illustrate the significant impact of psychosocial care on client intent. Identifies individual characteristics associated with high intent to adhere to care.

Diekelman, N: Pre-retirement counseling, Am J Nurs 78:1337, 1978.

Discusses nurse's role in helping older adults prepare for retirement. Presents major areas for assessment and describes anticipatory guidance to promote the older adult's successful retirement and health.

Ebersole, P, and Hess, P: Toward healthy aging: human needs and nursing responses, ed. 2, St. Louis, 1985, The C.V. Mosby Co.

Comprehensive gerontological nursing text. Approaches care of the older adult in the context of Maslow's hierarchy of needs. Identifies needs of the older client and describes appropriate nursing interventions. Includes theoretical foundations, roles, functions, and practice issues of gerontological nursing.

Foreman, MD: Acute confusional states in hospitalized elderly: a research dilemma, Nurs Res 35:34, 1986.

Review of the literature on acute confusional states. Includes information concerning classification, incidence, prevalence, etiology, and implication for nursing practice. Tables summarize information comparing acute confusional states with dementia.

Gropper-Katz, EI: Reality orientation research, J Gerontol Nurs 13(8):13, 1987.

Review and evaluation of five articles addressing reality orientation as an intervention for elderly persons with moderate to severe degrees of confusion.

Lappe, JM: Reminiscing: the life review therapy, J Gerontol Nurs 13(4):12, 1987.

Describes research study examining the use of reminiscing in the elderly. Findings suggest that life review is essential for adjustment to old age and acceptance of death.

Chapter 26
Loss, Death, and Grieving

PREREQUISITE READING

Read Chapter 26, pp. 660 to 683.

OBJECTIVES

Mastery of content in this chapter will enable the student to:

1. Define selected terms associated with loss, death, and the grieving process.
2. Identify the nurse's role in assisting clients with problems related to loss, death, and grief.
3. Describe and compare the phases of grieving from Engle, Kübler-Ross, and Martocchio.
4. List and discuss the five basic categories of loss.
5. Describe the six dimensions of hope.
6. Assess a client's reaction to grief and ability to cope.
7. Describe characteristics of a person experiencing grief.
8. Compare and contrast grief after loss, anticipatory grief, and resolved grief.
9. Give at least five examples of nursing diagnoses related to grief.
10. Develop a care plan for a client or family experiencing grief.
11. Implement interventions for grieving clients to provide therapeutic communication, maintain self-esteem, and promote a return to normal activities.
12. Describe how the nurse helps meet the dying client's needs for comfort.
13. Explain ways for the nurse to assist a family in caring for a dying client.
14. Discuss the purposes of a hospice.
15. List and discuss important factors in caring for the body after death.
16. Describe criteria to evaluate nursing care for grieving and dying clients.

REVIEW OF KEY CONCEPTS

1. Which statement concerning loss is accurate?
   a. Loss is only experienced when there is an actual absence of something valued.
   b. The more that an individual has invested in what is lost, the less the feeling of loss.
   c. Loss may be maturational, situational, or both.
   d. The degree of stress experienced is unrelated to the type of loss.
2. List and briefly describe the five categories of loss.
   a.
   b.
   c.
   d.
   e.
3. A form of sorrow involving thought, feeling, and behaviors is called:
   a. bereavement.
   b. grief.
   c. loss.
   d. denial.
4. The subjective experience that occurs in response to loss caused by death is called ______________.
5. Identify the four tasks that must be accomplished by the grieving person.
   a.
   b.
   c.
   d.
6. The process of grieving may promote personal growth. (true or false)
7. In the table below, list the phases of the grieving process proposed by each of the identified theorists.

Engle	Kübler-Ross	Martocchio
a.	a.	a.
b.	b.	b.
c.	c.	c.
	d.	d.
	e.	e.

8. All individuals experiencing loss will progress through each phase of the grieving process in a sequential manner. (true or false)
9. It is common for people to work through grief over more than 1 to 2 years. (true or false)
10. Match the behaviors described to the stage of dying identified by Kübler-Ross.
    a. _____ Becomes quiet, noncommunicative, and inattentive to personal appearance
    b. _____ Fearful of losing body functions or control
    c. _____ Gives away personal possessions; reminisces about the past
    d. _____ Demanding and anxious with feelings of low self-esteem

e. _____ Fails to comply with medical therapy; unable to deal with treatment decisions

1. Anger
2. Depression
3. Denial
4. Acceptance
5. Bargaining

11. Identify and briefly define the six dimensions of hope.
a.
b.
c.
d.
e.
f.
12. Recognition and reaction to loss are age dependent. (true or false)
13. The developmental stage in which the child is first able to understand logical explanations about death is:
a. toddler years.
b. preschool age.
c. school age.
d. adolescence.
14. Match the developmental stage with the most characteristic description.
a. _____ Infant
b. _____ Toddler
c. _____ Preschooler
d. _____ School age
e. _____ Adolescent
f. _____ Young adult
g. _____ Middle adult
h. _____ Older adult

1. Least likely of any age group to accept loss of life
2. Perception of death associated with destruction
3. Concept of death primarily derived from religious or cultural beliefs
4. Difficulty separating fact from fantasy; prevents comprehending death
5. Often fear events surrounding death more than death itself
6. Response to loss first requires development of attachment
7. Perceives death as a kind of sleep or temporary departure
8. Recognizes life as finite; considers options to gain personal fulfillment

15. Identify five needs of spouses when attempting to cope with their mate's impending death.
a.
b.
c.
d.
e.
16. Bereavement recovery occurs more rapidly when the death is sudden and unanticipated. (true or false)
17. Violent deaths are more difficult for survivors to accept. (true or false)
18. Identify five risk factors that increase a person's potential for suffering psychological or physical illness during bereavement.
a.
b.
c.
d.
e.
19. Persons experiencing bereavement may have physical symptoms of grief. (true or false)
20. Define anticipatory grief.
21. Identify four goals appropriate for the family or client engaged in the grieving process.
a.
b.
c.
d.
22. Donna Kane has just been told that she has cancer and will require extensive surgery. Ms. Kane tells the nurse, "I know that the test is wrong. I feel just fine." The best response by the nurse at this time would be to:
a. reassure Ms. Kane that her cancer is curable.
b. tell Ms. Kane that the test is very reliable and accurate.
c. convey a willingness to be available to, and talk with, Ms. Kane.
d. acknowledge that Ms. Kane looks healthy and should request a second opinion.
23. Refusal to die or accept the feeling of helplessness is a motivator for the terminally ill client. (true or false)
24. Identify five goals of care appropriate for terminally ill clients and their families.
a.
b.
c.
d.
e.
25. List four ways the nurse or family can provide spiritual comfort to the dying client.
a.
b.
c.
d.
26. What is the purpose of a hospice program?
27. A hospice program emphasizes:
a. curative treatment and alleviation of symptoms.
b. palliative treatment and control of symptoms.
c. hospital-based care.
d. prolongation of life.
28. Identify the physiological changes after death that the following nursing interventions are intended to minimize.
a. Remove tape and dressings gently. __________
b. Elevate head. __________________

c. Position body in normal alignment.

APPLICATION OF KEY CONCEPTS

Activities to reinforce skills and techniques

1. Review your institution's policy and procedure manual to determine:
   a. policies and procedure for obtaining autopsy consent.
   b. policies and procedure for requesting tissue and organ donations.
   c. procedure for care of the body after death.
2. Observe or assist a nurse caring for the body after death.
   a. Identify actions that were taken to minimize the physiological changes in the body after death.
   b. Identify actions that reflected the nurse's sensitivity for the dignity of the body.
   c. Describe your feelings and reactions to observing or participating in care of the body.
   d. Share these feelings and reactions with your instructor.

Activities to reinforce theoretical concepts

1. Discuss the importance of the nurse's self-assessment as a first step in assisting persons experiencing loss.
2. Experiential exercise: personal loss
   Identify a situation in which you have experienced a personal loss.
   a. Determine the category or type of loss that was experienced.
   b. Identify the physical and emotional responses that you experienced.
   c. Describe strategies that you used in coping with your loss.
   d. Share this information, verbally or in writing, with a friend, another student, or your instructor.
3. Talk with one or more of the following individuals about their experiences with dying clients and their families: social worker, clinical specialist, hospice volunteer, hospice staff member, hospital staff nurse, student nurse, instructor. Question the individual about:
   a. interventions used in assisting clients and families.
   b. personal coping strategies used in dealing with dying clients and their families.
4. Experiential exercise: losses associated with a chronic illness
   Interview a client with a chronic illness.
   a. Identify actual and potential losses faced by the individual as a result of chronic illness.
   b. Determine the meaning of each loss to the client.
   c. Describe the potential impact of the loss on physical and psychological functioning.
   d. Identify nursing interventions to minimize loss and maximize physical and psychological function in the presence of the chronic illness.
   e. Share your conclusions with your instructor for feedback.
5. Experiential exercise: nursing assessment of the client experiencing loss
   a. Perform a nursing assessment of a grieving client using any comprehensive assessment tool.
   b. Based on your assessment describe how each of the following variables are influencing the client's grief reaction.
      (1) Age
      (2) Personal relationships
      (3) Nature of loss or death
      (4) Cultural and spiritual beliefs
      (5) Sex roles
      (6) Socioeconomic status
   c. Based on identified client behaviors, identify the client's stage of grieving according to:
      (1) Engle.
      (2) Kübler-Ross.
      (3) Martocchio.
   d. Identify at least one intervention that the nurse may use to support a client's hope in each of the following dimensions.
      (1) Affective
      (2) Cognitive
      (3) Behavioral
      (4) Affiliative
      (5) Temporal
      (6) Contextual
6. Clinical situation: needs of spouses; survivor's risks
   Mr. and Mrs. Merton have been married for 54 years. Mrs. Merton has been admitted to the hospital in the terminal phase of congestive heart failure. The physician has informed Mr. and Mrs. Merton of the seriousness of the illness and its very grave prognosis.
   a. Identify five needs that Mr. Merton may have in attempting to cope with Mrs. Merton's impending death. Describe at least two nursing interventions that could assist in meeting each of the identified needs.
   b. Mr. Merton is at risk for psychological and physical illness during bereavement. Identify six risk factors that should be assessed and describe at least two nursing interventions to minimize the identified risk.
   c. The Mertons' daughter, Caroline, tells the nurse about Mr. Merton's anger and frequent emotional outbursts before Mrs. Merton's admission. She expresses concern that Mr. Merton will never recover from his wife's death.
      (1) What explanation could the nurse provide about Mr. Merton's anger and emotional outbursts?
      (2) How long a period of time should Caroline expect her father to need in order to resolve his loss?
      (3) What behaviors should be considered normal for Mr. Merton during his bereavement?
      (4) What behaviors would alert Caroline to the fact that her father is experiencing dysfunctional grief?

7. Experiential exercise: the dying person's bill of rights
   - a. Select three of the dying person's rights that you consider to be most important.
   - b. Discuss why you value these rights.
   - c. Identify at least three nursing interventions that assist in preserving each of these rights.
   - d. Share this information individually with a peer or instructor or during a small group discussion.
8. Experiential exercise: nursing care of the dying client
   Observe or assist a nurse caring for a terminally ill client, or independently provide nursing care to a dying client.
   - a. Perform a nursing assessment of the client utilizing a comprehensive assessment tool.
   - b. Formulate and prioritize three nursing diagnoses for the client.
   - c. Develop a nursing care plan for the client that includes the following goals. For each goal, state at least one expected outcome and two individualized nursing interventions.
     - (1) Promote comfort
       - (a) Outcome
       - (b) Interventions
     - (2) Maintain independence
       - (a) Outcome
       - (b) Interventions
     - (3) Conserve energy
       - (a) Outcome
       - (b) Interventions
     - (4) Prevent loneliness and isolation
       - (a) Outcome
       - (b) Interventions
     - (5) Promote spiritual comfort
       - (a) Outcome
       - (b) Interventions
     - (6) Support the grieving family
       - (a) Outcome
       - (b) Interventions

ADDITIONAL READINGS

Engle, GL: Grief and grieving, Am J Nurs 64(9):93, 1964.
Discusses the experience of the grieving process and behaviors characteristic during each stage. Offers potential interventions for assisting the grieving client.

Hampe, SO: Needs of the grieving spouse in a hospital setting, Nurs Res 24:113, 1975.
Study that identified common needs of grieving spouses. Information presented may be helpful in designing family-centered care of the dying client and fostering improved coping for spouses of the terminally ill.

Johnson, SH: 10 ways to help the family of a critically ill patient, Nurs 86 16:50, 1986.
Describes 10 strategies for working with families of the critically ill. Cites examples that more clearly illustrate the application of strategies to actual clinical practice.

Martocchio, B, and Dufault, K: Symposia on (1) hospice and (2) compassionate care and the dying experience, Nurs Clin North Am 20(2), 1985.
Two separate but related symposia. "Hospice" presents a comprehensive overview of issues and practices associated with hospice programs. "Compassionate Care and the Dying Experience" explores the physical and psychosocial needs of dying clients and their families.

Miles, HS, and Hays, DR: Widowhood, Am J Nurs 75:280, 1975.
Summarizes common problems facing the newly widowed. Discusses the nursing role in supporting the grieving spouse.

Musgrave, CF: The ethical and legal implications of hospice care: an international overview, Canc Nurs 10:183, 1987.
Analyzes the basic rights of the dying client. Discusses unique religious beliefs and their effect on care of the terminally ill. Compares laws related to terminal care in the United States, Great Britain, and Israel.

Strickney, SK, and Gardner, ER: Companions in suffering, Am J Nurs 84:1491, 1984.
Discusses grief experienced by family members and nurses caring for dying clients. Proposes approaches to increase coping abilities of family members and care givers.

Taylor, PR, and Gideon, MD: Holding out hope to your dying patient, Nurs 82 12:42, 1982.
Discusses clinical situations in which nurses fostered hope to support dying clients. Redefines the concept of hope in relation to unique client situations. Contends that hope may be honest and realizable even in the final stages of illness.

UNIT 6 Human Needs in Health and Illness

Chapter 27
Basic Human Needs

PREREQUISITE READING

Read Chapter 27, pp. 686 to 699.

OBJECTIVES

Mastery of content in this chapter will enable the student to:

1. Define selected terms associated with basic human needs.
2. Discuss each component of Maslow's hierarchy of needs.
3. Describe assessment techniques for identifying unmet needs.
4. Identify actual or potential conditions that threaten fulfillment of a client's needs.
5. Identify nursing diagnoses appropriate for unmet basic needs.
6. Describe the basic nursing implications concerning unmet needs.
7. Describe relationships among the different levels of needs.
8. State factors that influence the individual client's need priorities.

REVIEW OF KEY CONCEPTS

1. What are basic human needs?
2. Build the hierarchy of human needs by writing in the five levels of basic needs identified by Maslow.

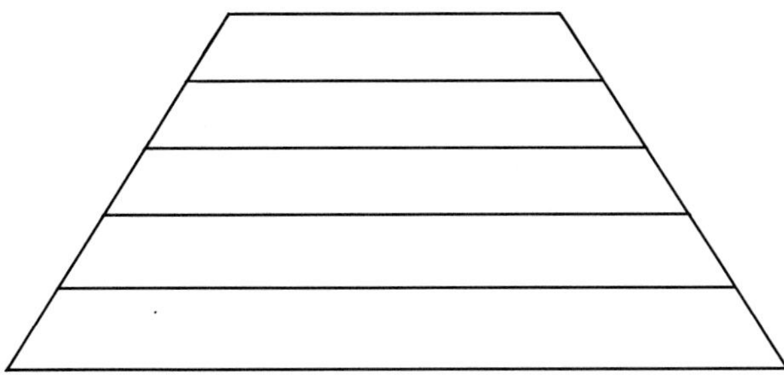

3. Which statement concerning the hierarchy of basic needs is incorrect?
   - **a.** Priorities assigned to basic human needs are the same in all individuals.
   - **b.** Unmet needs place the individual at risk for development of illness.
   - **c.** Environmental and social factors may influence ability to meet needs.
   - **d.** Hospitalized clients have basic needs that are actually or potentially unmet.
4. List the eight physiological needs in Maslow's hierarchy, and star (or circle) the need that has highest priority.
   - **a.**
   - **b.**
   - **c.**
   - **d.**
   - **e.**
   - **f.**
   - **g.**
   - **h.**
5. Identify four client groups who frequently require assistance in meeting physiological needs.
   - **a.**
   - **b.**
   - **c.**
   - **d.**
6. Identify the two age groups at greatest risk for unmet fluid needs.
   - **a.**
   - **b.**
7. Clients with appropriate body weight may still have nutritional deficits. (true or false)
8. Sexual need refers exclusively to an individual's need for physical sex. (true or false)
9. Nancy Williams is an 18-year-old nursing student assigned to care for a 20-year-old man with a spinal cord injury. Nancy identifies that sexual needs may be unmet in this client because of his paralysis but recognizes that she is very uncomfortable discussing this topic. Which action would be most appropriate for Nancy to take at this time?
   - **a.** Ignore the subject since the client has not mentioned any concerns regarding sex.
   - **b.** Design a plan of care that addresses other physical needs that have higher priority.
   - **c.** Try to talk with the client about sexual matters, no matter how uncomfortable it may be.
   - **d.** Identify another health care worker who can talk with the client about sexual matters.
10. Safety needs may take precedence over a physiological need. (true or false)

11. Which factor is of greatest importance in determining the impact of a body image change on self-esteem?
    a. Magnitude of the change
    b. Nature of the illness precipitating change
    c. Person's self-perception after the change
    d. Extent to which changes can be seen by others
12. List six characteristics that indicate than an individual has achieved self-actualization.
    a.
    b.
    c.
    d.
    e.
    f.
13. Match the description or term with the most closely associated basic need.
    a. _____ Cyanosis
    b. _____ Interstitial spaces
    c. _____ Self-confidence
    d. _____ Privacy with spouse
    e. _____ Skin breakdown
    f. _____ Activity patterns
    g. _____ Glucose
    h. _____ Community resources
    i. _____ Body image
    j. _____ Oliguria
    k. _____ Fear of the unknown
    l. _____ Significant others, peers
    m. _____ Shivering

    1. Oxygen
    2. Fluids
    3. Nutrition
    4. Temperature
    5. Elimination
    6. Shelter
    7. Rest
    8. Sex
    9. Physical safety
    10. Psychological safety
    11. Love and belonging
    12. Esteem
    13. Self-actualization
14. It is appropriate for the nursing care plan to address needs in more than one level of the hierarchy at a time. (true or false)
15. Identify four factors that influence need priorities.
    a.
    b.
    c.
    d.

APPLICATION OF KEY CONCEPTS
Activities to reinforce theoretical concepts

1. Experiential exercise: personal needs
    a. Assess your personal needs and classify them in relation to Maslow's hierarchy.
    b. Determine relationships among your identified needs.
    c. Identify those needs that you consider to be priorities and describe factors that influence your ranking.
    d. Identify available resources to assist you in meeting these needs (for example, personal strengths, family, friends, colleagues, educational setting, health care institution, community).
    e. Identify ways in which needs from different levels may be met simultaneously.
    f. Share the results of this exercise with a friend, peer, family member, or your instructor.
2. Experiential exercise: assessment of client needs
    Conduct a comprehensive nursing assessment of a client in any health care setting.
    a. Identify actual and potential needs of the client.
    b. Formulate nursing diagnoses for each identified client need.
    c. Describe data that support the presence of the actual or potential need and nursing diagnosis.
    d. Categorize each need and nursing diagnosis according to Maslow's hierarchy, ranking these according to priorities.
    e. Describe conditions creating barriers to successful attainment of the identified needs.
    f. Describe nursing actions to assist the client in meeting the identified needs.

ADDITIONAL READING

Sorenson, KC, and Luckmann, J: Meeting human needs through the nursing process, Basic nursing: a psychophysiologic approach, ed. 2, Philadelphia, 1986, W.B. Saunders Co.

Describes basic human needs and discusses their importance in maintaining health. Explores role of nursing in meeting needs of clients through the nursing process.

Chapter 28
Adaptation to Stress

PREREQUISITE READING

Read Chapter 28, pp. 700 to 721.

OBJECTIVES

Mastery of content in this chapter will enable the student to:

1. Define selected terms associated with stress and adaptation.
2. Discuss the limitations of homeostatic control.
3. Discuss four models of stress as they relate to nursing practice.
4. Describe how adaptation occurs in each of the five dimensions.
5. Describe two forms of local physiological adaptation.
6. Describe the three phases of the general adaptation syndrome.
7. List and discuss behaviors that are responses to stress.
8. List and discuss the most common ego-defense mechanisms that are responses to stress.
9. Discuss the effects of prolonged stress on each of the five dimensions of a person's functioning.
10. Describe stress management techniques that nurses can help clients use.
11. Discuss techniques of crisis intervention.
12. Describe stress management techniques that can benefit nurses themselves.

REVIEW OF KEY CONCEPTS

1. Define stress.
2. Define homeostasis.
3. Which statement concerning homeostasis is inaccurate?
   a. Homeostatic mechanisms are primarily a result of conscious behavior.
   b. Homeostatic mechanisms are self-regulatory.
   c. Homeostatic mechanisms function through negative feedback.
   d. Illness may inhibit normal homeostatic mechanisms.
4. Homeostatic mechanisms provide both long-term and short-term control over the body equilibrium. (true or false)
5. Mr. Riley, a business executive, has had to meet six major deadlines during the past 3 weeks. Presently, he enters an outpatient setting complaining of headaches, insomnia, and anorexia. Which model of stress correlates best with Mr. Riley's stress response?
   a. Adaptation model
   b. Process model
   c. Psychosomatic model
   d. Social environmental model
6. Which nursing intervention is best used when applying the adaptation model of stress?
   a. Intervention to improve vital signs
   b. Intervention to reduce anxiety
   c. Intervention to maintain fluid balance
   d. Intervention to promote reality orientation
7. Which stress model emphasizes assessment of the work environment?
   a. Adaptation model
   b. Process model
   c. Psychosomatic model
   d. Social environmental model
8. The process model of stress emphasizes:
   a. changing the stress response.
   b. group process.
   c. nursing process.
   d. changing the stressor.
9. List the four characteristics of stress that influence a person's response.
   a.
   b.
   c.
   d.
10. List the four requirements for successful family adaptation.
    a.
    b.
    c.
    d.
11. List the five human dimensions and briefly describe how adaptation occurs in each.
    a.
    b.
    c.
    d.
    e.

12. Identify four of the body responses to localized stress.
   a.
   b.
   c.
   d.
13. List the five characteristic signs and symptoms of the inflammatory response.
   a.
   b.
   c.
   d.
   e.
14. The body systems primarily involved in the general adaptation syndrome (GAS) are the:
   a. central nervous system and cardiovascular system.
   b. endocrine system and respiratory system.
   c. musculoskeletal system and immunological system.
   d. autonomic nervous system and endocrine system.
15. List (in sequential order) and briefly describe the three stages of the GAS.
   a.
   b.
   c.
16. Match the physiological response to the stage of the GAS.
   a. _____ Death
   b. _____ Release of epinephrine, norepinephrine
   c. _____ Hormone levels return to normal
   d. _____ Increased blood sugar
   e. _____ Diminished physiological regulation
   f. _____ Vital signs return to normal
   g. _____ Increased blood volume
   h. _____ Dilated pupils

   1. Alarm
   2. Resistance
   3. Exhaustion
17. Psychological adaptive behaviors may be constructive or destructive. (true or false)
18. Identify and briefly describe the two general types of psychological adaptive behaviors (coping mechanisms).
   a.
   b.
19. List six commonly observed ego-defense mechanisms.
   a.
   b.
   c.
   d.
   e.
   f.
20. Identify eight physical indicators of stress.
   a.
   b.
   c.
   d.
   e.
   f.
   g.
   h.
21. Identify at least one indicator of stress characteristic of each developmental stage listed below.
   a. Infant
   b. Toddler
   c. Preschool-age child
   d. School-age child
   e. Adolescent
   f. Young adult
   g. Middle-aged adult
   h. Older adult
22. Identify the four factors that influence an individual's reaction to stress.
   a.
   b.
   c.
   d.
23. List 10 behavioral and emotional indicators of stress.
   a.
   b.
   c.
   d.
   e.
   f.
   g.
   h.
   i.
   j.
24. List four intellectual indicators of stress.
   a.
   b.
   c.
   d.
25. List two spiritual indicators of stress.
   a.
   b.
26. Identify stress reduction methods for each stress management goal listed below.

Reducing stressful situations	Decreasing physiological responses	Improving responses to stress
a.	a.	a.
b.	b.	b.
c.	c.	c.
d.	d.	
e.		

27. List the three factors essential to crisis resolution.
   a.
   b.
   c.

APPLICATION OF KEY CONCEPTS

Activities to reinforce theoretical concepts

1. Experiential exercise: concepts of stress
   Identify and analyze a recent situation in which you felt stressed. After your analysis, respond to the following questions.
   a. What did you perceive as the primary stressor?
   b. From which human dimension did the stressor arise?
   c. Would the stressor be classified as internal or external? Why?
   d. Identify your response to the stressor in each of the human dimensions.
      (1) Physical-developmental
      (2) Emotional
      (3) Intellectual
      (4) Social
      (5) Spiritual
   e. Describe the nature of the stressor in each of the following areas, and analyze how each influenced your response.
      (1) Intensity of the stressor
      (2) Scope of the stressor
      (3) Duration of the stressor
      (4) Number and nature of other stressors
   f. Which stress model did you use in coping with the stressor? How was this helpful?
   g. Would a different model have been more helpful in understanding and responding to the stressor? Which model? Why?
2. Clinical situation: response to stress, crisis intervention
   John Trout, a sales representative for a local pharmaceutical company, enters the emergency room following an automobile accident. He has sustained several lacerations (cuts) and a fractured left arm.
   His admission assessment includes the following: temperature—37.2, pulse—106, respirations—26, blood pressure—140/90, pupils: large, equal, and reactive to light, speech rapid, asking many questions about medical and nursing care, requesting the same information from different care givers, extremely angry and critical about the "inefficiency" of the hospital staff.
   No one else was injured in the accident. Mr. Trout's car was totaled, and he is very concerned about business losses that will occur because of the accident and his injuries. He tells the staff that he is the "best sales representative in the midwest" and requests the opportunity to come and speak to the staff about his company's products.
   a. Which stage of the GAS is Mr. Trout experiencing? What characteristic signs and symptoms of this stage does he display?
   b. Based on the data provided, identify the indicators of stress that Mr. Trout displays and categorize these into each of the human dimensions.
   c. Based on the situation, describe each of the localized stress responses Mr. Trout may experience. (Name at least five.)
   d. The trauma of the lacerations will precipitate the inflammatory response.
      (1) What signs and symptoms should Mr. Trout expect to have as a result of inflammation?
      (2) Identify and describe each of the three phases of this response.
   e. What type of crisis does the automobile accident represent for Mr. Trout?
   f. Based on principles of crisis intervention, describe interventions you would use in caring for Mr. Trout in the emergency room.
3. Experiential exercise: nursing process and adaptation to stress
   Perform a comprehensive nursing assessment of a client in any health care setting.
   a. Identify indicators of stress in each of the dimensions of adaptation.
   b. Formulate a list of nursing diagnoses that are directly associated with the client's stress.
   c. For the priority diagnoses, identify two goals for care.
   d. For each goal, describe one expected outcome and three specific, individualized nursing interventions.
4. Experiential exercise: stress management
   Nursing school, like any educational situation, presents students with multiple stressors. Since it is impossible to eliminate all stressors, it is important to develop strategies to manage stress.
   a. Formulate at least three strategies for each of the major goals of stress management. Be sure the strategies that you select are realistic for you and your personal situation.
      (1) Reducing stressful situations
      (2) Decreasing physiological response to stress
      (3) Improving behavioral and emotional responses to stress
   b. Select a deadline for implementation of your strategies and write the date selected on your paper.
   c. Photocopy your paper and share your strategies and deadline with a friend, relative, peer, or instructor.
   d. Set a time and date, after the identified deadline, to review, evaluate, and (if necessary) revise your strategies.

ADDITIONAL READINGS

Aguilera, DC, and Messick, JM: Crisis intervention: theory and methodology, ed. 5, St. Louis, 1986, The C.V. Mosby Co.

A classic, comprehensive text that presents the theoretical concepts and practical helping techniques related to crisis intervention. Information from this text is frequently cited in nursing literature addressing care of clients in crisis.

MacNeil, JM, and Weisz, GM: Critical care nursing stress, Heart Lung 16:274, 1987.

Study that examines stress experienced by critical care

nurses. Refutes generally held beliefs by revealing that critical care nurses generally experience less work-related distress than nurses working in noncritical care areas.

Norbeck, JS: Types and sources of social support for managing job stress in critical care nursing, Nurs Res 34:225, 1985.

Study that identifies job stress in the ICU and explores potential sources of support. Information presented would be useful in developing strategies to reduce job stress in any health care setting.

Qamar, SL: The stress-curative model of nursing practice, Focus Crit Care 13(6):15, 1986.

Describes a model for nursing practice that combines the concepts of stress and caring. The holistic model that addresses needs of clients, families, and nurses, although directed to the ICU setting, may be applicable to any practice environment.

Thomas, SP, and Groer, M: Relationship of demographic life style and stress variables to blood pressure in adolescents, Nurs Res 35:169, 1986.

Study conducted to determine the relationship of specific variables to the blood pressure of freshmen high school students. Identifies significant predictors of diastolic pressure elevation and highlights areas for risk reduction.

Wilson, VS: Identification of stressors related to patient's psychologic responses to the surgical ICU, Heart Lung 16:267, 1987.

Utilizes Neuman's health care systems model to examine the stressors experienced by clients in the ICU. Describes a study to determine the incidence of impaired psychological response in the ICU and to determine the relation between response and self-identification of stressors. Describes interventions at the primary, secondary, and tertiary levels of nursing care.

Chapter 29
Self-Concept

PREREQUISITE READING

Read Chapter 29, pp. 722 to 748.

OBJECTIVES

Mastery of content in this chapter will enable the student to:

1. Define selected terms associated with self-concept.
2. Describe development of self-concept.
3. Discuss factors that influence each of the four components of self-concept: identity, body image, self-esteem, and roles.
4. Describe the five processes of socialization.
5. Identify stressors that affect each of the four components of self-concept.
6. Explain the processes that can lead to role conflict, role ambiguity, and role strain.
7. Discuss identity confusion as a developmental aspect of adolescence and as a problem of self-concept.
8. Discuss ways in which the nurse's self-concept and nursing activities can affect the client's self-concept.
9. Describe behavior or defining characteristics that may indicate each of the following: identity confusion, disturbed body image, low self-esteem, and role conflict.
10. For each of the four components of self-concept, state a common nursing diagnosis related to a self-concept disturbance.
11. Describe goals of care, specific nursing interventions, and outcome/evaluation measures for a client with a self-concept disturbance.

REVIEW OF KEY CONCEPTS

1. Define self-concept.
2. Identify five sources from which self-concept is derived.
   - **a.**
   - **b.**
   - **c.**
   - **d.**
   - **e.**
3. Define body image.
4. A person's body image is always consistent with the actual body structure or appearance. (true or false)
5. Define self-esteem.
6. Match the developmental stage with the most characteristic aspect of self-concept or body image described.
   - **a.** _____ Expands self-concept through games
   - **b.** _____ Unable to differentiate self from environment
   - **c.** _____ Self-concept complicated by societal confusion in gender behavior, meaning of sexuality, and role conflicts
   - **d.** _____ Considers distal body parts as separate from self
   - **e.** _____ Changes in appearance and function negatively impact self-concept
   - **f.** _____ Body acts as primary source for acceptance or rejection by others
   - **g.** _____ Hormonal changes produce physical alterations and self-concept realignment
   - **h.** _____ Body boundaries and gender become defined

   1. Infant
   2. Toddler
   3. Preschool age
   4. School age
   5. Adolescent
   6. Young adult
   7. Middle adult
   8. Older adult
7. At which developmental level do children usually establish a positive or negative self-concept?
   - **a.** Toddler years
   - **b.** Preschool age
   - **c.** School age
   - **d.** Adolescence
8. Sensory changes associated with the aging process may produce negative personality changes. (true or false)
9. List the four components of self-concept.
   - **a.**
   - **b.**
   - **c.**
   - **d.**
10. Which developmental stage is particularly crucial for identity development?
    - **a.** Infancy
    - **b.** Preschool age

c. Adolescence
d. Young adult years

11. A person's sense of identity, once developed, will not change in response to life circumstances. (true or false)
12. Define sexual identity.
13. Which of the following statements concerning body image is correct?
    a. Physical changes are quickly incorporated in a person's body image.
    b. Body image refers only to the external appearance of a person's body.
    c. Body image is a combination of the person's actual and perceived (ideal) body.
    d. Perceptions of others have no influence on the person's body image.
14. Extreme disparity between ideal self and self-concept is characteristic of many persons with mental illness. (true or false)
15. List and briefly describe the five methods through which children learn socially approved behaviors.
    a.
    b.
    c.
    d.
    e.
16. The process by which a person acquires values, behaviors, skills, and roles from social norms and significant others is called ________________.
17. Robert, 2 years old, is praised for using his potty instead of wetting his pants. This is an example of learning a behavior by:
    a. identification.
    b. imitation.
    c. substitution.
    d. reinforcement-extinction.
18. A client constantly tells his nurse about his achievements at work, his wonderful wife, and his new $250,000 home. His comments may indicate problems associated with:
    a. body image.
    b. self-esteem.
    c. role as husband.
    d. identity.
19. Identify the role stressor category for each example provided.
    a. ____________ Mr. Jones is admitted to the hospital with symptoms of a myocardial infarction (heart attack).
    b. ____________ Jean Wallace, 15 years old, experiences menarche.
    c. ____________ Ms. Hamet receives a job promotion requiring a cross-country move.
20. Define role conflict.
21. Match the most characteristic type of role conflict with the situation described.
    a. _____ A college student wishes to study all weekend, but his parents expect him to participate in a family reunion.
    b. _____ A nurse who believes that life is sacred must care for a teenager who has made repeated suicide attempts.
    c. _____ A woman who is a wife, mother of three school-age children, and part-time grocery clerk returns to college to earn a degree.
    d. _____ A client expects the nurse to let him sleep during the night. The doctor writes orders to arouse the client every 2 hours.

    1. Interpersonal
    2. Interrole
    3. Person-role
    4. Role overload
22. Unclear role expectations and an inability to predict the reactions of others to one's behavior is characteristic of ________________.
23. In which developmental stage is role ambiguity most common?
    a. Older adult years
    b. Middle adult years
    c. Young adult years
    d. Adolescence
24. A feeling of frustration associated with perceived inadequacy in a role is called ______________.
25. Match the component of self-concept most likely to be impacted by the stressor listed.
    a. _____ Mastectomy
    b. _____ Unemployment in family
    c. _____ Parent-child relationship
    d. _____ Puberty
    e. _____ Parental abuse or spouse battering
    f. _____ Child assuming adult responsibilities
    g. _____ Unrealistically high personal aspirations
    h. _____ Alcohol or drug abuse

    1. Identity
    2. Body image
    3. Self-esteem
26. Describe three messages to be conveyed in order to provide an environment that supports the client's self-concept.
    a.
    b.
    c.
27. Match the assessment finding with the self-concept disturbance it most characteristically represents.
    a. _____ Demonstrates inability to relate to family, friends, or caretakers
    b. _____ Expresses feelings of depression about physical changes or deterioration
    c. _____ Is unable to communicate feelings, needs, or ideas
    d. _____ Expresses feelings of alienation from others, suspicious of others

e. _____ Demonstrates self-destructive acts
f. _____ Refuses to acknowledge or look at changes in body structure
g. _____ Demonstrates change in social involvement or relationships with others
h. _____ Demonstrates lack of confidence in self-care or performance of activities of daily living

1. Identity confusion
2. Body image
3. Self-esteem
4. Role function

28. List the four stages of adaptation in their usual sequence.
  a.
  b.
  c.
  d.

29. Identify three behaviors that are involved in establishing rapport with a client.
  a.
  b.
  c.

30. List the five sequential levels of intervention for assisting a client to attain a positive self-concept or adapt to changes in self-concept.
  a.
  b.
  c.
  d.
  e.

31. What action should be taken by the nurse when the client experiences a severe alteration in self-concept?

32. Following a major life change, adjustment of self-concept requiring more than 1 year should be considered maladaptive. (true or false)

33. A minor change in function, appearance, or role can create a severe self-concept problem. (true or false)

APPLICATION OF KEY CONCEPTS
Activities to reinforce theoretical concepts

1. Clinical situation: components of self-concept, self-concept stressors
Andy Sawchuck, a 44-year-old professional golfer, has developed a severe back problem that will require spinal surgery. He has reduced sensation in his left leg and is developing a limping gait.

Mr. Sawchuck is a highly valued golf professional at the most respected country club in the city. He is accustomed to entering several national tournaments each year and finishing in the top five. His physician has informed him that he will not be able to resume golfing for at least 1 year after his surgery, and then it should be restricted to nine holes weekly.

Mr. Sawchuck has recently remarried. He has two teenage children from a former marriage. These children visit him frequently during the school year and live with him during the summer months. His back problem has altered his sexual relationship with his wife. His wife, however, has been very supportive. Mr. Sawchuck is very depressed and worried about his future. Golf is his and his family's sole means of financial support.

  a. What normal developmental events are expected at Mr. Sawchuck's present age? What impact could the situation described have on his normal developmental tasks?
  b. Describe at least two stressors and the dynamics that are actually affecting or could potentially affect each component of Mr. Sawchuck's self-concept. (Keep in mind the client's normal developmental tasks as well as the information presented in the situation.)
    (1) Body image
    (2) Self-esteem
    (3) Role
    (4) Identity
  c. What factors should the nurse examine and attempt to understand before assisting Mr. Sawchuck? Why is this step crucial to Mr. Sawchuck's care?
  d. Describe how the nurse can create a therapeutic environment that will facilitate Mr. Sawchuck's self-concept adaptation.

2. Experiential exercise: role stressors
Identify a personal situation in which you experienced role transition.
  a. Categorize the type of role transition you experienced as developmental, situational, or health-illness.
  b. Role transitions frequently impact self-concept and result in role conflict, role ambiguity, or role strain. Describe which of these results you may have experienced. Be sure to relate the theoretical concept described in your text with the feelings that you experienced.
  c. Identify coping strategies that you utilized in adapting to the role transition. Did you feel that these were adaptive or maladaptive?
  d. Describe alternative strategies that you believe could be implemented in future role conflict, ambiguity, or strain.
  e. If desired, seek assistance from a counselor, teacher, or nursing instructor in clarifying or developing alternative coping strategies to address role stress.

3. Clinical situation: altered self-concept and the nursing process
Mrs. Cruz, a 30-year-old mother of a 6-year-old son and an 8-year-old daughter, is recovering from a motor vehicle accident. Mrs. Cruz suffered severe facial lacerations. She will require several surgical procedures to reconstruct her face, and she will be left with some permanent facial scarring.

Mrs. Cruz avoids eye contact with people talking to her, including her husband and children. She seems very quiet and stays in her bed sleeping most of the time. She refuses to look in a mirror.

One day after visiting hours, the nurse sees Mr. Cruz sitting in the lounge with his head buried in his hands. The nurse talks with Mr. Cruz for about half an hour. She learns that Mr. Cruz is very worried about his wife because she says she wishes she would have died in the accident. He tells the nurse that he really doesn't know what to do to help his wife. He says she seems to ignore her children and tells him not to bring them to visit anymore. He says that when he tells his wife the children miss her, she just turns away from him.

a. Based on the information provided, write three nursing diagnoses related to an altered self-concept.

b. Which of the adaptation continuums would you consider to be the most appropriate for Mrs. Cruz? Provide a rationale to support your answer.

c. Using the five levels of intervention as a guide:

(1) Write two short-term goals and one long-term goal consistent with the priority nursing diagnosis you stated above.

(2) Identify the sequential level of intervention for self-concept disturbance that each goal represents.

(3) For each goal, identify one expected outcome and evaluative measures you would use to determine goal achievement.

(4) Formulate three nursing interventions for each goal.

(5) State the rationale for the interventions you selected.

ADDITIONAL READINGS

Molla, PM: Self-concept in children with and without physical disability, J Psych Nurs 19(6):22, 1981.

Discusses self-concept and body image in the context of the developmental process. Explores the impact of physical disability on children's self-concept. Makes recommendations for nursing approaches to promote more positive self-concept in children with physical disability based on research findings.

Morris, D: Self-concept as altered by diagnosis of cancer, Nurs Clin North Am 20(4):611, 1985.

Study that reviews current literature in an attempt to validate behavioral and emotional defining characteristics of the nursing diagnosis of altered body image. Information presented may facilitate nursing assessment of clients with cancer or other disorders who are at risk for altered body image.

Murray, R, editor: Symposium on the concept of body image, Nurs Clin North Am 7(4), 1972.

Series of articles addressing development of body image through the life cycle. Also explores body image changes associated with specific acute and chronic illness states. Discusses nursing interventions to promote body image, including the underlying principles guiding selection of appropriate nursing actions.

Norris, J, and Kunes-Connell, M: Self-esteem disturbance, Nurs Clin North Am 20(4):745, 1985.

Detailed examination of self-esteem disturbance as a nursing diagnosis. Describes study conducted to support clinical validation of nursing diagnosis. Identifies defining characteristics and explores potential contributing factors of self-esteem disturbance.

Oldaker, S: Identity confusion: nursing diagnosis for adolescents, Nurs Clin North Am 20(4):763, 1985.

Describes research that investigated developmental health and psychological symptoms among high school adolescents. Explores potential causes of adolescent identity confusion, identifies diagnostic criteria, and correlates this information with developmental task achievement.

Rubin, R: Body image and self-esteem, Nurs Outlook 16(6):20, 1968.

Explores the fundamental concepts of body image and self-esteem.

Chapter 30
Sexuality

PREREQUISITE READING

Read Chapter 30, pp. 750 to 791.

OBJECTIVES

Mastery of content in this chapter will enable the student to:

1. Define selected terms associated with sex and sexuality.
2. Identify personal attitudes, beliefs, and biases related to sexuality.
3. Discuss the nurse's role in maintaining or enhancing a client's sexual health.
4. Define sexuality as a component of personality.
5. Describe key concepts of sexual development during infancy, childhood, adolescence, and adulthood.
6. Identify male and female genitalia and describe functions related to sexual stimulation/response and reproduction.
7. Describe the sexual response cycle (Masters and Johnson model).
8. Describe physical, therapeutic, and psychological issues affecting sexuality.
9. Identify potential causes of sexual dysfunction.
10. Assess a client's sexuality.
11. Define appropriate nursing diagnoses for sexuality.
12. Identify and describe nursing interventions to promote sexual health.
13. Evaluate a client's sexual health.
14. Identify sexual concerns outside the nurse's level of expertise, and identify potential referral resources.

REVIEW OF KEY CONCEPTS

1. Compare the meanings of the terms sex and sexuality.
2. An individual's sense of being feminine or masculine is known as ____________________.
3. The clear, persistent, erotic preference of a person for one sex or the other is called ________________.
4. An individual whose inner sense of sexual identity does not match the biological body is known as a:
   a. lesbian.
   b. gay.
   c. transsexual.
   d. transvestite.
5. Identify four major factors that influence an individual's sexual attitudes and behaviors.
   a.
   b.
   c.
   d.
6. What is the most common concern people have about their sexuality?
7. Complete the table below, outlining the physiology of the female reproductive system.

Structure/Organ	Function(s)
Vulva	
Labia minora	
Labia majora	
Clitoris	
Vestibule	
Introitus	
Bartholin's glands	
Hymen	
Vagina	
Uterus	
Cervix	
Body	
Myometrium	
Endometrium	
Fallopian tubes	
Ovaries	
Breasts	

8. Fill in the name of the hormone or hormones responsible for the menstrual cycle beside the anatomical component of the feedback loop.
   Hypothalamus **a.** ____________________
   Pituitary **b.** ____________________
   c. ____________________
   Ovaries **d.** ____________________
   Corpus luteum **e.** ____________________
9. The follicular phase of the menstrual cycle is characterized by:
   a. increasing levels of progesterone.
   b. reduction in ovarian production of estrogen.
   c. inhibition of follicle-stimulating hormone.
   d. rupture of the Graafian follicle.
10. Which statement concerning the uterine secretory phase of the menstrual cycle is accurate?

a. The secretory phase is the time before ovulation.
b. The uterus is under the influence of high levels of estrogen.
c. Cervical mucus becomes more clear, slippery, and stretchable.
d. In the absence of pregnancy, the endometrium begins to slough.

11. List four signs or symptoms experienced by women with PMS.
a.
b.
c.
d.

12. Complete the table below, outlining the physiology of the male reproductive system.

Structure/Organ	Function(s)
Penis	
Scrotum	
Testis	
Seminiferous tubules	
Epididymis	
Vas deferens	
Ampulla	
Seminal vesicles	
Prostate gland	
Bulbourethral (Cowper's) glands	

13. The removal of the foreskin or prepuce from the penis is called ___________________.

14. At what age is it particularly important for children reared in single-parent families to be exposed to same-sex adults?
a. Infancy
b. Toddlerhood and preschool years
c. School age
d. Adolescence

15. In the school-age child, learning and reinforcement of gender-appropriate behaviors are most commonly derived from:
a. parents.
b. teachers.
c. siblings.
d. peers.

16. The onset of the menstrual cycle is called ___________________.

17. Adolescent females experiencing menarche and males experiencing first ejaculations should assume that they are fertile. (true or false)

18. Identify four sexual issues that should be addressed with adolescents.
a.
b.
c.
d.

19. The capacity for sexuality is lifelong. (true or false)

20. Identify four areas of concern that affect sexual functioning in the older adult.
a.
b.
c.
d.

21. Sequentially list and briefly describe the four phases of the sexual response cycle (according to Masters and Johnson).
a.
b.
c.
d.

22. Which statement concerning sexual response in the older adult is correct?
a. The resolution phase is slower.
b. The orgasm phase is prolonged.
c. The plateau phase is prolonged.
d. The refractory phase is more rapid.

23. Normal pregnancy presents no physiological contraindications to sexual intercourse. (true or false)

24. Why is it important for a woman, during the second half of pregnancy, to select intercourse positions other than lying flat on her back?

25. Describe two ways in which sexual intercourse or nipple stimulation may accidentally or therapeutically stimulate or accelerate labor.
a.
b.

26. Which of the following statements concerning sexuality during the postpartum period is incorrect?
a. Couples should refrain from sexual intercourse until vaginal bleeding has stopped and discomfort subsides.
b. In the early postpartum period, breast-feeding couples need not be concerned about using contraceptives.
c. The demands of the new baby may negatively influence sexual desire in both partners.
d. Hormonal changes will decrease the amount of vaginal lubrication necessitating use of water-soluble lubricants during intercourse.

27. An unwanted pregnancy can affect the health of the:
a. mother.
b. child.
c. community.
d. all of the above.

28. Identify seven questions to explore with a client when clarifying values and providing information about contraception.
a.
b.
c.
d.
e.
f.
g.

29. In the following outline, identify examples of contraception methods for each general classification listed.

a. Biological
(1)
(2)
(3)
(4)
b. Chemical
(1)
(2)
c. Chemical-mechanical
(1)
d. Mechanical
(1)
(2)
(3)
(4)
e. Surgical
(1)
(2)

30. The most effective means of preventing pregnancy is ______________.
31. The least effective means of pregnancy prevention is:
a. coitus interruptus.
b. calendar (rhythm) method.
c. body temperature method.
d. mucus method.
32. A client wishes to use the rhythm method for contraception. She reports cycles between 24 and 32 days in length. Which days of the cycle should she refrain from intercourse?
33. A client wishes to use the basal body temperature (BBT) as a method to prevent conception. Client education should include which of the following points?
a. BBT rises 0.4° to 0.8° just before ovulation.
b. Schedule changes and illness will not affect the use of BBT.
c. BBT is most accurately measured in the late afternoon or early evening.
d. Conception is possible if intercourse occurs several days before BBT elevation.
34. How can cervical mucus be used to predict ovulation?
35. Which contraceptive method is most effective in protecting men and women against sexually transmitted diseases?
a. Spermicide
b. Condom
c. Diaphragm
d. Oral contraceptive
36. Males may remain fertile for 6 to 8 weeks following vasectomy. (true or false)
37. Infertility is primarily a female problem. (true or false)
38. Which statement concerning abortion is correct?
a. Women who decide to abort an unwanted fetus will not experience any guilt.
b. Nurses are obligated to participate in abortion, even if this is in conflict with personal values.
c. The male partner may experience loss and grief, requiring professional support.
d. Women who abort a deformed fetus will not experience any sense of loss or grief.
39. Sexually transmitted diseases (STDs) infect and are transmitted only through genital organs. (true or false)
40. Match the sexually transmitted disease with the characteristics described.
a. _____ Treatable but not curable
b. _____ Painless chancre
c. _____ Incurable and fatal
d. _____ Cluster of painful blisters
e. _____ Dysuria; whitish genital discharge
f. _____ Fever; diarrhea; weight loss; fatigue
g. _____ Sterility if untreated
h. _____ Central nervous system damage in the tertiary stage

1. Gonorrhea, *Chlamydia*
2. Syphilis
3. Herpes simplex II
4. AIDS

41. Identify four measures to promote safe sex.
a.
b.
c.
d.
42. The only 100% effective method to avoid sexually contracting a disease is:
a. using condoms.
b. avoiding sex with partners at risk.
c. knowing the sexual partner's health history.
d. abstinence.
43. List the three body systems that must be intact for sexual behavior to occur.
a.
b.
c.
44. Illnesses that do not affect systems directly involved in sexual behavior may still influence feelings of desirability and arousal. (true or false)
45. Identify two simple ways that the nurse may assist clients in learning to meet sexual needs in the hospital setting.
a.
b.
46. Mr. James has demonstrated persistent sexual acting out since he was admitted for a myocardial infarction. This behavior has occurred with several female nurses. Which action by the head nurse would be most appropriate at this time?
a. Tell Mr. James that his behavior is inappropriate and unacceptable.
b. Assign only male nurses to Mr. James.
c. Tell the nurses to avoid interacting with Mr. James.
d. Obtain a consultation from a psychiatric nurse specialist.

47. Identify six general psychological factors that may contribute to sexual dysfunction.
    a.
    b.
    c.
    d.
    e.
    f.
48. Which sexual dysfunction in females is most often associated with physiological factors?
    a. Primary orgasmic dysfunction
    b. Secondary orgasmic dysfunction
    c. Dyspareunia
    d. Vaginismus
49. List four physiological conditions contributing to sexual dysfunction.
    a.
    b.
    c.
    d.
50. Identify and briefly describe the four major factors affecting sexuality.
    a.
    b.
    c.
    d.
51. State two general sex-related questions that may be used to initially determine if the adult client has any sexual concerns.
    a.
    b.
52. State two general sex-related questions that may be used to initially determine if a child's parents have any concerns related to the child's sexuality.
    a.
    b.
53. Mary Webb visits the postpartum clinic 4 weeks after delivering her first child. When the nurse begins to talk about contraception, Ms. Webb looks away and changes the subject. How should this behavior be interpreted?
    a. Ms. Webb isn't interested in talking about contraception.
    b. Ms. Webb doesn't want to use contraception.
    c. Ms. Webb may have a problem or concern related to her sexuality.
    d. Ms. Webb probably understands contraception since her pregnancy was planned.
54. Identify six interview strategies to enhance the client's and nurse's comfort when eliciting a sexual history.
    a.
    b.
    c.
    d.
    e.
    f.
55. State five questions that the nurse could use in eliciting a brief sex history from a client.
    a.
    b.
    c.
    d.
    e.
56. Kegel exercises minimize problems with urinary incontinence in men and women. (true or false)
57. Describe two Kegel exercises.
    a.
    b.
58. What major factor determines whether the nurse diagnoses sexual dysfunction or altered patterns of sexuality?
59. State four general goals appropriate for the client experiencing actual or potential alterations in sexual functioning.
    a.
    b.
    c.
    d.
60. What action should the nurse take when sexual dysfunctions such as ongoing premature ejaculation, vaginismus, or concerns over transsexual dressing are identified?

APPLICATION OF KEY CONCEPTS

Activities to reinforce theoretical concepts

1. Experiential exercise: sexual history
    a. Examine nursing assessment and health history forms used in your institution. Identify information elicited through the tool that would be useful in evaluating a client's sexuality.
    b. Formulate two general sex-related questions that you could routinely use in determining if a client has any sexual concerns.
        (1) Practice asking these questions by standing in front of a mirror, audiotaping or videotaping, or asking another person.
        (2) Repeat this exercise until you feel comfortable asking your questions.
    c. Utilizing guidelines described in your text, structure a questionnaire to be used in eliciting a brief sexual history for an adult client. Try to limit the tool to 10 or fewer questions.
    d. Practice taking a sexual history by answering the questions in a self-developed questionnaire.
        (1) If any concerns were identified, determine resources you could contact to receive needed assistance. (Your instructor, counselor, or personal health care provider could assist you in making any needed contacts.)
        (2) Identify questions with which you were comfortable and those that were more difficult to ask or answer. Attempt to analyze your feelings and consider whether an alternative approach or another health care provider would be needed to address these questions when you are working with a client. (If you found questions difficult to ask, it might be most

helpful to discuss this matter with your instructor.)

(3) Utilize the tool to elicit a sexual history from a peer, friend, or family member. The assessment could be realistic and factually based, or your "client" could simulate a fictitious client situation. If possible, audio tape or videotape the interaction. Analyze the interaction, including your comfort, the client's comfort, and alternative approaches that might be used.

2. Clinical situation: sexual development
For each of the following situations, discuss the information you would share with the client based on the stage of sexual development described.

a. Mrs. Williams is very concerned because her 5-year-old son Robert frequently touches or holds his genitalia. Mrs. Williams tells the nurse that this is very embarrassing—particularly when they are out in public. What information would you include in discussing Mrs. Williams' concerns?

b. Mrs. McArthur, 47 years old, is experiencing difficulty sleeping at night and has frequent "hot flashes." She realizes she's "going through the change of life." As her nurse, what information could you provide to assist her in adjusting to the physiological changes she is experiencing?

c. John Dempsey, 12 years old, visits his pediatrician for a well-child visit. John's mother, a single parent, is concerned because John seems much more withdrawn and is easily embarrassed when any sexual issues are brought up for discussion.

(1) As the nurse, what information would you provide to John's mother?

(2) What approach or approaches could be effective in meeting John's needs?

(3) What information would be most important to share with John during this office visit?

(4) What information concerning sexuality should be presented to John?

3. Experiential exercise: aging and sexual response

a. Design an in-service or community informational program on "Sexuality and the Older Adult." Limit your presentation to approximately 15 to 20 minutes. Include a discussion of common concerns that older adults have that may affect sexual functioning.

b. Present your program to a peer group or group of students or staff nurses. If possible, audio tape, videotape, or have an instructor or experienced staff nurse monitor the presentation to provide feedback for evaluation.

c. If possible, using your instructor as a resource person, present your program to a selected community group or clients in a health care setting.

4. Clinical situation: contraception
Miss Atkinson, 18 years old, is planning to be married. She and her fiancé do not want to have children until their college educations have been completed. She asks you, a community health nurse, about the best method of contraception for them to use.

a. What additional information would be important for you to determine before designing a teaching plan for Miss Atkinson?

b. Prepare a chart or table that lists six of the more effective nonpermanent methods of contraception, including advantages and disadvantages of each method, to use in the client-teaching situation.

c. Should Miss Atkinson's fiancé be involved in the educational process? Why or why not? How could you approach this issue?

d. Miss Atkinson tells you that many of her friends use "birth control pills" and have encouraged her to select this contraceptive method. In order to assist in clarifying Miss Atkinson's values and provide accurate information about this method, what specific questions (and answers) concerning oral contraceptives would you address in your teaching plan?

5. Experiential exercise: safe sex, STDs

a. Design an informational presentation on "safe sex" for college-age students. Include in the presentation what is meant by safe sex, the nature of transmission and warning signs of sexually transmitted diseases, and how one can engage in responsible sexual practices.

b. Practice presenting this information to a peer group, requesting peer and instructor feedback, or videotape the session.

c. If feasible, using an instructor as a resource person, present this information to a selected college-age student population.

6. Experiential exercise: sexual dysfunction

a. Conduct a comprehensive nursing assessment or review the medical records of a client in any health care setting.

b. Describe physical or psychological conditions that could actually or potentially contribute to sexual dysfunction.

c. Review the actions and side effects of the medications that have been prescribed for the client. Identify any medications that could contribute to sexual dysfunction and describe their impact on the client's sexuality or sexual function.

7. Clinical situation: attitudes toward sexuality
Role-play each of the following situations with a peer, implementing appropriate communication skills. Audio tape the role-playing situation and critique it to determine your level of effectiveness and assess your comfort level when dealing with sexually sensitive nursing procedures. Share your experience and feelings with your instructor for feedback.

a. Mr. Wenzel, a 26-year-old single professional football player, is admitted to the hospital for repair of an inguinal hernia. Postoperatively you must frequently assess the scrotal area for bruising and swelling. Role-play how you would inform Mr. Wenzel about the need for frequent assessment during his postoperative period and how you would approach your initial postoperative assessment.

b. Mr. Henry, a 68-year-old retired farmer, has been admitted to the hospital for prostate surgery. Following the preoperative teaching session with Mr. Henry, he says, "I've heard that this operation will prevent me from . . . performing with my wife, if you know what I mean. Is that true?" Role-play your response.

c. Ms. Spooner is a 25-year-old single businesswoman who has decided to use the diaphragm as a nonpermanent contraceptive method. Role-play how you would instruct Ms. Spooner about the technique of diaphragm insertion.

8. Clinical situation: sexuality and the nursing process
Mrs. Livingston, 35 years old, has been admitted to the hospital for a hysterectomy. She has been troubled by heavy menstrual bleeding for the past 6 months. Her physician has informed her that she has uterine fibroids; therefore her uterus must be removed, but her ovaries will be left intact.

Mrs. Livingston has two sons, 10 and 12 years old. She says she is "happily married" and that she and her husband have a "good" relationship, but she asks a lot of questions that allude to her "role as a wife and mother after this surgery." She says, "It's so final, but my doctor says there is no alternative because the fibroids will just get bigger and cause me more problems."

During Mr. Livingston's visit, Mrs. Livingston seemed happy, but after her husband left, she says, "I wish I knew what my husband will really think of me after my surgery. He always talked about having a big family."

a. Identify two nursing diagnoses related to Mrs. Livingston's sexuality.

b. For each diagnosis, formulate at least one goal related to Mrs. Livingston's actual or potential sexual alteration and describe the expected outcomes that could be used in determining goal achievement.

c. For each goal, describe at least three nursing interventions to be implemented.

ADDITIONAL READINGS

Boyle, CA, Berkowitz, GS, and Kelsey, JL: Epidemiology of premenstrual symptoms, Am J Public Health 77(3):349, 1987.

Study of selected population to identify the prevalence of specific premenstrual symptoms and common associated factors. Presents detailed information in table format.

Fogel, CI, and Woods, NF: Health care of women: a nursing perspective, St. Louis, 1981, The C.V. Mosby Co.

Comprehensive text addressing health and health care of women across the life span. Includes special sections discussing common health problems encountered by women at various developmental stages.

Muscarei, ME: Obtaining the adolescent sexual history, Pediatr Nurs 13(5):307, 1987.

Discusses the importance of self-awareness and interviewing skills in obtaining an adolescent sex history. Emphasizes the significance of clearly understanding and comfortably articulating information and issues associated with adolescent sexuality.

Schuster, E: Symposium on sexuality and nursing practice, Nurs Clin North Am 17(3):365, 1982.

Series of articles exploring nursing practice in the area of human sexuality. Addresses nursing role in dealing with selected physical, psychosocial, and pathological conditions impacting human sexuality.

Shipes, E: Sexual functioning following ostomy surgery, Nurs Clin North Am 22(2):303, 1987.

Addresses physical and psychological impact of ostomy surgery on sexual function. Provides guidelines for counseling clients about sex and sexuality after ostomy or other cancer therapies.

Shipes, E, and Lehr, S: Sexuality and the male cancer patient, Ca Nurse 5(5):375, 1982.

Examines male sexuality in health and illness, including the effects of cancer and cancer therapies. Offers guidelines for therapeutic, holistic care for men to promote or maintain male sexuality.

Chapter 31
Spiritual Health

PREREQUISITE READING

Read Chapter 31, pp. 792 to 805.

OBJECTIVES

Mastery of content in this chapter will enable the student to:

1. Define selected terms associated with spiritual health.
2. Discuss the relationship of spiritual health to physiological and psychosocial health.
3. Contrast spiritual and religious aspects of health.
4. Assess components of spiritual health.
5. Describe a spiritually healthy person.
6. Describe the signs of unmet spiritual needs.
7. List interventions in the nursing plan for spiritual care.
8. Evaluate attainment of spiritual health.
9. Identify resources that can help clients attain spiritual health.

REVIEW OF KEY CONCEPTS

1. Define spiritual health.
2. Define faith.
3. Spiritual distress can lead to physical or emotional illness. (true or false)
4. An individual's affiliation with a denomination or sect is called __Religion__.
5. The spiritual dimension of health care is limited to the client's religious affiliation and practices. (true or false)
6. Which faith group is most likely to resist complying to medical treatment?
   - **a.** Hindus
   - **b.** Buddhists
   - **c.** Conservative Muslims
   - **d.** Reformed Jews
7. Match the religion to the religious belief described.
   - **a.** __4__ Views illness as a result of misuse of body
   - **b.** __3__ Use faith healing as psychological support
   - **c.** __2__ Consider visiting the sick as a religious obligation
   - **d.** __1__ Generally opposed to blood transfusions
   - **e.** __5__ Family available for physical and emotional care

   1. Jehovah's Witnesses
   2. Judaism
   3. Islam
   4. Hinduism
   5. Buddhism
8. Mrs. Smith, in her fourth month of pregnancy, has just aborted the fetus for life-threatening medical reasons. What bearing would the client's religious practices have on the manner in which the fetus should be disposed of, if Mrs. Smith is a:
   - **a.** Reformed Jew
   - **b.** Roman Catholic
   - **c.** Follower of Islam
9. Mrs. F. is in the terminal stages of an illness, and death is imminent. What religious practices or rites would the nurse anticipate occurring before and after Mrs. F. dies, if she is a(n):
   - **a.** Hindu
   - **b.** Moslem
   - **c.** Roman Catholic
   - **d.** Orthodox Jew
   - **e.** Lutheran
   - **f.** Jehovah's Witness
10. What dietary restrictions might be imposed if a client is a:
    - **a.** Hindu
    - **b.** Follower of Islam
    - **c.** Orthodox Jew
    - **d.** Mormon
    - **e.** Roman Catholic
    - **f.** Baptist
11. State six questions that may provide information concerning a client's spiritual health.
    - **a.**
    - **b.**
    - **c.**
    - **d.**
    - **e.**
    - **f.**
12. In the table below, identify client behaviors that reflect spiritual health and spiritual distress.

Spiritual health	Spiritual distress
a.	**a.**
b.	**b.**
c.	**c.**

13. What is the nurse's primary responsibility in meeting the client's spiritual needs?

14. It is appropriate for a nurse who is comfortable with prayer to pray with a client when requested to do so. (true or false)
15. List five resources that may be of assistance in maintaining or promoting a client's spiritual health.
    a.
    b.
    c.
    d.
    e.
16. State five questions that may be asked in evaluating interventions directed toward a client's spiritual health.
    a.
    b.
    c.
    d.
    e.
17. It is appropriate for nurses to seek personal assistance from pastoral care associates to meet spiritual needs of clients. (true or false)

APPLICATION OF KEY CONCEPTS

Activities to reinforce theoretical concepts

1. Talk with an associate of the pastoral care department at your institution to determine:
   a. the role of the associate in meeting clients' spiritual needs.
   b. the associate's perception of the role and responsibilities of the nurse in meeting clients' spiritual needs.
   c. the assistance available to clients and nurses through the pastoral care department.

   (If your institution does not have a pastoral care department, you might ask to speak with clergy who are on call for the institution or direct these questions to your own spiritual advisor.)
2. Experiential exercise: resources for spiritual health Independently, or in a small group:
   a. Identify resources available in your institution to assist clients and health team members in restoring or maintaining spiritual health.
   b. Identify at least four resources available in your community to assist clients and health team members in restoring or maintaining spiritual health.
3. Experiential exercise: spiritual assessment
   a. Utilizing suggested questions presented in your text, develop a brief spiritual assessment tool.
   b. Perform a self-assessment of spiritual health. Analyze the data obtained. If spiritual distress is present, make an appointment to talk with your spiritual advisor or member of a pastoral care team.
   c. Perform a spiritual assessment of a peer, friend, or family member. Analyze the data obtained. If spiritual distress is present, encourage the individual to seek assistance from his or her spiritual advisor or other appropriate resource.
4. Clinical situation: spiritual health and the nursing process

   Mr. Samanski, a 38-year-old construction worker, has been admitted to the hospital with the diagnosis of acute leukemia. He is aware that his prognosis is poor. Mr. Samanski is married and has two children, 6 and 8 years old. His wife is employed part-time as a clerk in a department store. He has listed his religion as Christian but has not stated a specific denomination.

   One day, while the nurse is making Mr. Samanski's bed, he says, as his eyes fill with tears, "You know, I guess I don't really mind dying . . . if that's what He has planned for me. But I really need to stay alive to help my kids grow up. Boy, it really makes me wonder what I've done wrong." The nurse remains silent, quickly finishes the bed, and says, "Is there anything I can get for you?" Mr. Samanski replies, quietly, "No, I . . . I guess I'm fine." The nurse leaves the room.
   a. What information is presented that would support a diagnosis of spiritual distress?
   b. What factors could have influenced the nurse's reluctance to openly respond to Mr. Samanski's comment about his spiritual beliefs?
   c. Formulate possible responses that the nurse could have utilized to support Mr. Samanski and help him explore his feelings. (If possible, role-play this situation with a peer. Analyze your feelings and behaviors orally or in writing.)
   d. Based on the nursing diagnosis of spiritual distress, develop a nursing care plan for Mr. Samanski. Include one short-term goal and three appropriate nursing interventions.
   e. Identify what assistance you as the nurse might need in providing needed spiritual care for Mr. Samanski.
   f. Submit your care plan and analysis to your instructor for feedback.

ADDITIONAL READINGS

Brallier, LW: The nurse as holistic health practitioner, Nurs Clin North Am 13(4):643, 1978.

Presents overview of holistic health theory and practices. Places emphasis on the role of the nurse in addressing needs of clients in a comprehensive [holistic] manner through treatment of mind, body, and spirit.

Dickenson, SC: The search for spiritual meaning, Am J Nurs 75(10):1789, 1975.

Defines spiritual care in the context of nurse-client relationship. Emphasizes the therapeutic use of self in meeting clients' spiritual needs.

Highfield, MF, and Cason, C: Spiritual needs of patients: are they recognized? Ca Nurse 6(3):187, 1983.

Study to identify nurses' awareness of clients' spiritual concerns. Data presented indicate that nurses were unaware of many behaviors and conditions associated with clients' spiritual needs. Makes recommendations about interventions to more effectively address the spiritual domain of clients' needs.

Miller, JF: Inspiring hope, Am J Nurs 85(1):22, 1985.

Explores the relationship between hope and client survival. Identifies ways the nurse can inspire hope—even in the face of serious and prolonged illness—by helping the client develop and utilize personal resources.

Peck, ML: The therapeutic effect of faith, Nurs Forum 22(2):153, 1981.

Defines faith. Cites research which indicates that faith is associated with a psychic energy that has a curative power. Validates the belief that traditional customs and faith practices aid in restoring health.

Stoll, R: Guidelines for spiritual assessment, Am J Nurs 79:1574, 1979.

Compares spiritual and religious beliefs. Provides guidelines for questions that may help to determine the client's state of spiritual health.

Chapter 32
Hygiene

PREREQUISITE READING

Read Chapter 32, pp. 808 to 879.

OBJECTIVES

Mastery of content in this chapter will enable the student to:

1. Define selected terms associated with client hygiene.
2. Identify common skin problems and related interventions.
3. Describe factors that influence personal hygiene practices.
4. Discuss conditions that may put a client at risk for impaired skin integrity.
5. Describe the types of bathing techniques used depending on a client's physical condition.
6. Explain rationale for technique used in bathing an infant.
7. Successfully perform a complete bed bath and backrub.
8. Discuss factors that influence the condition of the nails and feet.
9. Explain the reason it is important for a diabetic client to understand foot care.
10. Describe the methods used for cleaning and cutting the nails.
11. Describe clients at risk for poor oral hygiene.
12. Discuss measures used to provide special oral hygiene.
13. Successfully provide oral hygiene.
14. List common hair and scalp problems and describe related nursing interventions.
15. Explain the rationale for assessing client's hair care practices.
16. Discuss how to assess the needs of clients requiring eye, ear, and nose care.
17. Describe the steps followed in making an occupied, an unoccupied, and a surgical hospital bed.

REVIEW OF KEY CONCEPTS

1. List five factors that influence the manner in which a person performs personal hygiene.
   a.
   b.
   c.
   d.
   e.
2. Briefly describe the hygienic care that would be provided for each of the following:
   a. Morning or after-breakfast care
   b. Evening or hour-of-sleep care
   c. Early morning care
   d. Afternoon care
3. For each of the skin functions listed below, describe at least two factors that will guide nursing actions when bathing a client.
   a. Protection
      (1)
      (2)
   b. Sensation
      (1)
      (2)
   c. Temperature regulation
      (1)
      (2)
   d. Excretion and secretion
      (1)
      (2)
4. Match the term with the most appropriate description.
   a. _____ Resident skin bacteria
   b. _____ Secrete heavy, oily substance to protect ear
   c. _____ House glands, hair follicles
   d. _____ Secrete oily lubricant for hair and skin
   e. _____ Located in axillary and genital areas
   f. _____ Replaces cells shed from skin's outer surface
   g. _____ Assist in temperature control through evaporation
   h. _____ Responsible for skin pigmentation
   i. _____ Serves as heat insulator

   1. Epidermis
   2. Melanocyte
   3. Dermis
   4. Normal flora
   5. Eccrine glands
   6. Apocrine glands
   7. Ceruminous glands

8. Sebaceous glands
9. Subcutaneous tissue

5. Which assessment finding would indicate an abnormal skin characteristic?
   a. Skin intact without abrasions
   b. Skin warm to touch
   c. Skin color variation from body part to body part
   d. Skin slowly returns to resting position after pinching
6. Complete the table below by identifying the skin problem and describing at least two related interventions.

Description	Skin problem	Interventions
a. Inflammatory, papulopustular skin eruption usually involving bacterial breakdown of sebum	______	(1) (2)
b. Scraping or rubbing away of epidermis	______	(1) (2)
c. Excessive growth of body and facial hair	______	(1) (2)
d. Flaky, rough skin texture on exposed areas	______	(1) (2)
e. Skin eruptions	______	(1) (2)
f. Abrupt onset of skin inflammation	______	(1) (2)

7. For each developmental stage listed, briefly describe the normal conditions that predispose the individual to alteration in skin integrity.
   a. Neonate
   b. Toddler
   c. Adolescent
   d. Older adult
8. Identify six factors to be assessed to determine a client's self-care ability related to performing personal skin care.
   a.
   b.
   c.
   d.
   e.
   f.
9. List six general conditions that place clients at risk for impaired skin integrity.
   a.
   b.
   c.
   d.
   e.
   f.
10. Larry Noah, a well-nourished 19-year-old, is hospitalized for a fractured right femur. The fracture is being treated with skeletal traction, so Larry is confined to bed. Larry has also had a fever and episodes of diaphoresis. Which of the following risk factors for skin impairment would not be applicable for this client?
    a. Immobilization
    b. Secretions and excretions on the skin
    c. Age
    d. Presence of external devices
11. The purposes of a cleansing bath and skin care include all of the following except:
    a. stimulating circulation.
    b. providing exercise.
    c. promoting comfort.
    d. reducing local inflammation.
12. State three goals for clients receiving skin care.
    a.
    b.
    c.
13. Describe each type of therapeutic bath by completing the table below.

Therapeutic bath	Purpose	Safety factors to consider
Tepid sponge bath		
Sitz bath		
Hot water tub bath		
Warm water tub bath		
Cool water tub bath		
Soak		

14. A physician's order is required for baths designed for therapeutic purposes. (true or false)
15. When giving a bed bath, in which position would the nurse place the patient and the hospital bed?
    a. Move the patient away from the nurse, and put the bed in low position.
    b. Move the patient away from the nurse, and put the bed in high position.
    c. Move the patient toward the nurse, and put the bed in low position.
    d. Move the patient toward the nurse, and put the bed in high position.
16. When changing the hospital gown of a patient with an IV line, remove the gown from the arm with the IV line first. (true or false)
17. Describe the technique for washing a client's eyes.
18. What action by the nurse will promote the safety of a client taking a tub bath or shower?
    a. Adjusting the water temperature to 120° F
    b. Checking on the client every 10 minutes
    c. Instructing client to remain in tub 20 to 30 minutes
    d. Draining the tub before client gets out
19. Describe what is meant by a partial bed bath.
20. As a safety precaution, clients should be instructed to stay in the bathtub for no longer than:
    a. 5 minutes.
    b. 10 minutes.
    c. 20 minutes.
    d. 40 minutes.
21. When implementing a tepid sponge bath to reduce a fever, the nurse should:

a. measure pulse and temperature immediately before and after the procedure.
b. measure pulse and temperature immediately before and every 15 minutes during the procedure.
c. measure pulse and temperature before the procedure and 1 hour later.
d. measure pulse and temperature every 30 minutes for 1 hour after the procedure.

22. What is the correct temperature of tepid water?
23. What are the four guidelines that the nurse should follow when assisting or providing a client with any type of bath?
    a.
    b.
    c.
    d.
24. Fill in the correct rationale for each of the following actions taken when bathing an infant.
    a. Keeping the infant covered as much as possible
    b. Using plain water (no soaps) for bathing
    c. Avoiding use of lotions and oils
    d. Eliminating use of cotton-tipped swabs for cleansing ears or nares
    e. Application of alcohol or triple dye to the umbilical cord
    f. Drying gently but thoroughly
25. The grayish-white, cheeselike substance covering the skin of the newborn is ________________.
26. Which of the following nursing actions would be inappropriate for the infant following circumcision?
    a. Frequent tub baths to reduce discomfort
    b. Loose application of the diaper
    c. Gentle removal of blood with clean cotton balls
    d. Thorough cleansing of the anal area after bowel movements
27. All of the following are true about perineal care except:
    a. the nurse should wear disposable gloves during the procedure.
    b. the client should be allowed to perform self-care whenever possible.
    c. perineal care includes cleansing of external genitalia and surrounding skin.
    d. perineal care may be omitted when the client and nurse are opposite sexes.
28. Which is the correct procedure for delivering perineal care to a female client?
    a. Separate the labia with a gloved hand and wipe from the pubic area to the rectum using a circular motion.
    b. Separate the labia with a gloved hand and wipe from the pubic area to the rectum in one smooth stroke.
    c. Separate the labia with a gloved hand and wipe from the rectum to the pubic area using a circular motion.
    d. Separate the labia with a gloved hand and wipe from the rectum to the pubic area in one smooth stroke.
29. An effective backrub takes:
    a. 1 to 3 minutes.
    b. 3 to 5 minutes.
    c. 5 to 10 minutes.
    d. 10 to 15 minutes.
30. Which method of massage should be used at the end of a backrub?
    a. Kneading skin by grasping tissue between thumb and fingers
    b. Firm, slow strokes across the width of the back
    c. Light strokes moving in a circular pattern up the back
    d. Long stroking movements laterally along the sides of the back
31. It is important for nurses to assess pulse and blood pressure following backrub for which of the following clients?
    a. Clients with rib fractures
    b. Clients with dysrhythmias
    c. Clients with vertebral fractures
    d. Clients with burns to the thorax
32. Match the following foot or nail problem with the most characteristic description.
    a. _____ Cone-shaped, round, raised often painful areas on toes
    b. _____ Fungal lesion on sole of foot
    c. _____ Unusually long curved nail
    d. _____ Flat, painless, thickened areas, often on undersurface of foot
    e. _____ Inflammation of tissue surrounding nail
    f. _____ Fungal infection of the foot with scaling, cracking, and blistering

    1. Callus
    2. Corn
    3. Plantar wart
    4. Tinea pedis
    5. Ram's horn nail
    6. Paronychia
33. Why is it important for diabetics to carefully inspect their feet on a daily basis?
34. Elderly clients with chronic foot problems should be encouraged to use over-the-counter preparations in order to optimally care for their feet and nails. (true or false)
35. A client with complex foot and nail problems should be referred to a ________________.
36. State three goals for clients receiving nail and foot care.
    a.
    b.
    c.
37. Identify four client groups at risk for foot or nail problems.
    a.
    b.
    c.
    d.

38. When caring for a client's feet and nails, the nurse routinely:
   a. checks the femoral pulses.
   b. cuts the nails straight across below the tops of the toes.
   c. soaks the patient's feet for 10 to 20 minutes before trimming nails.
   d. trims away calluses with a sterile blade or scissors.
39. Describe seven foot care guidelines to include when advising clients with diabetes or peripheral vascular disease.
   a.
   b.
   c.
   d.
   e.
   f.
   g.
40. Deciduous is a term that refers to:
   a. baby teeth.
   b. permanent teeth.
   c. changes in teeth associated with dental decay.
   d. changes in teeth associated with the aging process.
41. State four questions that could provide the nurse with helpful information concerning a client's dental care.
   a.
   b.
   c.
   d.
42. Match the oral problem with the most characteristic description.
   a. _____ Bad breath
   b. _____ Transparent coating on the teeth composed of mucin, carbohydrates, and bacteria
   c. _____ Inflammation of the gums
   d. _____ Cavities
   e. _____ Inflammation of the mouth
   f. _____ Cracking of the lips, especially at the corners of the mouth
   g. _____ Inflammation of the tongue
   h. _____ Dead bacteria that collects along the gum line

   1. Caries
   2. Plaque
   3. Stomatitis
   4. Halitosis
   5. Glossitis
   6. Cheilosis
   7. Gingivitis
   8. Tartar
43. What are the best measures to take to prevent tooth loss?
44. Describe why each of the following clients is at risk for oral problems.
   a. Client receiving radiation therapy
   b. Client with diabetes
   c. Right-handed client with a stroke affecting the right side
   d. Client who has had oral surgery
   e. Client with a nasogastric tube and continuous nasal oxygen
   f. Depressed client
45. Describe at least three assessment findings associated with oral malignancy.
46. State four goals for clients in need of oral hygiene.
   a.
   b.
   c.
   d.
47. Healthy clients of all ages should have a dental checkup at least every:
   a. 3 months.
   b. 6 months.
   c. 12 months.
   d. 2 years.
48. An effective oral hygiene program involves:
   a. brushing the teeth twice each day.
   b. using a hard bristle brush to maximize cleaning.
   c. holding the toothbrush at a 90-degree angle to the gum surface.
   d. flossing at least once each day.
49. Which of the following oral hygiene products would place the client at risk for oral problems?
   a. Hydrogen peroxide and water
   b. Moi-Stir salivary supplement
   c. Lemon-glycerin sponges
   d. Fluoride toothpaste
50. Which of the following observations is most important to determine before providing oral hygiene to the unconscious client?
   a. Presence of a functioning gag reflex
   b. Presence of dental caries or halitosis
   c. Color, texture, or bleeding of gums
   d. Dryness or discoloration of the tongue
51. Mrs. Crystal is an 18-year-old who is unconscious as a result of a head injury. When providing mouth care, the nurse should:
   a. position the client in a semi-Fowler's position to prevent aspiration of secretions.
   b. swab the client's mouth with a gloved finger while she is lying in a reverse Trendelenburg position.
   c. position the client on her side and have suction equipment available to remove secretions.
   d. position the client on her back and use a padded tongue blade to keep the teeth separated.
52. The nurse should wear disposable gloves when providing oral hygiene. (true or false)
53. Excessive fluoridation can result in discoloration of tooth enamel. (true or false)
54. When caring for a client with dentures, the nurse:

a. stores the dentures in a clean dry container.
b. uses hot water to ensure thorough cleansing of dentures.
c. rinses dentures in cold water to promote client comfort.
d. assists the client in brushing gums, palate, and tongue.

55. What action should be taken when a tick is found on a client's skin?
56. Fill in the correct term for each of the following parasitic conditions.
    a. ___________ Tiny grayish-white parasites found in pubic hair
    b. ___________ Tiny grayish-white parasites that are difficult to see, often clinging to clothing
    c. ___________ Tiny grayish-white parasites found on the scalp and attached to hair strands
57. State two goals for clients in need of hair and scalp care.
    a.
    b.
58. Combing the hair helps keep it clean and distributes oil along the hair shafts. (true or false)
59. The nurse should request the permission of the client in order to:
    a. shave a beard or mustache.
    b. braid the hair.
    c. cut tangled or matted hair.
    d. all of the above.
60. Identify two groups of clients for whom it is preferable to use an electric razor for shaving.
    a.
    b.
61. Identify at least two factors to assess in determining a client's knowledge and use of each sensory aid listed.
    a. Eyeglasses
        (1)
        (2)
    b. Artificial eye
        (1)
        (2)
    c. Hearing aid
        (1)
        (2)
62. Identify at least four factors to assess in determining a client's knowledge and use of contact lenses.
    a.
    b.
    c.
    d.
63. State two goals for clients requiring special hygienic care related to the eyes, ears, or nose.
    a.
    b.
64. Describe the special eye care that may be required for the unconscious client.
65. To safely remove a contact lens from an unconscious or immobilized client, the nurse should first make sure that the lens is placed directly over the:
    a. cornea.
    b. medial aspect of the sclera.
    c. lateral aspect of the sclera.
    d. conjunctiva.
66. A client wearing contact lenses complains of blurred vision. The possible cause of the blurring could include:
    a. dirty or damaged lenses.
    b. lens placed in the opposite eye.
    c. corneal irritation.
    d. all of the above.
67. Identify three situations in which the client's contact lenses should be removed immediately.
    a.
    b.
    c.
68. Describe each of the following techniques necessary in caring for an artificial eye.
    a. Removal
    b. Cleansing
    c. Reinsertion
    d. Storage
69. Excessive or impacted cerumen is most effectively removed by:
    a. gentle use of cotton-tipped applicators.
    b. bulb syringe irrigation with hot water.
    c. Water Pik irrigation with cold water.
    d. mineral oil drops and tepid water irrigation.
70. Draw a simple stick figure diagram to describe each of the following positions.
    a. Fowler's
    b. Semi-Fowler's
    c. Trendelenburg
    d. Reverse Trendelenburg
71. Match the specialized bed or mattress to the most accurate description.
    a. _____ Mattresslike pad constructed of silicone or polyvinyl chloride gel
    b. _____ Air forced through tiny ceramic microspheres
    c. _____ Rubberized mattress that fits over regular bed mattress; intermittently inflates and deflates
    d. _____ Rotates clients from extreme left to extreme right lateral position
    e. _____ Bed frame–turning mechanism that rotates vertically in a circular fashion
    f. _____ Foam mattress with peaks designed to disperse and distribute weight

    1. CircOlectric bed
    2. Rotokinetic table
    3. Clinitron bed
    4. Flotation pad
    5. Egg crate mattress
    6. Air mattress

72. Whenever possible, the nurse should make the bed while it is unoccupied. (true or false)
73. Which of the following points should the nurse remember when making a client's bed?
    - **a.** Shake and refold used linen.
    - **b.** Place dirty linen directly on the floor.
    - **c.** Place the hem of the bottom sheet "seam up."
    - **d.** Carry the dirty linen away from the body.
74. After making the bed, the nurse should:
    - **a.** lower the bed as close to the floor as possible.
    - **b.** secure the call light within the client's reach.
    - **c.** assist the client to a comfortable position.
    - **d.** all of the above.

APPLICATION OF KEY CONCEPTS
Activities to reinforce skills and techniques

1. Use of hospital room equipment
    - **a.** Arrange to visit an unoccupied room on your assigned nursing division to examine and practice working with the room equipment including:
        - **(1)** The nursing call system
        - **(2)** Room lights
        - **(3)** Overbed table
        - **(4)** Bedside stand
        - **(5)** Shower or tub fixtures
    - **b.** In your nursing laboratory or on your nursing division, practice the following activities using an empty hospital bed:
        - **(1)** Unlocking and locking the bed wheels
        - **(2)** Raising and lowering the side rails
        - **(3)** Positioning the bed in Fowler's, semi-Fowler's, Trendelenburg, and reverse Trendelenburg positions
    - **c.** When you have practiced each of the skills using an empty hospital bed, have a peer climb into the bed and perform each of the techniques again.
2. Oral hygiene technique
    - **a.** Examine your institution's procedure for administering oral hygiene.
    - **b.** Write a list of all the equipment and supplies needed to provide oral hygiene to an unconscious client and locate these on your nursing division.
    - **c.** Practice administering oral hygiene to a partner while a peer observes and critiques your performance based on the steps described in your text.
    - **d.** Elicit an instructor's evaluation of your technique for administering oral hygiene.
3. Bathing techniques
    - **a.** Examine your institution's procedure concerning hygienic care.
    - **b.** Write a list of all the equipment and supplies needed to administer a complete bed bath and locate these items on your assigned clinical area.
    - **c.** Practice giving a bed bath to a demonstration mannequin or a peer in your nursing laboratory. Utilizing the procedure steps listed in your text, critique your performance or have the peer critique your performance.
    - **d.** Volunteer to have another student give you a bed bath. Describe how it feels to have someone give you a bath. Identify actions that made you feel more comfortable. Identify actions that made you feel uncomfortable. Formulate approaches that would reduce your discomfort.
    - **e.** Observe or assist a nurse administering a bed bath to a client. Compare the techniques you observed with those described in your text. Attempt to determine the rationale for modification of the techniques your observed. Discuss your observations with your instructor.
    - **f.** Elicit an instructor's evaluation of your bed bath technique.
4. Sponge bath technique for infant
    - **a.** Examine your institution's procedures for bathing an infant.
    - **b.** Write a list of all the equipment and supplies needed to bathe an infant.
    - **c.** Practice giving a sponge bath to a doll while a peer observes and critiques your performance. (If you wish, practice bathing a doll independently and perform a self-evaluation.)
    - **d.** Elicit an instructor's evaluation of your infant bathing technique.
5. Shaving technique
    - **a.** Examine your institution's policies concerning shaving clients using safety razors or electric shavers.
    - **b.** Practice shaving a peer, friend, or family member.
6. Perineal care technique
    - **a.** Examine your institution's procedure for administering perineal care.
    - **b.** Write a list of the equipment and supplies needed to administer perineal care.
    - **c.** Using a demonstration mannequin in your nursing laboratory, practice administering perineal care while a peer observes and critiques your performance based on the steps described in your text.
    - **d.** Independently or in a role-playing situation, practice explaining the steps of perineal care in a simulated setting. Audio tape your explanation. Review and critique your performance.
    - **e.** Elicit an instructor's evaluation of your perineal care technique.
7. Backrub technique
    - **a.** Practice administering a backrub to a partner while a peer observes and critiques your performance.
    - **b.** Elicit an instructor's evaluation of your backrub technique.
8. Bed-making technique
    - **a.** In the nursing laboratory, practice the following bed-making techniques while a peer observes and critiques your performance based on the steps described in your text:

(1) Open, unoccupied bed
(2) Closed, unoccupied bed
(3) Surgical, recovery, or postoperative bed

b. In the nursing laboratory, practice making an occupied bed with a partner acting as the client. Ask your partner to observe and critique your performance.

c. Observe or assist another nurse making an occupied bed. Compare the techniques to the steps described in your text. Attempt to determine the rationale for modifications in the nurse's technique. Discuss your observations with your instructor.

d. Elicit an instructor's evaluation of your bedmaking technique.

Activities to reinforce theoretical concepts

1. Clinical situation: special hygiene needs
Helen Ziegler, a 55-year-old black music teacher, requires total care following a stroke. She is unable to speak or write and unable to move her right arm or leg. She has upper dentures. She has no blink reflex in her left eyelid. She has an indwelling Foley catheter for urinary drainage. Mrs. Ziegler has a history of diabetes mellitus.
   a. What factors must be considered before initiating Mrs. Ziegler's hygiene?
   b. Identify the conditions that currently place Mrs. Ziegler at risk for skin breakdown. Briefly describe the physiological basis for these risks.
   c. Identify the conditions that currently place Mrs. Ziegler at risk for oral problems. Briefly describe the physiological basis for these risks.
   d. Discuss the procedure and related rationale for providing Mrs. Ziegler with each of the following:
   (1) Oral hygiene
   (2) Eye care
   (3) Perineal care
   (4) Skin care
   (5) Hair care
2. Experiential exercise: assisting with client hygiene
   a. Following an observational experience or when assigned to provide hygienic care to a client, perform a self-care ability assessment to determine the level of assistance required.
   b. Include each of the following areas in your assessment:
   (1) Balance
   (2) Activity tolerance
   (3) Muscle strength
   (4) Coordination
   (5) Vision
   (6) Ability to sit without support
   (7) Hand grasp
   (8) Extremity range of motion
   (9) Cognitive function
   c. Describe modifications in technique that would be required based on your assessment.
3. Experiential exercise: bathing an infant
   a. Prepare a teaching plan to instruct a new parent on bathing an infant. Include equipment and supplies needed. (If possible, visit a local store to determine the cost of equipment and supplies.)
   b. Formulate a rationale for each step of the procedure.
   c. Obtain a doll and demonstrate the technique. Have a peer observe and critique your performance, or if possible videotape the simulated session for self-evaluation.
4. Experiential exercise: diabetic foot care
   a. Develop a teaching booklet addressing foot care for clients in the community with diabetes or peripheral vascular disease.
   b. Practice teaching the basic principles of foot care to a small group of peers based on the information presented in the teaching booklet. If possible, videotape or audio tape the simulated teaching session. Ask your peers to critique the teaching session and formulate your own self-evaluation.
   c. Submit your teaching booklet to your instructor for feedback.
   d. With your instructor as a resource and proctor, present your teaching session or booklet to a group of older adults in the community.

ADDITIONAL READINGS

Gannon, EP, and Kadezabek, E: Giving your patients meticulous mouth care, Nurs 80 10(3):70, 1980.
Photographic text illustrating oral hygiene. Includes techniques for patient-initiated and nurse-administered oral hygiene.

Greer, ME: Hair care for the black patient, Am J Nurs 76:1781, 1976.
Describes techniques for hair care in black patients. Emphasizes the psycho-socio-cultural, in addition to the physical, needs met through hair care.

Michelson, D: How to give a good backrub, Am J Nurs 78:1197, 1978.
A photographic text illustrating techniques for back rub. Briefly describes the importance of the procedure as a nonverbal communication tool in development of the nurse-client relationship.

Osguthorpe, NC: If your patient has contact lenses, Am J Nurs 84:1255, 1984.
Describes how to locate, remove, and protect contact lenses. Describes eye care appropriate for client with contact lenses. Includes photographs depicting lens removal.

Poland, JM: Comparing Moi-Stir to lemon glycerine swabs, Am J Nurs 87:422, 1987.
Summarizes a review of the literature addressing use of lemon-glycerine swab sticks for mouth care. Describes a study comparing lemon-glycerine swabs with Moi-Stir swabs (a salivary supplement), which revealed the superiority of Moi-Stir in client satisfaction as well as dental and gingival health.

Slattery, J: Dental health in children, Am J Nurs 76: 1159, 1976.
Discusses prevention of dental disorders in pediatric clients. Includes detailed dental history that may be adapted to any developmental level and included in assessment interviews.

Sykes, J: Black skin problems, Am J Nurs 79:1092, 1979.
Describes nine common skin problems found in black clients. Photographs illustrate each condition described. Discusses characteristic signs, causes, and treatment of the identified skin conditions.

Winslow, EH, et al: Oxygen uptake and cardiovascular responses in control adults and acute myocardial infarction patients during bathing, Nurs Res 34:164, 1985.
Describes a study comparing physiological responses before, during, and after three types of baths [basin, tub, and shower] in a normal adult control group and clients with acute myocardial infarction. Findings revealed similar physiological costs for the various bathing methods, with differences in physiological response related primarily to subject variability.

Chapter 33
Nutrition

PREREQUISITE READING

Read Chapter 33, pp. 880 to 923.

OBJECTIVES

Mastery of content in this chapter will enable the student to:

1. Define selected terms associated with nutrition.
2. List the six categories of nutrients and explain why each is necessary for nutrition.
3. Explain how energy is measured and the importance of a balance between energy intake and energy output.
4. List the end products of carbohydrate, protein, and lipid metabolism.
5. Explain the significance of saturated, unsaturated, and polyunsaturated lipids in nutrition.
6. Describe the basic four food groups, and discuss their values in planning meals for good nutrition.
7. Explain recommended daily allowances (RDAs).
8. List seven dietary guidelines for health promotion.
9. Discuss the major areas of nutritional assessment.
10. Name some of the factors that influence a client's dietary patterns and nutritional status.
11. Identify three major nutritional problems and describe the clients at risk for these problems.
12. State the goals for enteral nutrition.
13. Describe the procedure for initiating and maintaining tube feedings.
14. List and discuss the complications of tube feedings.
15. Describe methods to avoid the complications associated with tube feedings.
16. State the goals of total parenteral nutrition.
17. Describe the procedure for initiating and maintaining total parenteral nutrition.
18. Discuss how to prevent and identify complications of total parenteral nutrition.
19. Discuss the importance of diet counseling in evaluation and client teaching before discharge.

REVIEW OF KEY CONCEPTS

1. Match the following terms with the definition provided.

   a. 3 Biochemical reactions that build body tissues
   b. 5 The proportion of essential nutrients in relation to total calories
   c. 2 Foods containing elements needed for body functions
   d. 6 Resting energy requirements
   e. 4 Biochemical reactions that break down body tissues
   f. 1 All biochemical reactions within the body

   1. Metabolism
   2. Nutrients
   3. Anabolism
   4. Catabolism
   5. Nutrient density
   6. BMR

2. List the six categories of nutrients and identify the one that is most important.
   a. water ✓
   b. carbohydrates
   c. proteins
   d. lipids
   e. vitamins
   f. minerals
3. Identify the two developmental age groups most vulnerable to water deprivation or water loss.
   a. infant
   b. elderly
4. Thirst is the most reliable guide for fluid needs in all clients. (true or false)
5. The preferred energy source for the body is found in:
   a. proteins.
   b. carbohydrates. ✓
   c. lipids.
   d. minerals.
6. Indicate the total calories produced by metabolism of each of the nutrients listed.
   a. 20 g of protein 80 cal
   b. 15 g of fat 135 kcal
   c. 50 g of carbohydrate 200 cal
7. What is a complete protein?
8. Complete the following table by listing three food sources for each protein classification.

Complete proteins	Incomplete proteins
a.	a.
b.	b.
c.	c.

9. Briefly describe what is meant by each of the following:
   a. Nitrogen balance
   b. Negative nitrogen balance
   c. Positive nitrogen balance
10. The primary role of protein is to:
    a. provide energy.
    b. promote tissue growth, maintenance, and repair.
    c. serve as a catalyst for the body's metabolic reactions.
    d. store energy.
11. Indicate the effect of ingestion of each of the following lipid forms on blood cholesterol levels.
    a. Polyunsaturated fatty acids
    b. Unsaturated fatty acids
    c. Saturated fatty acids
12. Most animal fats have a higher proportion of:
    a. saturated fatty acids.
    b. unsaturated fatty acids.
    c. polyunsaturated fatty acids.
    d. polyunsaturated and unsaturated fatty acids.
13. Identify three sources of essential fatty acids.
    a.
    b.
    c.
14. The body's form of stored energy is:
    a. amino acids.
    b. carbohydrates.
    c. fats.
    d. proteins.
15. Nutritional guidelines recommend a lipid intake in the adult diet of up to:
    a. 45% of the total caloric intake.
    b. 35% of the total caloric intake.
    c. 20% of the total caloric intake.
    d. 10% of the total caloric intake.
16. Which statement concerning water-soluble vitamins is correct?
    a. Vitamins A and K are examples of water-soluble vitamins.
    b. Water-soluble vitamins are stored in the body.
    c. Water-soluble vitamins must be provided through daily intake.
    d. Hypervitaminosis of water-soluble vitamins does not occur.
17. What is the primary role of minerals in biochemical reactions?
18. In the following table, describe the function of the vitamin or mineral, three major food sources, and the required daily allowance.

Nutrient	Function	Food sources	RDA
Water-soluble vitamins			
Vitamin C			
Vitamin B_1			
Vitamin B_2			
Niacin			
Vitamin B_6			
Folic acid			
Vitamin B_{12}			
Fat-soluble vitamins			
Vitamin A			
Vitamin D			
Vitamin E			
Vitamin K			
Macrominerals			
Calcium			
Magnesium			
Potassium			
Sodium			
Microminerals			
Copper			
Fluoride			
Iodine			
Iron			
Zinc			

19. Match the food substance with the enzyme that aids its digestion.
    a. ____ Lipase
    b. ____ Pepsin
    c. ____ Amylase
    d. ____ Trypsin
    e. ____ Bile
    f. ____ Lactase

    1. Proteins
    2. Carbohydrates
    3. Fats
20. The process that occurs when the body breaks down liver glycogen stores into glucose is:
    a. anabolism.
    b. emulsion.
    c. catabolism.
    d. absorption.
21. What is the primary advantage of the basic four food group plan?
22. Describe the characteristics of the basic four food groups by filling in the table below.

Food group	Nutrients supplied	Dietary sources	Daily amounts
Milk			
Meats			
Vegetables and fruits			
Bread and cereals			

23. The RDAs exceed the requirements for most healthy individuals. (true or false).

24. Identify five of the dietary guidelines for Americans issued by the USDA and the Department of Health and Human Services.

a.
b.
c.
d.
e.

25. Match the category of vegetarianism with the characteristic diet that is followed.

a. Consume only plant foods
b. Consume plant foods and milk but avoid eggs
c. Consume plant foods, eggs, and milk
d. Consume plant food, seafood, and poultry.

1. Lactovegetarians
2. Semivegetarians
3. Ovolactovegetarians
4. Vegans

26. The recommended nutritional source for infants during the first 6 months is:

a. breast milk.
b. prepared formula.
c. whole milk.
d. enriched rice cereal.

27. Identify three nutrients that must be supplemented for the breast-fed infant.

a.
b.
c.

28. At what age are solid foods best introduced?

29. Mrs. Carson asks the nurse what type of milk to purchase for her 16-month-old daughter. The nurse should advise Mrs. Carson to buy:

a. skim milk.
b. 1% fat milk.
c. 2% fat milk.
d. whole milk.

30. Adult women using oral contraceptives may require additional:

a. iron and vitamin C.
b. B and C vitamins.
c. calcium and protein.
d. calories.

31. Which statement concerning nutrition in pregnancy is inaccurate?

a. Poor nutrition can cause low birth weight and decreased neonatal survival.
b. Fetal nutritional needs are generally met at the expense of the mother.
c. The nutritional status of the mother at the time of conception is of little importance.
d. A maternal weight gain of 22 to 33 pounds is recommended.

32. Identify the daily requirements for the pregnant woman in each of the following areas:

a. milk group.
b. meat group.
c. vegetable-fruit group.
d. bread-cereal group.
e. margarine or butter.
f. water.

33. When compared to pregnancy, the lactating mother requires an increased amount of:

a. calcium and phosporus.
b. iron.
c. protein.
d. calories and water.

34. List four factors that influence the nutritional status of the older adult, and identify the one that is considered to be the most important.

a.
b.
c.
d.

35. List the four major components of a nutritional assessment.

a.
b.
c.
d.

36. List seven factors that influence dietary patterns.

a.
b.
c.
d.
e.
f.
g.

37. Describe three ways in which excessive ingestion of alcohol may contribute to nutritional deficiencies.

a.
b.
c.

38. For each of the following body areas describe at least two signs of poor nutrition.

a. General appearance
(1)
(2)

b. Weight
(1)
(2)

c. Hair
(1)
(2)

d. Skin
(1)
(2)

e. Mouth (lips, gums, teeth, mucous membranes)
(1)
(2)

f. Eyes
(1)
(2)

g. Gastrointestinal function
(1)
(2)

h. Cardiovascular function
(1)
(2)

i. Musculoskeletal function
(1)
(2)

j. Neurological function
(1)
(2)

39. List the five aspects of anthropometric measurements.
a.
b.
c.
d.
e.

40. The laboratory data most useful in determining protein-calorie malnutrition are:
a. Hemoglobin and hematocrit
b. Total lymphocyte count and red cell count
c. Serum albumin and transferrin
d. Blood urea nitrogen and urine creatinine

41. a. The eating disorder characterized by self-imposed starvation is ______________.
b. The eating disorder characterized by abnormal food craving, gorging, and induced vomiting is ______________.

42. Identify seven conditions that place a client at risk for nutritional problems.
a.
b.
c.
d.
e.
f.
g.

43. What are the five nutritional components provided through TPN?
a.
b.
c.
d.
e.

44. Identify three nursing measures to promote an environment that is conducive to eating.
a.
b.
c.

45. The regular hospital diet contains approximately:
a. 1500 calories.
b. 1800 calories.
c. 2200 calories.
d. 2500 calories.

46. Fill in the name of each special diet described below.
a. ______________ Transparent fluids, egg whites, gelatin
b. ______________ Foods from the regular diet that are easily chewed and digested
c. ______________ Limits fibers, milk and milk products, cheese, fried foods, fruits
d. ______________ Allows all foods, but minimizes those difficult to digest or fried
e. ______________ Foods are served warm or cool; eliminates any foods that are irritating, stimulating, or spicy
f. ______________ Foods that are liquid at room or body temperature
g. ______________ Foods simply prepared, easily digested, and quickly emptied from the stomach

47. Identify the two major modes of enteral feeding.
a.
b.

48. Tube feedings are appropriate for all of the following situations except:
a. a client who is unable to digest or absorb nutrients.
b. a client who is unable to ingest nutrients.
c. a client who is unable to adequately chew foods.
d. a client who is unable to swallow foods.

49. Which tube type is preferred for enteral tube feedings?
a. Large-bore nasogastric tubes
b. Large-bore rubber or plastic feeding tubes
c. Small-bore, flexible feeding tubes
d. Small-bore rigid feeding tubes

50. Describe the method for determining the appropriate tube length for feeding tubes placed in the:
a. Stomach
b. Duodenum or jejunum

51. Identify two methods for nurses to use at the bedside to determine gastric tube placement.
a.
b.

52. Auscultation of air is a reliable indicator to verify placement of small-bore feeding tubes. (true or false)

53. Define gastric residual.

54. How often should gastric residual be routinely checked in a client receiving continuous tube feedings?
a. Every 2 to 4 hours
b. Every 4 to 6 hours
c. Every 6 to 8 hours
d. Every 12 hours

55. Why is it important for the nurse to assess abdominal distention, nausea, and vomiting in a client receiving tube feedings through a small-bore tube?

56. The most reliable method for determining feeding tube placement is:
a. aspiration of gastric contents.
b. radiographic verification.
c. auscultation of air injection.
d. examination of the posterior oral pharynx.

57. In what position should the client be placed before administering a tube feeding?

58. Briefly describe the rationale for each of the follow-

ing actions associated with initiating and maintaining total parenteral nutrition.
- **a.** Trendelenburg position
- **b.** Valsalva maneuver
- **c.** Chest x-ray
- **d.** Sterile technique and dressings
- **e.** Infusion regulation via a pump
- **f.** Checking blood glucose (or urine glucose and acetone) frequently

59. A client receiving TPN displays the following signs and symptoms: headache, cold clammy skin, dizziness, tachycardia, and circumoral tingling. The most likely reason for these manifestations would be:
- **a.** fluid overload
- **b.** hyperglycemia
- **c.** hypoglycemia
- **d.** air embolism

60. If a TPN infusion falls behind schedule, the nurse should attempt to catch up to ensure that the client receives the prescribed amount. (true or false)

APPLICATIONS OF KEY CONCEPTS

Activities to reinforce skills and techniques

1. Feeding techniques
- **a.** Visit a day-care center and observe the feeding techniques and methods of assisting children during meals. Compare the techniques and methods of assisting with the developmental levels of the children.
- **b.** Observe a nurse or family member feeding or assisting an adult at mealtime. What techniques seemed effective or ineffective? What were the similarities and differences between the techniques you observed and those you have studied?
- **c.** Eat a meal with a peer. Take turns feeding each other. Be sure to include different food forms (for example, liquids, solids, semisolids) and use a variety of utensils (spoon, fork, straw, cup). Share how you felt in the role of nurse and the role of client. Based on your experiences, identify ways to make the client more comfortable during mealtime.

2. Enteral tube feeding techniques
- **a.** Examine your institution's policies and procedures regarding administration of tube feedings.
- **b.** In the nursing laboratory or on your clinical division, examine the various types of gastric and enteral tubes and associated equipment available for tube feeding clients.
- **c.** In the nursing laboratory or on your clinical division, examine any available pumps used to administer continuous enteral tube feedings.
- **d.** Talk with your institution's dietitian or nutritionist to determine the types of tube feeding preparations most often ordered for clients.
- **e.** Observe clients receiving tube feedings in the clinical area. Compare the techniques that you observed in monitoring the client and administering the tube feeding to those described in your text. Share your observations with your instructor.
- **f.** In the nursing laboratory, using a demonstration mannequin with a feeding tube in place, have a peer observe and critique your performance as you:
  - **(1)** practice the techniques of assessment specific to a client receiving tube feedings.
  - **(2)** practice the techniques of checking for feeding tube placement.
  - **(3)** practice the techniques of administering a tube feeding.
- **g.** Elicit an instructor's evaluation of your assessment of a client requiring tube feeding and your techniques for administering a tube feeding.

Activities to reinforce theoretical concepts

1. Experiential exercise: diet history
- **a.** Using the tool provided in your text, elicit a diet history from a peer or an assigned client. Formulate a list of nursing diagnoses based on the data obtained.
- **b.** Keep a dietary log of your own intake for 3 days, including a weekend. Analyze and describe your intake, and formulate recommendations in relation to:
  - **(1)** the basic four food groups.
  - **(2)** RDAs
  - **(3)** USDA dietary guidelines.
  - **(4)** Pennington food guide.

2. Experiential exercise: basic four food groups, dietary guidelines
- **a.** Select a specific developmental level (preschool, school age, adolescent, young and middle adult, older adult).
- **b.** Based on developmental characteristics and specific nutritional needs for the age group, develop a teaching plan that presents the basic four groups and USDA dietary guidelines.
- **c.** Present your teaching plan to a peer group and instructor for feedback.
- **d.** If possible, using your instructor as a resource, arrange to present your teaching session to the identified population in your community.

3. Experiential exercise: nutritional assessment
- **a.** Perform a comprehensive nursing assessment of a selected client (or review the medical record of the client).
- **b.** Identify data pertinent to the client's nutritional state including:
  - **(1)** factors influencing dietary patterns.
  - **(2)** anthropometric data.
  - **(3)** clinical signs of nutritional status.
  - **(4)** laboratory data.
- **c.** Formulate actual and potential nursing diagnoses pertinent to the client's nutritional status.
- **d.** Develop a plan of care to address the priority diagnosis.

4. Clinical situation: developmental nutritional variables
Outline a nutritional diet plan for the following clients:
   a. A 2-year-old admitted to the hospital with chronic diarrhea
   b. A 12-year-old who has just had oral surgery
   c. A 17-year-old pregnant teenager who has been seen in the prenatal clinic with diagnosis of alteration in nutrition related to lack of information
   d. An obese 40-year-old woman who is a teacher, wife, and mother
   e. A 53-year-old male who has recently had a myocardial infarction
   f. A 60-year-old woman with cancer who is receiving radiation therapy
   g. An 82-year-old with complaints of chronic constipation
5. Experiential exercise: special diets
   a. Review the nursing or dietary Kardex for clients in any health care setting.
   b. Identify the types of diets that are ordered for selected clients.
   c. Using the institution's diet manual or other appropriate resources, determine the characteristics of the special diets ordered.
   d. Determine the reason for the prescribed diet.
6. Experiential exercise: community resources
Independently, or in a small group, identify resources available in your community to assist clients in meeting their nutritional needs (at least two for each of the identified resource areas listed below).
   a. Government programs
   b. Private agencies
   c. Volunteer health agencies
7. Clinical solution: nutrition and the nursing process
Mrs. Kirk is a 72-year-old widow who lives alone on a limited income. Her apartment is about six blocks from the nearest grocery store. To reach a larger supermarket Mrs. Kirk must catch two buses. Mrs. Kirk has arthritis, which makes walking or carrying large, heavy bags of groceries very difficult and painful.

   Mrs. Kirk has been admitted to the hospital because of iron-deficiency anemia and low blood pressure. She complains of feeling very tired and weak "all the time."

   When questioned about her normal dietary patterns, Mrs. Kirk states that she usually has a small bowl of soup with crackers for lunch and tea and a piece of toast at supper. She states, "It's no fun eating alone, and I don't have much money to spend on food because I won't be able to pay my bills."

   Mrs. Kirk weighs 98 pounds (45 kg) and she is 5 feet 3 inches (157.5 cm) tall. She states, "I guess I've lost some weight lately because my clothes are much looser." At lunchtime the nurse notes that Mrs. Kirk has eaten very little of the roast chicken and vegetables. When asked if she didn't like the food, Mrs. Kirk replied, "Oh no, it tasted alright, I'm just too tired to eat."

   Develop a comprehensive care plan for Mrs. Kirk that addresses (1) her short-term nutritional needs while in the hospital and, (2) her nutritional needs after she is discharged.

ADDITIONAL READINGS

Atkins, JM, and Oakely, CW: A nurse's guide to TPN, RN 6:20, 1986.

One article in a series concerning TPN. Presents basic information about the role of the nurse in initiating, monitoring, and caring for clients receiving TPN. Emphasizes prevention of complications associated with TPN.

Birdsall, C: When is TPN safe? Am J Nurs 85:73, 1985.

Highlights major nursing actions to ensure safety for client receiving TPN.

Bodinski, L: A nurse's guide to diet therapy, New York, 1982, John Wiley & Sons, Inc.

A handbook describing the nurse's role in meeting the nutritional needs of clients. Includes topics related to health promotion, as well as specific nutritional care for disease states.

Butterworth, C: The skeleton in the hospital closet, Nurs Today 9:4, 1974

Notable articles calling attention to the problems of iatrogenic starvation of hospital clients. Points out the relationship between disease, nutritional state, and recovery.

Caly, J: Assessing adults' nutrition, Am J Nurs, 77:1605, 1977.

Detailed discussion of the areas to include in comprehensive nutritional evaluation. Presents case studies to illustrate methods for analysis of pertinent data.

Claggett, M: Anorexia nervosa: a behavorial approach, Am J Nurs 80:1471, 1980.

Proposes that the underlying psychopathological features of anorexia must be treated but contends that nutritional needs must receive initial attention. Emphasizes the nutritional component of therapy and presents interventions to include in a behavioral approach to treatment.

Moore, ME: Do you still believe these myths about tube feeding? RN 5:51, 1987.

Describes six common misconceptions that continue to guide nurses in administering tube feedings. Suggests that these misconceptions place the client at risk for injury and presents approaches to ensure client safety.

Munro-Black, J: The ABC's of total parenteral nutrition, Nurs, 84 14(2):50, 1984.

Photographic text describing the steps in caring for client requiring TPN from the time of catheter insertion through infusion and dressing changes.

Richardson, T: Anorexia nervosa: an overview, Am J Nurs 80:1470, 1980.

Presents the psychodynamics of anorexia nervosa. Includes discussion of diagnostic criteria, etiology, and medical treatment.

Williams, SR: Nutrition and diet therapy, ed. 5, St. Louis, 1985, The C.V. Mosby Co.

Comprehensive text addressing normal and therapeutic nutrition. Approaches nutritional needs from developmental, physical, psychological, and cultural perspectives.

Worthington, B, editor: Nutrition, Nurs Clin North Am 14(2), 1979.

Series of articles describing nutritional care. Highlights controversies in nutrition, client assessment, dietary counseling, obesity, special needs of women, and TPN.

Chapter 34
Sleep

PREREQUISITE READING

Read Chapter 34, pp. 924 to 945.

OBJECTIVES

Mastery of content in this chapter will enable the student to:

1. Define selected terms associated with sleep and sleep disorders.
2. Describe the differences and similarities between rest and sleep.
3. Explain the effect the 24-hour sleep-wake cycle has on biological function.
4. Discuss mechanisms that regulate sleep.
5. Describe the stages of a normal sleep cycle.
6. Explain the functions of sleep.
7. Compare and contrast the sleep requirements of different age groups.
8. Identify factors that normally promote and disrupt sleep.
9. Describe common sleep disorders.
10. Conduct a sleep history for a client.
11. Identify relevant nursing diagnoses related to sleep problems.
12. Identify nursing interventions designed to promote a normal sleep cycle for an adult and child.
13. Describe ways to evaluate sleep therapies.

REVIEW OF KEY CONCEPTS

1. Define rest.
2. Define sleep.
3. Identify the three basic conditions required for proper rest.
   a.
   b.
   c.
4. Which biological rhythm would describe the stage of sleep known as REM?
   a. Diurnal
   b. Infradian
   c. Ultradian
   d. Circadian
5. The 24-hour sleep-wake cycle continues to operate even when external factors influencing behavior are removed. (true or false)
6. Karen Finnigan is a 24-year-old registered nurse who works the day/night rotation on a general nursing division. When she switches from the day to the night shift, she has difficulty sleeping. An alteration in her biological sleep cycle:
   a. will occur immediately if Karen is healthy.
   b. often takes several weeks before her body will adjust.
   c. has little influence on Karen's actual physiological function.
   d. is unrelated to the environmental temperature or light.
7. Complete the table below comparing the cerebral mechanisms responsible for sleep regulation.

	Sleep mechanisms	Arousal mechanisms
Name	BSR	RAS
Anatomical location	PONDS & MEDIAL FOREBRAIN	UPPER BRAIN STEM REGION
Neurotransmitter	SEROTONIN	CATACHOLAMINES

8. Match the stage of sleep with the characteristic description.
   a. 3 Complete muscle relaxation
   b. 1 If awake, feels as if daydreaming
   c. 5 Responsible for mental restoration
   d. 2 Sound sleep, progressive relaxation
   e. 4 Responsible for restoring and resting body

   1. Stage 1: nonREM
   2. Stage 2: nonREM
   3. Stage 3: nonREM
   4. Stage 4: nonREM
   5. REM
9. The physical benefits derived from sleep include:
   a. preservation of cardiac function.
   b. production of growth hormone.
   c. energy conservation.
   d. all of the above.
10. The amount of time spent in REM sleep is greatest for:
    a. infants.
    b. school-age children.
    c. adolescents.
    d. elderly.
11. Sleep pattern changes in an elderly person are pri-

marily a result of psychological problems. (true or false)

12. Identify and briefly describe five factors affecting sleep.
    a.
    b.
    c.
    d.
    e.
13. A protein found in milk, cheese, and meats that may help a person to sleep is ____________.
14. Identify the sleep disorder described in each of the following client situations.
    a. 6 While engaged in an argument with a co-worker, Mr. Warren suddenly falls asleep at his desk.
    b. 3 Mrs. Lewis, who has been depressed for several weeks, awakens each day at 3:00 AM and is unable to get back to sleep.
    c. 7 Todd is awakened by his mother and is surprised to find himself standing in the middle of the family room.
    d. 1 Mr. Hoyle reports that he has had difficulty falling asleep for the past 6 months.
    e. 5 Mr. Glenn has recently gained 50 pounds. His wife reports that she is awakened by her husband's increased snoring. She has observed episodes when there is no sound of breathing but accentuated breathing movements.
    f. 8 Jimmy, 7 years old, begins to experience nightly bedwetting.
    g. 4 Mr. Smyth reports that since his wife's recent stroke, he has noted that she often stops breathing for 15- to 20-second periods during the night.
    h. 2 Mrs. Webster reports that she has been awakening three to four times every night for the past several weeks.

    1. Initial insomnia
    2. Intermittent insomnia
    3. Terminal insomnia
    4. Central sleep apnea
    5. Obstructive sleep apnea
    6. Narcolepsy
    7. Somnambulism
    8. Nocturnal enuresis
15. Define sleep deprivation.
16. In the table below, identify characteristic sleep deprivation symptoms.

Physiological symptoms	Psychological symptoms
a. Hand tremors	a. Moods
b. decrease reflexes	b. disorientation
c. Decreased reasoning	c. irritability
d. Cardiac dysrhythmias	d. fatigue

17. The most effective treatment for sleep deprivation is:
    a. utilization of CPAP.
    b. administration of hypnotic sleeping medications.
    c. provision of comfort measures to induce relaxation and sleep.
    d. elimination of factors disrupting the normal sleep pattern.
18. Identify seven areas to be assessed when obtaining a sleep history.
    a. medical history
    b. rituals
    c. sleeping patterns
    d. emotional, mental status
    e. Bed Partner
    f. environmental conditions
    g. sleep wake log
19. State three goals appropriate for a client needing rest or sleep.
    a.
    b.
    c.
20. Identify six areas to consider when promoting a client's normal sleep pattern.
    a. stress (emotional)
    b. environment
    c. Ritual
    d. illness
    e. patterns (sleeping)
    f. lifestyle - exercise
21. Which of the following interventions would be expected to promote safe, restful sleep in an infant?
    a. Keep the room softly lit.
    b. Provide a soft pillow and light blanket.
    c. Maintain the room temperature at 78° F.
    d. Position the crib near an open window for fresh air.
22. Which of the following interventions would be expected to promote safe, restful sleep in a confused adult?
    a. Position the bed's side rails up.
    b. Keep the room dimly lit.
    c. Provide additional covers.
    d. All of the above.
23. At which age do bedtime rituals become particularly important?
    a. Newborns and infants
    b. Toddlers and preschoolers
    c. School-age children
    d. Adolesence
24. Identify four bedtime rituals appropriate for an adult.
    a.
    b.
    c.
    d.
25. Describe five comfort measures that the nurse may initiate to promote a client's sleep.
    a.
    b.

c.
d.
e.

26. A client who has initial insomnia should be encouraged to stay in bed and concentrate on falling asleep. (true or false)

27. Roberta Kimball, RN, is working on the night shift. While making rounds at 1:00 AM, she finds a client who is unable to fall asleep. The most appropriate action by Ms. Kimball would be to:
   a. provide the client with a hypnotic medication.
   b. tell other staff members to avoid going into the client's room.
   c. talk with the client to determine factors contributing to the sleeplessness.
   d. encourage the client to stay in bed and read or watch television until he or she feels tired.

28. Brian, 5 years old, frequently awakens during the night. He tells his mother that he is afraid to stay in his room. The best approach to this problem would be to:
   a. allow Brian to get up and watch television until he feels sleepy.
   b. provide Brian with a snack of milk and cookies.
   c. let Brian come into his parents' bed until he falls asleep.
   d. talk with Brian about his fears and comfort him in his own bed.

29. Which of the following snacks would be appropriate for a client experiencing difficulty falling asleep?
   a. Hot tea and crackers
   b. Cocoa and bread with butter
   c. Wine and cheese
   d. Jello with fruit

30. Identify three problems or hazards associated with the use of hypnotic drugs for sleep.
   a.
   b.
   c.

APPLICATION OF KEY CONCEPTS

Activities to reinforce theoretical concepts

1. Experiential exercise: sleep history
   a. Develop a sleep history assessment tool based on the necessary components described in your text.
   b. Examine the nursing assessment form utilized in your health care setting. Identify areas of the tool that provide information pertinent to the client's rest and sleep patterns.
   c. Elicit a sleep history from a partner utilizing the tool you developed or the sleep questionnaire provided in your text. Based on your assessment, identify actual or potential sleeping problems. Formulate possible approaches to promote rest and sleep.

2. Experiential exercise: bedtime environment
   a. Arrange to observe clients on a general nursing division and, if possible, in an intensive care unit. (Although nighttime observation would be preferable, daytime assessment will provide useful information for the exercise.)
   b. Based on your observations, identify factors in each setting that actually or potentially interfere with clients' rest and sleep patterns.
   c. Describe any client behaviors you observed that could be associated with sleep deprivation.
   d. Discuss specific actions that could be taken to control environmental factors interfering with clients' rest and sleep.

3. Experiential exercise: normal sleep requirements
   a. Develop a teaching tool (chart, table, pamphlet, booklet) that could be used to teach parents about the sleep requirements of their children from infancy through adolescence. Include each of the following areas in the tool:
      (1) Each developmental age group (infants, toddlers, preschoolers, school age, adolescents)
      (2) Total amounts of sleep required
      (3) Frequency and duration of naps
      (4) Common factors that disrupt sleep patterns
      (5) Actions to minimize sleep pattern disruption
   b. Submit the tool to your instructor for feedback.
   c. If possible, using your instructor as a resource, arrange to use your tool as a basis for discussion with parents or child-care providers in a community setting. (Possible locations for your interaction may be day-care centers, schools, churches, or parent support groups.)

4. Clinical situation: factors affecting sleep

   Mr. Styles is a 39-year-old engineer for the city power company. He is married and has four children (2, 4, 5, and 8 years old). His wife does not work outside the home. Lately he has been increasingly irritable and fatigued. He states that regardless of the amount of time he spends sleeping, he still feels tired.

   Mr. Styles rotates from a straight day to an evening shift every 4 weeks. Whenever he comes home from work he typically drinks three or four cans of beer. Mr. Styles has been a smoker for 15 years and is approximately 40 pounds over the recommended weight for a man his size. He does not engage in any regular exercise program but does participate in summer softball and winter bowling leagues.

   a. What factors are present that may contribute to Mr. Styles' complaints of fatigue and irritability. Describe how these factors influence normal rest and sleep patterns.
   b. What modifications in life-style could be explored with Mr. Styles to promote rest and sleep?

5. Experiential exercise: factors affecting sleep
   a. Review the medical record of a selected client, including diagnosis, prescribed medications, and treatments.
   b. Analyze the data obtained to determine the influence of each of the following factors on the client's rest and sleep patterns.

(1) Medical diagnosis
(2) Medications
(3) Routine hospital care
(4) Treatments and procedures

c. Share your analysis with your instructor for feedback.

6. Clinical situation: nursing process with clients experiencing sleep problems
Mrs. McLean is a 58-year-old woman who is seen in the medical clinic for the first time. The nursing history reveals that Mrs. McLean has had great difficulty falling asleep since her discharge from the hospital 4 months ago. She indicates that before her hospitalization she used to sleep 7 or 8 hours every night but now she just "tosses and turns." She states: "My husband gets so angry when I can't relax. During the day, I feel so tired and irritable."
Mrs. McLean has had chronic bronchitis for several years and continues to smoke 1 to 2 packs of cigarettes per day. She tells the nurse, "I get short of breath sometimes when I lie flat." Her current medications include aminophylline (a bronchodilator) and prednisone (a corticosteroid). Several years ago Mrs. McLean took sleeping pills, but the physician will not prescribe them because of her current respiratory condition.
   a. Discuss additional assessment data that you would need from Mrs. McLean to address her current rest/sleep status.
   b. What factors may be contributing to Mrs. McLean's difficulty sleeping?
   c. Based on the information provided in the situation, formulate actual and potential nursing diagnoses related to Mrs. McLean's sleeping problems.
   d. Identify at least two goals for Mrs. McLean's care related to her need for sleep.
   e. For each goal, formulate at least one expected outcome and three individualized nursing interventions.

ADDITIONAL READINGS

Chuman, MA: The neurological basis of sleep, Heart Lung 12:177, 1983
Explores the physiological basis of sleep. Describes major sleep disturbances and their manifestations. Presents a brief discussion of usual medical therapies.

Hayter, J: The rhythm of sleep, Am J Nurs 80:457, 1980.
Describes the stages of sleep. Discusses nursing care implications related to alterations in sleep patterns and specific sleep pattern disturbances.

Hayter, J: Sleep behavior of older persons, Nurs Res 32:242, 1983.
Describes study intended to refine methodology for research of sleep behavior of older adults. Data reveal consistent sleep behaviors associated with advancing age.

Helton, MC, et al: The correlation between sleep deprivation and the intensive care unit syndrome, Heart Lung 9:464, 1980.
Describes a study in which mental status alterations associated with the ICU syndrome were examined and correlated to sleep deprivation. Makes recommendations about nursing actions to enhance sleep and extend duration of sleep cycles for clients in the ICU setting.

Hoch, C, and Reynbolds, C, III: Sleep disturbances and what to do about them, Geriatr Nurs 7:24, 1986.
Overview of the sleep stages. Identifies sleep disturbances according to cause: alterations in sleep-wake patterns, illness, psychological factors, or medications. Describes sleep assessment and presents specific strategies for intervention, including the scientific rationale.

Walseben, J: Sleep disorders, Am J Nurs 82:936, 1982.
Presents information about the role of sleep disorder centers in caring for clients with serious sleep disorders. Describes diagnostic tests utilized and correlates usual finding with the stages of sleep. Gives overview of insomnia, somnolence, and parasomnias, including causes, characteristic findings, and treatment. Cites additional resources for further information concerning this problem.

Weaver, TE, and Millman, RP: Broken sleep, Am J Nurs 86:146, 1986.
In depth exploration of obstructive and central sleep apnea. Describes pathophysiological mechanisms, clinical features, and treatments.

Webster, RA, and Thompson, DR: Sleep in hospitals, J Adv Nurs 11:447, 1986.
Reviews physiological basis of sleep and its benefits. Gives overview of factors influencing sleep in the hospital setting. Discusses specific nursing interventions to ensure adequate sleep for the hospitalized client.

Chapter 35
Comfort

PREREQUISITE READING

Read Chapter 35, pp. 946 to 979.

OBJECTIVES

Mastery of content in this chapter will enable the student to:

1. Define selected terms describing pain and pain therapies.
2. Discuss common misconceptions about pain.
3. Identify components of the pain experience.
4. Discuss the three phases of behavioral responses experienced with pain.
5. Explain the relationship of the gate-control theory to select nursing therapies for pain relief.
6. Perform an assessment of a client experiencing pain.
7. Describe guidelines for individualizing pain therapies.
8. Identify the techniques and rationale for selecting pain therapies.
9. Explain common causes for treatment of pain with analgesics.
10. Discuss the roles of pain clinics and hospices in pain control.

REVIEW OF KEY CONCEPTS

1. Pain is:
   - **a.** subjective and individualized.
   - **b.** influenced by psychosocial and cultural factors.
   - **c.** a protective mechanism or warning of tissue damage.
   - **d.** all of the above.
2. The way in which a nurse responds to a client's pain is often based on personal perceptions and value systems. (true or false)
3. Which of the following statements regarding pain is accurate?
   - **a.** Clients with a history of drug or alcohol abuse tend to overreact to pain.
   - **b.** Clients with minor illnesses have less pain than those with severe diseases.
   - **c.** Psychogenic pain is just as real as the pain associated with physiological disturbances.
   - **d.** Administering analgesics regularly will lead to a client's drug dependence.
4. Identify the three components of the pain experience.
   - **a.**
   - **b.**
   - **c.**
5. Define pain threshold.
6. Compare the two types of peripheral nerve fibers responsible for conducting painful stimuli by completing the table below.

	A fibers	C fibers
Fiber size		
Myelination status		
Transmission speed		
Nature of pain message		

7. What is an endorphin?
8. Which statement concerning endorphins is correct?
   - **a.** Transcutaneous electrical nerve stimulation depresses endorphin release.
   - **b.** Endorphin release is enhanced in clients with chronic pain.
   - **c.** Pleasure or pain experiences may activate endorphin release.
   - **d.** Anxiety associated with pain has no influence on endorphin release.
9. An individual's reaction to pain is physiological and behavioral. (true or false)
10. Place the letter "S" for sympathetic or "P" for parasympathetic to describe the physiological responses to pain.
    - **a.** ____ Increased pulse rate
    - **b.** ____ Nausea and vomiting
    - **c.** ____ Rapid, irregular breathing
    - **d.** ____ Dilated pupils
    - **e.** ____ Diaphoresis
    - **f.** ____ Decreased blood pressure
11. Identify and briefly describe the three phases of the pain experience.
    - **a.**
    - **b.**
    - **c.**
12. Define pain tolerance.
13. Briefly describe the basic concept underlying the gate control theory of pain.

14. The use of client distraction in pain control is based on the principle that:
   a. small C fibers transmit impulses via the spinothalamic tract.
   b. the reticular formation can send inhibitory signals to gating mechanisms.
   c. large A fibers compete with pain impulses to close gates to painful stimuli.
   d. transmission of pain impulses from the spinal cord to the cerebral cortex can be inhibited.
15. Identify four characteristics of acute pain.
   a.
   b.
   c.
   d.
16. Pain that has periods of remissions and exacerbations would most appropriately be described as:
   a. acute.
   b. intractable.
   c. chronic.
   d. psychosomatic.
17. List four symptoms associated with chronic pain.
   a.
   b.
   c.
   d.
18. The nurse's primary goal in caring for the client with chronic pain is to:
   a. foster feelings of hope for a cure.
   b. reduce the client's perception of pain.
   c. eliminate the source of the pain.
   d. alter the client's reaction to pain.
19. When Mr. Owens bends over the pain in his back seems to travel down his right leg. This is an example of:
   a. phantom limb pain.
   b. deep visceral pain.
   c. radiating pain.
   d. cutaneous pain.
20. Which assessment by the nurse is most likely to yield accurate information about the quality of the client's pain?
   a. "Tell me how you would rate your pain on a scale of 1 to 10."
   b. "Would you describe your pain as pricking, burning, or aching?"
   c. "Tell me what your pain feels like."
   d. "What events seemed to cause your pain?"
21. Whatever a client uses to safely and effectively relieve pain should also be tried by the nurse. (true or false)
22. Identify five potential pain relief measures.
   a.
   b.
   c.
   d.
   e.
23. Define concomitant symptom.

24. Identify the four major behavioral indicators of the effects of pain, and cite at least two examples for each indicator.
   a.
      (1)
      (2)
   b.
      (1)
      (2)
   c.
      (1)
      (2)
   d.
      (1)
      (2)
25. List three examples of coping resources that the client might utilize in dealing with pain.
   a.
   b.
   c.
26. Identify four situational factors that influence the client's pain experience.
   a.
   b.
   c.
   d.
27. State three goals appropriate to the client experiencing pain.
   a.
   b.
   c.
28. Teaching a child about painful procedures is best achieved through:
   a. early forewarning of the pain.
   b. relevant play directed toward the activities involved in the procedure.
   c. story telling about the upcoming procedure.
   d. avoiding any explanations until the pain is actually experienced.
29. Describe six general guidelines for individualizing a client's pain therapies.
   a.
   b.
   c.
   d.
   e.
   f.
30. Match the nursing measure with the principle for promoting client comfort.
   a. ____ Guided imagery
   b. ____ Application of a cold or warm compress
   c. ____ Turning a client alternately from back to sides
   d. ____ Distraction techniques
   e. ____ Encouraging fluids and fiber to avoid constipation
   f. ____ Giving a massage
   g. ____ Progressive relaxation techniques

1. Preventing pain reception
2. Lessening pain perception
3. Modifying pain reaction

31. What is TENS and how is it believed to reduce a client's pain? Transcutaneous electric nerve stimulator; stimulate larger fiber transmission, blocking smaller ones

32. Which type of pain is most likely to respond to the use of distraction?
   a. Intractable cancer pain
   b. Chronic pain of moderate intensity
   c. Acute, intense pain of short duration
   d. Chronic visceral pain

33. Which of the following actions are appropriate when using music to control pain?
   a. Encourage the client to concentrate on the music's rhythm.
   b. When pain is acute, reduce the music volume.
   c. When the client's mood is low, select music that is upbeat.
   d. Avoid selecting music based on client age and background.

34. Under certain circumstances, it is appropriate for the nurse to obtain a physician's order for relaxation therapy. (true or false)

35. The nurse has just taught a relaxation technique to a client with chronic tension headaches. The client subsequently develops a tension headache and finds that the technique is ineffective in reducing the pain. The best action by the nurse would be to:
   a. tell the client that the technique was probably done incorrectly.
   b. teach the client a new technique, since this one is ineffective.
   c. inform the client that relaxation techniques are inappropriate for tension headaches.
   d. assure the client that the technique may need to be practiced repeatedly to be effective.

36. Identify four areas to include when providing a client with anticipatory guidance concerning pain.
   a. occurrence, onset, & expected duration of pain
   b. quality, severity, & location of pain
   c. cause of pain
   d. Expectations of the client during a procedure

37. Identify six characteristics of an ideal analgesic.
   a. rapid onset
   b. effective over a prolonged time
   c. effective for all ages
   d. use orally & parenterally
   e. free of severe side effects
   f. Nonaddicting

38. Describe four major principles for the nurse to follow when administering an analgesic.
   a. Know the client's previous response to analgesics
   b. select the proper medication when more than one is ordered
   c. Know the accurate dosage
   d. assess the right time & interval for administration

39. Which principle concerning analgesic administration is correct?
   a. Injections provide longer, more sustained relief for clients with chronic pain.
   b. The same dose of a drug, when administered by a different route, will produce the same level of analgesia.
   c. The best time to administer analgesics is after the client has been active.
   d. More severe pain requires a greater amount of analgesic for relief.

40. What is PCA? Patient Control Analgesia

41. Describe three benefits of PCA.
   a. Clients have control over their pain
   b. Pain relief does not depend on nurse availability
   c. Clients tend to take less medication

42. Nursing care for clients receiving a local anesthetic includes:
   a. warning the client that loss of motor function occurs before loss of sensation.
   b. protecting the client from injury.
   c. explaining that the initial injection will be painless.
   d. encouraging the client to use the anesthetized body part.

43. Define placebo. Any treatment that produces an effect because of its intent & not its physical or chemical properties

44. The nurse may administer a placebo without the physician's order. (true or false)

45. Which of the following nursing actions would be inappropriate when administering a placebo?
   a. Promoting a relaxing environment before administration
   b. Explaining that the purpose of the placebo is to relieve pain
   c. Assessing the client's pain and evaluating the effect of the placebo
   d. Using the placebo as a way to determine the presence of genuine pain

46. The administration of a local anesthetic in the lumbosacral region of the spinal cord is known as an epidural or peridural nerve block

47. Surgically cutting the dorsal roots of a spinal nerve in order to control pain is called a posterior rhizotomy

48. A battery-powered device that blocks pain impulses through stimulation of a small, surgically implanted electrode is a:
   a. chordotomy.
   b. TENS.
   c. dorsal column stimulator.
   d. nerve block.

49. When providing analgesics to clients with the intractable pain of cancer, it is important to know that:
   a. medication addiction is high among these clients.
   b. the goal of treatment is to anticipate and minimize pain.
   c. administration of analgesics is best provided on a p.r.n. (as needed) basis.
   d. the overall goal of treatment is to cure the pain.

50. The best resource for evaluating the effectiveness of pain relief measures is the:
   a. client.
   b. nurse.

c. family member.
d. physician.

APPLICATION OF KEY CONCEPTS

Activities to reinforce skills and techniques

1. Massage techniques
   a. Practice the procedure for massage of a body part with a partner. Ask your partner to critique your performance and report subjective feelings during and following the massage.
   b. Elicit an instructor's evaluation of your massage technique.
2. Pain control techniques
   a. Observe client care in a clinic or on a nursing division where clients experiencing chronic or intractable pain receive care.
   b. Identify pain control modalities that are being used for the client. (for example, TENS, continuous morphine infusions, guided imagery, relaxation techniques)
   c. Identify the role of the nurse in applying or monitoring pain control equipment or modalities.
   d. Talk with the client concerning the pain experience, its impact on life-style, and the effectiveness of pain relief measures.
   e. Discuss your observations with your instructor.

Activities to reinforce theoretical concepts

1. Experiential exercise: personal perspectives
   a. Identify a personal experience in which you or someone you know experienced physiological pain.
   b. Describe the etiology of the pain and the individual's response to the painful stimuli.
   c. Discuss how other people (family, friends, health care providers) responded to the individual experiencing pain.
   d. Analyze how this experience has influenced your personal perspectives about pain and the pain experience.
   e. Explore how your personal perspective may influence the care you provide to clients experiencing pain.
   f. Share your analysis with your instructor for feedback.
2. Pain reception, perception, and reaction
   Using the example of stepping on a nail, trace the transmission of the pain impulse from reception through perception and reaction. (Be sure to identify the specific neurophysiological components involved.)
3. Experiential exercise: pain assessment
   a. Develop a pain assessment tool or questionnaire utilizing the guidelines provided in your text. Be sure to include:
      (1) Physical signs and symptoms (including behavioral indicators)
      (2) Descriptive pain scales
      (3) Location
      (4) Severity
      (5) Quality
      (6) Time and duration
      (7) Precipitating and aggravating factors
      (8) Relieving factors
      (9) Concomitant symptoms
      (10) Past experiences
      (11) Effects on activities of daily living
      (12) Available coping resources
   b. Identify the essential data (from the information listed above) that you would attempt to elicit if a client has acute, severe pain in an emergency room (before pain relief or reduction).
   c. Utilize the tool or questionnaire to assess a peer's or assigned client's pain.
   d. Based on the assessed data, formulate nursing diagnoses pertinent to the peer's or client's pain.
4. Clinical situation: anticipatory guidance
   Develop a teaching plan for each of the following clients requiring a venipuncture to obtain a blood specimen. Include the components of anticipatory guidance described in your text in designing a developmentally appropriate plan for a:
   a. 3-year-old toddler
   b. 9-year-old school child
   c. 22-year-old college student
5. Experiential exercise: analgesics
   a. Care for a client requiring analgesics for pain control (or review the medical records of a client experiencing pain who is receiving analgesics).
   b. Review the medical and nursing diagnoses to determine the source of the pain and variables influencing the client's reception, perception, and response.
   c. Review the medication record or Kardex to identify ordered analgesics. Prepare medication cards or papers that indicate the:
      (1) Medication classification
      (2) Indications for use
      (3) Usual dose and frequency of administration
      (4) Actions
      (5) Side and toxic effects
      (6) Antidote
      (7) Nursing implications
6. Clinical situation: pain assessment
   Mr. Williams is a carpenter who has had acute neck pain for the last 2 weeks. He describes it as "a sharp knife cutting into the muscle behind my head."
   State the questions you would ask Mr. Williams to more thoroughly assess his pain. (If possible, consider role-playing this situation with a peer and audio taping it for review and self-evaluation.)
7. Clinical situation: nursing process for pain management
   Maria Lombardo, a 32-year-old woman of Italian descent, is recovering from a cholecystectomy. She has a large abdominal dressing on the upper abdominal incision.
   Her physician has ordered the choice of a narcotic

analgesic meperidine (Demerol) to be given intramuscularly every 3 or 4 hours for severe pain or acetaminophen with codeine (Tylenol no. 3) to be given every 4 hours for mild to moderate pain. Mrs. Lombardo is to be assisted with ambulation and requires deep-breathing and coughing exercises every 2 hours.

Mrs. Lombardo is anxious "to get better," but she is also very tense and rigid when she gets up to walk. She is also reluctant to do her exercises because "it hurts too much." Her pain is described as "sharp and burning," and she also complains of a backache.

a. Develop a list of actual and potential nursing diagnoses for Mrs. Lombardo related to her current pain problem.

b. Identify the priority nursing diagnosis associated with her pain problem and formulate two short-term goals for care.

c. For each goal statement, describe at least three individualized nursing interventions and the rationale for their selection.

d. For each goal formulated, describe at least one outcome criterion to be used in evaluating the success of the plan of care.

ADDITIONAL READINGS

Baily, LM: Music's soothing charms, Am J Nurs 85:1280, 1985.

Brief discussion of music's effect on anxiety and fear associated with pain. Gives overview of responsibilities associated with use of music as a pain control treatment. Selected references cite experimental studies in which music was an effective technique for pain control.

Bast, C, and Hayes, P: Patient controlled analgesia, Nurs 86 1:25, 1986.

Brief overview of patient-controlled analgesia. Describes major benefits, placebo effects, safeguards, and major client teaching points.

DiMotto, JW: Relaxation, Am J Nurs 84:754, 1984.

Summarizes characteristics of relaxation methods and their impact on physical, cognitive, and behavioral functioning. Describes six specific relaxation methods. Information presented is useful for client care as well as the nurse's personal health-promotion activities.

Heidrich, G, and Perry, S: Helping the patient in pain, Am J Nurs 82:1828, 1982.

Describes the nursing role in pain management. Emphasizes methods for assessment and theoretical concepts to consider in selection and administration of ordered analgesics. Briefly describes alternative pain control methods.

McCaffrey, M: Relieving pain with noninvasive techniques, Nurs 80 10(12):54, 1980.

Describes three major noninvasive techniques for pain control. Includes information concerning when and how to implement these methods and the benefits to be expected by the client.

McCaffrey, M: Would you administer placebos for pain? These facts can help you decide, Nurs 82 12(2):80, 1982.

Describes common myths and misconceptions about administration of placebos. Presents circumstances in which placebos could be used and describes when and how these should be administered. Explores the legal and ethical issues surrounding placebo administration.

Moore, DE, and Blacker, HM: How effective is TENS for chronic pain? Am J Nurs 83:1175, 1983.

Discusses history and theoretical concepts underlying the use of TENS. Describes specific nursing care related to use of TENS. Discusses a study involving use of TENS by clients with chronic pain.

Rankin, MA, and Snider, B: Nurse's perceptions of cancer patient's pain, Canc Nurs 7:149, 1984.

Study of nurse's perception of pain experienced by clients with terminal or metastatic cancer. Reveals a disparity between nurses' perception that clients are receiving adequate medication and actual achievement of pain control. Points out that effective pain control may not be achieved because of the common perception that the goal of analgesia is reduction rather than relief of cancer client's pain.

Taylor, AG, et al: Duration of pain condition and physical pathology as determinants of nurses' assessment of patients in pain, Nurs Res 33:4, 1984.

Study to examine characteristic differences in manifestations of acute and chronic pain syndromes and the influence of these manifestations on nursing care. Explores the impact of client signs and symptoms on the nurse's assessment, attitudes, and pain relief actions when caring for clients in pain.

Wells, N: The effect of relaxation on postoperative muscle tension and pain, Nurs Res 31:236, 1982.

Presents a study that revealed a reduction in pain distress for postoperative clients using relaxation techniques.

Chapter 36
Oxygenation

PREREQUISITE READING

Read Chapter 36, pp. 980 to 1021.

OBJECTIVES

Mastery of content in this chapter will enable the student to:

1. Define selected terms associated with respiratory function and oxygenation.
2. Describe the gross structure and function of the respiratory system.
3. Identify processes involved in ventilation, perfusion, and exchange of respiratory gases.
4. Describe neural and chemical regulation of respiration.
5. Explain how a client's level of health, age, lifestyle, and environment can affect tissue oxygenation.
6. Identify causes and effects of hyperventilation, hypoventilation, and hypoxemia.
7. Perform a nursing assessment of the respiratory system.
8. Develop nursing diagnoses for altered oxygenation.
9. Describe nursing interventions to increase activity tolerance, maintain or promote lung expansion, promote mobilization of pulmonary secretions, maintain a patent airway, promote oxygenation, and restore cardiopulmonary function.
10. Develop evaluation criteria for a nursing care plan for the client with altered oxygenation.

REVIEW OF KEY CONCEPTS

1. Define ventilation.
2. The major inspiratory muscle is innervated by the __________________.
3. Spinal cord disruption impairing diaphragmatic function would be characterized by damage at which spinal cord level?
   - **a.** First thoracic level
   - **b.** Fourth cervical level
   - **c.** Second thoracolumbar level
   - **d.** Seventh cervical level
4. Match the activities involved in the work of breathing with the most accurate description.
   - **a.** ____ The pressure difference between the mouth and the alveoli
   - **b.** ____ The use of muscle groups to contract the lungs
   - **c.** ____ Ability of the lungs and thorax to expand
   - **d.** ____ The sternocleidomastoid group

   1. Compliance
   2. Airway resistance
   3. Active expiration
   4. Accessory muscles
5. An instrument used to measure the volume of air entering or leaving the lungs is called a __________.
6. Define perfusion.
7. The exchange of gases in pulmonary circulation occurs in the:
   - **a.** pulmonary artery.
   - **b.** pulmonary vein.
   - **c.** pulmonary capillary bed.
   - **d.** pulmonary venules.
8. Define diffusion.
9. Identify the four factors required for oxygen transport and delivery.
   - **a.**
   - **b.**
   - **c.**
   - **d.**
10. Identify and briefly describe the two regulatory mechanisms of respiration.
    - **a.**
    - **b.**
11. Match the physical condition or disease state with the mechanism affecting oxygenation.
    - **a.** ____ Fever
    - **b.** ____ Heart failure
    - **c.** ____ Anemia
    - **d.** ____ Stroke
    - **e.** ____ Rib fracture
    - **f.** ____ Hypovolemia
    - **g.** ____ Pregnancy
    - **h.** ____ Obesity
    - **i.** ____ Muscular dystrophy
    - **j.** ____ Cigarette smoking

1. Decreased oxygen-carrying capacity of the blood
2. Decreased cardiac output
3. Increased metabolism
4. Altered chest wall movement
5. Altered central nervous system function

12. Identify the three basic mechanisms contributing to anemia.
    a.
    b.
    c.
13. Anemia is characterized by:
    a. pallor and fatigue.
    b. decreased exercise tolerance.
    c. increased heart and respiratory rate.
    d. all of the above.
14. An abnormal increase in the number of erythrocytes in the blood is called ________________.
15. An abnormal condition of the vertebral column characterized by increased convexity of the thoracic spine is:
    a. pectus excavatum.
    b. kyphosis.
    c. flail chest.
    d. scoliosis.
16. The respiratory complication associated with inability to fully expand the lungs and mobilize pulmonary secretions is known as ______________.
17. Identify at least one physiological factor influencing tissue oxygenation for each developmental level listed.
    a. Premature infant
    b. Infant and toddler
    c. School-age child and adolescent
    d. Older adult
18. Living in an environment with smoking parents can have harmful effects on a child's respiratory function. (true or false)
19. List and briefly describe the five life-style factors that can influence respiratory function.
    a.
    b.
    c.
    d.
    e.
20. Define hyperventilation.
21. Hyperventilation is primarily associated with an increased respiratory rate. (true or false)
22. Identify three causes of hyperventilation.
    a.
    b.
    c.
23. List six signs and symptoms of alveolar hyperventilation.
    a.
    b.
    c.
    d.
    e.
    f.
24. Hypoventilation is best described as a state in which:
    a. the respiratory rate decreases.
    b. thoracic excursion decreases.
    c. carbon dioxide increases.
    d. inspired oxygen decreases.
25. Identify three causes of hypoventilation.
    a.
    b.
    c.
26. Briefly discuss why clients with chronic obstructive pulmonary disease (COPD) should not receive high concentrations of oxygen.
27. List five signs and symptoms of alveolar hypoventilation.
    a.
    b.
    c.
    d.
    e.
28. Define hypoxia.
29. List four major physiological conditions that can cause hypoxia.
    a.
    b.
    c.
    d.
30. List seven signs and symptoms of hypoxia.
    a.
    b.
    c.
    d.
    e.
    f.
    g.
31. Which statement concerning cyanosis is accurate?
    a. Cyanosis is an early sign of hypoxia.
    b. Cyanosis from hypoxemia is best observed in the fingernail beds.
    c. An absence of cyanosis indicates adequate oxygenation.
    d. Cyanosis is a result of desaturation of hemoglobin.
32. Define dyspnea.
33. Identify the nine areas to include in a nursing history for respiratory function.
    a.
    b.
    c.
    d.
    e.
    f.
    g.
    h.
    i.

34. Identify the five major characteristics to be included in a description of sputum.
   a.
   b.
   c.
   d.
   e.
35. A term for blood-tinged sputum is:
   a. hematemesis.
   b. hematuria.
   c. hemothorax.
   d. hemoptysis.
36. An abnormal condition in which the person must stand, sit, or use multiple pillows when lying down in order to breathe is called ________________.
37. Define wheezing.
38. Which of the following occupations could place the worker at risk for respiratory disease?
   a. Farmer
   b. Coal miner
   c. Insulation installer
   d. All of the above
39. Identify the possible cause for each of the following cardiopulmonary assessment findings.
   a. Peripheral cyanosis
   b. Dependent edema
   c. Neck vein distention
   d. Intercostal retractions
   e. Pale conjunctivae
   f. Corneal arcus
   g. Cyanotic mucous membranes
   h. Nail-bed clubbing
   i. Xanthelasma
40. Match the breathing pattern with the most accurate description provided.
   a. _____ Abnormally slow respiratory rate
   b. _____ Alternating periods of apnea and deep rapid breathing
   c. _____ Abnormally rapid, shallow breathing
   d. _____ Absence of coordinated rate or depth of respirations
   e. _____ Abnormally deep, rapid, sighing type of respiration
   f. _____ Normal respiratory rate

   1. Eupnea
   2. Tachypnea
   3. Bradypnea
   4. Kussmaul
   5. Ataxic
   6. Cheyne-Stokes
41. Describe what is meant by paradoxical breathing.
42. The sound produced by percussion over normal adult lung tissue during inspiration would be:
   a. resonance.
   b. hyperresonance.
   c. dullness.
   d. tympany.
43. Identify three conditions creating adventitious breath sounds.
   a.
   b.
   c.
44. Which of the following cardiovascular assessment findings would be considered normal?
   a. Presence of S_1 and S_2
   b. Presence of S_3 and S_4
   c. Carotid bruits
   d. Murmurs and rubs
45. The continuous measurement of capillary oxygen saturation through a cutaneous sensor is called ________________.
46. Complete the table below describing diagnostic tests used to evaluate respiratory function.

Diagnostic test	Test purpose	Nursing implications
Pulmonary function test (PFT)		
Complete blood count (CBC)		
Chest x-ray film		
Bronchoscopy		
Throat culture		
Sputum specimen		

47. What information concerning oxygenation is obtained through arterial blood gas studies?
48. State the normal hemoglobin value range for:
   a. Adult men
   b. Adult women
   c. Neonates
   d. Infants (through first 12 months)
   e. Children
49. In relation to safety, what is the most important information to present to a client before thoracentesis?
50. State the three major classifications of nursing diagnoses for clients with altered levels of oxygenation.
   a.
   b.
   c.
51. State five goals appropriate for clients with actual or potential oxygenation needs.
   a.
   b.
   c.
   d.
   e.
52. Describe selected nursing interventions used to promote and maintain adequate oxygenation by completing the following table. Include the purpose of the intervention and summarize the procedure, equipment, or supplies required.

Nursing interventions	Purpose	Procedure summary
Positioning the client		
Pursed-lip breathing		
Abdominal-diaphragmatic breathing		
Flow-oriented incentive spirometer		
Blow bottles		
Maintaining hydration		
Inserting an oral airway		

53. An acceptable postoperative inspiratory capacity for a client must equal:
a. the preoperative inspiratory volume.
b. one-half to three-fourths the preoperative volume.
c. one-fourth to one-half the preoperative volume.
d. one-eighth to one-fourth the preoperative volume.

54. What is the purpose of intermittent positive-pressure breathing?

55. A collection of air or other gas in the pleural space is a ______________.

56. The absence of fluctuation of the water level in the water-seal chamber of a chest tube may indicate that:
a. the client is lying on the tubing.
b. the tubing has been occluded by a clot.
c. the lung is reexpanded.
d. all of the above.

57. A client had a chest tube inserted for a pneumothorax 3 days ago. On entering the room, the nurse finds that there is continuous bubbling in the water-seal chamber. Which action should be taken immediately?
a. No action is required since this is an expected finding.
b. Check for any air leaks in the system.
c. Call for a chest x-ray film.
d. Clamp the tube until the physician can evaluate it.

58. Humidification is necessary for clients receiving oxygen therapy. (true or false)

59. Identify and briefly describe the three activities involved in chest physiotherapy (CPT).
a.
b.
c.

60. Chest percussion would be contraindicated in all of the following except:
a. a client with a bleeding disorder.
b. a client with osteoporosis.
c. a client with a rib fracture.
d. infants and children.

61. Vibration is contraindicated in chest physiotherapy for which age group?
a. Infants and toddlers
b. School-age children
c. Adolescents
d. Older adults

62. Vibration is performed during:
a. Inhalation
b. Exhalation
c. Either inhalation or exhalation

63. Liquification of pulmonary secretions can be achieved by all of the following except:
a. increased fluid intake.
b. inhaling humidified air.
c. chest physiotherapy.
d. nebulization.

64. In most situations, the client should be positioned so that the lung segment requiring postural drainage is:
a. dependent.
b. elevated.

65. List the three interventions used to maintain a patent airway.
a.
b.
c.

66. Describe the characteristics of coughing techniques by completing the table below.

Cough	Technique	Action/Benefits
Controlled cough		
Cascade cough		
Huff cough		
Quad cough		

67. Identify two criteria to utilize in evaluating the effectiveness of coughing.
a.
b.

68. Which principle governing suctioning techniques is correct?
a. Nasopharyngeal suctioning is indicated for clients unable to cough effectively.
b. Suction should be applied intermittently during catheter insertion.
c. Tracheal suctioning should always precede oropharyngeal suctioning.
d. The suctioning procedure should take 20 to 30 seconds.

69. What action does the nurse take to ensure that the suction catheter remains in the pharyngeal region?

70. The nurse auscultates rhonchi over an area of the left lung. To optimally suction from the left bronchus, the nurse positions the client's head:
a. to the left.
b. to the right.
c. in a neutral position.
d. forward, with chin touching the chest.

71. Clients with an artificial airway should be routinely suctioned every 1 to 2 hours. (true or false)

72. Describe the "five rights" of medication administration as they pertain to oxygen administration.
a.
b.

c.
d.
e.

73. Identify three safety measures to be instituted when a client requires oxygen administration.
   a.
   b.
   c.
74. Identify the three signs of cardiac arrest.
   a.
   b.
   c.
75. State the three goals of CPR.
   a.
   b.
   c.

APPLICATION OF KEY CONCEPTS

Activities to reinforce skills and techniques

1. Respiratory assessment
   a. Practice cardiopulmonary assessment with a partner. Validate your findings with your instructor or nursing laboratory supervisor.
   b. Record your assessment findings using correct medical terminology, and submit them to your instructor for evaluation.
   c. In any client care setting, identify individuals with normal and abnormal cardiopulmonary conditions and, with their permission, perform cardiopulmonary assessment. Confirm your findings with your instructor or other experienced staff members. Record your findings on a separate piece of paper and compare these with assessment findings reported in the client's medical record.
2. Breathing and coughing exercises
   a. Independently, or with a partner, practice the techniques of deep breathing, pursed-lip breathing, and abdominal-diaphragmatic breathing.
   b. Independently, or with a partner, practice the coughing techniques for controlled cough, cascade cough, and huff cough.
3. Incentive spirometry and blow bottles
   a. Examine the types of incentive spirometers and blow bottles used in your institution.
   b. Practice setting up incentive spirometers and blow bottles with the assistance of your instructor or laboratory supervisor.
   c. Practice using the incentive spirometers and blow bottles.
4. Care of chest tubes
   a. Examine your institution's policies concerning care of clients with chest tubes.
   b. In a clinical laboratory or hospital setting, examine equipment and supplies required by clients with chest tubes. Compare the parts of the water-seal bottle system to the Pleuravac system.
   c. With the assistance of an instructor or laboratory supervisor, practice setting up a water-seal drainage system.
   d. In the clinical setting, observe chest tube drainage systems being used by clients. Observe other staff as they monitor and provide care unique to the client with chest tubes.
5. Chest physiotherapy
   a. Observe a respiratory therapist, physical therapist, or experienced nurse administering chest physiotherapy.
   b. In the laboratory setting, practice the techniques of chest physiotherapy (percussion, vibration, postural drainage) with a partner. For the practice situation, position your partner to promote drainage from each of the following lung segments:
      (1) Left upper lobe
      (2) Right middle lobe
      (3) Posterior lower lobes
   c. Elicit an instructor's evaluation of your chest physiotherapy technique.
6. Artificial airways and suctioning technique
   a. Examine your institution's policies regarding airway management and suctioning techniques.
   b. Examine a variety of artificial airways (for example, endotracheal tubes, nasotracheal tubes, tracheal tubes, oral airways, nasal airways) provided by your instructor or available in your clinical setting.
   c. Formulate a list of all the equipment and supplies required for client airway suctioning.
   d. In the laboratory setting, practice the following techniques on a simulation mannequin:
      (1) Placement of an oral airway
      (2) Placement of a nasal airway
      (3) Oropharyngeal and nasopharyngeal suctioning
      (4) Nasotracheal suctioning
      (5) Suctioning a tracheal tube
7. Oxygen administration
   a. Examine your institution's policies regarding oxygen administration.
   b. Request a respiratory therapist, experienced respiratory care nurse, or your instructor to show you various oxygen delivery equipment and methods for setting up and changing systems.
   c. Practice setting up or changing the oxygen administration system in the laboratory setting.
   d. Observe other nursing staff as they care for clients receiving oxygen therapy. Identify actions taken that reflect the "five rights" and safety considerations associated with oxygen administration. Discuss your observations with your instructor.
8. Cardiopulmonary resuscitation
   Reading about CPR technique or limited independent practice in a laboratory setting is not adequate preparation for this lifesaving skill. It is of utmost importance that you enroll in a CPR course that provides repetition and reinforcement of the necessary psychomotor skills. This course may be offered through your nursing program, American Red Cross, or

American Heart Association. You should recertify in these skills on an annual basis.

Activities to reinforce theoretical concepts

1. Experiential exercise: Assessment of cardiopulmonary function and oxygenation
   a. Structure an assessment tool to be used specifically for clients with altered cardiopulmonary function or oxygenation (or identify the elements in the comprehensive assessment tool used by your institution that address cardiopulmonary function).
   b. Using an appropriate tool (self-developed or modified), assess a client or partner for evidence of cardiopulmonary dysfunction or diminished oxygenation levels.
   c. Request that an instructor or other experienced staff nurse confirm your cardiopulmonary assessment findings.
   d. Based on the data obtained, identify physiological factors, developmental stage, life-style, and environment that are influencing the client's respiratory state (positively or negatively).
   e. Based on the data obtained, identify actual or potential diagnoses that relate to the individual's respiratory status.
2. Experiential exercise: diagnostic tests
   a. Review a client's medical record for the presence of any laboratory or diagnostic tests associated with oxygenation and respiratory function.
   b. Determine if the findings are normal or abnormal. Identify factors that may be contributing to any abnormal findings (for example, disease process, physiological factors, developmental stage, life-style, environment). Describe how these findings may influence delivery of nursing care.
   c. Describe nursing responsibilities associated with at least two of the diagnostic tests.
3. Clinical situation: cardiopulmonary reconditioning —client education
   Mrs. Theiss is a 34-year-old homemaker who has been experiencing increased fatigue and shortness of breath with exertion. She states that she is tired all the time and seems anxious during her clinic visit. She reports no formal health maintenance behaviors. She has three children under 5 years of age. Her husband has recently been working two jobs to "make ends meet."
   The physician informs Mrs. Theiss, after examination and diagnostic testing, that there are no major physical problems contributing to her condition. The physician recommends cardiopulmonary reconditioning to assist in improving her activity tolerance.
   Structure a client teaching program for Mrs. Theiss that may assist in improving her activity tolerance. Be sure to include the major activities included in cardiopulmonary reconditioning that may be adapted to her home environment and financial situation.
4. Clinical situation: interpretation of physical findings
   Explain why cyanosis in an anemic client would reflect a more critical oxygenation problem than cyanosis in a client with polycythemia.
5. Water-seal systems
   Draw a picture of each of the water-seal systems listed below. Be sure to include the water-seal straws and water level. Label the tubes to client, to suction, or to air.
   a. One-bottle system
   b. Two-bottle system
   c. Suction–three bottle system
6. Chest physiotherapy
   Prepare a chart that illustrates the positions for postural drainage in the adult or pediatric client. Include in the chart the lung segment being treated with the appropriate client position.
7. Clinical situation: nursing process in clients with altered oxygenation
   Mr. Mathews is a 56-year-old bank manager admitted to the hospital. He states that he is having trouble "catching his breath" when he walks short distances. Occasionally he coughs and expectorates small amounts of tenacious greenish sputum. He smokes one and one-half packs of cigarettes per day.
   His thorax has bilateral chest wall movement. Vital signs are as follows: pulse, 112 beats per minute, regular, bounding; blood pressure, 168/102 mm Hg, temperature 99° F (37.2°C); respirations 28, labored, shallow, wheezy. His skin is warm and moist to the touch. He is 5 feet 10 inches tall (170 cm) and he weighs 190 pounds (86 kg).
   During the admission interview, Mr. Mathews readily attempts to answer all questions, but he has difficulty breathing when he speaks. He is unable to lie in a supine position. He indicates he has less difficulty breathing if he is sitting upright.
   a. Based on the data presented, state three nursing diagnoses related to Mr. Mathews' current respiratory state. Identify the data supporting each diagnosis.
   b. Write two goal statements for each nursing diagnosis. Identify expected outcomes that could be used to measure goal achievement.
   c. Describe nursing actions and rationale for two interventions addressing each goal.

ADDITIONAL READINGS

Duncan, CR, Erickson, RS, and Weigel, RM: Effect of chest tube management on drainage after cardiac surgery, Heart Lung 16(1):1, 1987.

Compares three methods of chest tube management on mediastinal drainage volume in postoperative cardiac surgery clients. Compares the efficacy of suction, intermittent stripping, single, and sump catheters.

Erikson, R: Chest tubes: they're really not that complicated, Nurs 81 11(5):34, 1981.

Describes chest tube management and related client care. Details physiological basis of chest tube drainage systems. Includes illustrations to clarify major points.

Gift, AD, Plant, SM, and Jacox, A: Psychologic and physiologic factors related to dyspnea in subjects with chronic obstructive pulmonary disease, Heart Lung 15(6):595, 1986.

Attempts to clarify nature of dyspnea. Describes study in which clinical manifestations of dyspnea were validated in relation to their presence and intensity. Examines physiological and psychological factors and their impact on the nature of dyspnea experienced by the client.

Hoffman, L, and Wesmiller, S: Home oxygen: transtracheal and other options, Am J Nurs 88(4):464, 1988.

Describes alternative home oxygen delivery systems. Particular attention is directed toward the transtracheal approach. Provides guidelines for nursing care of the client using transtracheal oxygen. Compares efficacy, advantages, and disadvantages of frequently used home systems.

Weaver, TE: New life for lungs . . . through incentive spirometers, Nurs 81 11(2):53, 1981.

Discusses types of incentive spirometers and mechanisms of function. Table provides guide to the 10 common brands and their characteristics. Information provided may assist in selection of the most appropriate spirometer for the client and assist in client education concerning spirometer use.

Chapter 37

Fluid, Electrolyte, and Acid-Base Balances

PREREQUISITE READING

Read Chapter 37, pp. 1022 to 1073.

OBJECTIVES

Mastery of content in this chapter will enable the student to:

1. Define selected terms associated with fluid, electrolyte, and acid-base balances.
2. Describe distribution and composition of body fluids.
3. Describe mechanisms by which body fluids move and are regulated.
4. Describe the regulation and imbalances of sodium, potassium, calcium, magnesium, chloride, bicarbonate, phosphate, and acid-base.
5. Describe the volume disturbances of dehydration and overhydration.
6. Discuss the variables affecting fluid, electrolyte, and acid-base balances.
7. Compile a nursing history and complete a physical examination for fluid, electrolyte, and acid-base balances.
8. Measure and record fluid intake and output.
9. Describe laboratory studies associated with fluid, electrolyte, and acid-base imbalances.
10. State nursing diagnoses associated with fluid, electrolyte, and acid-base imbalances.
11. Develop a nursing care plan for clients with fluid, electrolyte, and acid-base disturbance.
12. Describe fluids used for oral replacement of fluid losses.
13. Discuss the purpose of intravenous (IV) therapy.
14. Describe the different types of IV solutions.
15. Distinguish between peripheral and central venous lines.
16. Describe the procedure for initiating and maintaining an IV line.
17. Demonstrate how to calculate IV flow rate and use an infusion pump.
18. Demonstrate how to change IV solutions, tubing, and dressings and how to discontinue an infusion.
19. Discuss the complications of IV therapy.
20. Describe the blood groups and types of transfusion reactions.
21. Discuss the procedure for administering a blood transfusion and nursing actions for a transfusion reaction.

REVIEW OF KEY CONCEPTS

1. The portion of body fluids comprising the interstitial fluid and blood plasma are:
   a. intracellular.
   b. extracellular.
   c. hypotonic.
   d. hypertonic.
2. Define electrolyte.
3. List and briefly describe the four factors responsible for movement of body fluids and electrolytes.
   a.
   b.
   c.
   d.
4. The movement of body fluids and electrolytes that requires metabolic function and energy expenditure is:
   a. diffusion.
   b. osmosis.
   c. active transport.
   d. fluid pressure.
5. The pressure exerted by blood as it enters the capillaries is called:
   a. hydrostatic pressure.
   b. osmotic pressure.
6. a. A solution with the same osmotic pressure or osmolarity as blood plasma is called isotonic.
   b. A solution with a lower osmotic pressure or osmolarity than blood plasma is called hypotonic.
   c. A solution with a higher osmotic pressure or osmolarity than blood plasma is called hypertonic.
7. Briefly describe the physiological stimuli that trigger the thirst mechanism.

8. List the four organs of water loss.
   a.
   b.
   c.
   d.
9. Approximately what hourly urine output would be expected in a client weighing 55 kg?
10. Define insensible water loss.
11. For each of the hormones listed below, identify the stimuli for its release and its influence on fluid and electrolyte balance.

Hormone	Stimuli	Action
ADH		
Aldosterone		
Glucocorticoids		

12. The primary intracellular cation is:
    a. calcium.
    b. magnesium.
    c. potassium.
    d. sodium.
13. Give normal values, function, and regulatory mechanisms for the following major body electrolytes:
    a. Sodium
    b. Potassium
    c. Calcium
    d. Magnesium
    e. Chlorine
    f. Bicarbonate
    g. Phosphate
14. An increased acid component of the blood would be reflected by:
    a. an increased pH and a rising hydrogen ion concentration.
    b. a decreased pH and a falling hydrogen ion concentration.
    c. an increased pH and a falling hydrogen ion concentration.
    d. a decreased pH and a rising hydrogen ion concentration.
15. What is the normal value for an arterial blood pH?
16. Identify and describe the acid-base regulatory mechanisms for each of the following buffering systems.
    a. Chemical regulation
    b. Biological regulation
    c. Physiological regulation
17. Body pH is most rapidly regulated by:
    a. the lungs.
    b. the kidneys.
    c. biological buffering.
    d. carbonic acid–bicarbonate buffering.
18. Identify three ways in which the kidneys can regulate hydrogen ion concentration.
    a.
    b.
    c.
19. Define dehydration.
20. Match the fluid imbalance with the most accurate description or definition.
    a. _____ Isotonic extracellular fluid excess, hypervolemia
    b. _____ A loss of fluid from extracellular space, with sodium excess
    c. _____ Increased volume and dilution of extracellular fluid resulting in movement of water into the cells
    d. _____ Loss of fluid from extracellular space, without significant effect on the solutes within the plasma
    e. _____ Loss of sodium from the extracellular fluid in excess of water loss

    1. Hypernatremic dehydration
    2. Isotonic dehydration
    3. Hyponatremic dehydration
    4. Water intoxication
    5. Circulatory overload
21. List six signs of dehydration.
    a.
    b.
    c.
    d.
    e.
    f.
22. Identify three signs of circulatory overload (isotonic excess).
    a.
    b.
    c.
23. The abnormal accumulation of fluid in the interstitial spaces of the tissues is _______________.
24. For each electrolyte disturbance listed below, identify the diagnostic laboratory finding and at least four characteristic signs and symptoms.

Imbalance/Laboratory finding	Signs and symptoms
Hyponatremia	
Hypernatremia	
Hypokalemia	
Hyperkalemia	
Hypocalcemia	
Hypercalcemia	
Hypomagnesemia	
Hypermagnesemia	

25. Mr. Lusk, 65 years old, complains of stomach pains and ingests sodium bicarbonate eight times per day. For which acid-base imbalance is Mr. Lusk at risk?
    a. Respiratory acidosis
    b. Respiratory alkalosis
    c. Metabolic acidosis
    d. Metabolic alkalosis
26. Mary Ellen Wharton, 17 years old, is admitted to the hospital. Her respirations are very deep and rapid (32 per minute). She is disoriented. Her pH is 7.34 and her P_{CO_2} is 38 mm Hg. These findings are a probable indication of:

a. respiratory acidosis.
b. respiratory alkalosis.
c. metabolic acidosis.
d. metabolic alkalosis.

27. Mr. Donaldson enters the emergency room complaining of light-headedness and numbness and tingling of his extremities. Vital signs are as follows: blood pressure, 126/82; temperature, 98.6° F (37° C); pulse, 100; and respirations, 36. He states that he is "nervous and jumpy." He appears very uncomfortable and anxious. Based on the data presented, which acid-base disturbance would Mr. Donaldson most likely be experiencing?
a. Respiratory acidosis
b. Respiratory alkalosis
c. Metabolic acidosis
d. Metabolic alkalosis

28. Identify the five major factors that can affect fluid and electrolyte status:
a.
b.
c.
d.
e.

29. Briefly describe the influence of each life-style habit on fluid and electrolyte balance.
a. Diet
b. Stress
c. Exercise

30. Briefly discuss the fluid and electrolyte imbalances commonly experienced by clients in each of the following situations.
a. Following surgical trauma
b. Burns
c. Cardiovascular disorders
d. Renal disorders
e. Cancer

31. List six major categories of risk factors for fluid, electrolyte, and acid-base imbalances.
a.
b.
c.
d.
e.
f.

32. Indicate the possible fluid, electrolyte, or acid-base imbalance associated with each of the following assessment findings.
a. Weight loss
b. Irritability
c. Lethargy
d. Depressed fontanels (infant)
e. Periorbital edema
f. Sticky dry mucous membranes
g. Chvostek's sign
h. Distended neck veins
i. Dysrhythmias
j. Weak pulse
k. Low blood pressure
l. Third heart sound
m. Increased respiratory rate
n. Rales
o. Anorexia
p. Abdominal cramps
q. Poor skin turgor
r. Oliguria or anuria
s. Increased specific gravity
t. Muscle cramps, tetany
u. Hypertonicity of muscles on palpation
v. Decreased or absent deep tendon reflexes
w. Increased temperature
x. Velvety sheen to skin
y. Skin cold, clammy
z. 2^+ edema

33. Which of the following should be recorded as fluid intake?
a. Gelatin
b. Tube feedings
c. Intravenous fluids
d. All of the above

34. The nurse requires a physician's order to place a client on "intake and output." (true or false)

35. Indicate the effect of overhydration on each of the following laboratory studies, using the key provided. Key: I = increased value, D = decreased value, U = unchanged.
a. CBC
b. BUN
c. Urine specific gravity
d. Blood creatinine

36. Complete the table below comparing the differences in laboratory findings for each acid-base imbalance.

Laboratory value	Metabolic alkalosis	Metabolic acidosis	Respiratory alkalosis	Respiratory acidosis
pH				
PCO_2				
HCO_3				
K^+				

37. The laboratory test most useful in measuring kidney function is:
a. urine specific gravity.
b. blood creatinine.
c. CBC.
d. serum electrolytes.

38. What is the normal value for urine specific gravity?

39. State two goals appropriate for the client with altered fluid, electrolyte, and acid-base imbalance.
a.
b.

40. Calculate the fluid intake in metric measurements for the following meal:
a. 4 oz. tomato juice
b. 2 poached eggs
c. 2 slices bacon

d. One-half pint milk ______
e. 1 cup coffee ______
f. TOTAL ______

41. The preferred route for fluid replacement in most clients is:
a. oral.
b. nasogastric tube feedings.
c. jejunostomy feedings.
d. parenteral.

42. When a client is placed on fluid restriction, which of the following food forms would be considered fluids?
a. Ice cream
b. Ice chips
c. Liquid medications
d. All of the above

43. According to the recommendation described in the text, allocate a 1000 ml fluid restriction over a 24-hour period.
a. 0800 to 1600
b. 1600 to 2400
c. 2400 to 0800

44. State the primary goal of IV fluid administration.

45. Generally speaking, the fluids used for extracellular volume replacement are:
a. hypertonic.
b. hypotonic.
c. isotonic.

46. Which IV fluid additive would be expected when a client with normal kidney function is NPO?
a. Sodium
b. Potassium
c. Multivitamins
d. Calcium

47. Identify three groups of clients in whom venipuncture may be difficult.
a.
b.
c.

48. Briefly describe the differences between peripheral and central venous lines in relation to location, catheter size, and purpose.

49. Complete the following calculations:
a. 1000 ml D5W to run 12 hours: how many milliliters per hour?
b. 1000 NS to run over 8 hours (drop factor = 10 gtts/ml): how many drops per minute?
c. 500 ml Ringer's lactate to run over 6 hours (drop factor = 15 gtts/ml): how many drops per minute?
d. 50 ml D5W with 500 mg ampicillin to run over 30 minutes (drop factor = 60 gtts/ml): how many drops per minute?
e. 1000 ml D5W with 20 nEq KCl to run over 12 hours (drop factor = 10 gtts/ml): how many drops per minute?

50. List four factors that may affect IV flow rates.
a.
b.
c.
d.

51. Identify the two major purposes of infusion pumps.
a.
b.

52. When using volume control devices, such as a Volutrol or buret, how much fluid is routinely added to the device?
a. The total buret capacity (approximately 150 ml)
b. The total amount ordered for the shift
c. 2 hours' worth of solution
d. 1 hour's worth of solution

53. How often should a nurse routinely check on an IV infusion?
a. Every hour
b. Every 2 hours
c. Every 4 hours
d. Once per shift

54. Indicate the sequence to be followed when changing a gown of a client with an IV line.
a. ______ Place the IV bottle or bag and tubing through the sleeve of the clean gown.
b. ______ Remove the sleeve of the gown from the uninvolved arm.
c. ______ Place the uninvolved arm through the gown sleeve.
d. ______ Remove the IV bottle or bag from its stand and pass it and the tubing through the sleeve.
e. ______ Place the involved arm through the gown sleeve.
f. ______ Remove the sleeve of the gown from the involved arm.

55. Describe the instructions to be given to a client with a peripheral IV line who is able to ambulate independently.

56. What is the average infusion flow to keep the vein open (KVO)?
a. 5 ml/hr
b. 10 to 15 ml/hr
c. 25 to 50 ml/hr
d. 100 ml/hr

57. Complete the table below describing complications of IV therapy.

Complication	Assessment finding	Nursing action
Infiltration		
Phlebitis		
Fluid overload		
Bleeding		

58. List four interventions that can reduce the risk of infusion-related infections.
a.
b.
c.
d.

59. The nurse should apply disposable gloves when discontinuing an IV infusion. (true or false)

60. How long should pressure be applied to an IV site when an infusion has been discontinued?
61. Identify the three objectives for blood transfusion.
   a.
   b.
   c.
62. Complete the table below describing the major blood groups.

	Blood type			
	A	B	O	AB
Antigens present				
Antibodies produced				

63. a. The blood group of the universal donor is __________________.
   b. The blood group of the universal recipient is __________________.
64. Define autotransfusion.
65. In an emergency situation it is acceptable for the nurse to hang blood without double checking the information about the blood product and client with another registered nurse. (true or false)
66. Describe the rationale for each of the following nursing actions associated with blood transfusions.
   a. Confirm placement of an 18- or 19-gauge angiocath.
   b. Prime the tubing only with 0.9% normal saline.
   c. Ask the client if he or she has ever experienced a transfusion reaction.
   d. Obtain baseline vital signs.
   e. Begin the infusion slowly (2 ml/min) for the first 15 minutes and remain with the client.
67. The most common type of adverse reaction to blood transfusions is:
   a. febrile, nonhemolytic.
   b. allergic urticarial.
   c. hemolytic.
   d. anaphylactic.
68. List five signs and symptoms most commonly associated with transfusion reactions.
   a.
   b.
   c.
   d.
   e.
69. When a transfusion reaction is suspected in a client receiving blood, the nurse should:
   a. close the roller clamp to the blood and open the roller clamp to the 0.9% normal saline.
   b. slow the blood transfusion until the physician is notified.
   c. stop the transfusion and "piggyback" 0.9% normal saline into the IV line.
   d. continue the blood transfusion until symptoms clearly indicate a transfusion reaction.
70. How long should pressure be applied over an arterial puncture site?

APPLICATION OF KEY CONCEPTS

Activities to reinforce skills and techniques

1. Intake and output
   a. Obtain copies of the intake and output records used in your institution (or review the samples provided on pp. 178 and 179).
   b. Complete the records utilizing the information from a simulated 8-hour shift provided below.
      0730—voided 250 ml
      0800—50 ml D5W with 500 mg Keflin IVPB
      0815—1 cup coffee, 4 oz. cup juice
      0830—½ cup water
      0900—voided 300 ml
      1000—1 cup water
      1200—½ pint milk, 4 oz. cup juice, 1 cup iced tea
      1330—350 ml diarrhea
      1400—¾ cup water
      Voided 200 ml
      Hemovac drainage: 150 ml
      The infusion pump is set to deliver 100 ml/hr, and the 1400 reading indicates that 800 ml has infused since previous readings were cleared at 0600.
   c. Submit your completed I & O forms to your instructor for feedback.
2. IV calculation problems
   Complete the following calculation problems and submit them to your instructor for validation of the correct answer.
   a. 250 ml of packed cells to infuse over 2 hours (drip factor: 12 gtts/ml)
   b. 100 ml D5W with 40 mg gentamicin to infuse over 40 minutes (drip factor: 60 gtts/ml)
   c. 2500 ml D5W to infuse over 24 hours (drip factor: 10 gtts/ml)
   d. 2000 ml TPN solution to infuse over 24 hours via infusion pump. Infusion pump requires nurse to dial in the number of milliliters per hour. What is the correct setting?
   e. 450 ml of whole blood to infuse over 3 hours (drip factor: 15 gtts/ml)
3. Parenteral solution administration
   a. Review your institution's policies regarding IV fluid administration.
   b. In the nursing laboratory, or on the clinical division, examine the various types of fluids, vascular access devices, delivery systems, and equipment used for IV fluid administration.
   c. Write a list of all the equipment needed to:
      (1) Start an IV
      (2) Change IV tubing
      (3) Change an IV dressing
      (4) Discontinue an IV
   d. In the nursing laboratory practice each of the following skills using available equipment and, if

Barnes Hospital
DAILY INTAKE AND OUTPUT RECORD

B-8

17-4 Rev. 2/83

FROM 0700 / / **TO** 0700 / /

Addressograph Plate

INTAKE		OUTPUT	
Coffee mug - 180cc Ice tea container to clear line (without ice) - 250cc Ice cream container (melted) - 30cc Sherbet container (melted) - 50cc Juice container - 120cc Milk carton - 240cc Paper cup (1/4 from brim) - 240cc Soup bowl (broth) - 180cc Gelatin container (melted) - 100cc RATE GTTS/MIN. CC/HR.	ORDERS: (CIRCLE) NPO WATER CLEAR FLUIDS FULL FLUIDS AMT. DESIRED CC	SOURCE KEY: V = VOIDED C = CATHETER INC = INCONTINENT	SOURCE KEY: VOM. = VOMITUS LIQ. S. = LIQUID STOOL HV. = HEMOVAC L.T. = LEVIN TUBE T.T. = T. TUBE OTHER

	PARENTERAL			ORAL		URINE		OTHER	
TIME	SOLUTION IN BOTTLE KIND	AMT. (CC)	AMT. (CC) ABSORBED	KIND	AMT. (CC)	SOURCE	AMT. (CC)	SOURCE	AMT. (CC)
0700 0800									
0800 0900									
0900 1000									
1000 1100									
1100 1200									
1200 1300									
1300 1400									
1400 1500									
	8 HR. TOT.			**8 HR. TOT.**		**8 HR. TOT.**		**8 HR. TOT.**	
1500 1600									
1600 1700									
1700 1800									
1800 1900									
1900 2000									
2000 2100									
2100 2200									
2200 2300									
	8 HR. TOT.			**8 HR. TOT.**		**8 HR. TOT.**		**8 HR. TOT.**	
2300 2400									
2400 0100									
0100 0200									
0200 0300									
0300 0400									
0400 0500									
0500 0600									
0600 0700									
	8 HR. TOT.			**8 HR. TOT.**		**8 HR. TOT.**		**8 HR. TOT.**	
	24 HR. TOT.			**24HR. TOT.**		**24 HR. TOT.**		**24 HR. TOT.**	

B-17

BARNES HOSPITAL
24 HOUR
INTAKE AND OUTPUT SUMMARY
(Retain in Patient's Record)

STAMP ADDRESSOGRAPH PLATE HERE

		INTAKE		OUTPUT		
DATE	SHIFT	ORAL and/or TUBE FEEDING	IV (Incl. Blood and Plasma)	URINE	GASTRIC	OTHER (specify)
	07000 1500					
	1500 2300					
	2300 0700					
	TOTAL					
	07000 1500					
	1500 2300					
	2300 0700					
	TOTAL					
	07000 1500					
	1500 2300					
	2300 0700					
	TOTAL					
	07000 1500					
	1500 2300					
	2300 0700					
	TOTAL					
	07000 1500					
	1500 2300					
	2300 0700					
	TOTAL					
	07000 1500					
	1500 2300					
	2300 0700					
	TOTAL					
	07000 1500					
	1500 2300					
	2300 0700					
	TOTAL					

possible, a simulation mannequin. Have another student critique your performance and provide feedback concerning your technique.

(1) Changing the gown with an IV placed in the hand or forearm (If a mannequin is not available for this, tape the IV tubing to a partner's arm and attach the tubing to an IV bag or bottle.)

(2) Changing the IV bag or bottle but continuing to use the current tubing

(3) Changing the tubing but continuing to use the current IV fluid bottle or bag

(4) Changing the tubing and IV fluid bottle or bag at the IV catheter
(5) Changing the IV dressing

e. When you feel comfortable with the preceding skills, elicit an instructor's evaluation of your technique.
f. Observe an experienced nurse providing care to a client receiving parenteral fluids. Identify techniques that are specific to needs associated with parenteral fluid administration. Share your observations with your instructor.
g. In the nursing laboratory setting, practice the following infusion pump techniques with a partner:
(1) Setting up the pump
(2) Changing a client gown when the pump is in use
(3) Changing the IV tubing when the pump is in use
(4) Changing the flow rate on the pump
(5) Obtaining the total intake computed by the pump (if it has that capacity) and clearing the totals
(6) Responding to the various alarm modes

h. In the nursing laboratory setting, with the assistance of an instructor or laboratory supervisor, practice venipuncture techniques on an appropriate mannequin. When you have become proficient in your practice, request an opportunity to practice on a peer with the close supervision of an instructor.

4. Arterial puncture
   a. Review your institution's policies regarding arterial punctures or "sticks" with particular attention to the nursing role in this procedure.
   b. List the equipment required when assisting with an arterial puncture.
   c. Observe a qualified staff member obtaining an arterial blood sample. Be sure to interact with, and provide support to, the client. Share your observations with your instructor.
5. Blood transfusions
   a. Review your institution's policies regarding blood transfusions. Pay particular attention to the responsibilities of the nurse and compare these to the information presented in your text.
   b. In the laboratory setting, or on the clinical division, examine the equipment and supplies needed in order to transfuse a client.
   c. Observe or assist an experienced nurse caring for a client being transfused. Share your observations with your instructor.

Activities to reinforce theoretical concepts

1. Experiential exercise: monitoring fluid, electrolyte, and acid-base balance
   a. Perform a comprehensive assessment of an assigned client, or obtain the assessment data from the medical record, using a standard or self-developed form. (If it is not feasible to do this on an actual client, select a peer, friend, or family member as your "client.")
   b. Identify variables that influence the client's fluid, electrolyte, and acid-base balance.
   c. Identify factors in the health history that indicate that the client may be at risk for fluid, electrolyte, or acid-base disturbance. Describe why these place the client at risk.
   d. Identify signs and symptoms from your assessment that indicate that there is an actual or potential fluid, electrolyte, or acid-base disturbance.
   e. Review the medical records to identify pertinent laboratory data reflecting the client's current fluid, electrolyte, and acid-base status. Analyze whether these data are normal. If they are abnormal, attempt to determine the factors contributing to these findings.
   f. From the information obtained, describe specific nursing interventions for the client that relate to his or her fluid, electrolyte, or acid-base status.
2. Clinical situation: blood transfusions
   Mrs. Smith is receiving her second unit of whole blood when she demonstrates signs of an acute hemolytic transfusion reaction.
   a. List at least seven signs and symptoms that Mrs. Smith may demonstrate.
   b. List, in priority order, the actions you would take as Mrs. Smith's nurse.
3. Clinical situation: acid-base imbalance
   Ms. English, 22 years old, was admitted to the hospital because of repeated episodes of fainting while at work. While completing her nursing history, Ms. English tells the nurse she has been trying to lose weight. Her diet consists mostly of black coffee, diet cola, and some vegetables. She admits to taking a "water pill" the past two mornings and evenings.
   a. What is the most likely acid-base disturbance described in this situation?
   b. List the assessment criteria that support your conclusion.
   c. What additional data would you wish to obtain in order to better care for Ms. English?
   d. Identify at least three interventions specific to the acid-base disturbance identified.
4. Clinical situation: nursing process for clients with fluid and electrolyte imbalance
   Ms. Wanda Marconi, 16 years old, is admitted to the hospital after experiencing severe vomiting and diarrhea for the past 3 days. The onset of these symptoms was sudden. During the initial nursing assessment, Wanda states that she has had "a couple of glasses of ginger ale in the past few days but neither of them stayed down." She states she has been having loose green liquid stools every 2 or 3 hours accompanied by cramps.

   On admission, Wanda was able to void 75 ml of concentrated dark amber urine for a urinalysis; the specific gravity was 1.030. Her skin turgor is poor. Her lips are dry and cracked. Her tongue is covered with a white-gray coating. She says she is thirsty but is afraid to drink anything. Vital signs are as follows: temperature, 99° F (37.2° C); pulse, 116; respirations, 28 and shallow; blood pressure, 104/62 supine and 90/50 sitting.

a. What fluid, electrolyte, and acid-base disturbances are present or potentially exist in the client? Support your answer with the assessment data provided.

b. Identify laboratory data that you would review to gain a clearer understanding of the client's condition.

c. Formulate nursing diagnoses that relate to the client's fluid, electrolyte, or acid-base status.

d. For the primary diagnosis, identify three nursing goals.

e. For each goal, describe at least two interventions.

ADDITIONAL READINGS

Folk-Lightly, M: Solving the puzzles of patient's fluid imbalance, Nurs 84 14:34, 1984.

Describes assessment parameters specific to fluid balance. Provides guidance for interpretation of findings. Summarizes major fluid imbalances, their etiology, and nursing care.

Jones, S: New IV catheters that can do it all, RN 48:20, 1985.

Gives overview of latest technology available in intravenous access devices.

Messner, RL, and Gorse, GJ: Nursing management of peripheral intravenous sites, Focus Crit Care 14(2):25, 1987.

Analyzes research related to peripheral IV infections. Describes common factors predisposing clients to peripheral IV infection, characteristic manifestations, and preventive care techniques. Tables summarize essential steps in infection prevention and the related rationale.

Metheny, NM: Quick reference to fluid balance, Philadelphia, 1984, J.B. Lippincott Co.

A practical handbook that summarizes fluid and electrolyte disturbances. Overview of normal physiological mechanisms for fluid and electrolyte balance, common causes of imbalance, and nursing responsibilities related to client management. Special chapters are devoted to the fluid and electrolyte disturbances associated with specific disease states.

Metheny, NM: Overview of fluid and electrolyte balance: nursing considerations, Philadelphia, 1987, J.B. Lippincott Co.

An excellent, clear presentation of a complex and often confusing clinical topic. A comprehensive reference describing the normal regulation of fluids and electrolytes, and balance disturbances. Includes nursing assessment and care from a developmental perspective. Describes specific nursing care unique to each fluid or electrolyte disturbance. Discusses many special topics related to maintenance of fluid and electrolyte balance, including parenteral therapy and nutritional support. Also addresses fluid and electrolyte imbalance associated with disease states and treatment modalities.

Querin, J, and Stahl, L: Twelve simple steps for successful blood transfusions, Nurs 83 13(11):34, 1983.

A continuing-education program article. Describes step-by-step guidelines for safe blood transfusions. Includes tables that compare various transfusion products, including their description, indications for use, equipment required for transfusion, administration techniques, and special considerations in administration. Also includes a chart comparing the causes, onset, clinical manifestations, and nursing actions appropriate for transfusion reactions.

Smith, LG: Reactions to blood transfusions, Am J Nurs 84:1096, 1984.

An excellent resource for clinical practice. Provides a detailed table comparing possible transfusion reactions. Includes a summary of characteristic signs and symptoms, pathophysiological mechanisms, laboratory findings, differential diagnosis, management, and prevention.

Chapter 38
Urinary Elimination

PREREQUISITE READING

Read Chapter 38, pp. 1074 to 1115.

OBJECTIVES

Mastery of content in this chapter will enable the student to:

1. Define selected terms associated with urinary elimination.
2. Explain the function of each organ in the urinary system.
3. Describe the process of urination.
4. Identify factors that commonly influence urinary elimination.
5. Compare and contrast common alterations in urinary elimination.
6. Obtain a nursing history for a client with urinary elimination problems.
7. Identify nursing diagnoses appropriate for clients with alterations in urinary elimination.
8. Obtain urine specimens.
9. Describe characteristics of normal and abnormal urine.
10. Describe the nursing implications of common diagnostic tests of the urinary system.
11. Discuss nursing measures to promote normal micturition.
12. Describe nursing measures to reduce episodes of incontinence.
13. Insert a urinary catheter.
14. Discuss nursing measures to reduce urinary tract infection.
15. Irrigate a urinary catheter.

REVIEW OF KEY CONCEPTS

1. List and summarize the function of each organ in the urinary system.
   a.
   b.
   c.
   d.
2. The functional unit of the kidney responsible for the formation of urine is the ________________.
3. All of the following substances are normally filtrated through the glomerulus except:
   a. protein.
   b. glucose.
   c. creatine.
   d. electrolytes.
4. All the substances filtered through the glomeruli are excreted as urine. (true or false)
5. Renal alterations may be indicated by a urinary output of:
   a. 1500 ml in 24 hours.
   b. 1800 ml in 24 hours.
   c. 60 ml per hour.
   d. 25 ml per hour.
6. Excessive urination at night is called __________.
7. The process by which urine is expelled from the urinary bladder is called:
   a. urination.
   b. micturition.
   c. voiding.
   d. all of the above.
8. Number the steps describing the normal act of micturition in their correct order.
   a. ______ Parasympathetic impulses from micturition center cause detrusor muscle to begin contracting.
   b. ______ External bladder sphincter relaxes.
   c. ______ Impulses travel to cerebral cortex, making the person conscious of the need to void.
   d. ______ Detrusor muscle contracts.
   e. ______ Internal urethral sphincter relaxes, allowing urine to enter urethra.
   f. ______ Urine passes through urethral meatus.
   g. ______ Volume of urine stretches bladder walls, sending impulses to spinal cord.
9. Full control of micturition generally occurs at age:
   a. 12 to 16 months.
   b. 18 to 24 months.
   c. 2 to 3 years.
   d. 4 to 5 years.
10. The process of aging causes all of the following changes in urination except:
    a. increased concentration of urine.
    b. loss of bladder tone.
    c. increased frequency.
    d. urinary retention.

11. Briefly explain how each of the following factors can influence urinary elimination.
    a. Anxiety
    b. Childbirth
    c. Long-term use of indwelling catheter
    d. Increased fluid intake
    e. Diabetes mellitus
    f. Narcotic analgesics
12. The accumulation of urine in the bladder with the inability of the bladder to empty fully is ________________.
13. What are the mechanisms associated with "retention with overflow"?
14. List three factors that may cause urinary retention.
    a.
    b.
    c.
15. The most common cause of infection in the urinary tract is:
    a. poor perineal hygiene.
    b. bladder distention.
    c. instrumentation.
    d. sexual intercourse.
16. Blood-tinged urine is described as ____________.
17. List six signs or symptoms of urinary tract infections.
    a.
    b.
    c.
    d.
    e.
    f.
18. The loss of control over micturition is called ________________.
19. Define enuresis.
20. Match the types of urinary incontinence with the most accurate definition or description.
    a. ______ Involuntary passage of urine following a strong sense of the urge to void
    b. ______ Involuntary passage of urine when a specific bladder volume is reached
    c. ______ Strong urge to void, causing loss of urine before reaching appropriate facilities
    d. ______ Constant flow of urine at unpredictable times, unawareness of bladder filling or emptying
    e. ______ Dribbling of urine with coughing, laughing, vomiting, or lifting

    1. Total
    2. Functional
    3. Stress
    4. Urge
    5. Reflex
21. What is a urinary diversion?
22. The urinary diversion in which the end of one or both ureters are brought to the abdominal surface is called:
    a. an ileal loop.
    b. an ileal conduit.
    c. urethral fistula.
    d. ureterostomy.
23. List the three major factors to be explored during a nursing history concerning urinary elimination.
    a.
    b.
    c.
24. Match the common symptoms of urinary alterations with the correct description.
    a. ______ Voiding at frequent intervals
    b. ______ Leakage of urine despite voluntary control of urination
    c. ______ Difficulty initiating urination
    d. ______ Diminished urinary output
    e. ______ Painful or difficult urination
    f. ______ Feeling of the need to void immediately
    g. ______ Voiding a large amount of urine

    1. Urgency
    2. Dysuria
    3. Frequency
    4. Hesitancy
    5. Polyuria
    6. Oliguria
    7. Dribbling
25. List six factors affecting urination that need to be summarized during a nursing history assessing urinary elimination.
    a.
    b.
    c.
    d.
    e.
    f.
26. Which of the following is the best description of the normal bladder?
    a. Normally nonpalpable; when distended feels smooth and rounded
    b. Normally palpable just below symphysis pubis; feels smooth and rounded
    c. Normally nonpalpable; palpation may cause urge to urinate; when distended feels smooth and rounded
    d. Normally palpable; palpation causes urge to urinate
27. What physical examination technique may be used to assess the presence of kidney infection or inflammation?
28. A congenitally formed opening of the urethra on the undersurface of the penis is called ____________.
29. The scale on the outside of a urinary drainage bag may be used for accurate volume measurement. (true or false)
30. When urine is red, it is appropriate to assume that the client has hematuria. (true or false)
31. A sterile urine specimen may be collected from a urinary drainage bag. (true or false)

32. Which of the following assessment findings would be characteristic of normal urine?
   a. Clear, straw colored, and aromatic
   b. Pink tinged, clear, and aromatic
   c. Dark amber, clear, and smelling of ammonia
   d. Cloudy, thick, and smelling of ammonia
33. When a clean voided specimen is collected, the nurse follows all of the following principles except:
   a. send to the laboratory within 15 minutes, or refrigerate the specimen.
   b. collect a midstream specimen.
   c. discard the first specimen and obtain a second specimen in 30 to 45 minutes.
   d. wash the urethral meatus of the female from above urethral orifice toward anus.
34. Which technique would be appropriate for obtaining a sterile specimen from an indwelling retention catheter?
   a. Clamp the tubing just above the site chosen for withdrawal.
   b. Cleanse the catheter with soap and water before obtaining the specimen.
   c. Insert the needle at a 90-degree angle.
   d. Use a small gauge (no. 23 or 25) needle on a sterile syringe.
35. Briefly describe the method for obtaining a timed urine collection.
36. Which measurement would be considered a normal value in a routine urinalysis?
   a. pH of 5.6
   b. Specific gravity of 1.035
   c. Protein of 10 mg/100 ml
   d. Glucose of 2^+
37. An accurate measurement of urinary glucose and ketones always requires a double-voided specimen. (true or false)
38. Which of the following diagnostic tests allows direct visualization of the urinary structures?
   a. IVP (intravenous pyelogram)
   b. Renal scan
   c. Cystoscopy
   d. All of the above
39. Identify four nursing interventions appropriate for the client following cystoscopy.
   a.
   b.
   c.
   d.
40. State four goals appropriate for promoting normal urinary elimination for the client.
   a.
   b.
   c.
   d.
41. List five techniques that may be used to stimulate the micturition reflex.
   a.
   b.
   c.
   d.
   e.
42. Describe two pelvic floor (Kegel) exercises.
   a.
   b.
43. A client with urge incontinence is likely to benefit most from:
   a. catheterization.
   b. diuretics.
   c. anticholinergic medications.
   d. cholinergic medications.
44. The physician has ordered bethanechol (Urecholine) for a client with retention and overflow incontinence. Nursing actions to enhance the effectiveness of the medication include:
   a. administration immediately after voiding.
   b. administration immediately before micturition.
   c. administration 3 or 4 hours after last voiding.
   d. restriction of oral fluids.
45. State the goal of bladder retraining.
46. Match the client situation with the most appropriate type of catheterization.
   a. ____ Mr. Powers received 10 mg of morphine every 4 hours for the past 12 hours. His bladder is palpable, but he cannot void.
   b. ____ Ms. Spencer lives in a nursing home. She cannot sense the need to void. She has severe excoriation of her perineum.
   c. ____ Ms. Pine enters the clinic with a high fever. Her doctor suspects urinary infection and orders a specimen. Ms. Pine is unable to void.
   d. ____ Mr. Ahrens is admitted to the hospital with severe congestive heart failure. In order to treat his fluid volume overload, the physician requests that the nurses monitor his intake and output hourly.

   1. Intermittent catheterization
   2. Indwelling catheterization
47. Indicate the catheter size appropriate for:
   a. Children
   b. Women
   c. Men
48. To ensure easy insertion of a urinary catheter into a male client, the best technique would include:
   a. Lowering the penis and introducing the catheter as the client bears down to void.
   b. lifting the penis perpendicular to the body and asking the client to breathe deeply.
   c. lifting the penis perpendicular to the body, applying light traction, and asking the client to bear down.
   d. holding the penis at a 45-degree angle to the body and applying light traction.

49. When urine flows out of the end of a retention catheter during insertion, how much further should it be advanced?
 a. 2.5 cm
 b. 5 cm
 c. 7.5 cm
 d. 10 cm

50. The nurse should never raise a drainage bag and tubing above the level of the client's bladder. (true or false)

51. All of the following would be routine methods for maintaining the patency of the urinary drainage system except:
 a. irrigating the tubing using sterile saline.
 b. checking for kinks or bends in the tubing.
 c. avoiding positioning the client on the drainage tubing.
 d. observing for clots or sediment that may occlude the collecting tubing.

52. State two important principles to follow when removing an indwelling catheter.
 a.
 b.

53. It is normal for the client to experience dysuria immediately following removal of an indwelling catheter. (true or false)

54. Describe a suprapubic catheter.

55. Identify two precautions that should be taken to ensure client safety and comfort when using a condom catheter.
 a.
 b.

56. Identify three general measures to prevent urinary tract infection in clients without indwelling urinary catheters.
 a.
 b.
 c.

57. Describe six ways to minimize the risk of urinary tract infection in catheterized clients.
 a.
 b.
 c.
 d.
 e.
 f.

58. All of the following would be appropriate foods for acidifying the urine in order to inhibit growth of microorganisms except:
 a. orange or grapefruit juice.
 b. meats and eggs.
 c. whole grain breads.
 d. cranberries and plums.

59. A physician's order is required for catheter irrigations. (true or false)

60. A client with a ureterostomy is at risk for all of the following problems except:
 a. skin breakdown.
 b. fluid and electrolyte alterations.
 c. body image alterations.
 d. bladder infections.

61. What is the best way to remove urine from the skin?

APPLICATION OF KEY CONCEPTS

Activities to reinforce skills and techniques

1. Obtaining urine specimens
 a. Review your institution's procedures for obtaining routine urinalysis, clean voided specimens, timed (24-hour) collections, and specimens for glucose and acetone. Locate the needed equipment for collection and laboratory requisitions (or computer menu) on your clinical division.
 b. Obtain a sample of your own urine and practice each of these skills in the laboratory setting: specific gravity, Keto-Diastix, Multistix. Have an instructor or laboratory supervisor validate your findings.
 c. In the laboratory setting, using indwelling catheter demonstration equipment, practice the technique for obtaining a sterile specimen from a catheter. Have another student observe and critique your performance. Elicit an instructor's evaluation of your technique.

2. Use of bedpans and urinals
 a. In the nursing laboratory, or on the clinical division, examine the various types of bedpans and urinals available in your institution. Review institutional procedures regarding distribution and cleaning of these items.
 b. In the nursing laboratory, practice assisting a partner on and off a regular and orthopedic (fracture) bedpan.

3. Urinary catheterization
 a. Review your institution's procedure for intermittent and indwelling catheterization.
 b. Examine equipment used for catheterization insertion, drainage, and maintenance in your nursing laboratory or on the clinical division.
 c. In the nursing laboratory, using demonstration mannequins or models (male and female), practice the techniques of intermittent catheterization and indwelling catheterization. Have another student observe and critique your performance. Elicit an instructor's evaluation of your technique.
 d. In the nursing laboratory, using a demonstration mannequin or model, practice removing an indwelling catheter. Have another student observe and critique your performance. Elicit an instructor's evaluation of your technique.
 e. In the nursing laboratory, using a demonstration mannequin or model, practice the techniques of perineal care and catheter care.
 f. In the nursing laboratory, tape a urinary catheter to the leg of a partner and attach the catheter to a urinary drainage bag. Practice each of the follow-

ing techniques: turning and positioning in bed, dangling, moving from bed to wheelchair, ambulation. Be sure to monitor the level of the drainage bag, tube patency, and the tension on the tubing during these maneuvers.

g. In the nursing laboratory, using a demonstration mannequin or model, practice application of a condom catheter.

Activities to reinforce theoretical concepts

1. Trace the formation and flow of urine from the glomerulus to the urethra.

2. Clinical situation: urinary tract infection
Ms. Giles is a 58-year-old woman with a lower urinary tract infection. She is alert and reports no other acute or chronic health problems.

a. Describe normal physiological mechanisms that prevent urinary tract infections.

b. Describe the criteria to be used in collecting a nursing history on Ms. Giles.

c. Identify the signs and symptoms that would be expected for a lower urinary tract infection.

d. What laboratory examinations would you expect to be ordered for Ms. Giles? What results would indicate a urinary tract infection?

e. Formulate a discharge teaching plan for Ms. Giles that is directed toward prevention of future urinary tract infections.

3. Clinical situation: diagnostic examinations
Mr. Kent is a 58-year-old business executive with a long history of pipe smoking and recent onset of lower abdominal discomfort and hematuria. He has entered the hospital for diagnostic studies to determine the source of his symptoms.

a. The physician has ordered lower GI studies, including a barium enema, and an IVP. Which test should be scheduled first? Why?

b. What is the purpose of an IVP?

c. Describe at least five nursing responsibilities before the procedure.

d. What responsibilities does the nurse have during the IVP? (Name at least two.)

e. What specific nursing interventions are appropriate when Mr. Kent returns from the IVP?

4. Experiential exercise: pelvic floor exercises

a. Develop a teaching tool (chart, table, paper, pamphlet, booklet) to assist clients in learning pelvic floor (Kegel) exercises.

b. Practice these exercises yourself, following the directions in the teaching tool.

c. Practice explaining or teaching these exercises to a partner (or audio tape for practice and self-evaluation).

d. Submit your teaching tool to your instructor for feedback before using in an actual client education situation.

5. Clinical situation: bladder retraining
Mrs. Sharp is a 37-year-old woman who sustained a bladder injury during a traumatic childbirth 3 months ago. Since that time she has experienced problems initiating voiding and urge incontinence. Formulate a bladder retraining program for this client.

6. Clinical situation: nursing process for clients with alteration in urinary elimination
Mrs. Pender is a 63-year-old woman with urinary retention. Her problem developed 1 year ago after having surgery for a vaginal tumor. Mrs. Pender is a highly anxious person and becomes embarrassed when outflow of urine accidentally occurs. She states that this problem has caused her to curtail all social activities and prevents her from attending church services. She also suffers from degenerative arthritis and has pain in her knees with joint motion.

a. List actual and potential nursing diagnoses associated with Mrs. Pender's elimination problem.

b. Identify one goal for each of the top two priority nursing diagnoses.

c. For each goal, describe at least three interventions. (State the rationale for the interventions selected.)

ADDITIONAL READINGS

Bielski, M: Preventing infection in the catheterized patient, Nurs Clin North Am 15:703, 1980.
Explores factors associated with nosocomial urinary tract infections. Discusses pathophysiology, epidemiology, and strategies for control and prevention of urinary tract infection.

Burgener, S: Justification of closed intermittent urinary catheter irrigation/instillation: a review of current literature and practice, J Adv Nurs 12:229, 1987.
Reviews current literature on pathogenesis of urinary tract infection, catheter irrigation techniques, and specific outcomes. Based on findings cited, recommends use of closed system technique in both catheter irrigations and instillations.

Demnerle, B, and Bantol, MA: Nursing care of the incontinent person, Geriatr Nurs 1:246, 1980.
Describes practical approaches in caring for incontinent clients based on levels of physical and mental functioning. Explores information to incorporate in a data base for development of a care plan aimed at prevention and management of incontinence.

Erickson, PJ: Ostomies: the art of pouching, Nurs Clin North Am 22:311, 1987.
Describes practical approaches for the technique of pouching a stoma. Information useful for students as well as more experienced nurses. Information presented may be easily incorporated into a client teaching plan.

Mandelstam, D: Strengthening pelvic floor muscles, Geriatr Nurs 1:251, 1980.
Gives overview of the physiological mechanisms of voiding. Describes pelvic floor exercises. Provides information to include when developing a written or verbal teaching plan for clients.

Petillo, MH, editor: Enterostomal therapy, Nurs Clin North Am 22(2), 1987.
A series of articles addressing urinary and intestinal ostomy therapy. Includes specific information about management of urinary and intestinal ostomies. Discusses special topics applicable to ostomy clients including devel-

opmental implications of an ostomy, psychosocial considerations, sexuality, and skin care.

Petillo, MH: The patient with a urinary stoma, Nurs Clin North Am 22:261, 1987.

Detailed discussion of specific nursing care measures appropriate for clients with a urinary stoma.

Wilde, MH: Living with a Foley, Am J Nurs 86:1121, 1986.

Describes variations in technique required when a client has a long-term indwelling urinary catheter. Makes specific recommendations for procedure modification appropriate to the home setting.

Chapter 39
Bowel Elimination

PREREQUISITE READING

Read Chapter 39, pp. 1116 to 1153.

OBJECTIVES

Mastery of content in this chapter will enable the student to:

1. Define selected terms associated with bowel elimination.
2. Discuss the role of gastrointestinal organs in digestion and elimination.
3. Describe four functions of the large intestine.
4. Explain the physiology of normal defecation.
5. List and discuss psychological and physiological factors that influence the elimination process.
6. Describe common physiological alterations in elimination.
7. Assess a client's elimination pattern.
8. Perform a guaiac test for occult blood.
9. List nursing diagnoses related to alterations in elimination.
10. Describe nursing implications for common diagnostic examinations of the gastrointestinal tract.
11. Administer an enema.
12. List nursing measures aimed at promoting normal elimination.
13. Discuss the relationship between the structure and function of a colostomy and nursing care required.

REVIEW OF KEY CONCEPTS

1. Briefly list and describe the four functions of the colon.
   a.
   b.
   c.
   d.
2. The medical term for intestinal gas is ________.
3. Waste products reaching the sigmoid portion of the colon are called ________.
4. Permanent dilations of the rectal veins are called ________.
5. Indicate the correct sequence of mechanisms involved in normal defecation.
   a. ____ Increased intraabdominal pressure or the Valsalva maneuver occurs.
   b. ____ The external sphincter relaxes.
   c. ____ The internal sphincter relaxes, and awareness of the need to defecate occurs.
   d. ____ The levator ani muscles relax.
   e. ____ Sensory nerves are stimulated via rectal distention.
6. Describe the Valsalva maneuver.
7. List six changes occurring in the GI system of the aging adult that impair normal digestion and elimination.
   a.
   b.
   c.
   d.
   e.
   f.
8. What mechanism causes high-fiber diets to promote elimination?
9. Identify four types of foods considered high in fiber.
   a.
   b.
   c.
   d.
10. General anesthesia and surgery tend to stimulate peristalsis. (true or false)
11. Describe the effect of each medication on elimination.
    a. Mineral oil
    b. Dicyclomine hydrochloride (Bentyl)
    c. Narcotics
    d. Anticholinergics (atropine, glycopyrrolate)
    e. Antibiotics
12. Chronic use of cathartics can make the large intestine less responsive to laxatives. (true or false)
13. What treatment would be anticipated in a client who has had a barium examination procedure?
14. All of the following describe constipation except:
    a. it is a symptom.
    b. it is a decrease in frequency of bowel movements.
    c. it is passage of hard, dry stools.
    d. it is the inability to have a daily bowel movement.
15. Identify and briefly describe four causes of constipation.
    a.
    b.
    c.
    d.

16. Identify three groups of clients in whom constipation could pose a significant health hazard.
a.
b.
c.

17. How can the Valsalva maneuver be avoided?

18. Define fecal impaction.

19. List four signs and symptoms of fecal impaction.
a.
b.
c.
d.

20. Define diarrhea.

21. Identify the two major complications associated with diarrhea.
a.
b.

22. Mr. Wilms had an appendectomy 2 days ago. He currently complains of abdominal pain and shortness of breath. The nurse observes abdominal distention. The most likely cause of Mr. Wilms' current condition is:
a. increased peristalsis.
b. flatulence.
c. constipation.
d. slowed esophageal emptying.

23. An artificial opening in the abdominal wall is called a ________________.

24. A surgical opening formed from the ileum to the abdominal wall is an ________________.

25. A surgical opening formed from the colon to the abdominal wall is a ________________.

26. Feces with the most normal consistency and appearance would be expected from:
a. an ileostomy.
b. a sigmoid colostomy.
c. a transverse colostomy.
d. an ascending colostomy.

27. Colostomy and ileostomy clients have similar needs. Which need would be unique to the management of a client with an ileostomy?
a. Skin care
b. Monitoring of electrolytes
c. Promoting body image
d. Encouraging a low-fiber diet

28. List eight factors to be included in a nursing history for clients with altered elimination status.
a.
b.
c.
d.
e.
f.
g.
h.

29. The nurse auscultates the abdomen for bowel sounds before performing palpation because:
a. the action minimizes the client's anxiety.
b. it is less intrusive than palpation.
c. palpation may change the frequency of bowel sounds.
d. palpation may alter the location of bowel sounds.

30. Identify the possible cause for each of the following abdominal assessment findings.
a. Increased pitch or "tinkling" bowel sounds
b. Hypoactive or absent bowel sounds
c. Hyperactive bowel sounds
d. Percussion of tympanic sounds
e. Percussion of dull sounds

31. To increase client comfort by relaxing the anal sphincter during rectal examination, the nurse instructs the client to:
a. bear down.
b. deep breathe.
c. pant.
d. hold breath.

32. For each of the fecal characteristics below, indicate the possible cause.
a. White or clay colored
b. Black or tarry
c. Melena
d. Liquid consistency
e. Narrow, pencil shaped

33. Nurses should wear disposable gloves when handling specimens. (true or false)

34. Mr. Rogers has been receiving an anticoagulant (Coumadin) for a clotting disorder. The nurse notes that Mr. Rogers' stools appear darker. The test most likely to be ordered for Mr. Rodgers would be a:
a. sigmoidoscopy.
b. stool for guaiac.
c. proctoscopy.
d. stool for culture.

35. a. State three risk factors for colon cancer.
(1)
(2)
(3)
b. Identify two warnings signs of colon cancer.
(1)
(2)

36. Which diagnostic examination requires that the client remain NPO before the test?
a. Sigmoidoscopy
b. Guaiac
c. Gastroscopy
d. Proctoscopy

37. List four nursing interventions appropriate for clients following gastroscopy.
a.
b.
c.
d.

38. Identify five goals appropriate for clients with elimination problems.
a.
b.

c.
d.
e.

39. Identify three ways to promote regular bowel habits in the hospitalized client.
a.
b.
c.

40. The proper technique for positioning a client on a bedpan includes:
a. Place client high in bed, raise head 30 degrees, assist client in bending knees and lifting hips upward.
b. Place client high in bed, position head of bed flat, instruct client to bend knees and raise hips.
c. Place client low in bed, elevate head 30 degrees, instruct client to extend back and raise hips.
d. Raise head of bed 30 degrees, roll client to side, place pan over buttocks, roll client to supine position.

41. When is the best time to administer cathartic suppositories?

42. Match the laxative classification to its primary action.
a. ______ Intestinal mucosa is irritated to increase motility.
b. ______ Osmotic effect increases pressure in bowel to stimulate peristalsis.
c. ______ High fiber content absorbs water and increases intestinal bulk.
d. ______ Fecal contents are coated, allowing for easier passage.
e. ______ Detergents lower surface tension of feces, allowing penetration of water and fat.

1. Bulk forming
2. Emollient (wetting)
3. Saline
4. Stimulant cathartics
5. Lubricants

43. The safest solution to use for repeated enemas would be:
a. tap water.
b. saline.
c. soapsuds.
d. sterile water.

44. Which enema would be ordered to provide relief from gaseous distention?
a. Carminative (MGW)
b. Medicated (Kayexalate)
c. Oil retention
d. Soapsuds

45. What height would be appropriate for elevation of the enema bag or bottle for a cleansing enema?
a. 12 inches or less above the hips
b. 12 to 18 inches above the hips
c. 18 to 24 inches above the hips
d. Slightly below the hips

46. What is the meaning of the order "enemas 'til clear"?

47. It is acceptable to give an enema while the client is seated on the toilet. (true or false)

48. The most appropriate action to take when a client complains of abdominal cramping during an enema would be to:
a. remove the rectal tube.
b. encourage the client to change positions.
c. temporarily lower the container or clamp the tubing.
d. take no action (this is expected).

49. A physician's order is necessary for the nurse to remove a fecal impaction. (true or false)

50. Why is it necessary to assess a client's heart rate when digitally removing stool?

51. Identify five factors to consider when selecting a pouching system for an ostomate.
a.
b.
c.
d.
e.

52. A nurse with special education in the care of clients with an ostomy is called an ________________.

53. Which observation about a sigmoid colostomy would be abnormal?
a. Intermittent passage of gas and formed stool
b. Shiny stoma appearance
c. Mucous drainage from the stoma
d. Dark purple stoma color

54. List six contraindications to colostomy irrigation.
a.
b.
c.
d.
e.
f.

55. Describe two exercises for prevention of constipation in the bedridden client.
a.
b.

56. The most effective means of local heat application for painful hemorrhoids would be:
a. warm soaks.
b. sitz baths.
c. a heating pad.
d. a heat lamp.

57. A client is experiencing discomfort from postoperative flatulence. Which actions will assist in decreasing flatus or promoting its escape?
a. Drinking soda
b. Sucking on hard candy
c. Maintaining a right, side-lying position
d. Ambulation

58. Baby powder or cornstarch offers effective skin protection for debilitated, incontinent clients. (true or false)

59. Describe four interventions that may assist in re-

storing self-concept in a client with bowel elimination problems.
a.
b.
c.
d.

60. Mr. Clancy has an ascending colostomy. What information would be appropriate to include in his individualized teaching plan?
   a. Techniques for colostomy irrigation
   b. Daily use of stool softeners
   c. Skin care and pouching techniques
   d. Activity and exercise restrictions

APPLICATION OF KEY CONCEPTS

Activities to reinforce skills and techniques

1. Obtaining stool specimens
   a. Review your institution's procedures for obtaining the following stool specimens: guaiac stools, stools for ova and parasites, fecal fat.
   b. Obtain a Hemoccult slide testing kit from your nursing laboratory and practice a guaiac test on your own stool sample.
2. Positioning for bowel elimination
   a. In the nursing laboratory, practice the following maneuvers with a partner:
      (1) Positioning on a regular bedpan using a hip-lift approach
      (2) Positioning on a regular bedpan using a rolling technique
3. Enema administration
   a. Review your institution's procedure for giving enemas.
   b. In the nursing laboratory, or on the clinical division, locate and examine the equipment needed to administer the following enemas: soapsuds, saline, MGW.
   c. In the nursing laboratory, using an appropriate mannequin or simulation model, practice administering a tap water enema. Have another student observe and critique your performance. Elicit an instructor's evaluation of your technique.
4. Ostomy care
   a. Review your institution's procedure for ostomy care.
   b. In the nursing laboratory, or on the clinical division, locate and examine the equipment available in your health care setting for care of the client with an ostomy.
   c. In the nursing laboratory, using an appropriate mannequin or simulation model, practice the following skills with a partner:
      (1) Skin and stoma care
      (2) Pouching the ostomy
      (3) Changing the ostomy pouch
      (4) Irrigating the colostomy
   d. Identify clinicians or experienced nurses in your health care setting with expertise in the care of the client with an ostomy. Determine the mechanisms for client and staff referral.

Activities to reinforce theoretical concepts

1. Trace the pathway of ingested foods through the entire GI tract. Include the anatomical structures and primary functions of each section of the tract.
2. Experiential exercise: assessment of bowel elimination
   a. Formulate an assessment tool to evaluate a client's bowel elimination status (or examine the assessment tool used in your health care setting and identify those components that are pertinent to the assessment of bowel elimination.)
   b. Use the formulated or modified form to evaluate bowel elimination of an assigned client or partner.
   c. From the information obtained, identify factors promoting or impairing effective elimination and any other actual or potential abnormalities in GI function.
   d. Formulate pertinent nursing diagnoses based on your findings.
3. Clinical situation: care of the client with chronic constipation
   Mr. Truscott, a 58-year-old business executive, has come to the clinic for his annual employment physical. During the assessment interview, Mr. Truscott tells the nurse that he travels extensively and most of his mornings are rushed by trying to catch early-morning flights to his next business destination. He reports that he frequently ignores the urge to defecate. Most of his meals are in restaurants or at fast food outlets. His fluid intake is limited to mealtimes, which are often rushed. His "normal" bowel elimination pattern varies. It is not uncommon for Mr. Truscott to have only one bowel movement every 5 to 7 days. His stool is hard and dry. He frequently requires a lot of straining to pass the stool. He often experiences pain, and occasionally bleeding, with bowel movements. When he is not traveling, he takes laxatives to relieve his constipation.
   a. What factors are currently influencing Mr. Truscott's elimination status?
   b. Develop a teaching plan for Mr. Truscott that promotes regular bowel habits. Be sure to individualize the plan to his life-style and developmental level.
4. Experiential exercise: medications
   Following a client care experience, or after reviewing a selected client's medication records, identify each of the following:
   a. The effect of prescribed medications on GI function
   b. Medications that are laxatives or cathartics
   c. In the case of laxatives or cathartics, identify the particular classification, action, side effects, and nursing implications for safe administration
5. Clinical situation: care of the client with diarrhea
   Jamie Rose is a 9-month-old with gastroenteritis. Ja-

mie's mother reports that he has had 10 or more greenish watery stools each day for the past 2 days.

a. Describe at least three major nursing diagnoses appropriate for Jamie at this time.
b. State at least one goal for each nursing diagnosis formulated.

6. Clinical situation: Ms. Bowen is a single, 35-year-old secretary. Two weeks ago Ms. Bowen had an ileostomy for treatment of inflammatory bowel disease.

   Outline a discharge teaching plan for Ms. Bowen that reflects her developmental level and the nature of her bowel diversion. Include good health practices (fluids, foods, exercise, comfort), self-concept, sexuality, and specifics concerning care of the ostomy.

7. Clinical situation: bowel training
   James Hamet is a 48-year-old college professor with multiple sclerosis. Recently Dr. Hamet has had an exacerbation of his symptoms, including problems with bowel control. He has responded well to treatment and continues to have the ability to ambulate with the assistance of a walker. He is alert and oriented and hopes to return to work following his hospitalization. He is, however, extremely concerned about regaining bowel control. He reports that his office is near a bathroom, but that his classrooms are not always accessible to toilet facilities.

   Describe and appropriately modify the components of a successful bowel training program based on Dr. Hamet's age, disease state, work environment, and developmental level.

ADDITIONAL READINGS

Alterescu, V: The ostomy, what do you teach the patient? Am J Nurs 85:1250, 1985.

Discusses client education appropriate for the preoperative and postoperative ostomate. Presents information to include in a discharge plan including common "do's and don't's" and sample instruction sheets.

Aman, RA: Treating the patient, not the constipation, Am J Nurs 80:1634, 1980.

Describes a program directed at evaluating the effectiveness of specific stool softeners, laxatives, enemas, and suppositories in preventing and treating constipation. Discusses development of a protocol to prevent constipation in the institutionalized elderly population. Information presented could be applied to any health care setting.

Erickson, PJ: Ostomies: the art of pouching, Nurs Clin North Am 22:311, 1987.

Describes practical approaches for the technique of pouching a stoma. Information useful for students as well as more experienced nurses. Information presented may be easily incorporated into a client teaching plan.

Petillo, MH, editor: Enterostomal therapy, Nurs Clin North Am 22(2):1987.

A series of articles addressing urinary and intestinal ostomy therapy. Includes specific information about management of urinary and intestinal ostomies. Discusses special topics applicable to ostomy clients including developmental implication of an ostomy, psychosocial considerations, sexuality, and skin care.

Smith, DB: The ostomy: how is it managed? Am J Nurs 85:1246, 1985.

Describes nursing interventions for ostomy management.

Watt, R: The ostomy: why is it created? Am J Nurs 85:1242, 1985.

Describes conditions for which an ostomy is indicated. Includes actual photographs and compares these with drawings depicting the specific surgical diversions that have been created.

UNIT 8 Providing a Safe Environment

Chapter 40 Safety

WEEK #4

PREREQUISITE READING

Read Chapter 40, pp. 1156-1183.

OBJECTIVES

Mastery of content in this chapter will enable the student to:

1. Define selected terms associated with client safety.
2. Describe how unmet basic physiological needs for oxygen, fluids, nutrition, and temperature can threaten a client's safety.
3. Discuss methods to reduce physical hazards.
4. Describe current methods to reduce the transmission of pathogens and parasites.
5. Describe present methods of pollution control.
6. Discuss the specific risks to safety as they pertain to the client's developmental age.
7. Describe the four categories of risks in a health care agency.
8. State nursing diagnoses associated with risk to a client's safety.
9. Develop a nursing care plan for clients whose safety is threatened.
10. Describe nursing interventions specific to the client's age for reducing risks of falls, fires, poisonings, and electrical hazards.
11. Describe methods to evaluate interventions designed to maintain or promote a client's safety.

REVIEW OF KEY CONCEPTS

1. List five characteristics of a safe environment.
   a.
   b.
   c.
   d.
   e.
2. An individual's safety would be threatened by:
   a. lack of an adequate water supply.
   b. unrefrigerated fresh vegetables.
   c. atmospheric carbon dioxide.
   d. atmospheric humidity of 70%.
3. List three general measures to decrease physical hazards in the home.
   a.
   b.
   c.
4. Define pathogen.
5. Define parasite.
6. The process by which resistance to infectious disease is produced or augmented is ________________.
7. Which of the following would be considered a source of environmental pollution?
   a. Vehicle exhaust
   b. Flooding
   c. Rock concert
   d. All of the above
8. Identify four potential problems associated with sensory overload.
   a.
   b.
   c.
   d.
9. List five factors that influence a client's safety in the community.
   a.
   b.
   c.
   d.
   e.
10. The greatest risk of death from home accidents occurs in children:
    a. less than 5 years old.
    b. between 5 and 8 years old.
    c. between 9 and 12 years old.
    d. between 12 and 16 years old.
11. Accidents involving children are largely preventable through parental education. (true or false)
12. Information about safe sexual practices and birth control is often appropriate to provide to the adolescent client. (true or false)
13. Threats to an adult client's safety are frequently related to life-style habits. (true or false)
14. Describe eight physiological changes that increase the risk of falls in the aging client.
    a.
    b.
    c.
    d.
    e.
    f.
    g.
    h.

15. Identify the four major risks to client safety in the health care environment.
a.
b.
c.
d.

16. When an accident involving a client occurs, the nurse should do all of the following except:
a. notify the attending physician.
b. complete an incident report.
c. document the incident and its effect on the client in the medical record.
d. document in the medical record that an incident report was completed.

17. Which client is characteristically at highest risk for falls during hospitalization?
a. Client with language barriers
b. Client with history of substance abuse
c. Client with hearing impairment
d. Client with neurological disorder

18. Incorrect administration of a medication to a client is an example of:
a. a client-inherent accident.
b. a procedure-related accident.
c. an equipment-related accident.

19. List six electrical hazards that increase the risk of injury or fire.
a.
b.
c.
d.
e.
f.

20. The nurse experiences a small shock when unplugging a suction machine from a wall outlet. The nurse should:
a. plug the machine back into the same outlet and unplug it again to determine if the shock can be replicated.
b. plug the machine into a different outlet to determine if the shock was caused by a defective outlet.
c. ignore the incident, since the client no longer requires the suction machine.
d. label the machine as defective and report the incident.

21. State three goals appropriate in meeting a client's safety needs.
a.
b.
c.

22. List four signs that could indicate potential depression in the school-age child.
a.
b.
c.
d.

23. Select the nursing intervention that best promotes safety in a hospitalized toddler.
a. Provide child-size knife, fork, and spoon at mealtime.
b. Allow unattended bathtub play in less than 3 inches of water.
c. Provide miniature (matchbox) cars for group play.
d. Cover electrical outlets with protective covers.

24. Describe five measures to reduce the risk of accidents in adolescents.
a.
b.
c.
d.
e.

25. List the three most common injuries in the older adult.
a.
b.
c.

26. Identify eight measures to prevent falls in the health care setting.
a.
b.
c.
d.
e.
f.
g.
h.

27. Mr. Brimford, an active 72-year-old, is admitted to the hospital for prostate surgery. He tells you he usually gets up to go to the bathroom at least twice each night. As a safety precaution the nurse should:
a. apply a restraint jacket so he cannot get up at night.
b. leave a night-light on so he can see where he is going.
c. insist that he use the urinal in bed instead of getting up.
d. put the side rails up on his bed so he won't fall out.

28. State the four purposes for restraints.
a.
b.
c.
d.

29. Any restraint applied to a bedridden client should be secured to the:
a. side rail.
b. head board.
c. bed frame.
d. most easily accessible spot.

30. Restraints should be removed at least:
a. every 30 minutes.
b. every 60 minutes.
c. every 2 hours.
d. every 4 hours.

31. Mr. George is confused and frequently pulls out his peripheral IV. The restraint method most appropriate for this problem would be:
    a. jacket restraint.
    b. bilateral wrist restraints.
    c. mitten restraints.
    d. mummy restraint.
32. Short-term restraint of a small infant or child for treatments involving the head or neck is best accomplished by:
    a. jacket restraint.
    b. mummy restraint.
    c. mitten restraints.
    d. clove-hitch restraints.
33. Although Mr. Norton is confused at times, he enjoys sitting in a chair and watching the activity around him. To prevent Mr. Norton from falling out of his chair, the nurse can apply a(n):
    a. elbow or arm restraint.
    b. close-hitch restraint.
    c. mitten restraint.
    d. jacket restraint.
34. What is the best method for preventing falls in a confused client confined to bed?
35. Describe six fire containment guidelines.
    a.
    b.
    c.
    d.
    e.
    f.
36. List three nursing priorities when a fire occurs in a health care agency. Identify which of the three should always take highest priority.
    a.
    b.
    c.
37. The electrical cord on a heating lamp has started to smoke. Which fire extinguisher would be most appropriate for controlling this type of fire?
    a. Soda and acid
    b. Water pump
    c. Antifreeze
    d. Dry chemical
38. What is the substance of choice for inducing vomiting after accidental poisoning?
39. Vomiting may be induced for accidental poisoning from:
    a. household cleaners.
    b. petroleum products.
    c. medications.
    d. all of the above.
40. If a client receives an electrical shock, the nurse's first action should be to:
    a. assess the client's pulse.
    b. assess the client for thermal injury.
    c. notify the physician.
    d. notify the maintenance department.

APPLICATION OF KEY CONCEPTS

Activities to reinforce skills and techniques

1. Application of restraints
    a. Review your institution's policies regarding the use of restraints.
    b. In the nursing laboratory, practice applying each of the following types of restraints to a partner (as client) in bed or in a chair:
        (1) Jacket restraint
        (2) Belt restraint
        (3) Extremity restraint (commercially prepared or clove hitch)
        (4) Mitten restraint
    c. In the nursing laboratory, practice applying each of the following types of restraints to an infant mannequin:
        (1) Mummy restraint
        (2) Elbow restraint
2. Fire containment
    a. Review your institution's fire containment policies.
    b. Identify your institution's method for reporting a fire.
    c. Request an opportunity to have your institution's safety, security, or maintenance department review the use of fire extinguishers and fire hoses found in client care areas.
    d. Visit a client care area and locate each of the following:
        (1) Fire escape routes
        (2) Oxygen and electrical outlet shutoff valves
        (3) Fire alarm boxes
        (4) Fire extinguishers or hoses

Activities to reinforce theoretical concepts

1. Experiential exercise: accident prevention in children
    Complete the following table to identify methods to assist in protecting children from hazards located in their home and environment. For each injury, identify at least one safety precaution specific to each age group.

Injury	Age group	Safety precautions
Burns	Infant	
	Toddler	
	Preschooler	
Falls	Infant	
	Toddler	
	Preschooler	
Poisons	Infant	
	Toddler	
	Preschooler	
Asphyxiation	Infant	
	Toddler	
	Preschooler	
Motor vehicle accidents	Infant	
	Toddler	
	Preschooler	
	School-age child	

Injury	Age group	Safety precautions
Playing	Infant	
	Toddler	
	Preschooler	
	School-age child	
Acquisition of communicable diseases	Infant	
	Toddler	
	Preschooler	
	School-age child	

2. Experiential exercise: clients at risk for hospital falls
   a. Using the risk and fall assessment tool in your text, complete an assessment on a selected client.
   b. From the information gathered, indicate whether the individual is at high risk or risk prone for falls. Discuss the factors that contribute to the identified risk.
   c. Formulate nursing interventions that will prevent or minimize the client's risk of experiencing a fall.

3. Experiential exercise: environmental assessment
   a. Perform an assessment of your home or residence to identify environmental hazards. Summarize your findings of safety hazards and potential solutions for each of the following areas:
      (1) Falls
      (2) Electrical safety
      (3) Fire
      (4) Toxic substances (poisoning)
   b. Perform an environmental assessment of your home and identify modifications that would be required if your environment included:
      (1) A 5-month-old infant
      (2) An 18-month-old toddler
      (3) A 4-year-old preschooler
      (4) An 8-year-old school-age child
      (5) An 88-year-old person who needs a walker for ambulating
   c. Survey any health care setting to identify:
      (1) Safety promotion activities being implemented
      (2) Actual or potential safety hazards
   d. Share your observations with your instructor, and be sure to bring any hazards to the immediate attention of your instructor or supervisor.

4. Experiential exercise: adolescent safety
   a. Formulate a teaching session to present measures for adolescent accident prevention.
   b. Incorporate teaching strategies appropriate to the adolescent developmental level.
   c. Present the teaching session to a peer group (or audio tape or videotape) for evaluation.
   d. With your instructor as a resource, present this session to a selected group (for example, teenagers, parents of teenagers, teachers).

5. Experiential exercise: accident prevention for the elderly
   a. Select one of the three accidents responsible for the majority of injuries in the elderly population: falls, automobile accidents, or burns.
   b. Develop a teaching tool (paper, chart, pamphlet, booklet) focusing on one of these three areas.
   c. Submit your teaching tool to your instructor for feedback.
   d. Utilize your tool in presenting a safety session to a population of elderly clients in the community (or families or health care providers who work with the elderly population in the community).

6. Clinical situation: application of restraints
Mrs. Ferris is a 70-year-old woman who recently sustained a fractured femur. Following surgery to repair the fracture, Mrs. Ferris is restless, confused, and picking at her intravenous site.
   a. What factors must be considered before applying any type of restraint on Mrs. Ferris?
   b. If a decision is made to restrain Mrs. Ferris, what guidelines must be followed? (Include the rationale for the nursing actions taken.)
   c. What type of restraint might be appropriate for Mrs. Ferris? Why?
   d. If the situation is presenting a hazard to Mrs. Ferris' safety and the nurse is unable to immediately obtain a physician's order before applying restraints, what actions must be taken?

7. Clinical situation: fire containment
Ms. Varga is a paraplegic. After entering her room you smell smoke. Upon investigation you realize that Ms. Varga has fallen asleep while smoking and that her mattress is smoldering.
   a. Describe the sequence of actions you would take. Include the rationale for each action.
   b. What type of fire extinguisher could be used to put out this fire?

8. Clinical situation: hospital falls
During the night, Mr. Jackson, 74 years old, gets up to go to the bathroom. While in the bathroom, he slips and falls.
   a. List and describe four possible factors that could have contributed to this accident.
   b. State a nursing diagnosis (related to safety) that the nurse could include on Mr. Jackson's nursing care plan.
   c. List five nursing interventions and their rationale that may have prevented this accident.

ADDITIONAL READINGS

Baptiste, MS, and Feck, G: Preventing tap water burns, Am J Public Health 70:727, 1988.

Describes epidemiological study to determine and describe tap water burns as a basis for prevention. Recommends 120° F as preferred, and 130° F as acceptable, in terms of diminished severity of burns and decreased energy consumption.

Cooper, KL: Electrical safety: the electrically sensitive ICU patient, Focus 10:17, 1983.

The electrical hazards present in the ICU are identified, with emphasis on the physiological alterations present in the ICU clients that place them at even higher risk for injury.

Cooper, S: Common concern—accidents and older adults, Geriatr Nurs 2:287, 1981.

Presents data describing accidental injury in older adults and possible contributing factors. Describes practical measures to prevent injury from the three most common accidents experienced by elderly adults: burns, automobile accidents, and falls.

Hernandez, M, and Miller, J: How to reduce falls, Geriatr Nurs 2:97, 1986.

Describes a program developed to decrease falls in geropsychiatric setting. Identifies common risk factors. Presents an assessment tool used to gather risk-related data and assist in development of a protocol for "fall precautions." Makes specific recommendations for nursing care to minimize risk of falls.

Hoffman, Y: Surviving a child's suicide, Am J Nurs 87:955, 1987.

Personal reflections on the loss of a child from suicide.

Jankin, JK, Reynolds, BA, and Swiech, K: Patient falls in the acute care setting: identifying the risk factors, Nurs Res 35:214, 1986.

Describes retrospective chart reviews on hospitalized older adults to determine factors that increase risk of client injury. Variables identified assist in determining clients and risk and modifying care to prevent client injury in the acute care setting.

Jones, MK: Fire, Am J Nurs 84:1368, 1984.

Graphically describes the disaster inherent when fires occur in the health care setting. From data based on interview with survivors, makes specific recommendations about appropriate actions when a fire occurs.

Lynn, FH: Incidents—need they be accidents? Am J Nurs 80:1098, 1980.

Describes classifications of accidents occurring in the hospital environment. Based on studies, identifies times when most accidents occur, clients at risk, and specific prevention strategies.

Chapter 41

WEEK #4

Body Mechanics

PREREQUISITE READING

Read Chapter 41, pp. 1184 to 1231.

OBJECTIVES

Mastery of content in this chapter will enable the student to:

1. Define selected terms related to mobility and body mechanics.
2. Describe the roles of the skeleton, skeletal muscles, and nervous system in regulation of movement.
3. Describe normal body alignment for standing, sitting, and lying down.
4. Discuss physiological influences on body alignment and joint mobility.
5. Discuss pathological influences on body alignment and joint mobility.
6. Assess for alterations in body alignment and joint mobility.
7. State the correct nursing diagnoses for impaired body alignment and joint mobility.
8. Write nursing care plans for impaired body alignment and joint mobility.
9. Describe correct procedures for lifting.
10. Describe positioning techniques for the supported Fowler's position, supine position, prone position, side-lying position, and Sims' position.
11. Describe the procedure for assisting a client to move up in bed.
12. Describe the procedure for moving a helpless client up in bed.
13. Describe the procedure for repositioning a helpless client.
14. Describe the procedure for assisting a client to a sitting position.
15. Describe the procedure for assisting a client to a sitting position at the side of the bed.
16. Describe the procedure for transferring a client from bed to chair.
17. Describe the procedure for a three-person carry.
18. Describe the complete range of joint motion (ROJM) exercises.
19. List types of mechanical devices used for walking.
20. Describe how to measure a client for crutches.
21. Describe crutch safety.
22. Describe the five crutch gaits.
23. Describe how to get into a chair with crutches.
24. Evaluate the nursing plan for maintaining body alignment and joint mobility.

REVIEW OF KEY CONCEPTS

1. Define body mechanics.
2. Define friction.
3. Identify three techniques the nurse may use to decrease friction when moving a client.
   a.
   b.
   c.
4. List three systems responsible for coordinated body movements.
   a.
   b.
   c.
5. Identify the five functions of the skeletal system.
   a.
   b.
   c.
   d.
   e.
6. Weight bearing associated with activities of daily living may cause fractures in clients with osteoporosis. (true or false)
7. Match the terms with the most accurate descriptions or definitions.
   a. _____ Tissues connecting muscles to bone
   b. _____ Connection between ribs and sternum
   c. _____ The hip
   d. _____ Nonvascular supporting connective tissue
   e. _____ Tissue binding joints together
   f. _____ Connection between tibia and fibula
   g. _____ The sacrum

   1. Synostatic joint
   2. Ligament
   3. Cartilaginous joint
   4. Tendons
   5. Fibrous joint
   6. Cartilage
   7. Synovial joint
8. Muscle contraction that occurs when increased muscle tension results in shortening of the muscle is _____________________.

9. Muscle contraction that causes an increase in muscle tension without shortening the muscle is ____________________.
10. Posture and movement can be reflections of personality and mood. (true or false)
11. The normal state of balanced muscle tension is:
    a. posture.
    b. muscle movement.
    c. muscle tone.
    d. balance.
12. Muscles that permit the individual to maintain a sitting posture are called:
    a. antagonistic muscles.
    b. antigravity muscles.
    c. synergistic muscles.
    d. complementary muscles.
13. Awareness of the body's spatial position and muscular activity is called ____________________.
14. Maintenance of balance is primarily achieved by the:
    a. cerebral cortex.
    b. proprioceptors.
    c. motor strip and spinal cord.
    d. cerebellum and inner ear.
15. Proper body mechanics is as important to the nurse's health as it is to the client's. (true or false)
16. Which statement about the principles of body mechanics is correct?
    a. Equilibrium is maintained with least effort when the base of support is narrow.
    b. Lifting requires less force than pushing, pulling, or sliding an object.
    c. Stooping with hips and knees flexed and trunk in good alignment helps to prevent back strain.
    d. Relaxation of stabilizing muscles preparatory to activity prevents injury to ligaments and joints.
17. Match the developmental stage with the most descriptive characteristics of body alignment and mobility.
    a. _____ Tremendous but frequently uneven growth spurt
    b. _____ Shift of gravity toward anterior, complaints of back pain
    c. _____ Decreased ROM and muscle mass
    d. _____ Spinal flexion, complete ROM
    e. _____ Swaybacked, broad-based gait with feet everted
    f. _____ Improved balance, coordination, fine motor movement

    1. Infant
    2. Toddler
    3. School-age child
    4. Adolescent
    5. Pregnant woman
    6. Older adult
18. Match the name of each postural abnormality described with the list provided.
    a. _____ Dorsiflexion, inability to invert foot because of peroneal nerve damage
    b. _____ Hip instability with limited abduction of hips
    c. _____ Increased convexity in curvature of the thoracic spine
    d. _____ Medial deviation and plantar flexion of the foot
    e. _____ Exaggeration of the anterior, convex curve of the lumbar spine
    f. _____ Lateral curvature of the spine, unequal heights of hips and shoulders

    1. Lordosis
    2. Kyphosis
    3. Scoliosis
    4. Clubfoot
    5. Congenital hip dysplasia
    6. Foot-drop
19. The functional activity of bone cells that involves the processes of bone resorption and formation is called:
    a. modeling.
    b. remodeling.
    c. repair.
    d. metabolism.
20. List three major conditions that produce altered joint mobility.
    a.
    b.
    c.
21. Match the disorder of bone or muscle with the most accurate description.
    a. _____ Excessive longitudinal growth in the cartilage of all epiphyseal plates
    b. _____ Absolute loss of bone volume caused by altered ratio of bone formation to resorption
    c. _____ Loss of calcification of the matrix with decreased bone density
    d. _____ Abnormal bone formation resulting from a deficiency in vitamin D, calcium, or phosphorus
    e. _____ Excessive bone destruction and unorganized repair of unknown cause
    f. _____ Progressive pathological changes in skeletal muscles

    1. Osteoporosis
    2. Paget's disease
    3. Marfan's syndrome
    4. Rickets
    5. Osteomalacia
    6. Muscular dystrophy
22. Mr. Moore has sustained a cerebrovascular accident (stroke) in the right cerebral hemisphere. The nurse would anticipate that Mr. Moore would manifest motor weakness or paralysis on the:

a. left side of his body.
b. right side of his body.
c. bilaterally in the lower extremities.
d. bilaterally in the upper extremities.

23. In order for the nurse to accurately assess body alignment, the client must be standing. (true or false)
24. Describe five objectives to be achieved during assessment of body alignment.
a.
b.
c.
d.
e.
25. List and briefly describe the three components to include when assessing client mobility.
a.
b.
c.
26. Indicate the correct sequence for the activities of walking.
a. _____ Push-off
b. _____ Heel strike
c. _____ Swing
d. _____ Stance
27. Physiological effects of exercise include:
a. increased alveolar ventilation.
b. increased triglyceride levels.
c. decreased cardiac output.
d. increased glycogen storage.
28. Define activity tolerance.
29. For each domain, describe three factors influencing a client's activity tolerance.
a. Physiological
b. Emotional
c. Developmental.
30. State four goals appropriate for clients with improper body alignment or impaired mobility.
a.
b.
c.
d.
31. State the four criteria to be assessed before lifting a client or object.
a.
b.
c.
d.
32. What is the maximal weight that may be safely lifted by a nurse weighing 130 pounds?
33. Which of the following violates principles of body mechanics and therefore could cause injury to the nurse when moving a client?
a. Standing with feet together
b. Standing with feet apart
c. Bending at the knees
d. Using body weight to assist with movement
34. In the following table, indicate the correct use for each positioning device listed.

Device	Uses
Pillow	
Footboard	
Trochanter roll	
Sandbag	
Hand-wrist splint	
Trapeze bar	
Side rail	
Bed board	

35. In an emergency situation, it would be acceptable to tie restraints to a side rail. (true or false)
36. List three general guidelines to apply when positioning clients.
a.
b.
c.
37. Describe five general guidelines to apply in any transfer procedure.
a.
b.
c.
d.
e.
38. When a client is experiencing pain, it is best to provide analgesic medications:
a. before moving, positioning, or transferring.
b. after moving, positioning, or transferring.
39. Identify four areas for the nurse to consider in order to determine if assistance is required when moving a client in bed.
a.
b.
c.
d.
40. Exercises in which the nurse moves each of the client's joints through its range of motion are called:
a. active.
b. passive.
41. In most situations, range of motion (ROM) exercises should be as active as the client's health and mobility allow. (true or false)
42. Define contracture.
43. Which principle about ROM exercise is correct?
a. Passive ROM should begin 48 hours after ability to move an extremity or joint is lost.
b. Each movement should be performed twice during the exercise.
c. Nurses should gently force a joint slightly beyond its capacity.
d. Nurses should support the joint and extremity being exercised.
44. To maintain the functional position of the hand means that:
a. the thumb is slightly adducted and the fingers are extended.
b. the thumb is abducted and the fingers extended.
c. the thumb is slightly adducted and the fingers are slightly flexed.
d. the thumb is abducted and the fingers flexed.

45. Describe five steps to be taken by the nurse in preparing to assist the client to walk.
   a.
   b.
   c.
   d.
   e.
46. When ambulating a client with hemiplegia or hemiparesis, the nurse should:
   a. stand on the unaffected side, holding the client's arm.
   b. stand on the affected side, holding the client's arm.
   c. stand on the unaffected side, with one arm around the client's waist and the other around the inferior aspect of the client's upper arm.
   d. stand on the affected side, with one arm around the client's waist and the other around the inferior aspect of the client's upper arm.
47. Mr. Taylor has a left leg paralysis following a stroke. Which assistive walking device would be appropriate?
   a. Straight-legged cane
   b. Quad cane
   c. Lofstrand (forearm) crutch
   d. Axillary (wooden) crutch
48. Which guideline for ambulation with a single straight-leg cane is correct?
   a. The cane should be kept on the weaker side of the body.
   b. The cane should be placed forward about 6 to 10 inches before moving the legs.
   c. The stronger leg is moved forward first.
   d. The stronger leg should never be advanced past the cane.
49. Describe the appropriate measurements for axillary crutches.
50. Identify four crutch safety guidelines to be taught to clients before walking independently.
   a.
   b.
   c.
   d.
51. The required space between the client's axilla and the top of the crutch is necessary to:
   a. reduce the hazard of pressure on the axilla.
   b. decrease friction with the floor surface.
   c. maintain proper elbow alignment.
   d. maintain proper body alignment.
52. Match the crutch stance or gait with the most accurate description.
   a. ______ Weight is placed on the supported legs; the client places the crutches one stride in front and then swings to or through the crutches; the sequence is repeated.
   b. ______ Weight is borne on the uninvolved leg and then on both crutches; the sequence is repeated.
   c. ______ Crutches are placed 6 inches (15 cm) in front of and to the side of each foot.
   d. ______ Each leg is moved alternately with each crutch so that three points of support are on the floor at all times.
   e. ______ Each crutch is moved at the same time as the opposing leg, so crutch movements are similar to arm motion during normal walking.

   1. Swing-through
   2. Two-point gait
   3. Three-point gait
   4. Four-point gait
   5. Tripod position
53. List the sequence of movement for ascending the stairs on crutches.
   a. ______ Weight shifts from crutches to unaffected leg.
   b. ______ Unaffected leg is advanced between crutches to the stairs.
   c. ______ Client aligns both crutches on the stairs.
   d. ______ Body weight is transferred to crutches.
54. When descending the stairs while on crutches, the unaffected leg is moved to the lower step before the crutches. (true or false)
55. When preparing to sit in a chair while using crutches, the client:
   a. places the posterior aspect of the legs against the seat of the chair.
   b. holds both crutches in the hand on the same side as the affected leg.
   c. supports the body weight on the affected leg and crutches.
   d. all of the above.

APPLICATION OF KEY CONCEPTS

Activities to reinforce skills and techniques

1. Positioning in bed
   a. In the nursing laboratory, practice positioning a partner in each of the following bed positions:
      (1) Fowler's
      (2) Supine
      (3) Prone
      (4) Lateral side-lying
      (5) Sims'
   b. After you have positioned your partner, evaluate the partner's body alignment, pressure points, and comfort level.
   c. When you have practiced these positions, elicit an instructor's evaluation of your partner's body alignment.
   d. In the nursing laboratory, or on the clinical division, identify positioning devices available in your institution. Practice using these devices when positioning your partner.
2. Assisting with ambulation
   a. In the nursing laboratory, practice each of the following with a partner as the client:

(1) Preparation for walking
(2) Ambulation
(3) Lowering a fainting client to the floor

b. In the nursing laboratory, with the assistance or supervision of an instructor, practice ambulation with each of the following assistive devices:
(1) Walker
(2) Single-legged cane
(3) Quad cane
(4) Crutches (tripod position, two-point gait, three-point gait, four-point gait, swing to–swing through)

c. After you have practiced walking with an assistive device, teach another student to safely use the assistive device in the laboratory. If possible, spend part of a day ambulating with the device. Share your experience and perceptions with other students and your instructor.

3. Assisting with exercise
a. In the nursing laboratory, practice performing passive ROM on a partner. Attempt to put each joint on one side of the body through ROM. Switch places and have your partner perform passive ROM on you. Elicit an instructor's evaluation of your technique.
b. Observe nurses caring for clients in any health care setting. Identify active ROM that the nurse performs while caring for clients.

4. Lifting and moving
a. In the nursing laboratory, incorporate good body mechanics as you practice each of the following techniques with one or more partner(s):
(1) Pulling a client up in bed
(2) Three-person carry
(3) Moving a bed
(4) Lifting a box
b. Elicit an instructor's evaluation of your technique.

5. Transfer techniques
a. In the nursing laboratory, practice each of the following techniques with a partner:
(1) Assisting a client to a sitting position in bed
(2) Assisting a client to a sitting position on the side of the bed
(3) Assisting a client to transfer from the bed to a chair
(4) Assisting a client to transfer from a chair to a bed
b. Elicit an instructor's evaluation of your technique.

Activities to reinforce theoretical concepts

1. Experiential exercise: principles of body mechanics
From the following list, explain why each principle is important and identify clinical situations in which it may be regularly applied.
a. Moving an object by pulling increases friction.
b. A wide base of support increases stability.
c. A lower center of gravity increases stability.
d. The center of gravity passes through the base of support.
e. A person should face in the direction of motion.
f. Use more than one muscle group if possible.

2. Experiential assessment: body alignment and mobility
a. Using the guidelines provided in your text, perform an assessment of an assigned client or partner that includes the following:
(1) Body alignment standing
(2) Body alignment sitting
(3) Body alignment lying
(4) ROM
(5) Gait
(6) Exercise tolerance
b. Summarize your findings.
c. Formulate actual or potential nursing diagnoses based on your findings.

3. Clinical situation: nursing process of clients with altered mobility
Mr. Cobb is a 68-year-old retired train engineer. He has been admitted to the hospital for a total hip replacement. He has a history of degenerative arthritis that has resulted in limited range of joint movement in his arms, hands, and both legs.

Mr. Cobb likes to be independent, but because of his limited mobility, he often finds this very difficult. His wife had been assisting him with his activities of daily living before his hospitalization.

Mr. Cobb's physician informed him that he will be confined to bed for at least 5 or 6 days postoperatively. He will be able to be turned from his back to his unoperative side as long as a splint, designed to keep his leg in an abducted position, is in place.

Mr. Cobb is within normal weight for his age and height. He states he would feel much better if he could be more independent. He is hoping the surgery will enable him to be more mobile.
a. Identify areas that will need to be considered in order to determine the number of persons required to safely move Mr. Cobb in bed.
b. State three nursing diagnoses that would be related to Mr. Cobb's mobility.
c. Formulate one goal for each nursing diagnosis.
d. Formulate at least two nursing interventions and the rationale for each goal.

ADDITIONAL READINGS

Other pertinent articles addressing the related topic of immobility will be found in Chapter 42.

Bergstom, N, et al: The Braden Scale for predicting pressure sore risk, Nurs Res 36:205, 1987.
Provides criteria to evaluate in determining clients at risk for pressure formation. The reliability and validity of the tool permit early intervention to prevent or minimize risk of pressure sores.

Goldberg, WG, and Fitzpatrick, JJ: Movement with the aged, Nurs Res 29:339, 1980.
Explores the importance of movement and activity in the self-concept of the elderly client.

Gordon, M: Assessing activity tolerance, Am J Nurs 76:72, 1976.

Provides guidelines for assessment before and during activity. Analysis of the various parameters and their interpretation in relation to client activity tolerance are presented.

Viellion, G: Assessment: examining joints of the upper and lower extremities, Am J Nurs 81:763, 1981.

A self-paced programed instruction in musculoskeletal assessment. Includes numerous pictures and illustrations to reinforce content. Posttest included to validate learning.

Winslow, EH, and Weber, TM: Progressive exercises to combat hazards of bedrest, Am J Nurs 80:440, 1980.

Describes a progressive exercise program based on the needs of clients with cardiac disease. Presents normal, expected exercise response and the signs and symptoms warning of more serious problems and dictating the need to stop or slow exercise progression.

Chapter 42
Hazards of Immobility

PREREQUISITE READING

Read Chapter 42, pp. 1232 to 1261.

OBJECTIVES

Mastery of content in this chapter will enable the student to:

1. Define selected terms associated with immobility and hazards of bed rest.
2. Describe mobility and immobility.
3. Discuss benefits and hazards of bed rest.
4. Identify changes in metabolic rate associated with immobility.
5. Describe altered protein metabolism.
6. Describe fluid changes associated with immobility.
7. Describe alterations in exchange of nutrients associated with immobility.
8. Describe alterations in gastrointestinal functioning associated with immobility.
9. Describe alterations in respiratory function associated with immobility.
10. Discuss the mechanism of orthostatic hypotension.
11. Describe how immobilization increases cardiac work load.
12. Describe the mechanism of thrombus formation.
13. Describe musculoskeletal changes associated with immobility.
14. List the classes of decubitus ulcers.
15. Discuss factors that contribute to decubitus ulcer formation.
16. Discuss effects of immobilization on urinary and bowel elimination.
17. Describe psychosocial effects of immobilization.
18. Describe developmental effects of immobilization.
19. Complete a nursing assessment of an immobilized client.
20. List nursing diagnoses associated with immobility.
21. Develop a nursing care plan for an immobilized client.
22. List appropriate nursing interventions for an immobilized client.
23. State evaluation criteria for the immobilized client.

REVIEW OF KEY CONCEPTS

1. List five conditions that may result in immobility.
   a.
   b.
   c.
   d.
   e.
2. List three therapeutic benefits of bed rest.
   a.
   b.
   c.
3. Bed rest has physiological and emotional benefits only if the client finds it restful. (true or false)
4. Immobility disrupts normal metabolism as evidenced by:
   a. increased metabolic rate.
   b. increased anabolic processes.
   c. increased nitrogen excretion.
   d. decreased catabolic processes.
5. Describe how each of the following factors associated with immobility contributes to respiratory complications.
   a. Decreased hemoglobin
   b. Reduced lung expansion
   c. Generalized muscle weakness
   d. Stasis of secretions
6. List three cardiovascular system changes associated with immobility.
   a.
   b.
   c.
7. Orthostatic hypotension occurs when the client's blood pressure:
   a. increases by 15 mm Hg.
   b. decreases by 15 mm Hg.
   c. increases by 35 mm Hg.
   d. decreases by 35 mm Hg.
8. Why is cardiac work load increased in an immobilized, horizontal client?
9. Identify the three conditions required for thrombus formation.
   a.
   b.
   c.
10. List four musculoskeletal changes associated with immobility.
    a.
    b.

c.
d.

11. Identify the two major alterations in the skeletal system caused by immobilization.
    a.
    b.
12. A joint contracture is characterized by:
    a. a temporary change in the joint.
    b. flexion and fixation of the joint.
    c. overuse of the joint and extremities.
    d. maintenance of full joint range of motion (JROM).
13. Bone resorption is best described as:
    a. bone formation.
    b. calcium reabsorption from the GI tract.
    c. destruction of bone cells.
    d. movement of calcium into the bone.
14. Passive ROM:
    a. maintains joint mobility.
    b. prevents disuse osteoporosis.
    c. prevents muscle atrophy.
    d. all of the above.
15. Define decubitus ulcer.
16. Identify two mechanisms contributing to decubitus ulcer formation.
    a.
    b.
17. Skin breakdown may be precipitated by leaving an immobilized client in a position for longer than 2 hours. (true or false)
18. Define ischemia.
19. A compensatory response to ischemia in which the tissues become reddened because of increased blood flow is called ____________________.
20. Indicate the stages of decubitus ulcer formation from the descriptions provided.
    a. _____ Destruction of subcutaneous layers and underlying capillary bed
    b. _____ Reddening and edema that do not disappear; induration of superficial tissue
    c. _____ Destruction of subcutaneous capillaries and muscle mass; potential exposure of bone
    d. _____ Reddening of skin; disappears when pressure is relieved
21. Define shearing force.
22. State what each of the following contributes to decubitus formation:
    a. Moisture
    b. Poor nutrition
    c. Anemia
    d. Infection
23. List three urinary elimination changes associated with immobility.
    a.
    b.
    c.
24. List the four emotional alterations most commonly observed in immobilized clients.
    a.
    b.
    c.
    d.
25. Immobilization can retard a child's intellectual development. (true or false)
26. For each of the systems listed in the table below, describe abnormal findings characteristic of physiological hazards of immobility.

System	Abnormal findings
Metabolic	
Respiratory	
Cardiovascular	
Musculoskeletal	
Skin	
Elimination	

27. A respiratory assessment for clients with restricted activities should be performed:
    a. every 8 hours.
    b. every 4 hours.
    c. every 2 hours.
    d. every 1 hour.
28. Describe three assessment findings associated with deep vein thrombosis.
    a.
    b.
    c.
29. State eight goals appropriate for clients at risk for hazards of immobility.
    a.
    b.
    c.
    d.
    e.
    f.
    g.
    h.
30. For each system listed in the table below, identify at least three interventions to prevent or minimize hazards of immobility.

System	Interventions
Metabolic	
Respiratory	
Cardiovascular	
Musculoskeletal	
Skin	
Elimination	
Psychological	
Developmental	

31. Elastic stockings should be removed once per day during the bath. (true or false)
32. Appropriate nursing interventions when deep vein thrombosis is suspected should include all of the following except:
    a. immediately reporting the condition.
    b. leg elevation.

c. gentle massage.
d. avoiding direct pressure over the site.

33. Which cleansing agent would be appropriate for decubitus care when no necrotic tissue is present?
a. Antiseptic agents
b. Oxidizing agents
c. Enzymes
d. Dextranomer beads

34. The removal of necrotic tissue so that healthy tissue can regenerate is called:
a. escharotomy.
b. sloughing.
c. debridement.
d. wicking.

APPLICATION OF KEY CONCEPTS

Activities to reinforce skills and techniques

1. Application of elastic stockings
   a. In the nursing laboratory, measure a partner to determine the correct size of elastic hose to apply.
   b. Practice applying and removing an elastic hose without active assistance or cooperation of your partner (client). Keep in mind that often the client who requires elastic hose will be unable to assist in their application.
   c. Utilizing the steps presented in your text, evaluate your own performance.
2. Utilization of mechanical devices to prevent skin breakdown
   a. In the nursing laboratory, or in the client care setting, identify the devices available in your institution to minimize the complications of immobility.
   b. In the nursing laboratory, examine and practice application or utilization of each of the following devices:
      (1) Egg-crate mattress
      (2) Flotation pad
      (3) Sheepskin
      (4) Alternative pressure mattress
      (5) Clinitron bed
   c. If possible, visit a clinical division where you may observe special beds in use (for example, Clinitron, Guttman, Rotokinetic table, CircOlectric, or Stryker). Identify nursing responsibilities related to safe operation of these devices.

Activities to reinforce theoretical concepts

1. Experiential exercise: therapeutic benefits of bed rest
   a. Discuss the physiological and psychological benefits (rationale for) therapeutic bed rest.
   b. Review the nursing Kardex from a selected client area. Identify those clients on bed rest.
   c. Analyze information in the Kardex and medical record to determine the specific reason or reasons bed rest was ordered for a particular client.
   d. Discuss the physiological and psychological benefits of bed rest expected for the identified client.
2. Experiental exercise: multisystem effects of immobility
   a. Care for, assess, or review the medical records of a client who has been ordered on bed rest.
   b. Utilizing the table that follows, identify the specific effects of immobility that the client is experiencing and formulate at least two interventions to control or correct the identified complication.

Physiological effects	Client manifestations	Nursing interventions
Metabolic		
Fluid and electrolyte changes		
Bone demineralization		
Altered exchange of nutrients		
Altered exchange of gases		
Altered GI function		
Respiratory		
Decreased lung expansion		
Pooling of secretions		
Cardiovascular		
Orthostatic hypotension		
Increased cardiac work load		
Thrombus formation		
Musculoskeletal		
Decreased endurance		
Decreased muscle mass		
Atrophy		
Decreased stability		
Contracture formation		
Osteoporosis		
Skin		
Decubitus ulcer formation		
Elimination		
Renal calculi		
Stasis of urine		
Kidney infection		
Fecal constipation		
Fecal impaction		
Psychosocial		
Depression		
Behavioral changes		
Changes in sleep-wake cycles		
Decreased coping abilities		
Decreased problem-solving abilities		
Decreased interest in surroundings		
Increased isolation		
Sensory deprivation		
Developmental		
Increased rate of dependence		
Increased rate of loss of system functions		

3. Experiential exercise: ROM
   a. Observe a client, family member, or friend performing activities of daily living.
   b. Formulate a two-column table, with one column reflecting the activity observed and the second

column illustrating the ROM that is part of that activity. (See example below.)

ADL	ROM
Nodding head "yes"	Neck flexion and extension

4. Clinical situation: nursing process for immobilized clients
Mr. Concord, a 62-year-old businessman, has been hospitalized because of a cerebrovascular accident (stroke). The stroke has resulted in right-sided hemiplegia and dysarthria (difficulty clearly articulating words). The physician has ordered complete bed rest, soft diet, stool softeners, and a physical therapy consultation.
Mr. Concord is very quiet and withdrawn. His wife comes to visit him daily. Mrs. Concord is most anxious for her husband to "get better" and is very attentive to his needs. You notice that Mrs. Concord will frequently leave her husband's bedside and go to the visitor's lounge to cry.
   a. Develop a list of nursing diagnoses related to Mr. Concord's immobility.
   b. Develop a nursing care plan based on the priority nursing diagnosis. (Include at least two goals and four interventions.)
   c. Describe at least two outcome criteria for evaluation of the care plan.

ADDITIONAL READINGS

Other pertinent articles addressing the related topic of pressure ulcers will be found in Chapter 47.

Bergstom, N, et al: The Braden Scale for predicting pressure sore risk, Nurs Res 36:205, 1987.

Provides criteria to evaluate in determining clients at risk for pressure ulcer formation. The reliability and validity of the tool permits early intervention to prevent or minimize risk of pressure sores.

Byrne, N, and Feld, M: Overcoming the red menace: preventing and treating decubitus ulcers, Nurs 84 14:55, 1984.

Presents a specific, multidimensional plan for treatment of decubitus ulcers based on clinical staging of the ulcer.

Jones, PL, and Millman, A: A three part system to combat pressure sores, Geriatr Nurs 2:78, 1986.

Describes study at a large metropolitan hospital that included development of an assessment tool for identification of pressure sore risk. Discusses protocol developed for treatment based on the identified stage of the pressure sore.

Olson, EV, editor: The hazards of immobility, Am J Nurs 67:779, 1967.

A series of articles addressing the effects of immobility on each major body system. Discussion includes the effect of immobility on metabolism and psychosocial equilibrium.

Rubin, M: The physiology of bedrest, Am J Nurs 88:50, 1988.

Explores the normal physiological response to bed rest and its potential complications. Well referenced for additional pertinent reading.

Stoneberg, C, Petcock, N, and Myton, C: Wound care forum. Pressure sores in the homebound: one solution, Am J Nurs 86:426, 1986.

Describes study in which various home care techniques for pressure sore prevention were examined. Based on data obtained, makes specific recommendations for skin care and prevention of pressure sores in the homebound client.

Chapter 43

Infection Control

PREREQUISITE READING

Read Chapter 43, pp. 1262 to 1305.

OBJECTIVES

Mastery of content in this chapter will enable the student to:

1. Define selected terms related to immunological function and infection control.
2. Identify the body's normal defenses against infection.
3. Discuss the events in the inflammatory response.
4. Explain the differences between cell-mediated and humoral immunity.
5. Describe the nature of signs of a localized and systemic infection.
6. Describe characteristics of each link of the infection chain.
7. Identify clients most at risk for acquiring an infection.
8. Explain conditions that precipitate the onset of nosocomial infections.
9. Identify factors to assess a person's risk for infection.
10. Explain universal blood and body fluid precautions.
11. Identify principles of surgical asepsis.
12. Describe nursing interventions designed to break each link in the infection chain.
13. Correctly perform protective isolation techniques.
14. Perform proper procedures for hand washing.
15. Describe the zone of sterility for a sterile gown and sterile field.
16. Properly apply a sterile gown, sterile gloves, and surgical mask.

REVIEW OF KEY CONCEPTS

1. Define infection.
2. List the six elements making up the chain of infection.
   a.
   b.
   c.
   d.
   e.
   f.
3. Match the term associated with the chain of infection with the correct definition or description.
   a. ____ Resident pathogen
   b. ____ Carriers
   c. ____ Aerobic bacteria
   d. ____ Transient pathogens
   e. ____ Anaerobic bacteria
   f. ____ Virulence
   g. ____ Susceptibility

   1. Pathogenicity or strength of a disease-producing microorganism
   2. Microorganisms usually picked up by the hands during normal daily activities
   3. Degree of resistance to pathogens
   4. Microorganisms normally present on the skin, not easily removed by washing
   5. Persons or animals without symptoms of illness who are reservoirs of pathogens
   6. Bacteria requiring free oxygen for survival
   7. Bacteria that thrive in environments with little or no oxygen
4. The same microorganisms may be transmitted by more than one route. (true or false)
5. List the four major routes by which microorganisms may be transmitted from the reservoir to the host.
   a.
   b.
   c.
   d.
6. The severity of a client's illness will depend on all the following except:
   a. extent of infection.
   b. pathogenicity of the microorganism.
   c. susceptibility of the host.
   d. incubation period.
7. Match the stages of the course of infection with the correct description.
   a. ____ Prodromal
   b. ____ Convalescence
   c. ____ Illness
   d. ____ Incubation

1. Period of recovery
2. Interval between entrance of pathogen and symptoms
3. Appearance of nonspecific symptoms
4. Appearance of infection-specific symptoms

8. List the body's normal defenses against infection.

a. Normal flora
b. Body systems
c. Inflammatory response
d. Immune system

9. Normal flora:

a. cause disease.
✓**b.** maintain health.
c. produce cellular injury.
d. induce antibody production.

10. In the table below, identify at least one normal body system defense mechanism and the action by which infection is prevented.

System/Organ	Defense mechanism	Action
Skin		
Mouth		
Respiratory tract	p. 1269	
Urinary tract	table 43-4	
Gastrointestinal tract		

11. Define inflammation. Body's response to injury & infection

12. Signs of local inflammation are also signs of local infection. (true or false)

13. Identify five signs and symptoms of local inflammation.

a. REDNESS
b. Localized warmth
c. Swelling
d. Pain or tenderness
e. Loss of function

14. List the three major events making up the inflammatory response.

a. Vascular & cellular responses
b. Formation of inflammatory exudate
c. Tissue repair

15. Identify seven signs and symptoms of systemic inflammation.

a. Fever
b. Leucocytosis
c. MALAISE
d. ANOREXIA
e. NAUSEA
f. Vomiting
g. Lymph node enlargement

16. Match the term describing a component of immunity with the correct definition.

a. __3__ Immune response
b. __4__ Cell-mediated response
c. __2__ Humoral immune response
d. __5__ Antibodies
e. __1__ Foreign materials in the body
f. __7__ Complement
g. __6__ Interferon

1. Antigens
2. Synthesis of antibodies that destroy antigens
3. Body response to foreign materials
4. Proliferation of lymphocytes in response to a specific antigen
5. Immunoglobulins
6. Substance that interferes with ability of virus to produce disease
7. Enzyme activated when antigen and antibody bind, causing cytolysis

17. Indicate the sequence of events in the immune response.

a. Cell-mediated release of lymphocytes __2__
b. Antibodies circulate throughout the body __4__
c. Antigen enters the blood and lymphatic systems __1__
d. Synthesis of antibodies __3__
e. Antibodies destroy the foreign antigen __5__

18. Which component of the immune response is the basis of immunization against disease?

a. Antigen formation
b. Cell-mediated response
✓**c.** Antibody formation
d. Lymphocyte production

19. Fill in the term that best completes each sentence.

a. Infections resulting from health care delivery within a health care facility are __NOSOCOMIAL__ infections.
b. Infections resulting from diagnostic or therapeutic procedures are __IATROGENIC__ infections.
c. Nosocomial infections that are caused by microorganisms that do not exist as normal flora are __EXOGENUS__ infections.
d. Nosocomial infections that are caused by an alteration and overgrowth in the client's body flora are called __ENDOGENUS__ infections.

20. Describe at least three factors that increase a hospitalized client's risk of acquiring a nosocomial infection.

a. MEDICATIONS, Treatment, length of hosp. stay
b. NUMBER OF INVASIVE procedures / type of procedures
c. NUMBER OF Health care employees having direct contact w/ client

21. Which of the following clients would be at risk for infection because of inadequate primary defenses?

✓✓**a.** Chronic smoker
b. Client with anemia
c. Client with leukopenia
d. Client taking steroids

22. Identify six factors that influence an individual's susceptibility to infection.

a. age
b. nutritional status
c. Stress

d.
e.
f.

23. An individual is most susceptible to infection during which segments of the life span?
   a. Infancy and childhood years
   b. Infancy and older adult years
   c. Adolescence and young adult years
   d. Middle and older adult years

24. A negative nitrogen balance will result in:
   a. increased resistance to infection.
   b. decreased resistance to infection.
   c. enhanced wound healing.
   d. increased protein breakdown.

25. State three goals for the client with an actual or potential risk for infection.
   a.
   b.
   c.

26. Identify the two primary nursing responsibilities in controlling infection.
   a.
   b.

27. Match each of the terms related to asepsis with the correct definition.
   a. Asepsis ____
   b. Medical asepsis ____
   c. Surgical asepsis ____
   d. Sterile ____
   e. Contamination ____
   f. Disinfection ____
   g. Antiseptic ____
   h. Bacteriostatic ____
   i. Bacteriocidal ____

   1. Process by which an object becomes unsterile or unclean
   2. Substance that inhibits bacterial growth
   3. Term that describes an object free of microorganisms
   4. Absence of germs or pathogens
   5. Substance that kills bacteria but not spores
   6. Procedure used to eliminate microorganisms
   7. Process of destroying all pathogens except spores
   8. Procedures used to reduce the number of microorganisms and prevent their spread
   9. Substance that prevents bacterial growth

28. When cleaning equipment soiled by organic matter, the nurse should use:
   a.
   b.
   c.
   d.

29. The least expensive and most practical method for sterilizing items in the home is:
   a. soaking in isopropyl alcohol for 60 minutes.
   b. baking at 350 degrees for 30 minutes.
   c. boiling in water for 15 minutes.
   d. steaming in a pressure cooker for 10 minutes.

30. Match the nursing action with the element of the infection chain that is being controlled. (Answers may be used more than once.)
   a. Providing the client a well-balanced diet ____
   b. Proper disposal of contaminated needles ____
   c. Changing wet or soiled dressings ____
   d. Hand washing ____
   e. Cleaning soiled equipment ____
   f. Wearing gloves when handling body fluids or exudates ____
   g. Keeping the urinary drainage bag below the level of the client's bladder ____
   h. Wearing a mask when working with a mild cold ____
   i. Providing clients with a personal set of care items (bedpan, bath basin, thermometer) ____

   1. Control or eliminate infectious agents
   2. Control or eliminate reservoirs
   3. Control portals of exit
   4. Control transmission
   5. Control portals of entry
   6. Protect susceptible host

31. The most important, most basic, technique in preventing and controlling the transmission of pathogens is ____________.

32. Identify six situations in which it is recommended that nurses wash their hands.
   a.
   b.
   c.
   d.
   e.
   f.

33. The technique that is used to control the transmission of pathogens through barrier methods is:
   a. surgical asepsis.
   b. medical asepsis.
   c. protective asepsis.
   d. sterilization.

34. Identify and describe the two systems used for implementation of protective asepsis.
   a.
   b.

35. Describe the purpose of each category-specific isolation technique.
   a. Strict
   b. Contact
   c. Respiratory
   d. Enteric precautions
   e. Tuberculosis isolation
   f. Drainage and secretion precautions
   g. Universal blood and body fluid precautions
   h. Care of the severely compromised client

36. Place an "X" under the barriers required to maintain protective asepsis for each category-specific isolation technique in the following table.

Type of isolation	Room	Gown	Gloves	Mask
Strict				
Contact				
Respiratory				
Enteric precautions				
Tuberculosis isolation				
Drainage and secretion precautions				
Universal blood and body fluid precautions				
Care of the severely compromised client				

37. Health care workers should consider all clients as potentially infected with HIV and other blood-borne pathogens. (true or false)

38. List the nine guidelines for universal precautions according to the Centers for Disease Control.

a.
b.
c.
d.
e.
f.
g.
h.
i.

39. Describe four basic principles that may be applied to any protective asepsis system.

a.
b.
c.
d.

40. Identify two major areas of nursing care that may reduce the negative psychological effects of isolation.

a.
b.

41. Any individual visiting a client who is isolated should wash his or her hands:

a. before entering and immediately after leaving the isolation room.
b. after entering and before leaving the isolation room.
c. each and every time he or she touches the client.
d. after leaving the isolation room.

42. The primary reason for gowning during protective asepsis is to:

a. keep warm, since the isolation room is usually cool.
b. ensure that the client is not exposed to the organisms on the nurse's uniform.
c. maintain a sterile environment when providing client care.
d. prevent soiling of clothing during contact with client.

43. When gloves are used during protective asepsis, they should be changed after coming in contact with any infected material, even if the client's care has not been completed. (true or false)

44. When a client on respiratory isolation must be transported to another part of the hospital, the nurse:

a. places a mask on the client before he or she leaves the room.
b. obtains a physician's order to prohibit the client from being transported.
c. advises other health team members to wear masks and gowns when coming in contact with the client.
d. instructs the client to cover the mouth and nose with a tissue when coughing or sneezing.

45. To ensure maximal effectiveness of masks worn in an isolation room, the nurse should do all of the following *except:*

a. discard the mask if it becomes moist.
b. reuse the mask if it has not been contaminated.
c. change the mask every hour.
d. fit the mask snugly over the mouth and nose.

46. A single, impervious, sturdy bag is adequate for discarding or wrapping items removed from an isolated environment. (true or false)

47. Indicate the proper sequence that the nurse follows when removing protective clothing that has been worn in an isolation room.

a. Remove mask. ____
b. Wash hands. ____
c. Remove gloves. ____
d. Leave room. ____
e. Remove gown. ____

48. Identify five responsibilities of the infection control nurse.

a.
b.
c.
d.
e.

49. Surgical asepsis requires more stringent precautions than medical asepsis. (true or false)

50. Surgical aseptic techniques are only practiced in specialized areas such as the operating room or the labor and delivery area. (true or false)

51. State three teaching points that the nurse would emphasize in order to reduce the risk of client-associated contamination during sterile procedures or treatments.

a.
b.
c.

52. Based on principles of sterile technique, analyze each situation below and determine if sterile items remain sterile (S) or would be rendered contaminated (C).

a. A sterile tray is set up on a client's over-bed tray below the level of the nurse's waist. ____
b. A nurse's ungloved hand positions a sterile drape by grasping the outer 1-inch border. ____
c. A sterile tray is covered with a clean towel. ____
d. A client's sterile dressing is being applied while the roommate's bed is being made. ____
e. The nurse holds the tips of forceps, previously stored in disinfectant, with the tips down. ____
f. A sealed, sterile dressing package is placed on a wet table surface. ____

53. A staff nurse is performing a sterile dressing change assisted by the head nurse. The staff nurse thinks he or she may have contaminated his or her sterile glove by brushing against the client's arm. The nurse should:

a. ask the head nurse if he or she observed sterile technique being broken.
b. ask the client if he or she felt the nurse touch the arm.
c. continue with the dressing change.
d. stop and ask the head nurse to get another set of sterile gloves.

54. Indicate the sequence that should be followed to maintain sterile asepsis in the operating room.

a. Wash hands. ____
b. Don sterile gloves. ____
c. Apply mask and cap. ____
d. Put on sterile gown. ____

55. When a surgical mask becomes moist, the nurse in the delivery room should:

a. leave the delivery room and change masks.
b. reposition the mask so the area over the mouth and nose will be dry.
c. apply a second mask over the first.
d. remain in the room and change masks.

56. Describe the method for surgical hand washing using the following criteria:

a. Disposition of jewelry
b. Care of the nails
c. Areas to be washed
d. Duration of scrub
e. Equipment required
f. Position of hands and arms
g. Method for drying

57. When the color of a chemical tape on a sterile item remains unchanged, the item is considered sterile. (true or false)

58. When opening commercially packaged sterile items, the nurse tears the wrapper away from his or her body. (true or false)

59. When adding sterile supplies to a sterile field, it is acceptable to flip or toss objects onto the field to minimize contamination. (true or false)

60. In order to maintain sterility of solutions, it is important for the nurse to:

a. place the lid sterile side down on a clean surface.
b. pour a small amount of solution to cleanse the lip of the bottle.
c. hold the bottle high over the sterile field to avoid splashing.
d. pour the solution quickly to avoid contaminating the bottle.

61. What part of a sterile gown is considered sterile?

a. Back of the gown
b. Anterior surface—below the collar, to the waist
c. Anterior and posterior surface of the arms
d. All of the above

62. Describe the seven steps for application of a sterile drape with ungloved hands.

a.
b.
c.
d.
e.
f.
g.

63. In most home situations, it is acceptable for clients to utilize clean rather than sterile techniques. (true or false)

64. Identify seven topics that may be incorporated into a client teaching session addressing infection prevention and control.

a.
b.
c.
d.
e.
f.
g.

APPLICATION OF KEY CONCEPTS

Activities to reinforce skills and techniques

1. Hand-washing technique

a. Practice the proper procedure for hand washing while a peer observes and critiques your performance.
b. Elicit an instructor's evaluation of your hand-washing technique during a clinical laboratory experience.

2. Protective aseptic technique

a. Examine your institution's infection control policies. Determine if your institution utilizes category-specific or disease-specific isolation guidelines.
b. Reivew the contents of the isolation carts utilized by your institution.
c. Practice masking, gowning, and gloving techniques for protective asepsis while a peer observes and critiques your performance.
d. Elicit an instructor's evaluation of your masking, gowning, and gloving techniques for protective asepsis.
e. Identify a client who is hospitalized with a communicable disease and, using your institution's

infection control protocol, determine the barrier methods that must be applied.

f. Observe other hospital staff as they implement protective isolation techniques. Discuss your observations with your instructor.

3. Surgical aseptic technique

a. Examine your institution's policies concerning surgical hand-washing techniques.

b. Practice surgical hand-washing technique while a peer observes and critiques your performance.

c. Elicit an instructor's evaluation of your surgical hand-washing technique.

d. Practice the series of steps to maintain surgical aseptic technique (mask, cap, surgical hand washing, sterile gown and gloves) while a peer observes and critiques your performance.

e. Elicit an instructor's evaluation of your surgical aseptic technique.

f. Practice hand-washing and open gloving technique (used in general care areas) while a peer observes and critiques your performance.

g. Elicit an instructor's evaluation of your hand-washing and open gloving technique.

h. Observe other hospital staff as they utilize sterile technique. Discuss your observations with your instructor.

i. Practice setting up a sterile field with items provided by your instructor. Have a peer observe and critique your performance.

j. Elicit an instructor's evaluation as you set up a sterile field.

Activities to reinforce theoretical concepts

1. Clinical situation: James Miller, 83 years old, is admitted to the hospital for abdominal surgery. Although previously able to care for himself, Mr. Miller's appearance indicates that he has been unable to bathe himself or perform oral care. Because of his physical condition, Mr. Miller has also been unable to prepare or eat solid foods for several days and reports that his diet has been primarily composed of ginger ale and soup. He has a 50-year history of cigarette smoking. He currently has an IV line infusing in his right hand.

a. Which of Mr. Miller's normal body system defense mechanisms have been altered, increasing the risk of infection?

b. What other factors are present that increase Mr. Miller's susceptibility to infection? For each factor identified, describe the associated physiological changes that reduce resistance to infection.

c. The presence of an IV line predisposes Mr. Miller to local infection (phlebitis).

(1) What observations would indicate that this complication has occurred?

(2) Describe the physiological mechanisms that produce these signs and symptoms.

d. Postoperatively, Mr. Miller requires oral and nasotracheal suctioning. Explain why oral suctioning requires medical aseptic technique and nasotracheal suctioning requires sterile technique.

2. Experiential exercise: microorganism transmission
Following an observational or client care experience in the hospital setting, identify how microorganism spread may be facilitated in the hospital environment. For each of the four major routes of transmission, cite at least one method for organism transmission and at least one action that the nurse may take to break this link in the infection chain.

Route	Transmission method	Nursing action
Contact		
Air		
Vehicle		
Vectors		

3. Experiential exercise: nosocomial infections

a. Following an observational or client care experience in the hospital setting, identify at least two causes or sources of nosocomial infections for each of the sites listed.

b. For each of the causes or sources of infections identified, describe nursing actions you observed or enacted that helped to reduce the risk of nosocomial infection.

Site	Source or cause of infection	Preventive measures
Urinary tract		
Surgical wounds		
Respiratory tract		
Bloodstream		

4. Experiential exercise: protective isolation
Care for, interview, or review the medical record of a client who requires protective isolation. Answer the following questions and include specific examples to illustrate these concepts.

a. Identify the organism for which the client has been isolated.

b. What is the means of transmission for the identified organism?

c. What barrier methods must be employed to protect individuals coming in contact with the client? What is the rationale for the use of these methods?

d. What instructions should be given to the client's visitors regarding their use of isolation precautions?

e. Develop three nursing diagnoses that address the psychological implications of isolation. For each of the diagnoses identify one goal and describe at least two pertinent nursing interventions.

5. Clinical situation: client education
Terry Summers, 37 years old, is a single parent of two school-age children. Two weeks ago, Ms. Summers was in an automobile accident. The traumatic injury that she sustained was slow to heal and became infected. Although she has recovered sufficiently to return home, she continues to have a draining leg wound that is infected with *Staphylococcus*. A home

health nurse will be visiting to perform needed dressing changes to the infected leg.

Devise a teaching plan for Ms. Summers designed to promote compliance with infection control and prevention practices.

ADDITIONAL READINGS

AIDS precautions changing practice, Am J Nurs 88:372, 1988.

Describes modifications in care resulting from the CDC's revised guidelines in caring for AIDS victims. Examines OSHA standards in response to the CDC recommendations.

Bennett, J: Nurses talk about the challenge of AIDS, Am J Nurs 87:1150, 1987.

Eight clinicians discuss their concerns and views about care of the client with AIDS.

Grady, C, editor: AIDS, Nurs Clin North Am 23:4, 1988.

A series of articles addressing the epidemiology, pathophysiology, and treatment of AIDS. Examines complex nursing care needs of adults and children infected with human immunodeficiency virus (HIV). Discusses ethical and other practice-related issues associated with care of clients with HIV.

Hargiss, CO: The patient's environment: haven or hazard, Nurs Clin North Am 15(4):671, 1980.

Discusses factors that precipitate hospital-acquired infections. Briefly reviews category-specific isolation. Describes specific nursing interventions to reduce the risk of nosocomial infections.

Hargiss, CO, and Larson, E: Infection control guidelines for prevention of hospital acquired infections, Am J Nurs 81:2175, 1981.

One in a series of excellent articles included in a home study, continuing-education feature on infection control (putting principles into practice). Identifies the most frequent hospital-acquired infections and describes specific nursing measures to prevent their occurrence.

Labet, CG, and Roderick, MA: Infection control in the use of intravascular devices, Crit Care Q 3(4):67, 1981.

Describes a variety of intravascular devices found in the ICU environment but applicable to a variety of chronic and acute care settings. Sources of infection in clients with intravascular devices are clearly outlined. Emphasis is placed on practical approaches to the application of infection control guidelines in the clinical setting.

Marchiondo, K: The very fine art of collecting culture specimens, Nurs 79 9(4):34, 1979.

Emphasizes the importance of meticulous technique in obtaining culture specimens. Practical, detailed information on the correct methodology for obtaining commonly ordered culture specimens is presented. Stresses the role of the nurse in specimen acquisition and includes pertinent information for client education.

Chapter 44
Sensory Alterations

PREREQUISITE READING

Read Chapter 44, pp. 1306 to 1321.

OBJECTIVES

Mastery of content in this chapter will enable the student to:

1. Define selected terms associated with normal and altered sensory function.
2. Differentiate between the processes of reception, perception, and reaction to sensory stimuli.
3. Discuss common causes and effects of sensory alterations.
4. Discuss common sensory changes that normally occur with aging.
5. Identify factors to assess in determining sensory status.
6. Describe behaviors indicating sensory alterations.
7. Develop a plan of care for clients with visual, auditory, tactile, speech, and olfactory deficits.
8. List interventions for preventing sensory deprivation and controlling sensory overload.
9. Describe conditions in the health care agency or client's home that can be adjusted to promote meaningful sensory stimulation.
10. Discuss ways to maintain a safe environment for clients with sensory deficits.

REVIEW OF KEY CONCEPTS

1. List the three functional components necessary for any sensory experience.
   a.
   b.
   c.
2. All sensory impulses that enter the nervous system:
   a. are received.
   b. are perceived.
   c. elicit a response.
   d. all of the above.
3. Identify seven factors that may influence sensory function.
   a.
   b.
   c.
   d.
   e.
   f.
   g.
4. Define sensory deficit.
5. A condition in which inadequate quality or quantity of stimulation impairs an individual's perception is known as ________________.
6. Identify the three major types of sensory deprivation.
   a.
   b.
   c.
7. A condition in which there is a reception of multiple sensory stimuli that cannot be perceptually disregarded or selectively ignored is known as ________________.
8. For each type of alteration associated with sensory deprivation, describe at least two associated symptoms experienced by the client.
   a. Cognitive
   b. Affective
   c. Perceptual
9. Identify three client groups at high risk for sensory alterations during hospitalization.
   a.
   b.
   c.
10. Complete the table below by describing at least one assessment technique for the identified sensory function and one adult behavior that could indicate a sensory deficit.

Sense	Assessment technique	Deficit behavior
Vision		
Hearing		
Touch		
Smell		
Taste		
Position sense		

11. State five goals appropriate for clients with sensory alterations.
    a.
    b.
    c.
    d.
    e.

12. Identify four general measures to promote visual function.
    a.
    b.
    c.
    d.
13. List four ways to maximize residual hearing in an older adult.
    a.
    b.
    c.
    d.
14. All of the following interventions will enhance taste perception except:
    a. good oral hygiene.
    b. seasoning foods.
    c. chewing food thoroughly.
    d. blending or mixing foods.
15. Which nursing intervention would be appropriate for clients with hyperesthesia?
    a. Minimal use of direct touch
    b. Firm pressure when touching body parts
    c. Frequent back rubs
    d. Vigorous hair brushing
16. When ambulating a client with visual impairment, the nurse should:
    a. stand on the client's dominant side and grasp the client's arm.
    b. stand on the client's nondominant side, approximately one step behind the client, grasping the client's arm.
    c. stand slightly in front of the client, on the client's nondominant side, allowing the client to grasp the nurse's arm.
    d. stand on the client's dominant side slightly in front of the client, allowing the client to grasp the nurse's arm.
17. Painting the edge of a step with a bright color to prevent falls would be most helpful for clients with:
    a. reduced peripheral vision.
    b. color blindness.
    c. night blindness.
    d. altered depth perception.
18. All of the following communication methods would be appropriate for the client with aphasia except:
    a. allowing time for the client to respond.
    b. using short, simple sentences.
    c. speaking loudly and articulating clearly.
    d. using nonverbal clues.
19. Describe six communication methods appropriate for clients with hearing impairment.
    a.
    b.
    c.
    d.
    e.
    f.
20. An aphasic client should be considered intellectually impaired. (true or false)

APPLICATION OF KEY CONCEPTS

Activities to reinforce theoretical concepts

1. Experiential exercise: sensory deprivation
    a. Spend a limited time period (for example, 1 hour) during which you experience a simulated sensory deficit. Select only one of the following sensory modifications for your experience:
        (1) Touch: wearing disposable latex gloves
        (2) Hearing: wearing earmuffs or plugging ears with cotton
        (3) Vision: wearing sunglasses covered with petroleum jelly or with a portion of the lenses covered with black construction paper
    b. Be sure to have a partner who is not sensory impaired act as your monitor and ensure your safety.
    c. After an hour (or sooner if you find this experience problematic) switch roles with your partner.
    d. Summarize your perceptions of the experience and share them in a small-group discussion with peers or your instructor.
2. Experiential exercise: assessment of sensory function
    During a client care or observational experience, determine ways to evaluate the client's sensory function through your own observational skills. The goal is to determine how much information you are able to gather in the normal course of client care, without formal physical examination. Attempt to identify at least two observations for each of the sensory functions listed below.
    a. Vision
    b. Hearing
    c. Touch
    d. Smell
    e. Taste
    f. Position sense
3. Experiential exercise: maintaining meaningful stimuli
    a. During a client care or observational experience, identify at least three specific examples of environmental stimuli for each of the following areas:
        (1) Meaningful stimuli present
        (2) Stimuli to introduce
        (3) Excessive stimuli present
        (4) Methods to control excessive stimuli
    b. Sit in any hospital area for 15 minutes. Avoid any interactions; you are there merely to experience the sensory stimuli present. If possible, close your eyes a moment to hear, more clearly, the activity around you. Share the nature of the stimuli, your perceptions, and the effect of the experience with a small group or your instructor. Identify how the activity may modify care you provide to clients.
4. Clinical situations: promoting sensory function
    In each of the following situations, discuss nursing interventions that are needed in order to promote functioning of existing senses.

a. Mr. Abrams is reading his magazine by the light of a small bedside table. When the nurse says something to him about needing more light to read by, he says he "can see just fine."
b. A 12-year-old girl is seen with a radio headset on. When the nurse is 10 feet away from the client, she can clearly hear the music from the radio headset. When the nurse calls the adolescent's name, she does not respond.
c. Mrs. James complains to the nurse about the tasteless hospital food. It has been noted in the medical record that the 80-year-old Mrs. James has very poor oral hygiene habits.
d. Mr. Gray has had to remain in bed for 3 days because of flulike symptoms. He cannot even get out of bed to go to the bathroom. Nursing interventions thus far have been limited to changing his position to prevent pressure sores. He is complaining of numbness in his extremities.

5. Clinical situation: nursing process for the client with sensory impairment
Mrs. Everett is an active 65-year-old woman who enters the hospital for eye surgery. The physician has indicated that Mrs. Everett will have bilateral eye patches for the first 24 hours after surgery and a left eye patch throughout her hospital stay.
a. What nursing interventions related to Mrs. Everett's sensory function would be appropriate during the preoperative period?
b. Develop a postoperative nursing care plan for Mrs. Everett that focuses on her sensory needs.

ADDITIONAL READINGS

Blanco, KM: The aphasic patient, J Neurosurg Nurs 14:34, 1982.
Defines and classifies neurological communication disorders. Presents detailed comparison of expressive and receptive aphasia. Provides general nursing management and communication methods appropriate for aphasic clients.

Downs, FS: Bedrest and sensory disturbances, Am J Nurs 74:435, 1974.
Describes a study in which healthy young adults experienced moderate social isolation for limited time periods. Discusses distortions in sensory processes experienced. Makes recommendations to reduce sensory distortion associated with bed rest.

Kopac, CA: Sensory loss in the aged: the role of the nurse and the family, Nurs Clin North Am 18:373, 1983.
Describes effect of hospital environment on clients who enter with a sensory loss. Identifies common problems of vision, hearing, touch, taste, and smell found in the aged. Presents areas for assessment and specific interventions for sensory deficits. Identifies support of sensory function as an area for active family participation. Describes ways family members can be instructed to provide meaningful stimuli for sensory-impaired elderly persons. Information presented, while directed at the aged, could be applied to other clients with sensory loss.

Primental, PA: Alterations in communication, Nurs Clin North Am 21(2):321, 1986.
Describes the neurophysiological effects of stroke on communication. Provides guidelines for assessment and care of clients with aphasia, dysarthria, and right hemisphere syndromes.

Rubin, M: How bedrest changes perception, Am J Nurs 88:55, 1988.
Describes alterations in sensory stimuli associated with bed rest. Discusses perceptual changes that may commonly occur in clients on bed rest and offers suggestions for approaches to minimize alterations in perception.

Chapter 45
Substance Abuse

PREREQUISITE READING

Read Chapter 45, pp. 1322 to 1343.

OBJECTIVES

Mastery of content in this chapter will enable the student to:

1. Define selected terms associated with substance abuse and chemical dependency.
2. Discuss the general health risks related to the abuse of any substance.
3. Compare and contrast physiological and psychological dependence.
4. List nine major groups of drugs and substances and discuss their major effects.
5. Describe psychosocial causative variables associated with substance abuse.
6. Describe the disease of chemical dependency and its progression.
7. Discuss signs and symptoms of chemical dependency and physical, psychological, and social outcomes of the disease.
8. Describe the typical course of substance abuse.
9. State at least three special groups particularly at risk for substance abuse.
10. Describe the nurse's responsibility if a colleague may be abusing a substance.
11. Describe special assessment approaches for clients with substance abuse problems.
12. List three or more examples of nursing diagnoses related to substance abuse.
13. List and discuss seven general types of interventions appropriate for clients who are substance abusers.
14. Describe major characteristics of the evaluation process for nursing care of clients who are substance abusers.

REVIEW OF KEY CONCEPTS

1. Define substance.
2. Current research supports the hereditary nature of chemical dependency. (true or false)
3. Differentiate between the meaning of the following terms: drug use, drug misuse, and drug abuse.
4. A condition in which an individual experiences a withdrawal syndrome when a substance is abruptly stopped is:
   - **a.** psychological dependence.
   - **b.** physiological dependence.
   - **c.** drug misuse.
   - **d.** drug abuse.
5. An emotional reliance on a drug is called __________________.
6. Define FAS.
7. Which statement concerning substance abuse is accurate?
   - **a.** The majority of alcoholics come from lower socioeconomic levels.
   - **b.** Knowledge of the dangers of substance abuse will prevent addiction.
   - **c.** Continued abuse may be avoided through use of willpower.
   - **d.** Interventions for addicts may begin even before there is an expressed desire to "quit."
8. Alcohol is a central nervous system stimulant. (true or false)
9. Which group of drugs do not characteristically lead to physical or psychological dependence?
   - **a.** Tranquilizers
   - **b.** Opiates
   - **c.** CNS sympathomimetics
   - **d.** Hallucinogens
10. Over-the-counter analgesics such as aspirin and acetaminophen may be abused. (true or false)
11. In the table below, describe the psychological effect produced by each of the substances identified.

Substance	Psychological effect produced
Alcohol	
Opiates	
Barbiturates	
Antianxiety agents	
Cocaine	
Marijuana	
Hallucinogens	
Amphetamines	

12. Identify the two motivations that may explain why a person first misuses a substance.
   - **a.**
   - **b.**

13. Identify and briefly describe the four major theories of substance abuse.
    a.
    b.
    c.
    d.
14. Define binge drinking.
15. Alcohol is less destructive to body tissues than other abuse substances. (true or false)
16. The primary defense mechanism used by chemical dependents is:
    a. suppression.
    b. projection.
    c. denial.
    d. rationalization.
17. Alcohol consumption by pregnant women may have adverse effects on the fetus even when the mother is not an alcoholic. (true or false)
18. Briefly describe the nursing care focus for each level of chemical dependency care listed below.
    a. Primary prevention
    b. Secondary care
    c. Tertiary care
19. List the four interview techniques used to obtain needed information from a client admitted with a diagnosis of alcoholism.
    a.
    b.
    c.
    d.
20. Which interviewing style appropriate for the chemically dependent client is illustrated by the following interaction?

    Client: "I just have a few drinks after work; you know, social drinking . . . ."

    Nurse: "Exactly how many drinks do you usually have after work?"

    a. Empathetic style
    b. Clarifying style
    c. Giving advice
    d. Confrontation
21. Identify four goals of assessment when evaluating clients with potential chemical abuse problems.
    a.
    b.
    c.
    d.
22. State four goals of care appropriate for clients with a chemical dependency.
    a.
    b.
    c.
    d.
23. Identify the three major goals of chemical dependence treatment based on the principles of Alcoholics Anonymous (AA).
    a.
    b.
    c.
24. Removal of mood-altering chemicals from the chemically dependent person's body is called ________________.
25. Rapid removal of mood-altering chemicals from a chemically dependent person's body may cause:
    a. seizures.
    b. delirium tremens (DTs).
    c. death.
    d. all of the above.
26. Identify four interventions appropriate for family members of the chemically dependent client.
    a.
    b.
    c.
    d.
27. Mr. Jones is an alcoholic. The most appropriate self-help group to assist his wife would be.
    a. Alateen.
    b. Al-Anon.
    c. AA (Alcoholics Anonymous).
28. List the seven interventions the nurse can employ to assist clients with physiological chemical dependence during their treatment program.
    a.
    b.
    c.
    d.
    e.
    f.
    g.
29. Mr. West, a heroin addict who has undergone extensive rehabilitation therapy, is being discharged from the care unit. What are four forms of ongoing support that can be provided by the nurse?
    a.
    b.
    c.
    d.

APPLICATION OF KEY CONCEPTS
Activities to reinforce theoretical concepts

1. Experiential exercise: DAST, MAST
    a. Complete the DAST and MAST screening tools in your text (pp. 1332 and 1333).
    b. If you find that you score above three points on the MAST or DAST, make an appointment to talk with a qualified counselor to clarify your use of alcohol or drugs. This information, and the relationship with your counselor, may remain confidential.
2. Clinical situation: substance abuse in special groups

   One evening you are one of two RNs working on a busy clinical division. While you are at supper, one of your clients requests diazepam (Valium) for anxiety. Ms. Samuels, RN, reports that she administered the diazepam, but you assess that the client still is very anxious. You observe that Ms. Samuels appears slightly euphoric and that her speech is slurred.

a. What action should you take in relation to your client's anxiety?

b. What action should you take in relation to Ms. Samuels' behavior?

3. Clinical situation: nursing process for clients with chemical dependence

Mr. West is admitted to the hospital for evaluation and treatment of duodenal ulcers. The physician indicates that the ulcers are related to long-term alcohol abuse.

During assessment Mr. West's wife tells the nurse that Mr. West has been fired from his job as a sales representative because of poor attendance, appearance, and belligerence with clients. She reports that lately Mr. West has not been eating and that most of the grocery money for family food purchases has been spent on whiskey and beer. Mr. West reports difficulty sleeping but denies more than occasional social drinking.

a. What interviewing techniques would be appropriate to use in obtaining accurate information from Mr. West? (If possible, role-play this interview with another student, incorporating the interviewing techniques appropriate for the chemically dependent person.)

b. Describe at least four behaviors expected with alcohol abuse.

c. Describe at least four clinical manifestations that would be expected if Mr. West experiences withdrawal syndrome.

d. Based on the information presented in the clinical situation, and your understanding of chemical dependence, formulate nursing diagnoses appropriate for Mr. West.

e. Formulate at least three goals for Mr. West's care related to his chemical dependence.

f. For each of the following areas of nursing implementation, describe actions appropriate for Mr. West's care.

(1) Acute care period
(2) Verbal abuse to the hospital staff
(3) Family support
(4) Teaching and counseling
(5) Involvement in community programs (client and family)

ADDITIONAL READINGS

Adams, F: Drug dependency in hospital patients, Am J Nurs 88:4767, 1988.

Describes approaches to care of the chemically dependent client from initial interview through hospital discharge. Emphasizes the importance of health team members' ongoing interaction and consistency in care. Includes a chart summarizing controlled substances, actions, medicinal use (if any), common effects, and withdrawal characteristics.

Lawrence, F, et al: Admitting the intoxicated patient, Am J Nurs 84:617, 1984.

Describes the complex problems associated with care of the intoxicated client. Explores characteristic behaviors and makes recommendations for effective strategies in working with intoxicated clients. Although the focus of the article is on the admission process, strategies are applicable to any health care setting in which the nurse encounters intoxicated clients.

Powell, A, and Minick, M: Alcohol withdrawal syndrome, Am J Nurs 88:312, 1988.

Overview of pathophysiological basis of alcohol withdrawal syndrome. Describes characteristic symptoms and common medical treatment. Discusses nursing interventions to promote client safety during withdrawal.

Throwe, AN: Families and alcohol, Crit Care Q 8(4):79, 1986.

Explores the impact of alcoholism on the entire family unit. Discusses the family responses often encountered by the nurse in the acute care setting and offers approaches for assisting the alcoholic family.

Yowell, S, and Crose, C: Working with drug abuse patients in the ER, Am J Nurs 77:82, 1977.

Describes common characteristics of clients related to specific patterns of drug abuse. Provides concrete recommendations for interventions individualized to the client's personality and the actions of the identified drug.

Zahourek, R: Identification of the alcoholic in the acute care setting, Crit Care Q 8(4):1, 1986.

Defines and describes the extent of alcoholism in the acute care population. Describes characteristic signs of chemical dependence and additional subtle signs of alcoholism. Details assessment strategies and selected tools and explores the psychodynamics of alcoholism. Includes interventions appropriate to the acute care setting.

UNIT 9 Caring for the Perioperative Client

Chapter 46
The Surgical Client

PREREQUISITE READING

Read Chapter 46, pp. 1346 to 1393.

OBJECTIVES

Mastery of content in this chapter will enable the student to:

1. Define selected terms associated with care of the surgical client.
2. Explain the concept of perioperative nursing care.
3. Differentiate between classifications of surgery.
4. List factors to include in the preoperative assessment of a surgical client.
5. Properly witness a client's informed consent for surgery.
6. Demonstrate postoperative exercises: diaphragmatic breathing, coughing, turning, and leg exercises.
7. Design a preoperative teaching program.
8. Prepare a client for surgery on the morning of a scheduled operation.
9. Compare and contrast the actions and side effects of general, regional, and local anesthesia.
10. Explain the nurse's role in the operating room.
11. Describe the nurse's role in phase I and II recovery.
12. Identify factors to include in the postoperative assessment of a client in recovery.
13. Describe the rationale for nursing interventions designed to prevent postoperative complications.
14. Explain the differences and similarities in caring for outpatient versus inpatient surgical clients.

REVIEW OF KEY CONCEPTS

1. Define perioperative nursing.
2. List the three major classifications for all surgical procedures.
   - **a.**
   - **b.**
   - **c.**
3. Match the surgical procedure classification with the most accurate description.
   - **a.** ____ Extensive reconstruction or alteration in body parts
   - **b.** ____ Minimal alteration in body parts, often to correct deformities
   - **c.** ____ Performed on the basis of the client's choice
   - **d.** ____ Necessary for client health but not an emergency
   - **e.** ____ Must be done immediately to save a life or preserve a body part
   - **f.** ____ Surgical exploration to confirm a diagnosis
   - **g.** ____ Excision or removal of a diseased body part
   - **h.** ____ Relief or reduction of intensity of disease symptoms; will not produce a cure
   - **i.** ____ Restoration of function or appearance of tissues
   - **j.** ____ Replacement of malfunctioning organs or structures
   - **k.** ____ Restoration of function lost or reduced because of congenital anomalies

   1. Palliative
   2. Ablative
   3. Emergency
   4. Minor
   5. Urgent
   6. Major
   7. Reconstructive
   8. Constructive
   9. Elective
   10. Transplant
   11. Diagnostic
4. Describe four nursing responsibilities during the preoperative surgical phase.
   - **a.**
   - **b.**
   - **c.**
   - **d.**
5. Describe how each of the following conditions increases the risk associated with surgery.
   - **a.** Bleeding disorders
   - **b.** Diabetes mellitus
   - **c.** Heart disease
   - **d.** Respiratory infections
   - **e.** Liver disease
   - **f.** Fever
   - **g.** Chronic obstructive pulmonary disease (COPD)
6. Prescription drugs taken preoperatively are automatically continued during the postoperative period. (true or false)

7. Explain why a client who smokes is at greater risk for pulmonary complications following surgery.
8. Which preoperative assessment parameter would be of particular importance for clients anticipating spinal anesthesia?
   a. Level of hydration
   b. Self-concept
   c. Smoking habits
   d. Motor function
9. List and briefly describe three conditions that increase a person's surgical risk.
   a.
   b.
   c.
10. A risk factor that can directly interfere with postoperative wound healing is:
    a. the use of preoperative antibiotics.
    b. smoking.
    c. low serum potassium.
    d. poor nutrient intake.
11. In an elderly client, surgery poses a risk because:
    a. there is a stiffening of the rib cage and reduced range of diaphragmatic movement.
    b. the blood flow to the liver is reduced, increasing bleeding tendencies.
    c. the client has increased sensitivity to painful stimuli.
    d. the basal metabolic rate is increased.
12. Which preoperative diagnostic study would provide the most useful information about the risk of postoperative bleeding?
    a. Serum electrolytes
    b. CBC
    c. PT, PTT
    d. ECG
13. Which preoperative diagnostic test would be the most important for a client at risk for losing a large amount of blood during surgery?
    a. Type and cross match
    b. Sputum for culture and sensitivity
    c. Serum creatinine
    d. Serum sodium
14. State six goals appropriate for care of the preoperative client.
    a.
    b.
    c.
    d.
    e.
    f.
15. The primary responsibility for informing the client about the surgical procedure rests with the nurse. (true or false)
16. A client's signature on a consent form means that:
    a. the client understands the procedure that will be performed.
    b. the physician is not liable for errors made during the procedure.
    c. the client has been informed about the procedure.
    d. the client has read the information on the consent form.
17. Which of the following clients would be able to give informed consent?
    a. A 46-year-old who is illiterate
    b. A 24-year-old who has just received a sedative
    c. A 78-year-old who has a nursing diagnosis of confusion
    d. A 16-year-old who lives at home with parents
18. Describe the four ways in which structured preoperative teaching may influence a client's postoperative recovery.
    a.
    b.
    c.
    d.
19. The best time to initiate preoperative teaching is:
    a. the night before surgery.
    b. the day of surgery.
    c. several days before surgery.
    d. after the preoperative orders are written.
20. Describe six of the criteria developed by the AORN that may be used in determining the client's understanding of the surgical procedure.
    a.
    b.
    c.
    d.
    e.
    f.
21. State the basic rationale that supports the performance of each of the following postoperative exercises:
    a. Turning
    b. Coughing
    c. Deep breathing
    d. Leg exercises
22. Briefly discuss the purpose for each of the following orders.
    a. NPO after midnight
    b. Shower with antimicrobial soap the evening before surgery
    c. Soapsuds enema the evening before surgery
    d. Dalmane, 15 mg PO, at bedtime (night before surgery)
23. Shaving the surgical site preoperatively decreases the risk of postoperative infection. (true or false)
24. An effective way to reduce postoperative wound infection is to keep the client's preoperative hospital stay short. (true or false)
25. Why does the nurse complete a preoperative checklist?
26. List the 11 responsibilities of a nurse caring for a client the morning of surgery.
    a.
    b.
    c.
    d.
    e.

f.
g.
h.
i.
j.
k.

27. Match the purpose of nasogastric (NG) intubation with the correct description.
   a. ____ Removal of secretions and substances, relief of distention
   b. ____ Instillation of liquid nutrients when client is unable to swallow
   c. ____ Internal application of pressure to prevent internal hemorrhage
   d. ____ Irrigation of stomach for active bleeding, poisoning, or gastric dilation

   1. Lavage
   2. Decompression
   3. Gavage
   4. Compression

28. The nasogastric tube of choice for gastric decompression is the:
   a. Miller-Abbott.
   b. Levin.
   c. Dobhoff.
   d. Salem sump.

29. The nasogastric tube of choice for gavage is the:
   a. Dobhoff.
   b. Levin.
   c. Salem sump.
   d. Sengstaken-Blakemore.

30. List nine pieces of equipment that should be present in the postoperative bedside unit.
   a.
   b.
   c.
   d.
   e.
   f.
   g.
   h.
   i.

31. Match the nursing action with the area where it is most often performed. (There may be more than one answer for selected actions.)
   a. ____ Vital signs measured every 15 minutes
   b. ____ Nurse reviews consent forms
   c. ____ Nurse reviews medical record information
   d. ____ Intravenous catheter inserted
   e. ____ Nurse conducts physical assessment
   f. ____ Client positioned and surgical drapes applied

   1. Holding area
   2. Operating room
   3. Recovery room

32. During which stage of anesthesia does the surgeon perform the operation?
   a. Stage 1
   b. Stage 2
   c. Stage 3
   d. Stage 4

33. Epidural anesthesia is an example of which type of anesthesia?
   a. Local
   b. Regional
   c. General
   d. Nerve block

34. Which method of anesthesia is most commonly used for minor procedures in an ambulatory surgical setting?
   a. General
   b. Spinal
   c. Caudal
   d. Local

35. The circulating nurse in the operating room performs all of the following except:
   a. disposal of soiled equipment.
   b. keeping an accurate instrument count.
   c. helping reposition a client.
   d. handing the surgeon surgical instruments.

36. A client who has had spinal anesthesia:
   a. often experiences a rise in blood pressure because of the anesthetic.
   b. requires an endotracheal tube to maintain airway patency.
   c. is subject to burns or injury to the area anesthetized.
   d. commonly develops malignant hyperpyrexia.

37. A client receiving general anesthesia:
   a. may be positioned in almost any manner without injury to a body part.
   b. usually continues to have an effective cough reflex.
   c. maintains voluntary control of urination.
   d. experiences a loss of proprioception.

38. Who is responsible for informing the family about complications arising from the surgical procedure?
   a. Primary nurse
   b. Recovery room nurse
   c. Anesthesiologist
   d. Surgeon

39. Identify six areas of assessment to determine the respiratory status of a postoperative client.
   a.
   b.
   c.
   d.
   e.
   f.

40. List three major causes of airway obstruction in the postoperative client.
   a.
   b.
   c.

41. The preferred position for recovery of the postoperative client is:

a. supine with head turned to the side.
b. side-lying with neck flexed forward.
c. side-lying with face down and neck extended.
d. semi-Fowler's with neck extended.

42. Before removing an artificial airway in the recovering postoperative client, the back of the airway should be suctioned. (true or false)

43. How soon in the recovery period should the client begin coughing and deep-breathing exercises?
a. When responsive
b. When fully awake
c. When vital signs are stable
d. When preparing to leave the recovery room

44. List three areas for assessment to determine circulatory status of the postoperative client.
a.
b.
c.

45. In the table below, describe the characteristic findings associated with postoperative hemorrhage.

Area of assessment	Characteristic finding
Blood pressure	
Heart rate	
Respiratory rate	
Pulse volume	
Skin	
Client behavior	

46. Which of the following could be signs of hemorrhage?
a. Increased bloody drainage from an incisional drain
b. Incisional dressings saturated with blood
c. Swollen, tight incisional site
d. All of the above

47. Signs of internal hemorrhage include:
a. swelling of affected body part with elevation in blood pressure and pulse rate.
b. swelling of body part with fall in blood pressure and rise in pulse rate.
c. presence of bloody drainage from wound with fall in blood pressure and pulse.
d. fall in blood pressure, elevation in pulse, and appearance of bloody drainage on dressing.

48. Postoperative shivering is always a sign of hypothermia. (true or false)

49. When assessing the client's level of consciousness on arrival in the recovery room, the nurse should first:
a. apply a painful stimulus.
b. touch or gently move a body part.
c. call the client by name in a moderate tone of voice.
d. call the client's name in a loud tone of voice.

50. What action would be appropriate if the client requires painful stimuli for arousal in the recovery room?
a. No action is indicated; this is expected.
b. Notify the anesthesiologist.
c. Attempt to stimulate the gag reflex.
d. Increase the intensity of the painful stimulus.

51. How would the amount of drainage from a surgical wound be estimated?

52. Following anesthesia, voluntary control over urinary function may require up to 8 hours. (true or false)

53. All of the following will minimize nausea in the postoperative client in the recovery room except:
a. avoiding sudden movements.
b. irrigating nasogastric tube.
c. offering sips of water.
d. encouraging deep breathing.

54. Mucus suctioned from airways should be included in the client's output measurements. (true or false)

55. Pain can be perceived before the recovering client is fully conscious. (true or false)

56. The preferred route for analgesic administration in the immediate postoperative period is:
a. oral.
b. subcutaneous.
c. intramuscular.
d. intravenous.

57. During which phase of postoperative care should the nurse initiate client teaching?
a. Phase I
b. Phase II

58. Describe six pieces of information that must be presented to postoperative ambulatory surgical clients before discharge.
a.
b.
c.
d.
e.
f.

59. Identify nine criteria for evaluating recovery room discharge readiness.
a.
b.
c.
d.
e.
f.
g.
h.
i.

60. What task must the division nurse perform before the recovery room nurse leaves the client in his or her room?

61. A nurse may modify the frequency of ordered postoperative vital signs if the client appears normal during the initial assessment. (true or false)

62. State four goals appropriate for the postoperative client.
a.
b.
c.
d.

63. The respiratory complication in which alveoli col-

lapse and mucous secretions are retained is called:
a. pneumonia.
b. pulmonary embolism.
c. atelectasis.
d. hypoxia.

64. Identify three nursing interventions for each of the following areas of need in the postoperative client.

Area of need	Nursing interventions
Maintaining respiratory function	
Preventing circulatory stasis	
Promoting normal bowel elimination	
Promoting adequate nutrition	
Promoting normal urinary elimination	

65. Wound dehiscence is characterized by:
a. an invasion of wound tissue by pathogenic microorganisms.
b. separation of wound edges at the suture line.
c. protrusion of internal organs and tissue through the incision.
d. inflammation, purulent exudate, and fever.

66. A postoperative client complaining of sudden chest pain with dyspnea, cyanosis, tachycardia, and hypotension is most likely experiencing the complication of:
a. pneumonia.
b. hypovolemic shock.
c. pulmonary embolism.
d. wound infection.

67. A clean surgical wound usually regains strength against normal stress within:
a. 24 to 48 hours.
b. 3 to 6 days.
c. 15 to 20 days.
d. 4 to 6 weeks.

68. Describe five measures to maintain a client's self-concept during the postoperative period.
a.
b.
c.
d.
e.

APPLICATION OF KEY CONCEPTS

Activities to reinforce skills and techniques

1. Nasogastric intubation and irrigation
   a. Review your institution's procedure for nasogastric intubation and irrigation.
   b. In the nursing laboratory, or on the clinical division, examine the various nasogastric tubes and related equipment used in your institution.
   c. Formulate a list of all the equipment needed to insert a nasogastric tube. Locate this equipment on your clinical division.
   d. In the nursing laboratory, using a demonstration mannequin or simulation model, practice inserting, irrigating, and changing the tape on a nasogastric tube while another student observes and critiques your performance.
   e. Elicit an instructor's evaluation of your technique for nasogastric intubation and maintenance.
2. Preoperative client preparation
   a. Review your institution's policies regarding client preparation for surgery.
   b. Review policies regarding nurses' and student nurses' responsibilities in obtaining or witnessing informed consent.
   c. Obtain a preoperative checklist and review the tasks that must be performed to complete it correctly.
   d. Observe, assist, or provide care to a client preoperatively. Identify the care unique to the preoperative client. Compare the care provided to the care described in your text. Share your perceptions with your instructor.
3. The perioperative experience
   a. If possible, schedule an observational experience involving preoperative, intraoperative, and postoperative (recovery room) client care.
   b. Identify the nursing roles unique to each of these settings.
   c. Identify specific sensory stimuli that the client encounters in each phase of the perioperative experience.
   d. If possible, schedule an observational experience in an ambulatory surgical care area. Compare the role of the nurse and the client experiences to those observed in an inpatient setting.
4. Postoperative exercises
   a. In the nursing laboratory setting, practice teaching and performing the major postoperative exercises with a partner. Be sure to include methods of turning, coughing, deep breathing, and leg exercises.
   b. In the client care setting, provide preoperative teaching to a client that focuses on these postoperative exercises. Obtain feedback through demonstration and document the client's response to the teaching session.

Activities to reinforce theoretical concepts

1. Clinical situation: surgical risks
   For each of the following client situations, identify the risk factors that are present for surgical complications and describe the physiological basis of the identified risk. Discuss nursing actions to minimize the risks identified. Identify conditions present that assist in the recovery process.
   a. Mrs. Burns is a 36-year-old woman who previously had surgery for a benign tumor of the uterus. She is scheduled to have surgery for cancer of the colon after receiving a course of radiation treatments. Mrs. Burns smokes a pack of cigarettes

daily and only drinks an occasional glass of wine when dining out.

b. Mrs. Rush, a 78-year-old woman with a history of degenerative joint disease, is admitted for a total knee replacement. Although she experiences pain in more than one joint, she usually takes indomethacin (Indocin) and aspirin only for her knee pain. She is allergic to penicillin and shellfish. She is able to describe the procedure for replacing her knee joint and is hopeful that she will be able to walk again without pain. Mrs. Rush is 5 feet 3 inches and weighs 150 pounds. Her family reports that Mrs. Rush has at least two bourbon and soda drinks every evening before dinner and has a nightcap at bedtime.

c. Mr. Gregory is a 50-year-old man who has been hospitalized for 7 days following an automobile accident. During this time he has lost 15 pounds. He is currently receiving antibiotics for an infection from an abscess that developed in a wound suffered during the accident. Mr. Gregory is receiving intravenous fluids and has a Foley catheter in place. The surgeon is planning additional exploratory surgery to determine if Mr. Gregory has further internal injuries. Mr. Gregory has a history of hypertension and has been receiving hydrodiuril (Esidrex) and methyldopa (Aldomet) regularly for the past 3 years.

2. Experiential exercise: preoperative assessment
   a. Complete a preoperative assessment of an assigned client using a standardized or modified preoperative assessment tool.
   b. Based on the data elicited, formulate a list of client needs related to preoperative, intraoperative, and postoperative care.
   c. Identify the need for additional resources or referrals to assist the client during the perioperative period. With the assistance of your instructor, or co-assigned staff nurse, initiate the needed referrals.
   d. Formulate a preoperative teaching plan for the client, individualized to his or her unique characteristics or requirements.
   e. Before initiating your preoperative teaching plan, validate your interventions with a staff nurse or your instructor.

3. Experiential exercise: preoperative diagnostic screening

Complete the table below describing common diagnostic tests for a preoperative client.

Diagnostic test	Normal values	Significance to the preoperative client
Urinalysis		
CBC		
Chest x-ray film		
ECG		

4. Experiential exercise: preoperative teaching
   a. If possible, arrange for an observational experience that encompasses the three phases of perioperative care. As you observe, attempt to identify all the sensory experiences that the client would be exposed to in the course of a surgical experience (sight, sound, smell, touch, taste).
   b. Outline a preoperative teaching plan for a client that addresses:
      (1) Routine preoperative preparation
      (2) Perioperative sensory experiences
      (3) Prevention of postoperative complications
      (4) Return to normal or optimal physical functioning
   c. Present the preoperative teaching plan to a peer for critique and feedback.
   d. Elicit instructor evaluation of your teaching plan before utilizing it in an actual client-care situation.
   e. Implement the teaching plan and request client feedback before surgery and later, during the postoperative period.
   f. Care for the client during the postoperative period to evaluate the effectiveness of your teaching and its impact on the postoperative course.

5. Compare the use of general versus regional anesthesia in the table below.

	General anesthesia	Regional anesthesia
Vital sign changes		
Level of consciousness		
Nature of surgical procedure		
Postoperative nursing assessment		

6. Clinical situation: perioperative client care

Mrs. Wilson, 43 years old, is scheduled for a cholecystectomy tomorrow. She is aproximately 50 pounds overweight and smokes a pack of cigarettes every day. She has two children, 13 and 8 years old. Her husband is supportive and will be present on the day of surgery.

   a. What special considerations will be involved in conducting Mrs. Wilson's preoperative teaching?
   b. Why will it be important for Mrs. Wilson to be able to cough effectively?
   c. List at least five topics the nurse should discuss with Mrs. Wilson's family in preparing them for her surgery.
   d. What steps should be taken with Mrs. Wilson on the morning of surgery in relation to:
      (1) Her partial plate (partial dentures)
      (2) Her wedding ring
      (3) Her religious medal
      (4) Her shoulder-length hair
      (5) Her nail polish
      (6) Her complaints of thirst
   e. Complete the following table, which outlines common postoperative complications and the related nursing care for Mrs. Wilson.

Complication	Nursing intervention	Rationale
Thrombophlebitis		
Nausea/vomiting		
Atelectasis		
Urinary retention		
Wound infection		

f. Mrs. Wilson is experiencing acute incisional pain following surgery. Her incision line extends from the upper right abdominal quadrant and is approximately 12 cm (5 inches) long. Her dressing is intact, but she states that it feels like it's pulling on the incision. A drainage tube containing bile secretions extends from the wound site to a drainage bag. Describe at least four specific interventions for promoting Mrs. Wilson's comfort.

g. Mrs. Wilson has just examined her incision for the first time and expresses concern about "how ugly it looks, especially with that nasty green drainage." Develop one goal, two outcome criteria, and four interventions to address Mrs. Wilson's alteration in self-concept.

ADDITIONAL READINGS

Other resources that describe perioperative client care in relation to mobility, pain control, and wound healing may be found in Chapters 35, 42, and 47.

Blackwood, S: Back to basics, the preop exam, Am J Nurs 86:39, 1986.

Describes essential elements of the preoperative nursing assessment. Presents information in table form, summarizing areas to examine, examination techniques, and normal and abnormal findings.

Breslin, EF: Prevention and treatment of pulmonary complications in patients after surgery of the upper abdomen, Heart and Lung 10:511, 1981.

Explores the cause, incidence, and pathophysiology of atelectasis. Identifies populations at risk for developing this common respiratory complication. Proposes specific prevention and treatment strategies.

Burtman, F, and Salminer, CA: Back to basics: controlling postoperative infection, Nurs 84 14:43, 1984.

Presents a "5W" plan for preventing postoperative infections: wash, wind (spirometry), water (fluids), walk (ambulation), and wound care.

Gruendemann, BJ, and Meeker, MH: Alexander's care of the patient in surgery, ed. 7, St. Louis, 1983, The C.V. Mosby Co.

A comprehensive text addressing care of the client through all phases of the operative experience.

Lindeman, C, and Van Aernam, B: Nursing intervention with the pre-surgical patient—the effects of structured and unstructured preoperative teaching, Nurs Res 20:319, 1971.

Explores the influence of preoperative teaching on variables in the client's postoperative course.

McConnell, EA: Clinical considerations in perioperative nursing: preventive aspects of care, Philadelphia, 1987, J.B. Lippincott Co.

Overview of the perioperative experience for the nurse caring for surgical clients on the general surgical division. Describes client needs from a physical as well as an emotional perspective. Identifies nursing interventions specific to each phase of the perioperative experience, which are directed toward prevention of complications and promotion of optimal recovery.

McHugh, NG, et al: Preparatory information: what helps and why, Am J Nurs 82:780, 1982.

Discusses client education before diagnostic or therapeutic procedures. Describes studies in which sensory information was found to be the most critical in preparing clients. Provides several guidelines to follow when giving clients preparatory information.

Wells, N: The effect of relaxation on postoperative muscle tension and pain, Nurs Res 31:236, 1982.

Presents a study that revealed a reduction in pain distress for postoperative clients using relaxation techniques. Reinforces the importance of preoperative instruction in relaxation techniques to promote postoperative comfort.

Chapter 47
Nursing Care of Clients with Wounds

PREREQUISITE READING

Read Chapter 47, pp. 1394 to 1433.

OBJECTIVES

Mastery of content in this chapter will enable the student to:

1. Define selected terms associated with wounds and wound care.
2. Discuss normal stages of wound healing by primary intention.
3. Describe complications of wound healing and their usual time of occurrence.
4. Explain the factors that impair or promote wound healing.
5. Describe differences in assessing a wound in a stable versus an emergency setting.
6. Conduct an assessment of a closed and an open wound.
7. Identify nursing diagnoses related to clients with wounds.
8. Discuss principles of first aid in wound care.
9. Explain nursing care implications in the use of dressings.
10. Apply a sterile dry and wet-to-dry dressing.
11. Discuss the purpose of bandages and binders.
12. Describe the effects of hot and cold on wound healing.
13. Apply warm and cold applications safely to an injured body part.

REVIEW OF KEY CONCEPTS

1. Match the classification of wound type with the most accurate description.

   a. _____ Wound involving a break in skin or mucous membranes
   b. _____ Wound involving no break in skin integrity
   c. _____ Wound resulting from therapy
   d. _____ Wound occurring unexpectedly
   e. _____ Superficial wound involving scraping by friction
   f. _____ Wound involving break in epidermal, dermal, and deeper tissue layers
   g. _____ Penetrating wound from entry and exit of foreign object through an internal organ
   h. _____ Wound containing no pathogens
   i. _____ Wounds made under aseptic conditions but involving entrance into organs normally harboring microorganisms
   j. _____ Closed wounds caused by a blow to the body, a bruise
   k. _____ Bacterial organisms present in wound site ($>10^5$ organisms per gram of tissue)
   l. _____ Wound containing microorganisms
   m. _____ Tearing of tissues with irregular edges
   n. _____ Wound condition in which presence of microorganisms is likely
   o. _____ Wound that involved only epidermal layer of skin

   1. Clean-contaminated
   2. Unintentional
   3. Open
   4. Perforating
   5. Infected
   6. Closed
   7. Laceration
   8. Contusion
   9. Intentional
   10. Clean
   11. Colonized
   12. Contaminated
   13. Superficial
   14. Abrasion
   15. Penetrating

2. A surgical wound such as an appendectomy incision is most likely to heal by:
   a. primary intention.
   b. secondary intention.

3. Which type of wound is most likely to heal by secondary intention?
   a. A cholecystectomy incision
   b. A laceration on a finger from a knife cut
   c. A scalp laceration that requires suturing
   d. A deep burn on a hand

4. List, in the correct sequence, the four stages of the normal healing process.
   a.
   b.
   c.
   d.
5. The cells responsible for cleaning a wound and preparing it for tissue repair are called:
   a. neutrophils.
   b. macrophages.
   c. platelets.
   d. epithelial cells.
6. List at least four nutrients needed for wound healing and describe their contribution to the healing process.
   a.
   b.
   c.
   d.
7. A localized collection of blood underneath the tissues is called a ________________.
8. According to the CDC, what is the most important finding that indicates an infected wound?
   a. Purulent material draining from a wound
   b. A positive wound culture
9. Typically, a surgical wound infection develops around:
   a. the seventh postoperative day.
   b. the fourth or fifth postoperative day.
   c. the second or third postoperative day.
   d. within 24 to 48 hours.
10. Describe four signs and symptoms of wound infection.
    a.
    b.
    c.
    d.
11. Mr. Swan, an obese client, had abdominal surgery 2 days ago. Following a severe bout of coughing, he calls for the nurse, stating he feels "as though something has come loose under my dressing." The nurse observes Mr. Swan's wound: the sutures are intact, but there is an increase in serosanguineous drainage. What complication of wound healing could Mr. Swan be experiencing?
    a. Infection
    b. Dehiscence
    c. Evisceration
    d. Fistula
12. What action should the nurse take when a client's wound eviscerates?
13. An abnormal passage between two organs or between an organ and the outside of the body is called a ________________.
14. Which form of chronic fluid drainage would place the client at highest risk for skin breakdown?
    a. Urine
    b. Stool
    c. Pancreatic
    d. Bile
15. List three criteria for emergency wound inspection.
    a.
    b.
    c.
16. A client who experiences trauma from a dirty penetrating object would require a tetanus antitoxin injection if he or she has not received one within the last:
    a. month.
    b. 6 months.
    c. year.
    d. 5 years.
17. Under what two circumstances would a nurse inspect a wound that the physician has covered with a dressing?
    a.
    b.
18. Describe how each of the following impairs wound healing.
    a. Age
    b. Obesity
    c. Smoking
    d. Steroid medications
    e. Antibiotics
    f. Diabetes
    g. Radiation
19. List six areas for assessment of a wound in a stable setting (for example, after surgery or treatment).
    a.
    b.
    c.
    d.
    e.
    f.
20. Which wound description would be most indicative of a complication?
    a. Inflammation along outer edges of wound on the second postoperative day
    b. Bluish discoloration of tissue around incision site
    c. Yellowish brown discoloration of skin around incision site
    d. Redness and swelling around wound edges on the seventh postoperative day
21. Fill in the correct term describing the characteristic type of wound drainage.
    a. ____________ Thick yellow, green, or brown
    b. ____________ Clear, watery, straw color
    c. ____________ Pale, pink tinged, watery
    d. ____________ Fresh bleeding
22. Before collecting a wound culture, the nurse first cleans the wound to remove skin flora. (true or false)
23. Compare the techniques used to obtain an aerobic and anaerobic wound culture.
24. State six goals appropriate for the client with a wound.
    a.
    b.

c.
d.
e.
f.

25. List the four first aid interventions for clients with a traumatic wound.
   a.
   b.
   c.
   d.
26. Application of pressure to an injury site in which the potential for blood loss is high fulfills which objective of wound care?
   a. Promotion of hemostasis
   b. Promotion of wound healing
   c. Prevention of infection
   d. Prevention of further trauma
27. Which wound type should be allowed to bleed in order to remove contaminants?
   a. Abrasion
   b. Laceration
   c. Contusion
   d. Puncture
28. Identify six purposes of dressings.
   a.
   b.
   c.
   d.
   e.
   f.
29. Identify and briefly describe the purpose of each of the three layers of a surgical dressing.
   a.
   b.
   c.
30. When changing a dressing that adheres to a wound surface healing by primary intention, the nurse should:
   a. irrigate the dressing with warm tap water.
   b. gently pull off the dressing.
   c. irrigate the dressing with sterile normal saline.
   d. leave the contact dressing in place and reinforce outer layers.
31. Which dressing type is most appropriate for wounds requiring debridement?
   a. Self-adhesive transparent film (second skin)
   b. Nonadherent gauze (Telfa)
   c. Hydrogel
   d. Wet-to-dry
32. What is the meaning of the order: "reinforce dressing p.r.n."?
33. Describe the four guidelines for the dressing change procedure recommended by the CDC.
   a.
   b.
   c.
   d.
34. Identify four nursing actions appropriate in preparing a client for a dressing change.
   a.
   b.
   c.
   d.
35. To safely remove tape securing dressings, the nurse does all of the following except:
   a. gently pulls the outer end parallel with the skin.
   b. applies light traction to the skin toward the wound.
   c. pulls the tape in the direction of hair growth.
   d. pulls the tape gently toward the wound.
36. The most effective antiseptic solutions for skin care are:
   a. Tincture of chlorhexidine (Hibiclens) and iodophors (Betadine)
   b. 70% alcohol and Betadine
   c. Hibiclens and peroxide
   d. Peroxide and 70% alcohol
37. The nurse uses all of the following principles when cleansing a draining wound except:
   a. cleaning in the direction from the least contaminated to the most contaminated.
   b. using gentle friction when applying antiseptics to the skin.
   c. irrigating from the area of least contaminated to the most contaminated region.
   d. cleaning from a drain site toward the incisional area.
38. List the three purposes of wound irrigation.
   a.
   b.
   c.
39. Irrigation of an open wound requires sterile technique. (true or false)
40. Correct technique for wound irrigation includes:
   a. occluding the wound opening with the syringe.
   b. irrigating with the syringe tip in the actual drainage site.
   c. flushing the outer edges and contaminated areas first.
   d. using slow, continuous pressure to flush the wound.
41. Disposable gloves should be used to remove soiled dressings. (true or false)
42. Threads or wire used to sew body tissues together are called ____________________.
43. Describe a drainage evacuator.
44. Identify five purposes for use of a binder or bandage.
   a.
   b.
   c.
   d.
   e.
45. Describe four nursing responsibilities that must be performed before applying a bandage or binder.
   a.
   b.
   c.
   d.

46. The nurse should have a physician's order before loosening or removing a bandage applied by a physician. (true or false)

47. Using Montgomery ties to secure a dressing is advantageous because:
   a. pressure on the incision is reduced.
   b. skin irritation from frequent dressing changes is reduced.
   c. infection to the incision is reduced.
   d. drainage from the wound is reduced.

48. Identify whether heat (H) or cold (C) applications produce the physiological response described.
   a. _____ Vasodilation
   b. _____ Local anesthesia
   c. _____ Reduced muscle tension
   d. _____ Reduced cellular metabolism
   e. _____ Increased capillary permeability
   f. _____ Increased blood viscosity

49. Identify five conditions that increase risk of injury from heat or cold applications.
   a.
   b.
   c.
   d.
   e.

50. List six factors that influence the body's response to heat and cold therapies.
   a.
   b.
   c.
   d.
   e.
   f.

51. Describe the four areas to assess before application of heat or cold therapies.
   a.
   b.
   c.
   d.

52. Complete the safety chart describing "do's and don't's" for application of heat or cold therapy.

Do's	Don't's
a.	a.
b.	b.
c.	c.

53. Application of heat or cold requires a physician's order. (true or false)

54. Moist heat:
   a. has less risk of burns to skin than dry heat.
   b. does not cause skin maceration.
   c. penetrates deeply into tissue layers.
   d. retains temperature longer.

55. Optimal benefits from an aquathermic heating pad would be derived from which application schedule?
   a. Continuous application during waking hours
   b. Application for 2 hours, removal for 1 hour, reapplication
   c. Application for 1 hour, removal for 30 minutes, reapplication
   d. Application for 30 minutes, removal for 15 minutes, reapplication

56. Fill in the appropriate term for the heat or cold application described.
   a. ____________ A piece of gauze dressing moistened with a cool, prescribed solution
   b. ____________ Immersion of a body part in a warmed solution
   c. ____________ Immersion of the perineal area in warm fluid in a special tub, chair, or basin
   d. ____________ Exposure of superficial layers of the skin to a 40- to 74-watt light bulb

57. Identify the appropriate temperature for each of the following:
   a. Cold compresses or soaks
   b. Warm moist compresses
   c. Warm soaks
   d. Aquathermic pads

58. A client has an inflamed area on the right forearm from an infiltrated IV line. The client states that there is considerable discomfort. The nurse should obtain an order for:
   a. warm moist compresses.
   b. an ace bandage.
   c. a Telfa dressing.
   d. ice compresses.

59. When wrapping an extremity, apply a bandage first at the proximal end and progress distally. (true or false)

APPLICATION OF KEY CONCEPTS

Activities to reinforce skills and techniques

1. Wound management
   a. Review your institution's policies regarding wound care and dressing changes.
   b. In the nursing laboratory, or on the assigned clinical area, examine supplies and equipment used for wound management.
   c. On the client care areas, visit clients with traumatic or surgical wounds and observe the care that they receive. Compare the techniques for wound care and dressing changes used by the staff with those described in your text. If you note modifications in technique, attempt to determine the rationale for these changes. Discuss your analysis with your instructor.
2. Dressing changes
   a. In the nursing laboratory, practice each of the following dressing techniques using a demonstration mannequin or simulation model while a peer observes and critiques your performance:
      (1) Removing a soiled dressing
      (2) Cleansing a surgical wound with a drain in place

(3) Application of a dry sterile dressing
(4) Application of a wet-to-dry dressing
(5) Wound irrigation

b. Elicit an instructor's evaluation of your technique.

3. Special dressing applications
   a. In the nursing laboratory, practice application of each of the following binders on a demonstration mannequin while a peer observes and critiques your performance:
      (1) Abdominal binder
      (2) T binder (single or double)
      (3) Breast binder
   b. In the nursing laboratory, practice application of each of the following on a partner:
      (1) Arm sling (personally or commercially made)
      (2) Elastic bandage (arm, leg, head; to practice the various circling techniques described in your text)
4. Application of heat and cold
   a. Review your institution's policies regarding application of heat and cold.
   b. In the nursing laboratory, or on the clinical division, examine equipment and supplies used for heat or cold applications.
   c. In the nursing laboratory, practice application of each of the following thermal treatments with a partner. Be sure to assess and initiate the actions with regard for client safety and therapeutic effect.
      (1) Cold compress to finger
      (2) Heat lamp to forearm
      (3) Warm soak to hand
      (4) Aquathermic pad to calf
   d. In the nursing laboratory, or on the clinical division, gather and set up the equipment needed to provide a sitz bath for a client.

Activities to reinforce theoretical concepts

1. Experiential exercise: assessment for wound healing
   a. Conduct a comprehensive assessment of an assigned client.
   b. Based on the data obtained, identify factors that would facilitate or inhibit wound healing in this particular client.
   c. For those factors known to inhibit wound healing, identify nursing actions that could alleviate or minimize the client's risk.
2. Experiential exercise: wound assessment
   a. With the assistance of a designated staff nurse or your instructor, and the permission of the client, observe surgical or traumatic wounds of clients in the clinical setting.
   b. Formulate your own description of the wound using the following criteria:
      (1) Wound classification: status of skin integrity, cause, severity, cleanliness, other descriptive qualities
      (2) Stable wound assessment: appearance, characteristic drainage, presence of drains, wound closure, pain, cultures
      (3) Nature of healing: primary intention, secondary intention
   c. Submit your description to your instructor for critique.
3. Clinical situation: wound care in the emergency setting
   You are on a camping trip with a group of friends. The group leader falls and sustains an 8 cm laceration of the right forearm on a jagged rock. The group leader is right handed. You are about a 2-hour hike away from the campground and a 4-hour drive from any health care facility.
   a. Describe each of the assessment areas that you should evaluate related to the group leader's injury.
   b. Discuss the emergency care you would provide for the group leader's laceration. Include actions for each of the following areas:
      (1) Hemostasis
      (2) Cleansing
      (3) Protection
4. Clinical situation: application of heat and cold
   Ms. Claire is a 43-year-old schoolteacher with a deep vein thrombosis in her left leg. The physician's orders include strict bed rest, leg elevated at all times, and aquathermic pad p.r.n.
   a. What therapeutic benefits will an aquathermic pad have on Ms. Claire's condition?
   b. What factors would you assess before instituting the use of an aquathermic pad for Ms. Claire?
   c. What information will you present to Ms. Claire concerning:
      (1) The purpose of the treatment
      (2) The symptoms she may experience with temperature exposure
      (3) The precautions to take to prevent injury
   d. Which form of heat (moist or dry) would be preferable for Ms. Claire? Why?
   e. What aquathermic pad temperature setting would be safe for the client?
   f. What schedule would you design for application and removal of the pad to optimize client comfort and therapeutic effect?
5. Clinical situation: nursing process for client requiring wound care
   Mrs. Tucker, a 48-year-old nurse, has been hospitalized for the past 3 weeks. Initially she was admitted for a cholecystectomy, but she developed several complications in the postoperative period.

   At the present time, she is being treated for multiple abscesses under her incision. She has severe skin breakdown around the incision line and drain sites. Her dressing must be changed every 3 to 4 hours since there is a large amount of purulent drainage.

   Every time a nurse changes her dressing, Mrs. Tucker turns her face away and states that she "can't stand to look at that ugly mess." Mrs. Tucker's appetite is steadily decreasing. She recently has asked her husband not to bring the children in to visit.

a. Formulate a list of nursing diagnoses for Mrs. Tucker. Place the diagnoses in priority order.
b. Select the three priority diagnoses, and formulate a goal for each.
c. For each goal, identify at least one outcome criterion that will measure goal achievement.
d. For each goal, describe two nursing interventions and their rationale.

ADDITIONAL READINGS

Other resources addressing related topics of nutritional support, aseptic technique, and surgical trauma will be found in Chapters 33, 43, and 46.

Cuzzell, J: Artful solutions to chronic problems, Am J Nurs 85:163, 1985.

Identifies appropriate goals for chronic wound management. Describes selected wound care techniques appropriate for specific types of wounds and the rationale for their use. Analyzes pros and cons of the various wound care techniques described.

Cuzzell, J, and Willey, T: Wound care forum: pressure relief perennials, Am J Nurs 87:1157, 1987.

Presents a decision tree to use in determining the most appropriate mattress surface for clients. Includes color photographs illustrating characteristic stages of pressure ulcer development with descriptions and specific mattress recommendations.

Hotter, AN: Physiologic aspects and clinical implications of wound healing, Heart and Lung 11:522, 1982.

Detailed discussion of the physiological basis of wound healing. Describes common clinical conditions negatively impacting the healing process and makes recommendations to minimize their effect.

Mondoux, LA, editor: Pressure ulcers, Nurs Clin North Am 22(2), 1987.

A comprehensive series of articles addressing topics related to pressure ulcers including etiology and prevention, nutritional support needs, assessment, treatment strategies and supportive measures, client and family education, and current research.

Schummann, DL, editor: Wound healing, Nurs Clin North Am 14(4), 1979.

A comprehensive series of articles addressing topics related to wound healing. Includes nursing care directed toward prevention in the perioperative client, treatment strategies, and complex client management situations (such as wound sepsis and radical head and neck surgical procedures).

Young, M: Malnutrition and wound healing, Heart and Lung 17(1):60, 1988.

Discusses stages of wound healing and nutritional requirements necessary for normal wound healing. Overviews causes and physiological impact of malnutrition. Includes assessment criteria for identification of the client at high risk. Discusses nutritional support in the postoperative client.

UNIT 10 Contemporary Issues

Chapter 48
Nursing Leadership and Management

PREREQUISITE READING

Read Chapter 48, pp. 1436 to 1447.

OBJECTIVES

Mastery of content in this chapter will enable the student to:

1. Define selected terms describing nursing leadership and management.
2. Differentiate between leadership and management.
3. Compare and contrast the scientific management theory and the human relations movement in their perspectives for improving productivity.
4. Identify the primary principles of situational leadership theories.
5. Describe and give examples of the four classic leadership styles: authoritarian, democratic, laissez-faire, and situational.
6. Explain why leadership is important for nursing.
7. List and give examples of the four primary types of leadership skills student nurses can begin to develop.

REVIEW OF KEY CONCEPTS

1. Define leadership.
2. Define management.
3. Match the theorist with the appropriate leadership or management theory.
   - **a.** _____ Theory X and theory Y
   - **b.** _____ Management grid
   - **c.** _____ Scientific management movement
   - **d.** _____ Human relations movement
   - **e.** _____ System 4 management
   - **f.** _____ "Leader match" model
   - **g.** _____ Situational leadership theory

   1. Fiedler
   2. Fredrick Taylor
   3. Elton Mayo
   4. Hersey and Blanchard
   5. McGregor
   6. Blake and Mouton
   7. Likert
4. Identify the leadership theory for each description provided.
   - **a.** ____________ Management style is based on supportive relationships, group decision making, group methods of supervision, and high-performance goals.
   - **b.** ____________ Leadership theory that holds that every leader has a certain predominant style. Effective management should not attempt to change the leader's style but should choose a leader with the style most appropriate to the situation.
   - **c.** ____________ Theory that examines the four general styles of leaders with many variations on each continuum related to high and low consideration and structure.
   - **d.** ____________ Theory that assumes that human beings prefer to be directed, have little ambition, reject responsibility, and are most concerned about job security.
   - **e.** ____________ Time and motion studies were introduced to analyze tasks based on the belief that improving how tasks are performed would improve every aspect of the organization.
5. Which theory is based on the assumption that employees are capable of self-motivation and satisfaction if they are happy in the organization and committed to its goals?
   - **a.** McGregor's theory Y
   - **b.** Elton Mayo's human relations movement
   - **c.** Fiedler's leader match model
   - **d.** Blake and Mouton's management grid model
6. This type of leadership style is characterized by one-way communication in which the leader defines the roles of the followers and tells them what, how, when, and where to do the various tasks.
   - **a.** The high task/low relationship style
   - **b.** The high task/high relationship style
   - **c.** The high relationship/high task style
   - **d.** The high relationship/low task style
7. Mr. Massie is the team leader on a busy surgical

floor. The team members are upset with the evening client assignments. Mr. Massie tells the team members to work things out for themselves and that whatever they decide will be satisfactory. Mr. Massie's leadership style could best be described as:
a. authoritative.
b. democratic.
c. laissez-faire.
d. situational.

8. The effective nurse manager is able to use different styles and leadership skills depending on the specific situation and the maturity of the employees. This is an example of which leadership style?
a. Authoritative
b. Democratic
c. Laissez-faire
d. Situational

9. Identify the three key skills for effective leadership.
a.
b.
c.

10. Describe the differences between a formal and an informal leader.

11. The authoritarian leader:
a. promotes individual initiative and creativity.
b. is concerned primarily about tasks and goals.
c. establishes a two-way group communication pattern.
d. distributes authority and responsibility to others.

12. During a cardiac arrest, which leadership style would be most effective?
a. Autocratic
b. Democratic
c. Laissez-faire
d. Delegating-situational

13. Describe the four different leadership styles characteristic of situational leadership.
a. Style 1: directing
b. Style 2: coaching
c. Style 3: supporting
d. Style 4: delegating

14. Identify the four primary leadership skills for nurses and describe at least two behaviors characteristic of each skill.
a.
b.
c.
d.

APPLICATION OF KEY CONCEPTS
Activities to reinforce theoretical concepts

1. Discuss why it is important for student nurses to develop their leadership skills.

2. Experiential exercise: leadership styles
a. Identify a leader with whom you have worked. Describe the leadership style that this leader utilized. Support your position by providing examples of this person's actions that validate your conclusion.
b. Identify the leadership style or styles that you feel create the best environment for your work productivity and personal development. Are the leadership styles the same or different?
c. Identify the leadership style with which you are most uncomfortable in the work or educational setting. How can you effectively work with this particular leadership style?
d. Examine the primary leadership skills for nurses that appear in Chapter 48 of your text. In the table below, list the specific behaviors for each skill area and complete a self-assessment indicating which skills you feel you already possess and those that require additional development. For those that you need to develop, identify at least one strategy for your personal development plan. Share your plan with your instructor.

Leadership skills	Behaviors	Development strategies
Personal behaviors		
Communication		
Organization		
Self-examination		

3. Clinical situation: leadership styles
Ms. White, a recent graduate, has been assigned to provide care for five clients. She is having difficulty organizing her nursing activities to meet the demands of each of the clients as well as those imposed by the established routine of the nursing unit. The head nurse is aware of Ms. White's problem. Provide an example illustrating the possible approach each of the following head nurses would use when addressing Ms. White's problem using the situational leadership model.
a. The head nurse who uses style 1: directing
b. The head nurse who uses style 2: coaching
c. The head nurse who uses style 3: supporting
d. The head nurse who uses style 4: delegating

ADDITIONAL READINGS

Douglas, LM: The effective nurse: leader and manager, ed. 3, St. Louis, 1988, The C.V. Mosby Co.
A comprehensive text addressing a variety of topics related to leadership and management in the context of nursing practice. Management strategies are correlated with patterns of nursing care delivery and the nursing process. Special sections are devoted to discussion of communication skills, conflict resolution, control, and legal and ethical issues. Each section is well referenced for additional direction in reading.

Hein, E, and Nicholson, M: Contemporary leadership behavior: selected readings, ed. 2, Boston, 1986, Little, Brown & Co.
Presents a variety of leadership behaviors that may be incorporated into progressive nursing practice. Organizes the collection of articles into areas including the culture of nursing, modern leadership theories, contemporary

leadership behaviors, evolving health organization settings, and the future of nursing practice. Each section is well referenced for additional direction in reading.

Marriner, A, editor: Contemporary nursing management: issues and practice, St. Louis, 1982, The C.V. Mosby Co.

Discusses practical aspects of nursing management. Uses the components of the management process to organize articles addressing current management issues and practice. The diverse background of contributing authors provides a variety of fresh perspectives to the complex challenges of nursing management.

Chapter 49
Change Process and the Nurse

PREREQUISITE READING

Read Chapter 49, pp. 1448 to 1459.

OBJECTIVES

Mastery of content in this chapter will enable the student to:

1. Define selected terms associated with the concept and process of change.
2. Describe specific types of change.
3. Compare and contrast theories of change formulated by Lewin, Lippitt, and Rogers and describe examples of application.
4. Compare and contrast the systems, developmental change, and confrontation models of change and describe examples of application.
5. Describe the major concepts and examples of application for other models of change: traditional, elite corps, psychoanalytical, and scholarly consultation.
6. Analyze response to change, including interference and resistance, and factors that contribute to various reactions.
7. Compare steps of the nursing process to steps of the change process.
8. Describe characteristics, skills, and behaviors of the effective nurse change agent.
9. Relate the concept of power to skills and behavior of the nurse change agent.
10. Relate the role of change agent to other nursing roles.

REVIEW OF KEY CONCEPTS

1. Define change.
2. Match the type of change with its most accurate description.
   - **a.** _____ The biopsychosocial changes that occur within the life cycle experience
   - **b.** _____ Change that is effected by an individual or group carrying out the will of another without choice
   - **c.** _____ Change that occurs accidentally without control by any individual, group, or community
   - **d.** _____ Deliberate and collaborative attempts to alter the environment with specific consideration given to mutual goals of the individuals involved

   1. Planned
   2. Developmental
   3. Coercive
   4. Situational
3. List six characteristics of planned change.
   - **a.**
   - **b.**
   - **c.**
   - **d.**
   - **e.**
   - **f.**
4. Identify the individual associated with each of the following theories of change.
   - **a.** __________ Theory of change that states that the individual should be motivated and committed to the proposed change. Identified five stages of planned change: awareness, interest, evaluation, trial, and adoption.
   - **b.** __________ Theory of change that outlined several characteristic stages. An accurate diagnosis of the problem and an analysis of the potential solutions, with a trial period of change before full-scale implementation, are emphasized. Focuses on the ability of the change agent as crucial.
   - **c.** __________ The classical theory of change, which identifies three stages of the process: unfreezing, moving, and refreezing. Describes the need to determine variables that facilitate or impede change during the planning phase.
5. Complete the following table describing models of change and their characteristic concepts.

Model of change	Characteristic concepts
Traditional	
________________	Change occurs by direct confrontation, challenge, or criticism Change agent must remain calm and objective
Elite corps	
________________	Need for change grows out of structural stress or dysfunction in some part of system (inside or outside) Change agent defines or diagnoses dysfunction
Psychoanalytical	________________
Scholarly consultation	
________________	Change is required to respond to discrepancies between potential growth and actual growth, development, or change Change agent defines and diagnoses conflict areas and strategies to promote growth and development

6. Change is usually accompanied by feelings of anxiety, even when change is desired. (true or false)
7. Define resistance as it relates to change theory.
8. Identify seven reasons for resistance to planned change.
a.
b.
c.
d.
e.
f.
g.
9. Describe the activities needed to effect change as they relate to each step of the nursing process. Include at least one activity for the nursing diagnosis step and at least three activities for the other steps of the process.
a. Assessment
(1)
(2)
(3)
b. Diagnosis
(1)
c. Planning (goal establishment)
(1)
(2)
(3)
d. Intervention
(1)
(2)
(3)
e. Evaluation
(1)
(2)
(3)
10. When establishing goals for change:
a. input from all persons involved in the process should be gathered.
b. all people affected by the change should be involved.
c. consideration must be given to each suggested solution.
d. all of the above.
11. The most important characteristic in being an effective change agent is:
a. competence in organizational and management strategies.
b. competence in use of communication and interpersonal skills.
c. membership in the group as an informal leader.
d. membership in the group as the formal leader.
12. What three questions are of particular importance for the change agent in understanding personal motivation for participating in the change process?
a.
b.
c.
13. Describe four questions that may be asked to determine the capability of the nurse as change agent.
a.
b.
c.
d.
14. Define power in the context of change theory.
15. Identify the type of power in each situation described.
a. ____________ A psychiatric nurse consultant is recruited by the head nurse to teach the staff about care of the chemically dependent client.
b. ____________ A head nurse from the operating room is selected by the hospital director to observe the staff at work in the surgical intensive care unit and make recommendations concerning their care of the recovering surgical client.
c. ____________ The head nurse is given the authority, by the hospital administration, to hire three new staff nurses.
d. ____________ The RN provides direction and supervision to the nursing assistant in turning and positioning a client.
e. ____________ The voting membership of the state nurses' association elects a representative to vote on issues at the national convention.

16. Describe four ways in which resistance forces may be decreased during planned change.
    a.
    b.
    c.
    d.
17. Summarize the six actions that the nurse must perform in order to institute any change.
    a.
    b.
    c.
    d.
    e.
    f.

APPLICATION OF KEY CONCEPTS

Activities to reinforce theoretical concepts

1. Experiential exercise: the nurse as change agent
    a. Following a client care experience in any health care setting, identify situations in which the nurse actually or potentially could serve as a change agent.
    b. What model of change most closely matched the situation you observed?
    c. Describe characteristics, skills, and behaviors of the change agent (nurse) that would facilitate or inhibit planned change.
    d. What type of power did the nurse use in effecting change?
    e. What authority or power did the nurse have in this situation?
    f. Was there resistance to change? Was this handled effectively? (If yes, what was effective; if no, how could the approach be modified?)
2. Experiential exercise: planned change
    a. Identify a small change that you would like to promote in your home or residence environment.
    b. Identify the type of change involved.
    c. Select the model of change that best suits the problem identified.
    d. Develop a plan for change based on the change process.
    e. Examine your participation and role as the change agent.
    f. Evaluate the plan and analyze the response to change.
3. Clinical situation: resistance to change
    You are the head nurse on a clinical area that has been using nursing care plans in which each nurse formulates individual nursing diagnoses, rather than using the NANDA nursing diagnoses list. Several nurses on your clinical division recognize the usefulness of a standard approach to diagnosis of client problems, but efforts to introduce the use of the NANDA list have met with great resistance. In one of the clinical areas, the staff have openly refused to use the "new" list.
    a. What feelings may the staff have concerning this planned change?
    b. What reasons might the staff have for resisting change?
    c. What strategies for planned change could you implement in order to minimize resistance to use of the NANDA nursing diagnoses list?

ADDITIONAL READINGS

McGovern, W, and Rogers, J: Change theory, Am J Nurs 86:556, 1986.

Discusses client care situation in which change theory was applied. Clearly links theory to practice.

Nursing for the future: strategies for change, Am J Nurs 87:1643, 1987.

Report from a conference group that explored the future of nursing. Identifies change strategies for survival of the profession.

Rogers, J: Theoretical considerations involved in the process of change, Nurs Forum 12(2):161, 1973.

Describes the major models of change. Explores the process of change, resistance, power, and the problem-solving approach.

Ward, M, and Moran, S: Resistance to change: recognize, respond, overcome, Nurs Manage 15(1):30, 1984.

Describes the psychodynamics underlying resistance to change. Points out the positive function of resistance. Explores dangers of resistance and presents effective strategies to overcome resistance and facilitate planned change.

Welch, LB, editor: The nurse as change agent, Nurs Clin North Am 14(2), 1979.

A series of articles discussing change theory and strategies for the nurse to implement in the role of change agent. Information presented describes the nurse as change agent in both nursing service and nursing education.

...ers to Review of Key Concepts

CHAPTER 1

1. According to ICN: profession concerned with assisting an individual to perform activities contributing to health, recovery, or peaceful death. According to ANA: profession concerned with the diagnosis and treatment of human responses to actual and potential health problems.
2. False
3. True
4. d
5. **a.** 4
   b. 6
   c. 1
   d. 2
   e. 3
   f. 5
6. Goldmark report
7. Lysaught report
8. Any five:
   - Formulate legislation governing nursing practice and education.
   - Formulate regulations interpreting nurse practice acts so that nurses and nonnurses better understand the laws.
   - Develop curriculum plans for nursing education.
   - Establish criteria for measuring the quality of nursing care, education, and research.
   - Prepare job descriptions used by employers of nurses.
   - Guide the development of nursing care delivery systems.
   - Provide knowledge to improve nursing administration, practice, education, and research.
   - Guide research to establish an empirical knowledge base for nursing.
   - Identify the domain and goals of nursing.
9. **a.** 5
   b. 7
   c. 6
   d. 3
   e. 4
   f. 8
   g. 2
   h. 1
10. Refer to table at top of p. 250.
11. True
12. To prepare nurse clinicians capable of improving nursing care through advancement of nursing theory and sciences
13. Programs that help nurses remain current in skills, knowledge, and theory of nursing practice through formal, organized educational programs offered by educational and health care institutions
14. Any three:
    - To improve and maintain nursing practice
    - To promote and exercise leadership in effecting change in health care delivery systems
    - To fulfill professional learning needs
    - To help nurses become specialized in a particular area of practice
    - To teach nurses new skills and techniques
15. True
16. Instruction or training provided by a health care agency or institution, within the institution, designed to increase the knowledge, skills, and competencies of nurses and other personnel
17. Clinical ladder
18. **a.** Administrators and selected staff establish institutional/agency policies and procedures under which nurses must practice.
    b. Establish standards of practice that serve as guidelines for providing care and as criteria for evaluating care.
    c. Regulate licensure and define scope of nursing practice.
19. True
20. Shorter hospital stays, increased frequency of continuing nursing care in the home
21. **a.** Opportunistic infections associated with acquired immunodeficiency syndrome (AIDS)
    b. Increased critical care technology
    c. Increased frequency of organ transplantation
22. **a.** Increased number of elderly
    b. Increased number of clients with chronic illnesses
    c. Increased number of clients with functional impairments
23. Any four:
    - Health promotion
    - Health maintenance
    - Health education
    - Health management
    - Coordination and continuity of care within the community
24. **a.** Function with a high level of independence in providing a variety of health-related services within a designated community
    b. Provide health education; care for nonemergency illnesses; make referrals when more specialized health care is required
    c. Develop programs to increase worker health and safety; treat nonemergency acute illness; provide first aid; in emergency situations, provide immediate care and arrange hospital transport; make referrals to additional health resources
    d. Provide home-based nursing care, with particular attention to teaching the client or family members to perform nursing activities
25. **a.** Care giver
    b. Teacher

	Length of program	Educational institution	Degree granted	Program focus
Associate degree program	2 years	College, junior college	AD	Theoretical and practical course related to nursing practice
Diploma program*	2-3 years	Hospital based	Diploma	Same as AD
Baccalaureate program	4 years	College, university	BSN; BScN; BS, BN	Same as AD but with courses in the social sciences, basic sciences, and humanities to support nursing theory

*In Canada, the diploma programs are offered in community colleges or hospitals and are 2- or 3-year programs comparable to associate degree programs in the United States.

c. Manager
d. Comforter
e. Rehabilitator
f. Protector

26. Communicator

27. a. 3
b. 7
c. 4
d. 2
e. 5
f. 1
g. 6

28. a. Physician (MD [doctor of medicine], DO [doctor of osteopathy])
b. Physician assistant
c. Physical therapist
d. Occupational therapist
e. Respiratory therapist
f. Pharmacist
g. Social worker
h. Chaplain

29. a. A profession requires an extended education of its members, in addition to a basic liberal foundation—nursing requires that its members possess an appropriate education that incorporates current scientific and technological advances.
b. A profession has a theoretical body of knowledge leading to defined skills, abilities, and norms—there are several theoretical models of nursing that serve as frameworks for nursing curricula and clinical practice.
c. A profession provides a specific service—nursing is a vital component of the current health care delivery system.
d. Members of a profession have autonomy in decision making and practice—nurses are taking on independent practice roles in various settings and regulate accountability through nursing audits and standards of practice.
e. The profession as a whole has a code of ethics for practice—nursing has a code of ethics that defines the principles by which nurses function.

30. a. American Nurses' Association; to improve standards of health and availability of health care, to foster high standards for nursing, and to promote the professional development and general and economic welfare of nurses
b. Canadian Nurses Association; to improve standards of health and availability of health care, to foster high standards for nursing, and to promote the professional development and general and economic welfare of nurses
c. National League for Nursing; to improve nursing education, nursing service, and health care delivery in the United States
d. International Council of Nurses; to promote national associations of nurses, improve standards of nursing practice, seek a higher status for nurses, and provide an international power base for nurses
e. National Student Nurses' Association; to consider issues of importance to nursing students and often cooperate in activities and programs with the professional organizations (United States)
f. Canadian Student Nurses' Association; to consider issues of importance to nursing students and often cooperate in activities and programs with the professional organizations (Canada)

31. Any four:
- Technological advances
- Demographic changes
- Consumer movement
- Health promotion
- Women's movement
- Human rights movement

32. Any three:
- Learn about social needs.
- Become activists in influencing policies to meet social needs.
- Contribute time and money to nursing, professional organizations, and candidates.
- Become active in development of health care policies and practices.

CHAPTER 2

1. A dynamic state in which the individual adapts to changes in internal and external environments to maintain a state of well-being in all dimensions

2. A person's ideas, convictions, and attitudes about health and illness

3. Any three:
- Immunizations
- Proper sleep patterns
- Adequate exercise
- Adequate diet and nutrition

4. Any three:
- Smoking
- Drug abuse or alcohol abuse
- Poor diet
- Refusal to take prescribed medications

5. a. 2

b. 4
c. 5
d. 3
e. 1

6. d
7. c
8. Health prom
9. Illness preve
10. d
11. False
12. Any four:
   - Three meals every d
   - Breakfast every day
   - Moderate exercise two or thre
   - 7 to 8 hours of uninterrupted sleep each day
   - No smoking
   - Ideal body weight for sex, age, height, and body build
   - Alcohol only in moderation
13. **a.** 2
    b. 3
    c. 1
    d. 2
    e. 1
14. b
15. Any two for each category:
   - Genetic and physiological factors: pregnancy; obesity; family history of diabetes mellitus, cancer, coronary disease, renal disease
   - Age: increased age produces increased risk of cardiovascular disease, cancer, birth defects, complications of pregnancy; increased age accentuates or potentiates other risk factors that may be present
   - Environment: prolonged exposure to chemicals or toxic wastes; air, water, or noise pollution; living in high crime areas; poor living conditions and overcrowding; family conflicts and problems
   - Life-style: negative health practices such as overeating or poor nutrition, insufficient rest and sleep, poor personal hygiene, smoking, alcohol or drug abuse, involvement in dangerous activities (for example, skydiving), overexposure to the sun; severe or prolonged emotional stress
16. False
17. An abnormal state in which a person's physical, emotional, intellectual, social, developmental, or spiritual functioning is diminished or impaired compared with that person's previous experience
18. b
19. True
20. False
21. Any five:
   - The visibility and recognizability of the symptoms
   - The extent to which the person perceives the symptoms as serious (the person's estimate of the present and future risks)
   - The person's information, knowledge, and cultural assumptions and understanding related to the perceived symptoms
   - The extent to which symptoms disrupt family, work, and social activities
   - The frequency of the appearance of the symptoms and their persistence
   - The extent to which others exposed to the person tolerate the symptoms

b. Stage 2: assumption of the sick role—the point at which the person seeks confirmation from family and social group of illness and seeks to be excused from normal duties and role expectations
c. Stage 3: medical care contact—the point at which the client seeks expert validation and treatment of illness
d. Stage 4: dependent client role—the stage during which the client depends on health professionals for the relief of symptoms and accepts care, sympathy, and protection from the demands and stresses of life
e. Stage 5: recovery and rehabilitation—the time at which the client is able to resume an optimal level of functioning, or (in the case of chronic illness) makes the necessary adjustment to a prolonged reduction in level of health and functioning

23. False
24. c
25. Body image
26. Self-concept
27. All four:
   - The type of change
   - The adaptive capacity of the client and family
   - The rate at which the change takes place
   - The supportive services available to the client and family

CHAPTER 3

1. b
2. Medicare
3. Medicaid
4. c
5. d
6. a
7. The restoration of a person to normal or near-normal function after a physical or mental illness, injury, or chemical addiction
8. a
9. **a.** 5
   b. 2
   c. 6
   d. 1
   e. 4
   f. 3
10. **a.** Provide health services on an outpatient basis
    b. Provide health care, during the day, to specific client populations such as the elderly or individuals with emotional illnesses

c. Provide emergency psychiatric care and counseling to clients experiencing extreme stress or conflict, often involving suicide attempts or drug or alcohol abuse
d. Provide long-term care, and support during gradual return to the community, for clients with chemical drug dependency
e. Provide long-term medical, nursing, or custodial care for clients with chronic illnesses or disabilities
f. Provide therapy and training, in a residential setting, to restore a client to an optimal level of functioning and independence
g. Provide inpatient and outpatient counseling services to clients with behavioral or emotional illnesses

11. Any three:
    - Decreased length of hospital stays
    - Increased number of clients requiring acute care services in the home
    - Increased number of home health agencies
    - Higher priority to discharge planning at the time of hospital admission
    - Reduction of primary care in some institutions
    - Increased hiring of lower salaried, nonprofessional health care workers in some institutions
12. False
13. Informed consent
14. a. Traditional approach to health insurance obtained by the individual (or through a group plan), which is a retrospective fee-for-service (third-party-reimbursement) plan
    b. Include HMOs (health maintenance organizations) delivering care based on a prepaid fee, with emphasis on health promotion and illness prevention; PPOs (preferred provider organizations) made up of a group of physicians or a hospital agreeing to provide comprehensive health services at a discount to companies under contract; IPAs (individual practice associations), also a prospective payment health plan that involves a fixed annual payment from the client
    c. Insurance plan significantly impacted by federal budget cuts; increased amounts of copayment (Medicare and Medicaid) have increased cost to client; prospective payment (DRG plan) intended as incentive to control costs may reduce the quality of care in certain situations
15. a. High costs of care—influenced by increased population, demands for service, chronic illness, technology, inflation, specialization, aging population, survival of severely injured or ill as well as high risk neonates.
    b. Fragmentation of care—advanced knowledge and technology have resulted in increasing specialization of health care. Specialization has caused total care for the client to become fragmented, and care is not provided for the family as a unit or for the whole person. Fragmentation increases cost of health care and may diminish the efficacy of care. Primary nursing helps to reduce fragmentation.
    c. Inability to meet the special needs of the chronically ill and elderly—the current health care delivery system was designed primarily to meet the needs of the acutely ill. The lack of continuity of care in agency settings where the chronically ill or elderly seek care further compounds the problem. As the population ages, it is critical for the health care system to address the special care requirements of the chronically ill and elderly.
    d. Uneven distribution of services—while the number of health care workers in North America increases, low-income and rural areas still lack adequate health care professionals and services. Such communities may not have the fiscal resources to establish and maintain major health care services. Increased specialization has reduced the number of family and general practitioners available. Seasonal population fluctuations also change the needs for health care services to these populations.
16. a. Implementing cost containment measures
    b. Providing total care to coordinate the client's care and to decrease fragmentation
    c. Designing nursing strategies to meet the special needs of the elderly and chronically ill
    d. Providing low-income and rural regions with more nursing services

CHAPTER 4

1. Interaction that occurs when each person attempts to understand the other's point of view from his or her own cultural frame of reference
2. Areas of commonalities
3. c
4. True
5. A theory that analyzes the degree to which a person identifies with the dominant culture and his or her traditional culture
6. True
7. Culture
8. Ethnicity
9. Religion
10. Refer to table at top of p. 253.
11. The cause of illness within a belief system influenced by cultural, ethnic, or religious background
12. Traditional healers are aware of cultural and personal needs of the client and are able to understand the client within the context of his or her problems in today's world.
    - Although the traditional healer maintains an informal, friendly, affective relationship with the entire family, the physician deals primarily with the client.
    - The traditional healer comes to the house at any time, whereas the physician usually sees the client in an office or clinic.
    - The traditional healer uses a consultative approach during the diagnostic process by talking with the head of the house and other family members, building rapport and expectation of cure.
    - The physician deals primarily with the ill person, often dealing only with the person's illness and sometimes creating fear through an authoritarian manner.
    - The traditional healer is generally less expensive than the physician.
    - The traditional healer has rapport with the symbolic, spiritual, creative, or holy force. The physician is primarily secular, paying little attention to the religious beliefs of a client or the meanings that illness holds.
    - The traditional healer understands the life-style of the client, often speaking the same language and living in the same neighborhood or in similar socioeconomic conditions. The physician may not understand the life-style of the client, speak the same language, or live in the same neighborhood or in similar socioeconomic conditions.

	Heritage consistent	Heritage inconsistent
a.	Childhood development in country of origin or U.S. neighborhood of like ethnic group	Childhood development not in country of origin or like ethnic group
b.	Frequent visits to country of origin or the "old (ethnic) neighborhood"	No visits to country of origin or "old neighborhood"
c.	Family home in ethnic community	Family not in ethnic community
d.	Individual raised in extended family setting	Individual not raised in extended family setting
e.	Name not Americanized	Name Americanized
f.	Educated in nonpublic school with religious or ethnic philosophy	Educated in public schools
g.	Knowledgeable of ethnic culture and language	Not knowledgeable of ethnic culture or language
h.	Participates in traditional religious or cultural activities	Does not participate in these activities
i.	Incorporates elements of historical beliefs and practices into present philosophy	Does not incorporate these beliefs and practices into present philosophy

13. **a.** 3
b. 5
c. 2
d. 1
e. 4
f. 5
g. 1
h. 3
i. 4
j. 2
14. a
15. d
16. **a.** Intimate zone—extends up to 1½ feet. Allows adults the most body contacts for perception of breath and odor, not acceptable in public places. Visual distortions also present.
b. Personal distance—extends from 1½ to 4 feet. An extension of the self (like having a "bubble" of space surrounding the body). This distance allows the voice to be moderate, body odors may not be apparent, and visual distortions may disappear.
c. Social distance—extends from 4 to 12 feet. The distance reserved for impersonal business transactions. Perceptual information is much less detailed.
d. Public distance—extends 12 feet or more. Individuals interact impersonally. Communicators' voices must be projected, and subtle facial expressions may be lost.
17. c
18. b

CHAPTER 5

1. The provision of medically related professional and paraprofessional services and equipment to clients and families in their homes
2. Any four:
   - Health maintenance
   - Client and family education
   - Illness prevention
   - Diagnosis and treatment of disease
   - Palliation
   - Rehabilitation
3. To promote client and family independence through teaching of self-care
4. **a.** Home health agencies—provide intermittent professional and home health aide services that allow clients to live independently, usually with the help of family members. Reimbursement through government, private insurance, and private pay.
   b. Private duty agencies—provide professional and paraprofessional home health care services on a more continuous basis. Reimbursement provided primarily by private insurance and private pay.
   c. Durable medical equipment companies—provide medical equipment and supplies. Reimbursement through government and private insurance, with stringent guidelines for determining reimbursement for equipment.
5. Any four:
   - Decreased hospital funding because of changing government health care payment systems
   - Higher acuity level of clients at discharge from hospitals
   - Increased number of elderly and chronically ill
   - Advances in home care technology
   - Breakdown of the extended family
   - More households requiring more than one source of income (fewer family members at home to care for the elderly and disabled)
6. True
7. **a.** Insurance coverage
   b. Health care needs
   c. Family and home situation
8. Any five:
   - Physical assessment and history of body system, with emphasis on present illness
   - Psychosocial assessment
   - Family dynamics
   - Community resources
   - Environmental factors
   - Functional limitations
   - Client and family knowledge and attitudes toward illness and health behaviors
9. False
10. True
11. b

12. Any four:
    - New roles and responsibilities for nursing with greater emphasis on home health care in nursing education programs
    - Expanded research in the area of home health
    - Improvement in reimbursement for home health care, with improved response of insurers to this need, and increased orientation for preventive and long-term care
    - Direct involvement of physicians in home health, beyond the role of referral
    - Evolution of cost containment as a primary focus of home health care agencies
    - Expansion of computerization and high technology in the home health care industry

CHAPTER 6

1. A method for organizing and delivering care
2. **a.** Assessment
   b. Nursing diagnosis
   c. Planning
   d. Implementation
   e. Evaluation
3. **a.** Planning
   b. Assessment
   c. Evaluation
   d. Implementation
   e. Nursing diagnosis
4. Observations or measurements made by the data collector, based on an accepted standard
5. Clients' perceptions about their health problems
6. d
7. Any five:
    - Client
    - Family member or significant others
    - Health team members
    - Health record
    - Other records
    - Pertinent nursing and medical literature
8. a
9. **a.** Interview
   b. Nursing health history
   c. Physical examination
   d. Results of laboratory and diagnostic tests
10. a
11. a
12. b
13. **a.** Orientation phase: to familiarize the client, the nurse reviews the purposes for the interview, the type of questions that will be asked, the client's role in the interview, and the amount of time it will take. Part of the orientation phase also involves a few minutes getting acquainted with the client.
    b. Working phase: the nurse asks specific questions to formulate a data base from which the nursing care plan will be developed. This involves use of interviewing techniques and communication strategies.
    c. Termination phase: the nurse provides direct clues that the interview will be ending and provides specific information as to when there will be additional contact. It is important to ensure that the termination phase is positive and reflects concern for the client.
14. **a.** 4
    b. 6
    c. 1
    d. 9
    e. 8
    f. 3
    g. 10
    h. 5
    i. 7
    j. 2
15. To identify:
    a. Patterns of health and illness
    b. Presence of risk factors for physical and behavioral health problems
    c. Any deviations from normal
    d. Available resources for adaptation
16. False
17.
    - Nature of the onset: sudden versus gradual
    - Duration: always present, come and go, time (seconds, minutes, or hours)
    - Location of the pain
    - Intensity of the pain
    - Quality of the pain
    - Actions that precipitate the pain
    - Actions that make the pain worse
    - Actions that relieve the pain
18. The specific reactions that occurred (signs and symptoms) and the treatment (if any) that was given for the reaction
19. Life-style patterns or habits may place the client at risk for a variety of diseases.
20. When possible, these aspects of the client's life-style may be incorporated into the nursing care plan (the nurse may also identify areas for education concerning positive health habits).
21. b
22. To verify information obtained during interview and collect further data, which are compared with the standards to determine whether the findings are normal or abnormal
23. **a.** Auscultation
    b. Palpation
    c. Inspection
    d. Percussion
24. Any two:
    - Verify alterations identified in the nursing health history and physical examination
    - Provide baseline information about the client's response to illness and treatment
    - Evaluate success or failure of nursing or medical care
    - Identify actual or potential health care problems not identified by the client or examiner

CHAPTER 7

1. A statement of the client's potential or actual health problem that the nurse is licensed and competent to treat
2. **a.** Analysis and interpretation of data
   b. Identification of general health care problems
   c. Formulation of nursing diagnoses
3. Data clustering
4. **a.** Consulting another source
   b. Physical examination
   c. Results of laboratory and diagnostic tests

	Medical diagnosis	Nursing diagnosis
Nature of the diagnosis	Identification of a disease condition	Statement of potential or actual health problem that the nurse is licensed and competent to treat
Goal	Identify and sometimes cure disease	Identify actual and potential health problems of the client
Objective	Prescribe treatment	Develop a plan of care so the client and family may adapt to changes resulting from health problems

5. False
6. A group of signs and symptoms that results from data clustering and supports the presence of the nursing diagnosis
7. Part 1: the client's actual or potential health problem or need that can be affected by nursing interventions; part 2: the etiology or cause of the problem (represented by the phrase "related to")
8. The etiology (represented by the phrase "related to")
9. False
10. Refer to table at top of page.
11. Any three:
    - Facilitates communication among nurses about client's health and discharge planning
    - Serves as a focus for quality assurance and peer review
    - Eliminates potential problems in giving care
    - Maintains a focus on meeting the client's health care goals
    - Helps to ensure high quality care for clients and families
12. c
13. d
14. c
15. d

CHAPTER 8

1. **a.** Determining goals
   b. Setting priorities
   c. Projecting outcomes
   d. Formulating nursing care plan
2. **a.** 2
   b. 1
   c. 2
   d. 3
   e. 1
   f. 1
3. c
4. Short-term goals may be achieved quickly (during hospitalization, clinic visit, home visit). Long-term goals are achieved in the future and tend to focus on prevention, rehabilitation, discharge, and health education.
5. Any three:
    - Provide a direction for nursing activities
    - Provide observable client behaviors and measurable outcomes for each goal
    - Provide a projected time span for goal attainment
    - Provide an opportunity to state any additional resources required
    - Serve as criteria to evaluate effectiveness of nursing activities
6. b
7. d
8. c
9. Any four:
    - Document the client's health care needs
    - Coordinate nursing care
    - Promote continuity of care
    - Provide outcome criteria for evaluation of nursing care
    - Provide a means of communication to other nurses and health care professionals
10. **a.** Unique institutional format for writing/recording a nursing care plan; often involves the Kardex system
    b. Forms created for a specific clinical area that cares for a particular type of client; require the nurse to individualize standardized form to the specific client; help conserve nursing time
    c. An elaborate and detailed plan, unique to the specific educational program, which includes scientific rationale for nursing actions
11. b
12. **a.** What is the intervention?
    b. When should each intervention be implemented?
    c. How should the intervention be performed?
    d. Who should be involved in each aspect of the intervention?
13. c
14. **a.** When the nurse has identified a problem that cannot be solved using his or her knowledge, skills, and resources
    b. When the exact problem in a nursing situation remains unclear
15. **a.** Identifying the general problem area
    b. Identifying the appropriate professional for consultation
    c. Providing the consultant with pertinent information and resources about the problem area
    d. Avoiding consultant bias by eliminating subjective and emotional conclusions about the client and the problem
    e. Remaining available to discuss the consultant's findings and recommendations
    f. Incorporating the consultant's recommendations into the nursing care plan

CHAPTER 9

1. True
2. c
3. d
4. a
5. **a.** 2
   b. 4
   c. 8
   d. 7
   e. 1

f. 5
g. 3
h. 6
6. False
7. a. Reassessing the client: a partial assessment that may focus on a specific dimension (physical, psychological, spiritual, social, cultural) or body system
b. Reviewing and modifying the existing care plan: the client's status may change, requiring changes in the plan to provide appropriate nursing care
c. Identifying areas of assistance: to implement the plan of care, the nurse may require certain types of assistance (additional personnel, additional knowledge, or additional nursing skills)
d. Implementing nursing strategies: activities requiring theoretical knowledge and psychomotor skills that are directed toward achievement of the client-centered goals
e. Communicating nursing strategies: verbal interaction and written documentation concerning the need for nursing care, the nursing care plan, and the client's response to care
8. a. Additional personnel
b. Additional knowledge
c. Additional nursing skills
9. Any four:
- Assisting the client in ADL: assisting the client or performing for the client those activities usually performed in the course of a normal day such as eating, dressing, bathing, brushing the teeth, or grooming
- Counseling: assisting the client in using a problem-solving process to recognize and manage stress and other "normal" adjustment difficulties, and that enhances the client's interpersonal relationships
- Teaching: presenting information about health status as well as principles, procedures, and techniques of health care to the client and family
- Giving care to achieve the client's goals: initiating interventions to compensate for adverse reactions, using precautionary and preventive measures in providing care, applying correct techniques in administering care and preparing the client for special procedures, and initiating lifesaving measures in emergency situations
- Giving care to facilitate the client's attainment of health goals: providing an environment conducive to attaining health care goals, adjusting care in accordance with the client's needs, stimulating and motivating the client in order to achieve self-care and independence, and encouraging the client to accept care or adhere to the treatment regimen
- Supervising and evaluating the work of other staff members: delegating appropriate nursing interventions to another health care team member, which requires the nurse to ensure that the assigned team member is capable of performing and completing the task according to the standard of care

10. True

CHAPTER 10

1. Activities (behaviors) in which the nurse makes and records a determination about the extent to which the client's goals have been met
2. True
3. b
4. a
5. a. Establishing projected outcomes (evaluation criteria)
b. Comparing client response to criteria
c. Analyzing reasons for results and conclusions
d. Modifying the care plan
6. a
7. False
8. d
9. a. Improved quality of nursing care
b. Improved staff nurses' attitude and motivation to improve their knowledge and skills
c. Staff growth and development
10. Refer to table at top of p. 257.

CHAPTER 11

1. a. 2
b. 5
c. 3
d. 4
e. 1
2. a. The investigation is planned and conducted in a systematic and orderly fashion.
b. External factors not under direct investigation, which may influence relationship between phenomena, are controlled.
c. Empirical data are gathered directly or indirectly through human senses.
d. Goal is to understand phenomena so that knowledge may be applied generally, not just to isolated cases or circumstances.
e. Investigations are conducted to test or develop theories and thereby advance knowledge.
3. Systematic, controlled, empirical, critical investigation of natural phenomena guided by theory and hypotheses about the presumed relationship among the phenomena (Kerlinger, 1986)
4. Develops knowledge about health and health promotion over the life span, care of persons with health problems and disabilities, and nursing action to enhance the ability of individuals to respond effectively to actual or potential health problems (ANA Commission on Nursing Research, 1981)
5. d
6. a
7. a. 5
b. 4
c. 2
d. 1
e. 3
8. b
9. Any five:
- Promote health, well-being, and ability for self-care among all health care consumers
- Minimize and prevent behaviorally and environmentally induced health problems
- Minimize the negative effects of new health technologies
- Ensure that the care needs of particularly vulnerable groups are met effectively and acceptably
- Classify nursing practice phenomena
- Ensure that principles of ethics guide nursing research
- Develop instruments to measure nursing outcomes

Assessment	Diagnosis	Planning	Implementation	Evaluation
Purpose				
To gather, verify, and communicate data about a client so a data base is established	To identify health care needs of client and to identify nursing diagnoses	To identify client goals To determine priorities of care To design nursing strategies to achieve goals of care To determine outcome criteria	To complete nursing actions necessary for accomplishing plan	To determine extent to which goals of care have been achieved
Steps				
1. Collecting nursing health history 2. Performing physical examination 3. Collecting laboratory data	1. Interpreting data a. Data validation b. Data clustering 2. Formulating nursing diagnoses 3. Identifying client goals	1. Selecting nursing actions 2. Delegating actions 3. Consulting 4. Writing nursing care plan	1. Reassessing client 2. Reviewing and modifying existing care plan 3. Identifying areas of assistance 4. Implementing nursing strategies 5. Communicating nursing strategies	1. Establishing projected outcomes (evaluation criteria) 2. Comparing client response to criteria 3. Analyzing variables affecting outcomes and drawing conclusions 4. Modifying care plan

- Develop integrative methodologies for the holistic study of human beings
- Design and evaluate alternative models for delivering health care and for administering health care systems
- Evaluate the effectiveness of alternative approaches to nursing education
- Identify and analyze historical and contemporary factors that influence the shaping of nursing professionals' involvement in national health policy development

10. c
11. a
12. When the individual is concerned about the ethical aspects of the study
13. c
14. b
15. d
16. d
17. c
18. Any three:
- It should reflect something that could be improved in clinical practice.
- It should be a problem that occurs frequently in a particular client group.
- It should be able to be consistently and accurately measured.
- It should potentially change how nursing care is delivered.
- It may describe client phenomena.
- It may assist in devising measurement tools for research.

19. **a.** How much substantiating evidence is provided by other scientific studies that have obtained similar results?
b. Were the subjects and environment in the study similar to those in which the nurse practices?
c. What is the theoretical basis for present nursing care and its current effectiveness in solving clinical nursing problems?
d. How feasible is it to apply the findings in the nurse's clinical setting based on (1) ethical and legal limitations; (2) institutional policy; (3) changes in nursing services that might be required; and (4) potential costs in terms of personnel, time, money, and equipment?
20. Half of what a nurse learns today may be out-of-date within 5 years. To remain current in nursing, it is important to develop skills to read and understand nursing research studies.

CHAPTER 12

1. True
2. Hypothalamus
3. d
4. **a.** Metabolism
b. Muscle activity
c. Thyroid hormone
d. Sympathetic stimulation (vasoconstriction, shivering, piloerection)
5. **a.** 2
b. 1
c. 4
d. 3
6. **a.** Infants—thermoregulatory mechanisms are not fully developed, temperature influenced greatly by environment.
b. Elderly—thermoregulatory mechanisms deteriorate: vasomotor control unstable, subcutaneous tissue reduced, sweat gland activity reduced, metabolism reduced. (Also may lack physical ability to take action to control environmental temperature exposure.)
c. Clients with decreased level of consciousness or impaired thought processes—illness or injury may alter

awareness of the environment or ability to think rationally, potentially inhibiting the individual's ability to control environmental temperature exposure.

7. d

8. Body temperature above 38° C (100.4° F) measured rectally under resting conditions (This definition is commonly accepted but must be considered in light of the client's actual hypothalamic set point.)

9. a

10. False

11. Convulsions (or dehydration)

12. At least five:
- Measure vital signs when fever is suspected and on an ongoing basis as ordered (for example, every 2 to 4 hours) until body temperature returns to normal.
- Inspect and palpate skin and check for turgor.
- Ask the client how he or she feels.
- Note the presence of vomiting or diarrhea.
- Observe the client for behavioral changes.
- Monitor test results for electrolyte levels.
- Inspect the oral mucosa for dryness and lesions.

13. Prevent the hypothalamus from synthesizing prostaglandin E, which is responsible for elevating the hypothalamic set point.

14. d

15. b

16. **a.** A
b. R or A
c. R or A
d. A
e. O

17. True

18. Refer to table at bottom of page.

19. **a.** 38° C
b. 102° F
c. 36.6° C
d. 103° F

20. d

21. **a.** Pulse = 72
b. Cardiac output = 5760 ml
c. Yes

22. c

23. Any three:
- Impaired peripheral blood flow
- Abnormal or inaccessible radial pulse
- Infant or child
- Medications affecting heart rate
- Irregular heart rate

24. Apical pulse

25. **a.** Pulse rate
b. Rhythm
c. Strength
d. Elasticity
e. Equality

26. d

27. **a.** 4
b. 6
c. 2
d. 5
e. 1
f. 7
g. 3

28. Refer to table at top of p. 259.

29. **a.** 3

Site	Type of glass thermometer	Time left in place	Client's position	Special precautions
Oral	Slim tipped or stubby; may have blue tip	2 min (or based on agency policy)	Comfortable; mouth accessible	Not used for clients who are unable to hold thermometer in mouth or might bite thermometer; Infants; small children; confused or unconscious clients; clients after oral surgery, after face or mouth trauma, with oral pain, who are mouth breathers, with history of convulsions; clients experiencing shaking chills or receiving continuous oxygen administration. Wait 20-30 min after ingestion of hot or cold liquids or foods, smoking, or strenuous exercise.
Rectal	Stubby or pear tip	2 min (or by agency policy)	Sims	Not used for clients after rectal surgery, clients with rectal disorders, clients who cannot be positioned for proper placement or newborns. Expose only anal area, lubricate thermometer, never force thermometer, insert in direction of umbilicus 3.5 cm (1½ in) in adult, hold in place.
Axillary	Stubby or slim tip	5-10 minutes	Lying supine; sitting	Expose shoulder and arm, with arm placed across client's chest. Hold thermometer in position.

Site	Equipment needed	Length of time	Indications	Special techniques or precautions
Radial	Pen, vital sign graphic, wristwatch with second hand or digital display	Regular: 15 sec Irregular: 1 min	Usual nonemergency pulse site	Arm relaxed with wrist extended (see answer 23 on p. 258)
Apical	All the above, plus stethoscope and alcohol wipes	Regular: 30 sec Irregular: 1 min	See answer 23 on p. 258	Expose left side of chest, locate PMI, warm diaphragm in hand
Apical-radial	All the above, plus second nurse	1 min	Irregular pulse	Simultaneous assessment of apical and radial pulses by two nurses using exactly the same time period for measurement and using the same watch

b. 5
c. 2
d. 6
e. 4
f. 1

30. b

31. a. Decreased oxygen levels
b. Chronic lung conditions characterized by an elevation of carbon dioxide levels in the arterial blood, causing a loss of carbon dioxide as the normal stimulus for ventilation

32. a. Client splints or inhibits chest wall expansion; breaths are shallow.
b. Less oxygen is carried in the blood; client breathes faster to increase delivery of available oxygen.
c. Collapse of lung reduces chest wall movement on involved side, causes asymmetrical chest wall movement.
d. Chest appears barrel shaped; client actively uses neck and chest wall muscles to forcibly exhale.

33. a. Rate
b. Depth
c. Rhythm

34. d

35. a. Dyspnea
b. Respiratory stridor
c. Tachypnea
d. Apnea
e. Orthopnea

36. a. Hyperventilation (or Kussmaul)
b. Normal
c. Cheyne-Stokes

37. 12 to 20 per minute

38. a. Skin color
b. Level of consciousness
c. Difficult breathing
d. Sounds of breathing

39. a. The force exerted by the blood against a vessel wall
b. The maximal pressure exerted against the arterial walls, which occurs as the left ventricle pumps blood into the aorta
c. The minimal pressure exerted against the arterial walls at all times, which occurs as the ventricles relax

40. a. 50
b. 116
c. 66

41. a. DBP
b. DBP
c. IBP
d. IBP
e. IBP
f. IBP
g. DBP
h. IBP
i. IBP

42. When an average of two or more diastolic readings on at least two subsequent visits is 90 mm Hg or higher or when the average of multiple systolic blood pressures on two or more subsequent visits is consistently higher than 140 mm Hg

43. a

44. b

45. 156/88

46. a. 2
b. 6
c. 1
d. 4
e. 8
f. 5
g. 3
h. 7

47. c

48. Temporary disappearance of sound between first and second Korotkoff sound, may be seen in clients with hypertension

49. a. Palpation
b. Doppler (ultrasonic, electronic amplification)

50. True

CHAPTER 13

1. False

2. Any four:
- Gather baseline data about the client's health.
- Supplement, confirm, or refute data obtained in the nursing history.
- Confirm and identify nursing diagnoses.
- Make clinical judgments about a client's changing health status and management.
- Evaluate the physiological outcomes of care.

3. False

4. Any four:
   - Have good lighting.
   - Position and expose body parts so all surfaces can be viewed.
   - Inspect each area for size, shape, color, symmetry, position, and abnormalities.
   - Compare each area inspected with the same area on the opposite side of the body.
   - Use additional light (penlight, flashlight) to inspect body cavities.
5. c
6. **a.** Dorsum (back of hand)
   b. Fingertips
   c. Palm
   d. Fingertips
7. The sensing hand is relaxed and placed lightly over the client's skin. The active hand applies pressure to the sensing hand. The lower hand does not exert pressure directly and is able to retain the sensitivity needed to detect organ characteristics.
8. Location, size, and density of underlying structures
9. a
10. **a.** 4
    b. 1
    c. 3
    d. 2
11. b
12. True
13. Any three:
    - Privacy
    - Adequate lighting
    - Soundproof
    - No sources of noise
    - Steps to prevent interruptions
14. d
15. **a.** 1,3,5
    b. 1
    c. 5
    d. 2,4
    e. 2,4
16. b
17. One per age group:
    a. Infants and younger children
      (1) Gather all or part of the information from parent or guardian.
      (2) Offer parents support during the examination, do not pass judgment.
      (3) Call children by their first name, parent as Mr. or Mrs. ____________________.
    b. Older children
      (1) Interview older child, observe parent-child interaction.
      (2) Allow older child to provide information about health and current symptoms.
    c. Adolescents
      (1) Treat as adults and individuals.
      (2) Assure of right to confidentiality.
      (3) Confirm history with parents.
      (4) Speak alone with adolescent.
    d. Aging clients
      (1) Do not stereotype.
      (2) Recognize impact of aging on sensory or physical status and modify session as indicated.
18. **a.** General appearance and behavior
    b. Vital signs
    c. Height and weight
    d. Anthropometric measurements (including head circumference in infants)
19. Any eight:
    - Sex and race
    - Signs of distress
    - Body type
    - Posture
    - Gait
    - Body movements
    - Age
    - Hygiene and grooming
    - Dress
    - Body odor
    - Mood and affect
    - Speech
20. d
21. **a.** Weigh at the same time.
    b. Weigh in the same, or equivalent, clothes.
    c. Weigh on the same scale.
22. Position supine on firm surface with legs extended straight and soles of the feet supported upright. Measure with a tape measure from the soles of the feet to the vertex of the head.
23. Refer to table at top of p. 261.
24. Hyperpigmentation
25. a
26. Turgor is a measure of the skin's elasticity that is measured by grasping and then releasing a fold of the client's skin. Normally, the skin snaps back immediately to its original (resting) position.
27. Petechiae
28. Any five:
    - Location
    - Size
    - Type
    - Grouping
    - Distribution
    - Mobility
    - Contour
    - Consistency
29. **a.** Ulcer
    b. Atrophy
    c. Macule
    d. Pustule
    e. Vesicle
    f. Wheal
    g. Papule
    h. Nodule
30. **a.** The nurse applies firm pressure over the edematous area with the thumb for 5 seconds.
    b. The client has edema that, when pressure has been applied to the area, pits to a depth of 2 cm.
31. Any two:
    - Wear wide-brimmed hats and long sleeves to avoid exposure.
    - Use sunscreens before going into the sun and after swimming or perspiring.
    - Avoid tanning under direct sun (11 AM to 2 PM).
32. Endocrine disorder
33. b
34. Baldness or hair loss
35. True
36. d
37. Acromegaly

Skin color	Mechanisms	Causes	Assessment sites
Cyanosis	Increased deoxygenated hemoglobin, associated with hypoxia	Heart or lung disease, cold environment	Nail beds, lips, mouth, skin (severe cases)
Pallor	Reduced amount of oxy-hemoglobin	Anemia	Face, conjunctivae, nail beds, skin
	Reduced visibility of oxy-hemoglobin from de-creased blood flow	Shock	
	Congenital or autoimmune condition causing lack of pigmentation	Vitiligo	
Jaundice	Increased deposit of bili-rubin in tissues	Liver disease, de-struction of red blood cells	Sclera, mucous mem-branes, skin
Erythema	Increased visibility of oxyhemoglobin caused by dilation or increased blood flow	Fever, direct blush-ing, alcohol intake	Face, areas of trauma

38. **a.** Visual acuity
b. Extraocular movements
c. Visual fields
d. Pupil reflex

39. **a.** 6
b. 3
c. 1
d. 5
e. 4
f. 2

40. Ask the client to read printed material under adequate lighting.

41. Without correction (without glasses or contact lenses), the client standing 20 feet away can read a line that a person with normal vision can read at 60 feet.

42. d

43. **a.** Nystagmus
b. Exophthalmos
c. Ptosis
d. Conjunctivitis
e. Arcus senilis
f. Red reflex
g. Photophobia

44. Pupils equal, round, and reactive to light and accommodation

45. False

46. Any three:
- Clear, yellow optic nerve disc
- Reddish pink retina (white clients)
- Darkened retina (black clients)
- Light red arteries and dark red veins
- A 3:2 vein-artery ratio in size proportion
- Avascular macula

47. d

48. Any three:
- Hypoxia at birth
- Meningitis
- Birth weight less than 1500 grams
- Family history of hearing loss
- Congenital anomalies of skull or face
- Intrauterine viral infection
- Exposure to high noise levels

49. **a.** 4
b. 2
c. 1
d. 5
e. 3

50. False

51. b

52. b

53. **a.** Conduction hearing loss: interruption of sound waves traveling from the outer ear to the cochlea of the inner ear
b. Sensorineural hearing loss: failure of the inner ear, auditory nerve, or hearing center of the brain to transmit or interpret sound waves
c. Mixed hearing loss: involves combination of conduction and sensorineural loss

54. True

55. Bone conduction can be heard after air conduction sound becomes inaudible—a sign of conduction deafness.

56. False

57. **a.** Light pink, moist, and smooth
b. Medium red or pink, moist, slightly rough on top surface, smooth along lateral margins, midline with protrusion, undersurface highly vascular
c. Smooth, white, shiny
d. Pink, moist, and smooth (in black clients, patchy pigmentation)

58. **a.** Sore that bleeds easily and does not heal
b. Lump or thickening
c. Persistent red or white patch (leukoplakia) on the mucosa, especially under the tongue

59. d

60. a

61. Refer to table at top of p. 262.

62. c

63. Refer to table at bottom of p. 262.

64. **a.** Point of maximal impulse, the point where the apex of the heart actually touches the anterior chest wall
b. Third or fourth intercostal space, just to the left of the midclavicular line
c. Fourth to fifth intercostal space, midclavicular line
d. **(1)** Locate the angle of Louis between the sternal body and the manubrium (this is the second intercostal space). Count down to the fifth intercostal space

Assessment finding	Assessment skill used	Explanation or possible cause
Bulging	Inspection of ribs and intercostal spaces on expiration	Client using great effort to breathe
Reduced tactile fremitus	Palpation of chest wall	Mucous secretions, lung lesions, or collapsed lung tissue blocking vibrations
Reduced excursion	Palpation of lower rib cage: hands parallel with thumbs 5 cm (2 in) apart, pressing toward spine	Client not breathing deeply because of disease state or changes associated with aging
Resonance over posterior aspect of thorax	Percussion	Normal finding
Retraction	Inspection of ribs and intercostal spaces on inspiration	Client using great effort to breathe
Anteroposterior diameter 1:1	Inspection of chest contour	Aging, chronic lung disease, normal finding in small infants

on the left (by locating each intercostal space with the fingers), and locate the point lateral to this space in the midclavicular line.

(2) Gently place the palm of the hand (or fingertips) over the left part of the chest in the area of the fifth intercostal space and midclavicular line, and attempt to feel the apical impulse against the chest wall.

(3) When it is difficult to locate the PMI with the client in a supine position, assisting the client to the left side-lying position will move the heart closer to the chest wall.

65. Refer to Fig. 13-51, p. 282
Aortic area: S_2 louder than S_1
Pulmonic area: S_2 louder than S_1
Mitral area (apex): S_1 louder than S_2; S_3 and S_4 (if present) audible
Tricuspid area: S_1 louder than S_2

66. a

67. **a.** Timing
b. Location
c. Radiation
d. Intensity
e. Pitch
f. Quality

68. Thrill

69. Bruit

70. **a.** Examine one artery at a time; if both arteries are occluded during palpation, client could lose consciousness because of inadequate circulation to the brain.
b. Do not vigorously palpate or massage artery; carotid sinus in upper third of the neck may be stimulated and cause a reflex drop in heart rate and blood pressure.

71. False

72. False

73. c

74. **a.** 1
b. 2
c. 1
d. 2
e. 2
f. 1

75. **a.** Calf appears red and swollen.
b. Calf muscle is tender and firm. Homans' sign (pain in calf with forceful dorsiflexion of the foot) is positive.

Sound	Site of auscultation	Cause	Character
Pleural friction rub	Anterior lateral lung field (client upright)	Inflamed pleura	Grating quality heard on inspiration; does not clear with cough
Rhonchi	Primarily over trachea and bronchi; if loud, over most lung fields	Fluid or mucus in larger airways	Low-pitched, continuous, musical; loudest on expiration; may clear with cough
Wheezes	Over all lung fields	Severely narrowed bronchus	High pitched, continuous, musical, heard on inspiration or expiration, do not clear with cough
Crackles	Most common in dependent lobes, right and left bases	Sudden reinflation of groups of alveoli	Fine, short, interrupted crackling; during inspiration, expiration, or both; vary in pitch; may or may not clear with cough

76. True
77. b
78. **a.** N
b. A
c. N
d. A
e. A
f. N
79. Any five:
- Location
- Size in centimeters
- Shape
- Consistency
- Tenderness
- Mobility
- Discreteness (detectable boundaries of the mass)

80. Refer to Fig. 13-77, p. 298.
81. Costovertebral angle
82. Any four:
- Encourage client to empty bladder.
- Keep room warm.
- Keep client's upper chest and legs draped.
- Client remains supine with arms at side or folded across chest.
- Place small pillow under head or knees.
- Warm hands and stethoscope.
- Provide conversation to distract client.
- Work slowly and calmly.
- Ask client to report pain and point out tender areas.

83. d
84. True
85. **a.** 1
b. 4
c. 3
d. 2
86. b
87. c
88. Turn off the suction during auscultation.
89. 3 to 5 minutes
90. Borborygmi
91. c
92. Guarding
93. **a.** Examiner presses hand slowly and deeply into tender area and releases quickly.
b. Positive rebound tenderness test indicates inflammation of the abdominal cavity (peritonitis).
94. Bladder distention (full bladder)
95. Any three:
- Bleeding from rectum
- Black or tarry stools (melena)
- Rectal pain
- Change in bowel habits (constipation or diarrhea)

96. Refer to table at bottom of page.
97. False
98. True
99. False
100. **a.** Scoliosis
b. Hypotonic (hypotonicity)
c. Kyphosis
d. Crepitus
e. Lordosis
f. Hypertonic (hypertonicity)
101. b
102. Any two manuevers:
- Place hand firmly against client's upper jaw. Ask client to turn head laterally against resistance. (sternocleidomastoid muscle)
- Place hand over midline of client's shoulder, exerting firm pressure. Have client raise shoulders against resistance. (trapezius muscle)
- Pull down on forearm as client attempts to flex arm. (biceps muscle)
- As client's arm is flexed, apply pressure against the forearm. Ask client to straighten arm. (triceps muscle)
- When client is sitting, apply downward pressure to the thigh. Ask client to raise leg up, against resistance. (quadriceps muscle)
- Client sits, holding the shin of flexed leg. Ask client to straighten the leg against resistance. (gastrocnemius muscle)

103. True
104. Applying firm pressure with the thumb over the root of the fingernail
105. c
106. **a.** 3
b. 4
c. 1
d. 2
107. **a.** IX
b. XI
c. V
d. II
e. VII
f. I
g. X
h. III
108. True
109. Cerebellum
110. **a.** Any one maneuver:
- Client pats hand against thigh as rapidly as possible.

Assessment finding	Normal or abnormal	Assessment technique	Possible cause (if abnormal)
Bulging at inguinal ring	Abnormal	Inspection, palpation	Hernia
Smooth, round, firm prostate	Normal	Palpation	
Yellow drainage at cervical os	Abnormal	Inspection	Infection
Labia minora thin and darker in color than surrounding skin	Normal	Inspection	
Left testicle lower than right	Normal	Inspection, palpation	
Small, pea-sized lump on front of testicle	Abnormal	Palpation	Mass, possible testicular cancer

- Client alternately strikes thigh with the hand supinated and then pronated.
- Client touches each finger with the thumb of the same hand in rapid sequence.
- Client stands 2 feet away from nurse, alternately touching nurse's finger and client's nose.

b. Any one maneuver:
- Client performs Romberg test with feet together and eyes closed.
- Client closes eyes and stands on one foot and then the other.
- Client walks a straight line placing heel of one foot directly in front to toes of the other foot.

111. c
112. b

CHAPTER 14

1. False
2. Any order:
a. Accuracy
b. Conciseness
c. Thoroughness
d. Currentness
e. Organization
f. Confidentiality
3. Include first name initial, last name, status (for example, S. Blue, SN).
4. b
5. 2205
6. c
7. d
8. a
9. c
10. a. Information communicated in a telephone report may not be permanently documented in written form.
b. Information should be repeated back to the sender for verification.
11. c
12. Any event that is not consistent with routine client care or routine activities on a health care unit
13. False
14. To identify and eliminate significant problems in nursing practice or delivery of health care (or, for institutional use, to provide information for quality assurance and risk management)
15. a. 4
b. 1
c. 5
d. 3
e. 6
f. 2
16. The federal government and private insurance carriers audit medical records to determine client and health care agency financial reimbursement for health care costs. Thorough documentation ensures that maximal amounts of monies are recovered for the care delivered and that clients receive required care.
17. True
18. False
19. b
20. a
21. Advantage: care giver can easily locate proper section for making charting entries
Disadvantage: information is fragmented
22. Any three:
- Emphasizes clients and their problems
- Emphasizes clients' perceptions of their problems
- Requires continuous evaluation and revision of plan of care
- Provides greater continuity of care
- Enhances effective communication among health care team members

23. S: subjective data or information gathered from the client
O: objective data or information that may be observed or measured
A: conclusions drawn by the health care provider based on data obtained
P: plan of care, compared with plan in previous notes
24. P: problem or nursing diagnosis for the client
I: interventions or actions taken
E: evaluation of the outcomes of nursing interventions, client's response to nursing therapies
25. a. Preprinted, established guidelines used to care for clients with similar health problems
b. Any three:
- Establishes sound standards of care for similar groups of clients
- Easily located in a client's record
- Educates nurses who become familiar with client care requirements
- Increases continuity of care
- Documentation less time consuming

c. Nurse must still individualize approaches to care and modify and update care plan on a routine basis.

CHAPTER 15

1. a. 4
b. 1
c. 2
d. 3
2. d
3. a. Suspension
b. Troche (lozenge)
c. Capsule
d. Ointment (salve)
e. Syrup
f. Enteric-coated
g. Lotion
h. Tablet
i. Paste
j. Elixir
4. The nurse may be fined, be imprisoned, and lose license.
5. The study of how drugs enter the body, reach their site of action (distribution), are metabolized, and exit the body (excretion)
6. c
7. a
8. b
9. d
10. a

11. Intended or predicted physiological response caused by a drug
12. **a.** 5
    b. 4
    c. 2
    d. 3
    e. 1
13. The greater effect of a drug when given in combination with another drug
14. False
15. The time it takes for the excretion process to lower the serum drug concentration by half
16. **a.** Plateau
    b. Peak
    c. Duration
    d. Onset
17. Any three:
    - Hormonal differences between males and females
    - Age
    - Nutritional status
    - Disease states
18. True
19. True
20. c
21. c
22. d
23. True
24. Any two:
    - Drug should not be chewed.
    - Drug should not be swallowed.
    - Drug should not be taken with liquids, and liquids should not be taken until the drug is completely dissolved.
25. **a.** SQ (subcutaneous)
    b. IM (intramuscular)
    c. IV (intravenous)
    d. intradermal
26. Contamination of any of the materials or equipment may lead to infection.
27. **a.** Meters (m or M)
    b. Grams (g or Gm)
    c. Liter (l or L)
28. **a.** Left
    b. Right
29. **a.** Deciliter = 0.1 L
    b. Milligram = 0.0001 G
    c. Centimeter = 0.01 M
    d. Kiloliter = 1000 L
30. **a.** Gram
    b. Ounce
    c. Fluid ounce
    d. Minim
    e. Dram
31. gr iv
32.

Metric	Apothecary	Household
1 ml	15 minims	15 drops
15 ml	4 fluidrams	1 tablespoon
30 ml	1 fluid ounce	2 tablespoons
240 ml	8 fluid ounces	1 cup
480 ml (approx. 0.5 L)	1 pint	1 pint
960 ml (approx. 1 L)	1 quart	1 quart

33. **a.** 5 grams of glucose dissolved in 100 milliliters of water
    b. 1 milliliter of a liquid or 1 gram of a solid dissolved in 1000 milliliters of a fluid
    c. 250 milligrams in 1 milliliter of solution
34. **a.** 0.1
    b. 2500
    c. 0.5
    d. 2
    e. ¼
    f. 2
    g. 10
35. $\dfrac{\text{Dose ordered}}{\text{Dose on hand}} \times \text{Amount on hand} = \text{Amount to administer}$
36. $\dfrac{\text{Surface area of child}}{1.7\ \text{M}^2} \times \text{Normal adult dose} = \text{Child's dose}$
37. **a.** One-half tablet $\left(\dfrac{0.125\ \text{mg}}{0.25\ \text{mg}} \times 1\ \text{tab} = 0.5\ \text{tab}\right)$
    b. Broken in half on prescored line by using a knife edge or using the fingers holding the tablet in a clean paper towel or tissue
38. **a.** 0.75 ml
    $$\left(\text{gr. } 1/8 = 7.5\ \text{mg}\ \dfrac{7.5\ \text{mg}}{10\ \text{mg}} \times 1\ \text{ml} = 0.75\ \text{ml}\right)$$
    b. TB syringe to ensure accuracy of the dose
39. **a.** 25 ml $\left(\dfrac{200\ \text{mg}}{400\ \text{mg}} \times 5\ \text{ml} = 2.5\ \text{ml}\right)$
    b. Draw up appropriate amount in a syringe to ensure accuracy of the dose
40. 115 mg $\left(\dfrac{0.4\ \text{M}^2}{1.7\ \text{M}^2} \times 500\ \text{mg} = 115\ \text{mg}\right)$
    $$\dfrac{0.4\ \text{M}^2}{1.7\ \text{M}^2} = 0.23$$
41. **a.** 4
    b. 3
    c. 1
    d. 2
42. **a.** Prescribes medications
    b. Prepares, dispenses, and distributes prescribed medications
    c. Determines whether the drug should be administered at a given time; assesses the client's ability to self-administer drugs; provides medications at the proper time; monitors the effects of prescribed medications; educates family and client about drug administration and monitoring
43. c
44. Any seven:
    - Medical history; provides indications or contraindications for drug therapy
    - History of allergies; potential allergic response to prescribed medications
    - Purpose of drug order; determines whether a drug is needed or if other interventions may be as effective in creating the desired response
    - Client's current condition; determines whether or not the

drug should be given and how it should be administered
- Diet history; assists in planning dosage schedule more effectively
- Client's perceptual or coordination problems; determines if self-administration is possible, also provides clues that may be used in modifying approach to administering medications
- Client's knowledge and understanding of drug therapy; determines the willingness or ability to follow a drug regimen safely
- Client's attitude about the use of drugs; determines the level of client drug dependence
- Drug data; provides information needed by the nurse to safely administer medications
- Client's learning needs; determines the client's need for instruction

45. True
46. b
47. Any five:
- Keep each drug in its original, labeled container.
- Be sure labels are legible.
- Discard any outdated medications.
- Always finish a prescribed drug unless otherwise instructed (never save a drug for future illnesses).
- Dispose of drugs in a sink or toilet (not the trash within reach of children).
- Do not give someone a drug prescribed for someone else.
- Refrigerate medications that require it.
- Read labels carefully and follow all instructions.

48. b
49. **a.** The right drug
b. The right dose
c. The right client
d. The right route
e. The right time
50. **a.** Before removing the container from the drawer or shelf
b. As the amount of drug ordered is removed from the container
c. Before returning the container to storage (With the unit dose system, the label is checked a third time with the medicine ticket or form even though there is no storage container.)
51. d
52. **a.** Check the medicine ticket or form against the client's identification bracelet.
b. Ask the client to state his or her name.
53. b
54. a
55. d
56. **a.** 6
b. 4
c. 8
d. 1
e. 2
f. 5
g. 3
h. 7
57. False
58. True
59. **a.** Bevel
b. Shaft
c. Hub
d. Barrel
e. Plunger
60. **a.** Client size and weight
b. Tissue to be injected
c. Viscosity of fluid to be injected
61. d
62. One milliliter of insulin solution contains 100 units of insulin.
63. **a.** 2
b. 4
c. 3
d. 1
64. Ampule
65. Vial
66. **a.** Date solution was mixed
b. Concentration of drug per milliliter
67. **a.** Inject air into the vial
b. Between step 3 and step 4
68. **a.** Vent vial A (being careful not to touch solution with the needle).
b. Vent vial B and draw up the desired volume.
c. Return to vial A and draw up the desired volume.
69. **a.** Vent vial A (being careful not to touch solution with the needle).
b. Vent vial B and draw up the desired volume.
c. Apply a new needle to the syringe.
d. Draw up desired volume from vial A.
70. a
71. c
72. d
73. Any six:
- Use a sharp beveled needle in the smallest suitable length and gauge.
- Select the proper injection site, using anatomical landmarks.
- Apply ice to the injection site to create local anesthesia before cleansing and needle insertion.
- Insert the needle smoothly and quickly to minimize tissue pulling.
- Hold the syringe steady while the needle remains in tissues.
- Position the client as comfortably as possible to reduce muscular tension.
- Divert the client's attention from the injection through conversation.
- Massage the injected area gently for several seconds unless contraindicated.
- Increase the duration of the injection time.

74. Refer to Fig. 15-14, p. 402, in your text.
75. Abdominal wall
76. b
77. When using a 26-gauge needle, if 5 cm (2 inches) of tissue can be grasped, the needle should be inserted at a 90-degree angle; if 2.5 cm (1 inch) of tissue can be grasped, the needle should be inserted at a 45-degree angle.
78. d
79. **a.** 3 ml
b. Less than 2 ml
c. No more than 1 ml
80. a
81. c
82. d
83. **a.** Acromion process forms the base of a triangle in line with the midpoint of the lateral aspect of the upper arm. Injection site: in center of triangle (approximately 3 fingerbreadths below the acromion process).
b. Heel of hand placed over the greater trochanter (right hand for left hip, left hand for right hip). Nurse points thumb toward client's groin and fingers toward the head, with the index finger over anterior superior iliac

spine and middle finger back along iliac crest toward the buttock. Injection site: in center of the V-shaped triangle formed by the fingers.

c. Handbreadth above the knee to handbreadth below the greater trochanter of the femur. Injection site: midline of top of thigh to midline of lateral aspect of thigh.

d. Imaginary line is drawn between the posterior superior iliac spine and the greater trochanter of the femur. Injection site: above and lateral to the line (approximately 5 to 8 cm below the iliac crest).

84. b

85. The following points specific to the Z-track technique should be included:
   a. Nurse draws up solution with a 0.2 ml air lock.
   b. After preparing the site with an antiseptic swab, the nurse pulls the overlying skin and subcutaneous tissues approximately 2.5 to 3.5 cm laterally to the side.
   c. The skin is held taut while the needle is injected deep into the muscle.
   d. The nurse does not release the tissue during the injection process.
   e. After injection, the needle remains inserted for 10 seconds.
   f. The nurse withdraws the needle before releasing the skin.

86. **a.** 6
   b. 10
   c. 3
   d. 5
   e. 1
   f. 9
   g. 2
   h. 4
   i. 8
   j. 7

87. True
88. c
89. b
90. c
91. b
92. False
93. Wear gloves
94. False
95. c
96. a
97. a
98. b
99. b

CHAPTER 16

1. Personal belief about the worth of a given idea or behavior, a standard that influences behavior
2. b
3. True
4. Feelings toward a person, object, or idea
5. **a.** Observation
   b. Experience
6. **a.** Modeling: individual learns to behave by observing action of others
   b. Moralizing: individual held to a rigid standard of right and wrong prescribed by others
   c. Laissez-faire: individual acquires values informally, through unrestricted behavior
   d. Responsible choice: individual allowed choices in value selection in an environment that promotes freedom but that has specified boundaries or restrictions
7. Responsible choice
8. a
9. c
10. True
11. Values clarification
12. **a.** Choosing one's beliefs and behaviors
   b. Prizing one's beliefs and behaviors
   c. Acting on one's beliefs and behaviors
13. Any one:
   - Completing unfinished sentences: individual completes sentences that address certain values. Through sentence completion, the individual explores attitudes, beliefs, interests, and goals that are indicators of values. Completed sentences can be shared with others to enhance communication and affirm values held.
   - Rank ordering: individual selects priorities among different values listed. Priority assignment assists in identification and affirmation of values held.
   - Health value scale: individual prioritizes 10 values in order of importance. The placement of health in the rank order assists in determining the client's value of health. When the nurse is aware of the value that the client places on health, a more effective client teaching plan may be developed.

14. d
15. Any four:
   - Apathy
   - Flightiness
   - Uncertainty
   - Inconsistency
   - Drifting
   - Overconforming
   - Role playing

16. Any three:
   - Brief
   - Selective
   - Nonjudgmental
   - Thought provoking
   - Spontaneous

17. **a.** 2
   b. 1
   c. 3
   d. 4
18. b

CHAPTER 17

1. Principles or standards governing appropriate professional conduct
2. One of the following:
   - A situation in which there is a conflict in values and a person is unsure of what constitutes proper conduct
   - Situation in which a choice must be made between equally desirable or undesirable alternatives

3. True
4. d
5. c

6. False
7. Bioethics
8. a
9. a. 2
   b. 5
   c. 1
   d. 3
   e. 4
10. Any three:
    - To evaluate new professional practices
    - To reassess existing professional practices
    - To maintain standards of health care
    - To facilitate personal reflection, ethical thought, and personal growth of health professionals
    - To provide a basis for ethical decision making
11. a. To inform the client
    b. To support the client
12. a
13. c
14. Any four:
    - Nurses, as employees, work under policies established by others.
    - Conflicts arise between the professional model of nursing education and the bureaucratic model of health care institutions.
    - Nurses are often given responsibility and accountability but not authority.
    - Nurses experience role conflicts with other health care professionals.
    - Nurses experience conflicts between meeting a client's needs and following institutional procedures.
    - Nurses often have either limited or no input into decisions that they are responsible for implementing.
15. Any two:
    - Problem cannot be resolved solely through review of scientific data.
    - Problem is perplexing; one cannot easily think logically or make a decision about the problem.
    - Final answer to the problem will have profound relevance for several areas of human concern.
16. a. Recognize the ethical dilemma.
    b. Gather relevant factual information.
    c. Clarify the personal context of the ethical dilemma.
    d. Identify and clarify the ethical concepts.
    e. Construct and evaluate arguments for each issue.
    f. Take action.

CHAPTER 18

1. a. 3
   b. 4
   c. 1
   d. 2
2. a. Nursing practice acts
   b. Professional organizations
   c. Institutional policies
3. False
4. True
5. c
6. Tort
7. Carelessness or failure to meet appropriate nursing care standards, through action or inaction, resulting in client injury
8. a. Negligence
   b. Invasion of privacy
   c. Defamation of character
   d. Assault and battery
9. d
10. a. Nurse owed a duty to the client.
    b. Nurse did not perform the duty.
    c. Client was injured.
    d. Client's injury was a result of the nurse's failure to perform the duty.
11. d
12. b
13. Any two:
    - Follow standards of care.
    - Give competent care.
    - Develop empathetic rapport with the client.
14. False
15. b
16. Any four:
    - Person giving consent must be mentally and physically competent.
    - Person giving consent must be legally an adult.
    - Consent must be given voluntarily.
    - Person giving consent must thoroughly understand the procedure, risks, benefits, and alternatives.
    - Person giving consent must have an opportunity to have all questions answered satisfactorily.
17. d
18. False
19. c
20. Absence of brain function
21. True
22. True
23. d
24. To encourage health care professionals to assist in emergency situations by limiting liability and offering legal immunity
25. True
26. c

CHAPTER 19

1. The ongoing, dynamic series of events that involves transmission of information or feelings between two or more people
2. a. Intrapersonal: communication within the individual
   b. Interpersonal: communication between two people or a small group
   c. Public: communication with large groups of people
3. d
4. a. Receiver
   b. Intrapersonal variables
   c. Message
   d. Channels
   e. Sender
   f. Referent
5. b
6. a. 4
   b. 2
   c. 1
   d. 3
7. Both verbal and nonverbal involve transmission of a message. Verbal uses spoken or written words. Nonverbal occurs without use of words, through actions.

8. b
9. Any five:
   - Development: relates to neurological ability and intellectual development
   - Perceptions: individual's personal view of events
   - Values: standards that influence behavior
   - Emotions: subjective feelings about events
   - Sociocultural background: cultural origin
   - Knowledge: ability to understand words used
   - Roles and relationships: societal expectation of behavior in specific situations
   - Environment: setting in which communication occurs
   - Space and territoriality: Distances maintained by individuals during interaction
10. False
11. True
12. d
13. **a.** Intimate distance: 18 inches or less
    b. Personal distance: 1½ to 4 feet
    c. Social distance: 4 to 12 feet
14. a
15. False
16. Any four:
    - Face the client while he or she is speaking.
    - Maintain natural eye contact to show willingness to listen.
    - Assume a relaxed posture (avoid crossing legs and arms).
    - Avoid distracting body movements.
    - Nod in acknowledgment when client talks about an important point or looks for feedback.
    - Lean toward the speaker to communicate involvement.
17. Any two:
    - Listen without interrupting.
    - Provide verbal feedback that demonstrates understanding.
    - Be sure nonverbal cues match verbal communication.
    - Avoid arguing, expressing doubts, or attempting to change the client's mind.
18. False
19. b
20. **a.** 4
    b. 1
    c. 3
    d. 2
21. Any four:
    - Giving an opinion: takes decision making away from client, inhibits spontaneity and problem solving, creates doubt
    - Offering false reassurance: discourages open communication
    - Being defensive: suggests that the client has no right to an opinion, erodes client trust
    - Showing approval or disapproval: praise implies that behavior is the only acceptable one, disapproval implies that the client must meet the nurse's expectations, client may feel rejected
    - Stereotyping: inhibits uniqueness and oversimplifies the situation
    - Asking why: may be interpreted as an accusation, causes resentment, insecurity, and mistrust
    - Changing the subject: displays rudeness and lack of empathy
22. a
23. Relationship focusing on client needs and promoting a psychological climate to facilitate positive change and growth in the client
24. **a.** Trust: feeling that other individuals will be able and willing to assist
    b. Empathy: ability to understand and accept another person and accurately perceive that person's feelings
    c. Caring: having a positive regard for another person
    d. Autonomy: ability to be self-directed
    e. Mutuality: ability to share with another person
25. Empathy is a fair, sensitive, and objective look at another person's experiences. Sympathy is subjective; thinking or feeling as another person does. Empathy is therapeutic, sympathy is not.
26. **a.** 1
    b. 3
    c. 2
    d. 2
    e. 4
    f. 3
    g. 2
27. b
28. Any two:
    - Confrontation: nurse makes client aware of inconsistencies in behavior or thoughts
    - Immediacy: nurse focuses interaction on present situation, drawing attention to client's behaviors or statements
    - Self-disclosure: nurse reveals personal experiences, thoughts, ideas, values, or feelings in the context of the relationship
29. d
30. b
31. False
32. d
33. Any five:
    - Pad and felt-tipped pen or magic slate
    - Communication board with words, letters, or pictures
    - Call bells or alarms
    - Sign language
    - Use of eye blinks or movements of fingers for simple responses
    - Flash cards with common words or phrases the client may use
    - Language cards for non-English-speaking clients
34. Any three:
    - Regulating room temperature to a comfort level
    - Eliminating or reducing loud noises in the room
    - Making the client comfortable
    - Asking other staff or family (if appropriate) not to enter the room during the interaction
    - Reducing bright or glaring light
35. d
36. Any three:
    - Be sure hearing aid is clean, is inserted properly, and has a functioning battery.
    - Adjust volume of hearing aid to a comfortable level.
    - Speak slowly and articulate clearly.
    - Stand in front of client to provide opportunity for lip-reading.
    - Talk toward client's best ear.
    - Reduce background noise.
37. c
38. Any two:
    - Transmit clear, concise, and understandable messages.

- Gain a sense of trust in the nurse as care giver.
- Send and receive feedback.

CHAPTER 20

1. An interactive process consisting of a deliberate set of actions that helps individuals gain knowledge or perform new skills
2. Acquisition of knowledge or skills through reinforcement, practice, and experience
3. True
4. **a.** Promote health and prevent illness
   b. Restore health
   c. Cope with impaired function
5. False
6. **a.** 2
   b. 6
   c. 3
   d. 1
   e. 7
   f. 5
   g. 8
   h. 4
7. **a.** Affective
   b. Psychomotor
   c. Cognitive
8. **a.** Readiness to learn: that the individual is willing to take action to become involved in learning
   b. Ability to learn: that the individual has the physical, developmental, and cognitive capabilities necessary for learning to take place
   c. Learning environment: that conditions which support learning and interpersonal communication exist in the setting where learning is to take place
9. c
10. b
11. False
12. Any three:
    - Person believes that there is a susceptibility to the disease in question
    - Person believes there would be serious effects on life or life-style
    - Person believes that actions can be taken to reduce the chance of contracting the disease or lessen its severity
    - Person believes the threat of taking these actions is not as great as the threat of the disease
13. d
14. a
15. **a.** Developmental capability (cognitive level, knowledge)
    b. Age
    c. Physical capability
16. b
17. b
18. Any five:
    - Timing must be right (client ready).
    - Teaching material must be organized.
    - Nurse must speak the client's language.
    - Nurse must maintain learner attention and participation.
    - Teaching builds on existing knowledge.
    - Learner must be reinforced.
    - Nurse must match teaching methods with the learner needs.
19. c
20. True
21. c
22. **a.** 3
    b. 1
    c. 4
    d. 2
    e. 5
23. **a.** Learning needs
    b. Readiness to learn
    c. Ability to learn
    d. Teaching environment
    e. Resources for learning
24. d
25. **a.** Behavior: learner's ability to do something after the learning experience (involves an action verb)
    b. Content to be learned: precisely what is to be learned
    c. Conditions: situation under which the learned behavior will occur
26. c
27. b
28. b
29. a
30. To promote continuity of the teaching plan, particularly when several nurses are involved or several teaching sessions are needed
31. Teaching approach involves the nurse's tasks (for example, nondirective, directive, resource, facilitator) and relationship with the client. Teaching methodology refers to the techniques used to convey information (lecture, audiovisuals, discussion, and so on).
32. **a.** Physical sensations during the procedure are described (but not evaluated).
    b. Cause of the sensation is described.
    c. Only sensations commonly experienced by other clients are presented.
33. **a.** Specific content (what was taught)
    b. Evaluation of learning (behaviors demonstrated by the client indicating that learning has occurred)
    c. Method of teaching (how teaching was done)

CHAPTER 21

1. A group of interacting individuals making up a basic unit of society
2. b
3. **a.** Nuclear
   b. Origin
   c. Procreation
4. False
5. True
6. c
7. **a.** 3
   b. 2
   c. 5
   d. 4
   e. 1
8. d
9. Any five:
   - Collects and disseminates information to family members
   - Provides feedback to family members to guide them in interaction with the larger society

- Transmits beliefs, values, attitudes, and coping mechanisms to family members
- Guides family members in problem solving
- Provides practical services and concrete assistance
- Provides a safe, comfortable environment when family members need rest and recuperation
- Provides standards of behavior and attitudes against which family members can judge themselves
- Helps family members establish and reinforce identity
- Assists family members in controlling or working through negative emotions

10. **a.** 4
b. 6
c. 5
d. 1
e. 3
f. 2
11. True
12. Any three:
- Autonomy of family members
- Varied and regular communication
- Active coping
- Social ties within the community

13. Nurses may approach the family as environment or the family as client in providing effective nursing care. When the family is approached as the environment, the primary focus is on the health and development of an individual family member who exists within the environment that is the family. When the family is approached as the client, the nurse plans care that is directed toward each family member to achieve health and attain the developmental tasks of the family.
14. b
15. False
16. True
17. Any three:
- Clear communication
- Healthy child-rearing practices
- Support and nurturing among family members
- Active community participation
- Flexibility in roles and functioning

CHAPTER 22

1. d
2. True
3. Maturation
4. Development
5. Growth (physical growth)
6. **a.** Individual has adaptive potential for qualitative and quantitative changes by receiving stimuli from, and giving stimuli to, the environment.
b. Individual derives uniqueness from the interaction of heredity and environment.
c. Primary goal of development is achievement of potential (self-realization or self-actualization).
7. **a.** Development has direction, proceeding in an orderly and sequential fashion.
b. Development is complex yet predictable.
c. Development is unique to the individual and his or her genetic potential.
d. Development occurs through conflict and adaptation.
e. Development involves challenges for the individual.
f. Developmental tasks require practice and energy.
8. Refer to Table 22-1, p. 564, in your text.
9. False
10. **a.** 4
b. 2
c. 5
d. 3
e. 1
f. 6
11. Combination of genetic and environmental factors
12. Any agent capable of producing adverse effects in the fetus
13. Any three:
- Infections
- Drugs
- Smoking
- Alcohol

14. Fetus is capable of life outside the uterus, when organ systems are complete and capable of functioning.
15. Vernix caseosa
16. Lanugo
17. b
18. b
19. True
20. **a.** Patent airway
b. Stabilization of body temperature
c. Infection prevention
21. *Neisseria gonorrhoeae* (which may cause ophthalmia neonatorum, a severe conjunctival infection in the neonate)
22. **a.** Heart rate
b. Respiratory effort
c. Muscle tone
d. Reflex irritability
e. Color
23. c
24. Parents and neonate are capable and desire to explore and respond to each other.
25. False
26. When parents and newborn elicit reciprocal and complementary behaviors (parental behaviors: attentiveness, physical contact; neonatal behavior: maintenance of contact with the parent)
27. d
28. c
29. True
30. d
31. False
32. b
33. False
34. Unsuccessful attempts at controlling the environment through independent actions
35. b
36. b
37. Behavior in which the toddler returns to the parent, at periodic intervals, for encouragement and emotional support
38.

Play pattern	Age span	Characteristic behaviors
Cooperative	Late preschool	Take turns, join efforts to produce desired outcomes
Parallel	Toddler	Play next to, not with, another

Continued.

Play pattern	Age span	Characteristic behaviors
Associative	Early preschool	Play with others in similar activity; no formal organization or distribution of responsibility

39. d
40. True
41.

Stage	Age span	Average heart rate	Average respiratory rate
Fetus		130-160	0
Neonate	0-1 mo	120-140	30-50
Infant	1-12 mo	80-130	30-35
Toddler	1-3 yr	110	24
Preschooler	3-6 yr	90	24

42. A return to earlier patterns of behavior, most often occurring in response to stress
43. True
44. d
45. Any four:
    - Developmental age
    - Previous experiences with hospitalization
    - Available support persons
    - Coping skills
    - Seriousness of the illness
46. Denver Developmental Screening Test (DDST)
47. True
48. **a.** Minimizing separation anxiety
    b. Minimizing physical discomfort
    c. Promoting growth and development
    d. Providing diversional activities
49. **a.** Nursing personnel
    b. The child
    c. The family

CHAPTER 23

1. **a.** 2
   b. 1
   c. 1
   d. 2
   e. 1
   f. 1
   g. 2
   h. 1
2. False
3. a
4. a
5. **a.** 65-90
   b. 16-18
   c. 110/70
6. Provide nutritious snacks such as fruit, vegetables, and high-protein foods
7. Thinking about one's own thought processes
8. **a.** 2
   b. 1
   c. 2
   d. 2
   e. 1
   f. 1
   g. 1
9. True
10. c
11. c
12. Adolescence
13. Puberty
14. Primary sex characteristics are the physical and hormonal changes necessary for reproduction. Secondary characteristics are those external changes that differentiate males from females.
15. **a.** Increased growth rate of skeleton, muscle, and viscera
    b. Sex-specific changes, such as changes in shoulder and hip width
    c. Alteration in distribution of muscle and fat
    d. Development of the reproductive system and secondary sex characteristics
16. b
17. True
18. c
19. d
20. True
21. a
22. Sexually transmitted diseases
23. **a.** Developmental level
    b. Response to care
    c. History of prior health care
    d. Medical history
    e. Available support persons
24. External support system refers to significant others who the child is able to use for support. Internal supports are those actions or behaviors that the child independently initiates to assist with coping (for example, reading, listening to soft music, relaxation techniques).

CHAPTER 24

1. State in which independence and balanced development in physiological, psychosocial, and cognitive areas are attained
2. **a.** Early adult transition (separation from family, desire for independence; 18 to 20 years old)
   b. Entrance into the adult world (trying out careers and life-styles; 21 to 27 years old)
   c. Transition (major modifications in life activities; 28 to 32 years old)
   d. Settling down (experiences greater stability; 33 to 39 years old)
3. **a.** Achieve independence from parental controls.
   b. Begin development of strong friendships and intimate relationships outside the family.
   c. Establish a personal set of values.
   d. Develop a sense of personal identity.
   e. Prepare for life work and develop the capacity for intimacy.
4. **a.** 2
   b. 3
   c. 1
5. c
6. **a.** Conception
   b. Pregnancy
   c. Birth
   d. Lactation

7. Any four:
   - Make sure certain emotions are based on love rather than physical or sexual attraction.
   - Explore motivation for wanting to marry.
   - Develop clear communications.
   - Understand that any annoying behavior patterns and habits are unlikely to change after marriage.
   - Determine compatibility in important beliefs and values.
8. Any four:
   - Establish an intimate relationship.
   - Decide on and work toward material and economic goals.
   - Establish guidelines for power and decision-making issues.
   - Set standards for extrafamily interactions.
   - Find companionship with other couples for a social life.
   - Choose mores, values, and ideologies acceptable to both partners.
9. **a.** Parent relinquishes the parent role, establishes new relationship as fellow adult
   b. Focuses on meeting needs of the newborn
   c. Adoption of a parental self-image
   d. Offering structure and guidance to the toddler and early school-age child
   e. Permitting freedom for personal growth, while offering safety and guidance to the later school-age child and adolescent
10. Any six:
    - A sense of meaning and direction in life
    - Successful negotiation through transitions
    - Absence of feelings of being cheated or disappointed by life
    - Attainment of several long-term goals
    - Satisfaction with personal growth and development
    - When married, feelings of mutual love for partner; when single, satisfaction with social interactions
    - Satisfaction with friendships
    - Generally cheerful attitude
    - Not sensitive to criticism
    - No unrealistic fears
11. True
12. Any five:
    - Violent death and injury
    - Substance abuse
    - Unwanted pregnancies
    - Sexually transmitted diseases
    - Environmental or occupational factors
    - Life-style habits
    - Family history of heredity-associated diseases
13. Either one:
    - A man's, woman's, or couple's involuntary inability to conceive
    - Inability to conceive after a year or more of regular sexual intercourse
14. True
15. False
16. **a.** 3
    b. 1
    c. 2
    d. 2
    e. 3
    f. 1
    g. 1
    h. 3
17. A period of approximately 6 weeks following delivery during which the uterus returns to its approximate prepregnancy size
18. **a.** Lochia alba
    b. Lochia rubra
    c. Lochia serosa
19. d
20. b
21. Routine examinations of the pregnant woman by an obstetrician, nurse practitioner, or certified nurse-midwife to evaluate the health of the mother and the development of the fetus
22. 9 to 13 kg (19 to 30 lbs)
23. c
24. Any four:
    - Achieving adult civic social responsibility
    - Establishing and maintaining a standard of living
    - Helping teenage children become responsible and happy adults
    - Developing leisure activities
    - Relating to one's spouse as a person
    - Accepting and adjusting to the physiological changes of middle age
    - Adjusting to aging parents
25. c
26. Disruption of the cycle of menstruation and ovulation typically occurring between 45 and 60 years of age
27. Decrease in the level of androgens occurring in men in their late 40s or early 50s resulting in physiological changes in sexual response
28. True
29. Any four:
    - Sex: female
    - Age: declines for women after their early 50s, increases for men after their late 50s
    - Social isolation: absence of intimate, confiding relationships following a change in the nature of relationship with parents, children, or spouse
    - Losses: parental deprivation or loss of a mother before 14 years of age; other physical or emotional losses during midlife; departure of last child from home
    - Family history: history of depression in the family of origin
30. Any three:
    - Improved knowledge about the impact of risk factors on a person's level of health
    - Improved health promotion activities
    - Improved communication within the family structure
    - Fewer reports of illnesses, inability to problem solve, and so on

CHAPTER 25

1. Health specialty that deals with the physiology and psychology of aging and with diagnosis and treatment of diseases affecting the aged
2. The study of all aspects of the aging process and its consequences
3. b
4. Discrimination against people because of their increasing age
5. True
6. **a.** 2
   b. 5
   c. 1

d. 6
e. 4
f. 3

7. Any five:
   - Adjusting to decreasing health and physical strength
   - Adjusting to retirement and reduced or fixed income
   - Adjusting to the death of a spouse
   - Accepting oneself as an aging person
   - Maintaining satisfactory living arrangements
   - Realigning relationships with adult children
   - Finding meaning in life
8. **a.** A
   b. N
   c. N
   d. N
   e. A
   f. N
   g. N
   h. A
   i. A
   j. N
9. False
10. True
11. A syndrome involving progressive impairment of memory and other cognitive abilities, and personality change
12. SDAT (senile dementia of Alzheimer type)
13. Any three:
    - Infection
    - Drug reactions
    - Metabolic disorders
    - Depression
14. a
15. False
16. Any three:
    - Attention difficulties
    - Decreasing interest in life
    - Indifference to ceremony and courtesy
    - Forgetting nouns in speech
    - Vague, uncertain, and hesitant
17. d
18. b
19. True
20. True
21. Any four:
    - Financial provisions for retirement income
    - Available postretirement activities
    - Living arrangements
    - Role changes
    - Health care needs
    - Legal affairs
22. **a.** Isolation that occurs because society's bias against older adults prohibits social interactions with others
    b. Isolation that results from a person's unacceptable appearance or other factors involved in presenting oneself to others
    c. Isolation that results from behaviors that are unacceptable to others
    d. Isolation that occurs because of distance from family, urban crime, and barriers within institutions
23. Any four:
    - Activity level
    - Financial status
    - Accessibility of public transportation
    - Community activities
    - Environmental hazards
    - Support systems
    - Length of time arrangement will be appropriate
24. False
25. **a.** Heart disease
    b. Malignant neoplasms (cancer)
    c. Cerebrovascular disease
    d. Influenza or pneumonia
26. Sundown syndrome
27. b
28. **a.** Therapeutic communication: effective communication that establishes rapport and focuses on meeting the needs of the client
    b. Touch: therapeutic tool that can help provide stimulation, reduce anxiety, orient to reality, relieve physiological and emotional pain, and give comfort
    c. Reality orientation: communication technique that is directed toward restoring reality, improving awareness, promoting socialization, elevating client's independent function, and minimizing confusion or disorientation and regression
    d. Resocialization: identification and utilization of resources available to assist in expansion of the individual's social network
    e. Reminiscence: process of recalling the past to assign new meanings to experiences
    f. Body image interventions: actions to maintain the physical appearance of the individual
29. **a.** Clarity
    b. Independence
    c. Reinforcement
    d. Realism
    e. Consistency
    f. Repetition
    g. Individualization
30. Any four:
    - Select a small, quiet room that is well lit and has comfortable furniture.
    - Keep meetings short enough to promote learning without producing exhaustion (20 minutes).
    - Choose participants who are able to participate.
    - Consider sensory deficits when using audiovisual aids.
    - Present one topic for discussion at each meeting.
    - Make it clear that participation is voluntary.
31. **a.** Home care
    b. Hospice
    c. Day care
    d. Respite care
    e. Long-term care
32. **a.** Reflect consideration of factors that influence normal aging.
    b. Maintain independence as much as possible.
    c. Facilitate an optimal level of comfort and coping.

CHAPTER 26

1. c
2. **a.** Loss of external objects: loss of any possession that is worn out, misplaced, stolen, or ruined
   b. Loss of a known environment: leaving a familiar setting for a period of time or relocating permanently
   c. Loss of a significant other: loss of family, friends, acquaintances, or pets because of death, relocation, or job change

Engle	Kübler-Ross	Martocchio
a. Shock and disbelief	**a.** Denial	**a.** Shock and disbelief
b. Developing awareness	**b.** Anger	**b.** Yearning and protest
c. Reorganization and restitution	**c.** Bargaining	**c.** Anguish, disorganization, and despair
	d. Depression	**d.** Identification in bereavement
	e. Acceptance	**e.** Reorganization and restitution

d. Loss of an aspect of self: loss of a body part or of physical or psychological function
e. Loss of life: fear of pain, dependence, and loss of control associated with the dying process; fear of death

3. b
4. Bereavement
5. **a.** Accept reality of the loss.
b. Accept grief as painful.
c. Adjust to an environment that no longer includes the person who has died.
d. Reinvest emotional energy into new relationships.
6. True
7. Refer to table at top of page.
8. False
9. True
10. **a.** 2
b. 5
c. 4
d. 1
e. 3
11. **a.** Affective: sensations and emotions that are part of hoping
b. Cognitive: processes of wishing, imagining, perceiving, thinking, learning, or judging in relation to hope
c. Behavioral: actions taken to achieve hope
d. Affiliative: individual's involvement and relationships with others
e. Temporal: individual's experience in relation to hoping
f. Contextual: perception of hope in relation to interpretation of life situations
12. True
13. c
14. **a.** 6
b. 4
c. 7
d. 2
e. 1
f. 3
g. 8
h. 5
15. Any five:
- Need to be with the dying person
- Need to be helpful to the dying person
- Need for assurance of the spouse's comfort
- Need to be informed of the spouse's condition
- Need to be informed of the impending death
- Need to ventilate emotions
- Need for comfort and support of the family
- Need for acceptance, support, and comfort from health professionals

16. False
17. True
18. Any five:
- Low socioeconomic status
- Poor health
- Sudden death or short illness
- Perceived lack of available social support
- Lack of support from religious beliefs
- Lack of a supportive family or one that discourages grief expressions
- Strong tendency to cling to the person before death or preoccupation with the deceased's image
- Strong reactions of distress, anger, and self-reproach
- History of psychiatric illness or suicidal intention

19. True
20. Accomplishment of part of the grief work before the actual loss
21. **a.** Resolve grief.
b. Accept the reality of the loss.
c. Regain a sense of self-esteem.
d. Renew normal activities or relationships.
22. c
23. True
24. **a.** Promote comfort.
b. Maintain independence.
c. Prevent isolation.
d. Promote spiritual comfort.
e. Support the grieving family.
25. Any four:
- Apply techniques of therapeutic communication.
- Express empathy.
- Pray with the client.
- Read inspirational literature.
- Play music.

26. Providing family-centered care to assist the terminally ill client in maintaining comfort and a satisfactory life-style through the phases of dying
27. b
28. **a.** Algor mortis
b. Livor mortis
c. Rigor mortis

CHAPTER 27

1. Needs shared by all persons that are necessary for survival and health
2.

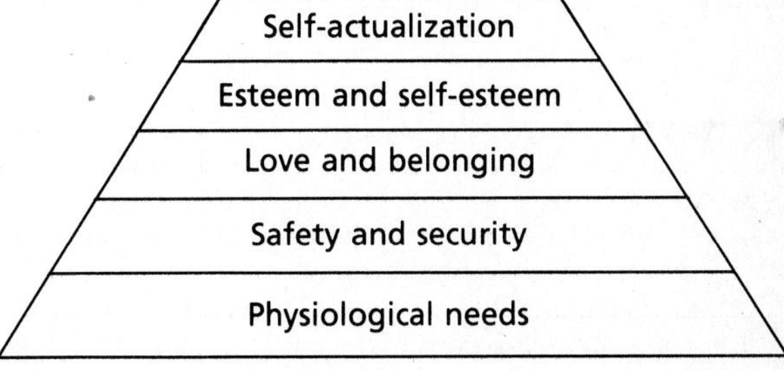

3. a
4. **a.** Oxygen
   b. Fluid
   c. Nutrition
   d. Temperature
   e. Elimination
   f. Shelter
   g. Rest
   h. Sex
5. Any four:
   - Very young
   - Very old
   - Poor
   - Ill
   - Handicapped
6. **a.** Very old (older adult or elderly)
   b. Very young (infants)
7. True
8. False
9. d
10. True
11. c
12. Any six:
    - Solves own problems
    - Assists others in problem solving
    - Accepts suggestions of others
    - Broad interests in work- and social-related topics
    - Possesses good communication skills both as a listener and as a communicator
    - Manages stress and assists others in managing stress
    - Enjoys privacy
    - Seeks new experiences and knowledge
    - Confident in abilities and decisions
    - Anticipates problems and successes
    - Likes self
13. **a.** 1
    b. 2
    c. 13
    d. 8
    e. 9
    f. 7
    g. 3
    h. 6
    i. 12
    j. 5
    k. 10
    l. 11
    m. 4
14. True
15. Any four:
    - Person's personality and mood
    - Person's state of health
    - Person's perception of need
    - Person's family structure
    - Interrelationship of needs

CHAPTER 28

1. State in which any nonspecific demand requires an individual to respond or take action
2. Either definition:
   - The body's tendency to maintain itself in a state of relative constancy
   - A dynamic form of equilibrium in the body's internal environment
3. a
4. False
5. c
6. b
7. d
8. d
9. **a.** Intensity of the stressor
   b. Scope of the stressor
   c. Duration of the stressor
   d. Number and nature of other stressors
10. **a.** Good communication skills
    b. Mutual respect for all family members
    c. Adequate resources available for adaptation
    d. Previous experience with stressors
11. **a.** Physical-developmental dimension: physical body changes of the LAS or GAS in response to internal or external environment; developmental task achievement
    b. Emotional dimension: psychological coping mechanisms including task-oriented behaviors and ego-defense mechanisms
    c. Intellectual dimension: gathering information, solving problems, communicating with others
    d. Social dimension: using individuals or organized groups to provide support, utilizing societal and community resources
    e. Spiritual dimension: believing in Supreme Being, unity with nature or positive sense of life's meaning and purpose
12. Any four:
    - Blood clotting
    - Wound healing
    - Accommodation of the eye to light
    - Response to pressure
    - Reflex pain
    - Inflammatory response
13. **a.** Localized pain
    b. Localized swelling
    c. Localized heat
    d. Localized redness
    e. Changes in function
14. d
15. **a.** Alarm reaction: physiological changes that prepare a person to adapt to a stressor
    b. Resistance stage: stabilization of the body to allow the person to make an adaptive response
    c. Exhaustion stage: if person is unable to alleviate the stress, energy insufficient for adaptation
16. **a.** 3
    b. 1
    c. 2
    d. 1
    e. 3
    f. 2
    g. 1
    h. 1
17. True
18. **a.** Task-oriented behaviors: use of direct problem-solving techniques
    b. Ego-defense mechanisms: unconscious, indirect methods of coping with stress
19. **a.** Compensation
    b. Conversion
    c. Denial

Reducing stressful situations	Decreasing physiological responses	Improving responses to stress
a. Habituation **b.** Change avoidance **c.** Time blocking **d.** Time management **e.** Environmental modification	**a.** Regular exercise **b.** Nutrition and diet **c.** Rest **d.** Relaxation techniques	**a.** Support systems **b.** Crisis intervention **c.** Enhancing self-esteem

d. Displacement
e. Identification
f. Regression

20. Any eight:
- Elevated blood pressure
- Increased muscle tension
- Elevated pulse and/or increased respiration
- Sweaty palms
- Cold hands and feet
- Slumped posture
- Tension headache
- Upset stomach
- Higher-pitched voice
- Change in appetite
- Changes in urinary frequency
- Restlessness; difficulty falling asleep or frequent awakening
- Dilated pupils
- Increased blood glucose

21. At least one behavior for each item
a. Distrust, withdrawal, or limited interaction with others in later years
b. Excessive dependence on others
c. Passive, inactive behavior toward the environment
d. Inability or unwillingness to develop friendships
e. Rebelliousness, depression, anxiety*
f. Increased discord at home and work, extremes in social activities (excessive participation or withdrawal), depression, anxiety*
g. Depression, anxiety*
h. Overdependence, strained family or social relationships*

22. a. Support systems
b. Prior experience with stressors
c. Coping mechanisms
d. Overall stress response

23. Any 10:
- Anxiety
- Depression
- Burnout
- Increased use of chemical substances
- Changes in sleep and activity patterns
- Mental exhaustion
- Loss of self-esteem
- Increased irritability
- Loss of motivation
- Emotional outbursts and crying
- Decreased productivity and quality of job performance
- Tendency to make mistakes; poor judgment
- Forgetfulness and blocking
- Diminished attention to detail
- Preoccupation—daydreaming or "spacing out"
- Inability to concentrate on tasks
- Increased absenteeism and illness
- Lethargy
- Loss of interest
- Accident proneness

24. Any four:
- Decreased ability to learn
- Reduced role performance
- Impaired communication
- Inability to resolve conflict
- Decreased ability to problem solve
- Increased dependence on others

25. Any two:
- Expressed anger with God or Supreme Being
- View of stressor as punishment
- Questioning meaning of life
- Abandoning earlier beliefs concerning meaning of life

26. Refer to table at top of page.

27. a. Perceiving the stressful event realistically
b. Having adequate support
c. Using adequate coping mechanisms

*Refer to answer 23 for additional responses.

CHAPTER 29

1. The person's subjective image of the self; the perception of physical, emotional, and social attributes or qualities

2. Any five:
- Reactions of others to the infant's or child's body and behavior
- Ongoing perceptions of others' reactions to the self
- Experiences with self and others
- Personality structure
- Perceptions of physiological and sensory stimuli that impinge on the self
- Prior and new experiences
- Present feelings about physical, emotional, and social self
- Expectations about the self

3. The mental picture of one's body, including the external, internal, and postural image of the body

4. False

5. Either definition:
- The evaluation that individuals maintain about themselves and convey to others verbally or through behaviors
- The acceptance of self because of basic worth, despite weaknesses, limitations, or deficiencies

6. a. 4
b. 1
c. 6
d. 2
e. 8

f. 5
g. 7
h. 3
7. b
8. True
9. a. Identity
b. Body image
c. Self-esteem
d. Roles
10. c
11. False
12. A person's image of self as male or female and the meaning that this has for the person
13. c
14. True
15. a. Reinforcement-extinction: behaviors that become common or avoided, depending on whether they are approved and reinforced or discouraged and punished
b. Inhibition: refraining from a behavior, even when motivated to do so, because of each reinforcement
c. Substitution: replacement of one behavior by another in order to provide the same gratification
d. Imitation: acquisition of knowledge, skills, or behaviors from members of a social or cultural group
e. Identification: internalization of beliefs, behaviors, and values of a role model into the person's unique, overt expression
16. Socialization
17. d
18. b
19. a. Health-illness transition
b. Developmental transition
c. Situational transition
20. Lack of congruent or compatible role expectations
21. a. 2
b. 3
c. 4
d. 1
22. Role ambiguity
23. d
24. Role strain
25. a. 2
b. 4
c. 1
d. 2
e. 3
f. 4
g. 3
h. 1
26. a. Whatever the client communicates is normal and acceptable.
b. The communication is not threatening or frightening to the nurse.
c. The nurse will not reject or isolate the client because of anything communicated.
27. a. 4
b. 2
c. 3
d. 1
e. 1
f. 2
g. 4
h. 3
28. a. Shock and panic
b. Defensive retreat
c. Acknowledgment
d. Adaptation
29. Any three:
- Relate to the client as an equal.
- Find a common interest or experience for initiating conversation.
- Establish a smooth, easy pattern of conversation.
- Convey a keen, sympathetic interest in the other person, give full attention, listen carefully, and indicate that there is time to listen.
- Adopt the client's terminology and conventions, and meet the client on his or her own ground to the extent possible.
30. a. Increased self-awareness
b. Self-exploration
c. Self-evaluation
d. Formulation of realistic goals
e. Commitment to goals and achievement through action
31. The nurse should seek assistance from other appropriate professionals.
32. False
33. True

CHAPTER 30

1. Sexuality is a holistic concept that involves biological, psychological, social, and ethical components constituting a person's sense of being female or male. Sex has a limited meaning describing the biological aspects of sexuality such as genital sexual activity.
2. Gender identity
3. Sexual orientation
4. c
5. a. Biology
b. Personality
c. Religious beliefs
d. Society
6. Whether their sexual attitudes, feelings, and actions are normal
7.

Structure/Organ	Function(s)
Vulva	
Labia minora Labia majora	Cover and protect vaginal and urinary openings; sensitive to touch, pressure, pain, and temperature
Clitoris	Sensitive to touch, pressure, and temperature, and sexual arousal and pleasure
Vestibule	
Introitus	Vaginal opening
Bartholin's glands	Small amount of lubrication of introitus during sexual arousal
Hymen	Membranous fold partly covering the introitus
Vagina	Passageway for menstrual flow, childbirth, and sexual pleasure
Uterus	
Cervix	Contains glands that secrete mucus, providing a plug for the opening to the uterus

Structure/Organ	Function(s)
Body	
Myometrium	Protective environment for developing fetus; contractions expel fetus during labor and delivery
Endometrium	Vascular, cushioned environment for ovum implantation and maintenance
Fallopian tubes	Conduit for passage of ovum and sperm
Ovaries	Produce ovum; secrete female hormones
Breasts	Milk production, sexual arousal and pleasure

8. **a.** Gonadotropin-releasing hormone
   b. Follicle-stimulating hormone (or luteinizing hormone)
   c. Luteinizing hormone (or follicle-stimulating hormone)
   d. Estrogen (small amounts of androgens also secreted)
   e. Progesterone
9. c
10. d
11. Any four:
    - Lower abdominal pain/discomfort
    - Breast fullness/tenderness
    - Weight gain
    - Fluid retention
    - Irritability
    - Depression

12.

Structure/Organ	Function(s)
Penis	Transmission of urine and seminal fluid, sexual arousal and pleasure
Scrotum	Houses and protects testicles, epididymis, and portion of vas deferens
Testis	Produces sperm and androgenic hormones, primarily testosterone
Seminiferous tubules	Location of actual sperm production
Epididymis	Duct transporting sperm from outside the testicle to the vas deferens
Vas deferens	Tube transporting sperm out of the scrotum to the ampulla
Ampulla	Reservoir for sperm
Seminal vesicles Prostate gland	Secrete seminal plasma to dilute and carry sperm and provide nutrition for the sperm; buffer vaginal acidity to aid in fertility
Bulbourethral (Cowper's) glands	Secrete clear, alkaline lubricating fluid during sexual arousal; may neutralize urethral acidity to create a more favorable environment for sperm

13. Circumcision
14. b
15. d
16. Menarche
17. True
18. Any four:
    - Dating issues
    - Masturbation
    - Emotional commitment in relationships
    - Virginity versus premarital sexual behavior
    - Contraception
    - Teen pregnancy and related issues (abortion, adoption, single parenthood)
    - Risks of STDs (sexually transmitted diseases)
19. True
20. Any four:
    - Monotony in sexual relationships
    - Career and financial concerns
    - Mental or physical fatigue
    - Overindulgence in alcohol
    - Illness
    - Fear of failure
21. **a.** Excitement: gradual increase in sexual arousal
    b. Plateau: heightened responses caused by vasocongestion and myotonia
    c. Orgasm: sudden release of pooled blood and tension in the muscles at the climax of sexual excitement associated with highly pleasurable feelings of physiological and psychological release
    d. Resolution:physiological and psychological return to an unaroused state
22. c
23. True
24. To avoid placing uterine weight on the major blood vessels, which could cause decreased maternal blood flow and therefore potential fetal hypoxia
25. **a.** Semen contains prostaglandins that may stimulate uterine contractions.
    b. Breast stimulation induces the release of oxytocin which may also stimulate uterine contraction.
26. b
27. d
28. Any seven:
    - How does the method work?
    - What are the risks involved in using the method?
    - Are there contraindications that rule out particular methods?
    - How will it affect lovemaking?
    - Does the partner object to it?
    - Will it cause any discomfort?
    - Is it readily available, affordable, and easy to use?
    - Will either partner feel embarrassed using it?
    - Is the risk of pregnancy acceptable?
    - Are there other alternatives?
29. **a.** **(1)** Abstinence
    (2) Calendar (rhythm) method
    (3) Mucus method
    (4) Basal body temperature method
    b. **(1)** Oral contraceptive pill
    (2) Spermicides
    c. **(1)** Vaginal sponge
    d. **(1)** Condom
    (2) Diaphragm
    (3) Cervical cap
    (4) Intrauterine device
    e. **(1)** Vasectomy
    (2) Tubal ligation
30. Abstinence
31. a
32. Either of the following:
    - Days 6-21 ($24 - 18 = 6$; $32 - 11 = 21$)
    - To increase effectiveness, days 1-21
33. d

34. Changes in cervical mucus correlated with ovulation. Just before ovulation, the amount of mucus increases. Women are most fertile when the cervical mucus is wet, abundant, slippery, stretchable, and clear.
35. b
36. True
37. False
38. c
39. False
40. **a.** 3
    b. 2
    c. 4
    d. 3
    e. 1
    f. 4
    g. 1
    h. 2
41. Any four:
    - Knowing one's sex partner or partners
    - Having a relationship with open communication enabling discussion about health, disease exposure, and use of protective devices
    - Limiting the number of sex partners
    - Avoiding sexual contact with intravenous drug users
    - Using condoms properly
42. d
43. **a.** Nervous system
    b. Vascular system
    c. Hormonal system
44. True
45. Any two:
    - Acknowledging the openness of the setting
    - Knocking or signaling before entering the client's space
    - Using a do-not-disturb sign
46. d
47. Any six:
    - Lack of knowledge about sexuality
    - Ignorance of sexual techniques
    - General misinformation about sexuality
    - Belief that sexual performance is inherently developed
    - Guilt and anxiety associated with early sexual learning
    - Fear of failure or rejection
    - Poor communications
    - Relationship problems
    - Fear of pregnancy
    - History of sexual abuse
48. c
49. Any four:
    - Diabetes mellitus
    - Alcohol
    - Neurological problems
    - Hormone imbalance
    - Pelvic disorders
    - Drugs (medications)
50. **a.** Physical factors: actual or anticipated pain or discomfort associated with sexual activity, illness, fatigue, medications; altered body image associated with changes in body structure or function
    b. Relationship factors: relationship issues may divert sexual desire, particularly when there are any interpersonal communication difficulties
    c. Life-style factors: use or abuse of alcohol, lack of time to devote to the relationship because of work or family commitments
    d. Self-esteem factors: reduced sense of personal value and lack of confidence in sexual skills negatively impacts sexual relationships as will any factor lowering an individual's self-esteem
51. Any two:
    - How do you feel about the sexual part of your life?
    - Have you noticed any changes in the way you feel about yourself as a man, woman, husband, wife, and so on?
    - How has your illness, medication, or impending surgery affected your sex life?
    - It is not unusual for people with your condition to be experiencing some sexual problems. Has that been a concern to you at all?
52. Any two:
    - Have you noticed your child exploring his or her body, for example, touching private parts?
    - Has your child begun to ask questions about where babies come from?
    - Have you talked with your child about sex, pregnancy, or contraception?
53. c
54. Any six:
    - Allow adequate time to conduct an uninterrupted interview.
    - Assure confidentiality and privacy.
    - Use a warm, empathetic approach.
    - Assume that all clients are uncomfortable talking about their sexuality.
    - Listen carefully, and notice nonverbal cues of the client.
    - Adapt the interview to the client's life-style and attempt to overcome cultural and language barriers.
    - Have a rationale for each question and be willing to share this with the client.
    - Assume that all clients are sexually experienced unless they tell you otherwise.
    - Avoid pressuring clients to respond to questions about their sexuality.
    - Move through questions from least sensitive to more sensitive.
    - Use open-ended questions that encourage more than a yes-or-no response.
    - Focus attention on the client, not on documenting responses.
55. **a.** What does the client see as sexual concerns?
    b. When did these sexual concerns begin and how have they changed over time?
    c. What does the client see as the cause of the concerns?
    d. What sort of treatment has the client sought to help alleviate this concern?
    e. How would the client like this concern to be resolved, and what are the client's goals for treatment?
56. True
57. Any two:
    - Contract the pubococcygeus muscle and hold this for 3 seconds.
    - Contract the pubococcygeus muscle rapidly.
    - Breathe deeply and tighten the pubococcygeus muscle during inhalation.
    - Bear down, then relax; during relaxation, tighten the pubococcygeus muscle.
58. Whether or not the client perceives problems in achieving sexual satisfaction (sexual dysfunction) or expresses concern regarding sexuality (altered patterns of sexuality)
59. **a.** To obtain knowledge of sexual development and functioning of women and men

b. To attain or maintain biologically and emotionally healthy sexual practices
c. To establish or maintain sexual satisfaction for self and partner if appropriate
d. To attain, maintain, or enhance positive self-esteem with integration of cultural/religious/ethical beliefs, sexual practices, past and present, and situational realities

60. Refer the client to a more appropriate expert.

CHAPTER 31

1. Either definition:
   - An awareness of and openness to a system of beliefs, Supreme Being, or God; a presence with or in each person and in the world
   - Meaning and purpose in life and love, and relatedness with other human beings
2. Either definition:
   - Response to the Supreme Being or God
   - A way of relating to self, others, and a Supreme Being that integrates the individual's past, present, and future with God as center
3. True
4. Religion
5. False
6. c
7. **a.** 4
   b. 3
   c. 2
   d. 1
   e. 5
8. **a.** Fetus would be buried
   b. Fetus would be baptized, buried
   c. Need to determine how far into the fourth month the pregnancy has progressed: if greater than 130 days, treated as fully developed human; only family and friends may touch the body
9. **a.** After death: priest ties thread around neck or wrist, pours water into mouth; only family touches and washes body before cremation.
   b. Before death: confessions of sins and asking forgiveness of family. After death: only family washes body, then turns toward Mecca; no autopsy.
   c. Before death: last rites (anointing of the sick). After death: other prescribed restrictions or rituals concerning burial.
   d. After death: oppose autopsy and cremation; occasionally body must be cleansed by members of a ritual burial society; burial carried out as soon as possible.
   e. After death: last rites optional.
   f. No special rituals before or after death.
10. **a.** May be vegetarian; prohibit meat and intoxicants
    b. Pork prohibited, daylight fasting during month of Ramadan (around June and July)
    c. Kosher dietary laws prohibit eating pork and shellfish, prohibit eating meat with milk or milk products, regulate food preparation
    d. Prohibit use of alcohol, coffee, tea, and tobacco
    e. Fast and abstain from meat on Ash Wednesday and Good Friday (older Catholics may continue to adhere to Friday abstinence); fast for one hour before Communion
    f. May prohibit use of alcohol, coffee, tea, or tobacco
11. Any six:
    - Who is the client's god? a Supreme Being? a governing principle? money? power? another human being?
    - What is the client's relationship with a Supreme Being or God—one of fear or of love?
    - How does the client express this spiritual relationship? Are spiritual or religious practices part of this expression?
    - Does the client view himself or herself positively or negatively? worthy of God's love?
    - Does the client act authentically and relate openly?
    - Does the client assume responsibility for behavior and its consequences?
    - How effectively does the client relate to family and friends?
    - How effectively does the client relate to health care personnel? to other clients? to strangers?
    - Does the client see illness as a Supreme Being's or God's punishment or as an indication of love?
    - Does the client view illness as threatening?
    - How have the client's diagnosis and therapy affected his or her self-concept? emotional state? will to live? co-operation with rehabilitation?
12. Three for each classification:

Spiritual health

Belief in a Supreme Being
View ultimate welfare and peace in terms of relationship to Supreme Being and world at large
Generally aware of personal limitations
Strive to act in accordance with personal beliefs
Assume life's responsibilities with joy and cheerfulness

Spiritual distress

Expresses concern with meaning of life and death or belief systems
Shows anger toward God (as defined by the person)
Questions meaning of suffering
Verbalizes inner conflict about beliefs
Verbalizes concern about relationships with deity
Questions meaning of own existence
Chooses not to participate in or is unable to choose usual religious practices
Seeks spiritual assistance
Questions moral and ethical implications of therapeutic regimen
Displaces anger toward religious representatives
Describes nightmares or sleep disturbances
Alters behavior or mood, evidenced by anger, crying, withdrawal, preoccupation, anxiety, hostility, or apathy
Regards illness as punishment
Does not believe that God is forgiving
Is unable to accept self
Engages in self-blame
Denies responsibilities for problems
Describes somatic complaints

13. To support and enhance the client's belief system, which sustains his or her spirituality; or find someone able to do so
14. True
15. Any five:
    - Family and friends

- Clergy
- Spiritual advisor
- Privacy
- Pastoral care department
- Administration of sacraments or rites
- Religious objects
- Taped meditation or music
- Religious services (attending or observing televised services)

16. Any five:
- Is the client's belief system stronger?
- Do the client's professed beliefs support and direct his or her actions and words?
- Does the client derive peace and strength from spiritual resources (such as prayer and ministers' visits) to face the rigors of treatment, rehabilitation, or impending death?
- Does the client seem more in control and have a clearer self-concept?
- Is the client at ease in being alone? in having life's plans changed?
- Is the client's behavior appropriate to the occasion?
- Has reconciliation of differences, if any, taken place between the client and family members or others?
- Are mutual respect and love obvious in the client's relationships with others?

17. True

CHAPTER 32

1. Any five:
- Body image
- Social practices
- Socioeconomic status
- Knowledge
- Cultural variables
- Personal preferences
- Physical condition

2. **a.** **(1)** Offering bedpan or urinal to client confined to bed
(2) Assisting with a bath or shower, oral hygiene, foot care, nail care, hair care
(3) Providing a backrub
(4) Changing client's pajamas
(5) Changing bed linens and straightening the bedside unit and room

b. **(1)** Offering bedpan or urinal to client confined to bed
(2) Changing soiled bed linens, pajamas
(3) Assisting the client in washing face and hands; oral hygiene
(4) Providing a backrub

c. **(1)** Offering bedpan or urinal to client confined to bed
(2) Assisting client in washing face and hands; oral hygiene

d. **(1)** Offering bedpan or urinal to client confined to bed
(2) Assisting client in washing face and hands, providing oral hygiene
(3) Straightening bed linen

3. At least two factors for each function (letter):

a.
- Epidermis is weakened by using dry razors, tape removal, and improper turning or positioning techniques.
- Excessive dryness causes breaks in the skin integrity that can allow bacteria to enter.
- Emollients and moisturizers prevent drying and protect the skin.
- Excessive exposure to moisture causes maceration, which promotes bacterial growth.
- Misuse of soap, detergents, and other skin preparations may cause skin irritation, drying, and changes from an acid to an alkaline pH, which may damage the skin surface and predispose to infection.
- Cleansing removes excess oil, sweat, dead skin cells, and dirt that can promote bacterial growth.

b.
- Friction should be used judiciously to avoid client discomfort.
- Removal of rings from the nurse's fingers prevents accidental client injury.
- Bath water temperature should be carefully checked.
- Bed linens should be smooth to avoid mechanical irritation.

c.
- Wet bed linens interfere with convection and conduction.
- Excess coverings can interfere with heat loss through radiation and conduction.
- Coverings can promote heat conservation.

d.
- Perspiration and oil can harbor bacterial growth.
- Bathing removes excess body secretions.
- Excessive bathing and misuse of skin care products may cause excessive drying.

4. **a.** 4
b. 7
c. 3
d. 8
e. 6
f. 1
g. 5
h. 2
i. 9

5. d

6. Two interventions for each skin problem listed:

a. Acne
- Wash hair and skin thoroughly each day.
- Wash with hot water and soap.
- Use cosmetics sparingly.
- Implement dietary restrictions if food-associated problems are noted.
- Use sunshine or heat lamp judiciously.

b. Abrasion
- Prevent abrasions through nurses' short nails and limited jewelry.
- Wash with mild soap and water.
- Avoid use of dressings or bandages.

c. Hirsutism
- Depilatories are most hazardous.
- Shaving is safest.
- Electrolysis, tweezing, and bleaching of hair can also be used.

d. Dry skin
- Bathe less frequently.
- Rinse body of all soap.
- Add moisture to air through humidifier.
- Increase fluid intake.
- Use moisturizing lotion.
- Use creams to clean skin.

e. Rash
- Wash area thoroughly.
- Apply antiseptic spray or lotion.
- Use warm soaks.

f. Contact dermatitis
- Identify causative agent.
- Remove causative agent.

7. a. Skin extremely thin, epidermis and dermis loosely bound together, poorly developed immune system
b. Active play and absence of established hygiene habits
c. Increased hormone levels, changes in skin texture, increased glandular activity (sebaceous, eccrine, apocrine)
d. Loss of resiliency and moisture, reduced glandular activity (sebaceous and eccrine), hormonal changes, thinning epithelium, and shrinking collagen fibers

8. Any six:
- Balance
- Activity tolerance
- Muscle strength
- Coordination
- Vision
- Ability to sit without support
- Hand grasp
- Range of motion
- Cognitive function

9. a. Immobilization
b. Reduced sensation
c. Nutritional alterations
d. Secretions and excretions on the skin
e. Vascular insufficiency
f. External devices

10. c
11. d
12. Any three:
- Skin will remain intact and free of body odors.
- Joint range of motion is maintained.
- Client achieves a sense of comfort and well-being.
- Client participates in and understands methods of skin care.

13. Refer to table at bottom of page.
14. True
15. d
16. False
17. Use plain warm water. Use different sections of the washcloth for each eye. Move the cloth from inner to outer canthus. Soak any crustations on eyelid for 2 or 3 minutes with damp cloth or cotton balls before attempting removal. Dry gently but thoroughly.
18. d
19. Bathing only body parts that would cause discomfort or odor if left unbathed (for example, hands, face, perineal area, axillae)
20. c
21. b
22. 37° C (98.6° F)
23. a. Provide privacy.
b. Maintain safety.
c. Maintain warmth.
d. Promote the client's independence.

24. a. Temperature control mechanisms are immature; exposure causes rapid cooling.
b. Soaps are usually alkaline and alter skin pH, increasing bacterial growth and the risk of infection.
c. Lotions and oils create a medium for bacterial growth and may also alter the skin pH, increasing the risk of infection.
d. Sudden movement could cause applicator to damage eardrum and mucous membranes.
e. Alcohol dries the cord and reduces the chance of infection.
f. Skin is very delicate and should be dried gently to avoid abrasion; thorough drying prevents evaporative heat loss.

25. Vernix caseosa
26. a
27. d
28. b
29. b
30. d
31. b
32. a. 2
b. 3
c. 5

Therapeutic bath	Purpose	Safety factors to consider
Tepid sponge bath	Lower body temeprature	Chilling must be avoided Water temperature of 37° C (98.6° F) Pulse and blood pressure may change (dysrhythmias)
Sitz bath	Cleanse and reduce inflammation	Water temperature of 43°-45° C (109.4°-113° F [danger of burns])
Hot water tub bath	Relieve muscle soreness or spasm	Water temperature of 45°-46° C (113°-114.8° F [danger of burns]) Pulse and blood pressure may change (hypotension)
Warm water tub bath	Relieve muscle soreness or spasm	Water temperature of 43° C (109.4° F)
Cool water tub bath	Relieve tension Lower body temperature (especially in small child)	See "Tepid sponge bath"
Soak	Remove dead tissue Soften crusted secretions Reduce pain and swelling	Aseptic technique if skin integrity altered

d. 1
e. 6
f. 4

33. Diabetics develop vascular insufficiency and neuropathy, increasing the risk for injury to the feet. Any trauma can easily lead to infection.
34. False
35. Podiatrist
36. Any three:
    - Skin and nail surfaces will remain intact and smooth.
    - Client achieves sense of comfort and cleanliness.
    - Client walks and bears weight normally.
    - Client understands and performs methods for foot and nail care correctly.
37. Any four:
    - Elderly
    - Diabetes
    - Heart disease (heart failure)
    - Renal disease
    - Cerebrovascular accident (stroke)
38. c
39. Any seven:
    - Wash and soak the feet daily using lukewarm water. Thoroughly pat the feet dry, and dry well between the toes.
    - Do not cut corns or calluses or use commercial removers. Consult a physician or podiatrist
    - If the feet tend to perspire, apply a bland foot powder.
    - If dryness is noted along the feet or between the toes, apply lanolin, baby oil, or even corn oil and rub gently into the skin.
    - File the toenails straight across and square; do not use scissors or clippers. Consult a podiatrist as needed.
    - Do not use over-the-counter preparations to treat athlete's foot or ingrown toenails. Consult a physician or podiatrist.
    - Teach the client to avoid wearing elastic stockings, knee-high hose, or constricting garters and not to cross the legs. Both impair circulation to the lower extremities.
    - Inspect the feet daily, including tops and soles of the feet, heels, and the area between the toes.
    - Wear clean socks or stockings daily. Socks should be free of holes and darns that might cause pressure.
    - Do not walk barefoot.
    - Wear properly fitting shoes. Soles of shoes should be flexible and nonslipping. Lamb's wool can be used between toes that rub or overlap. Shoes should be sturdy, closed in, and not restrictive to the feet.
    - Exercise regularly to improve circulation to the lower extremities: (Walk slowly; elevate, rotate, flex, and extend the feet at the ankle. Dangle the feet over the side of the bed 1 minute; then extend both legs and hold them parallel to the bed while lying supine for 1 minute, and finally rest for 1 minute).
    - Avoid applying hot-water bottles or heating pads to the feet. Use warm soaks or extra coverings instead.
    - Any minor cuts should be washed immediately and dried thoroughly. Only mild antiseptics, for example, neosporin ointment, should be applied to the skin. Avoid iodine or Mercurochrome. Contact a physician for treatment of cuts or lacerations.
40. a
41. Any four:
    - How often does the client brush his or her teeth?
    - What type of toothpaste or dentifrice is used?
    - Does the client have dentures? When and how are they cleaned?
    - Does the client use mouthwash or lemon-glycerin preparations?
    - Does the client floss? If so, how often?
    - When was the client's last dental visit?
    - How often does the client visit a dentist?
42. a. 4
    b. 2
    c. 7
    d. 1
    e. 3
    f. 6
    g. 5
    h. 8
43. Regular flossing and brushing
44. a. Causes soreness, dysphagia, dryness, and taste changes
    b. Prone to dryness of mouth, gingivitis, periodontal disease, and tooth loss
    c. Lacks upper extremity strength or dexterity needed to perform oral hygiene
    d. Tissues easily traumatized with swelling, inflammation, or break in integrity of the membranes
    e. Prone to dehydration and drying of mucous membranes; thick secretions develop on the tongue and gums; lips become cracked and reddened
    f. Unable or unwilling to attend to personal hygiene needs
45. Any three:
    - Any sore in the mouth that does not heal
    - History of pipe smoking or use of chewing tobacco
    - Lumps or ulcers in or around the mouth
    - Lumps or ulcers at the base of the tongue
46. Any four:
    - Oral mucosa is intact and well hydrated.
    - Teeth are without new dental caries.
    - Client is able to independently perform correct oral hygiene.
    - Client achieves sense of comfort.
    - Client understands oral hygiene practices.
47. b
48. d
49. c
50. a
51. c
52. True
53. True
54. d
55. Place a drop of oil or ether on the tick, or cover it with petroleum jelly, before removal.
56. a. Pediculosis pubis (crab lice)
    b. Pediculosis corporis (body lice)
    c. Pediculosis capitis (head lice)
57. Any two:
    - Hair and scalp will be clean and healthy.
    - Client achieves a sense of comfort and self-esteem.
    - Client will participate in hair-care practices.
58. False
59. d
60. Any two:
    - Clients receiving anticoagulant medications
    - Clients taking high doses of aspirin
    - Clients with bleeding disorders (hemophilia, leukemia)
61. Any two for each sensory aid listed:

a. Eyeglasses
  - Purpose for wearing glasses
  - Methods used to clean glasses
  - Presence of symptoms (blurred vision, headaches, irritation)

b. Artificial eye
  - Method used to insert and remove the eye
  - Method for cleansing the eye
  - Presence of symptoms (drainage, inflammation, pain in the orbit)

c. Hearing aid
  - Type of aid worn
  - Methods used to cleanse aid
  - Client's ability to change battery and adjust hearing aid volume

62. Any four:
- Type of lenses worn
- Frequency and duration of time lenses are worn (include sleep time)
- Presence of symptoms (burning, excess tearing, redness, irritation, swelling, sensitivity to light)
- Techniques used to cleanse, store, insert, and remove lenses
- Use of eye drops or ointments
- Use of emergency identification bracelet or card identifying that contact lenses are worn

63. Any two:
- Absence of infection
- Normal sensory organ function
- Understanding of methods used for care of the eyes, ears, and nose

64.
- More frequent eye care is needed.
- Eye patch may be necessary over involved eye.
- Lubricating eye drops may be given (according to physician's orders).

65. a
66. d
67. Any three:
- Client becomes unconscious
- Restricted hand movement
- Loss of clear judgment because of psychiatric illness
- Temporary mental confusion
- Substance abuse

68. **a.** Retract the lower eyelid and exert slight pressure just below the eye (alternative: use of small, rubber-bulb syringe or medicine dropper bulb to create a suction effect directly over the artificial eye to lift it from the socket).
b. Use warm normal saline for the prosthesis; use clean gauze soaked in warm saline or clean tap water for the edges of the eye socket and surrounding tissues.
c. Retract the upper and lower lids and gently slip the eye into the socket, fitting it under the upper eyelid.
d. Store in a labeled container filled with tap water or saline.

69. c
70. **a.** (head of bed elevated at least 45 degrees)

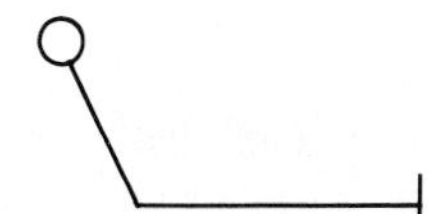

b. (head of bed elevated approximately 30 degrees)

c. (bed frame tilted head down)

d. (bed frame tilted foot down)

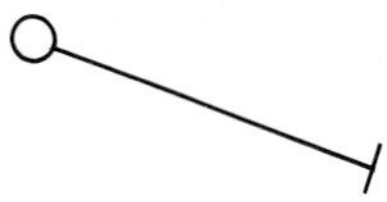

71. **a.** 4
b. 3
c. 6
d. 2
e. 1
f. 5
72. True
73. d
74. d

CHAPTER 33

1. **a.** 3
b. 5
c. 2
d. 6
e. 4
f. 1
2. **a.** Water (most important)
b. Carbohydrates
c. Proteins
d. Lipids
e. Vitamins
f. Minerals
3. **a.** Infants
b. Elderly
4. False
5. b
6. **a.** 80 (4 calories per gram × 20)
b. 135 (9 calories per gram × 15)
c. 200 (4 calories per gram × 50)
7. Protein that contains all the essential amino acids in sufficient quantity to support growth and maintain nitrogen balance (also known as high biological value proteins)
8. Any three for each classification:

Complete proteins	Incomplete proteins
Meat	Cereals
Fish	Legumes
Poultry	Vegetables
Milk	
Eggs	

9. a. Condition in which intake and output of nitrogen are equal
b. Condition in which body is losing more nitrogen than it is taking in (associated with body tissue destruction)
c. Condition in which body protein nitrogen is retained for building, repair, or replacement of body tissues (associated with periods of growth)

10. b

11. a. Decreases blood cholesterol
b. Minimal effect on blood cholesterol
c. Increases blood cholesterol

12. a

13. Any three:
- Safflower oil
- Soybean oil
- Corn oil
- Cottonseed oil
- Peanut oil

14. c

15. c

16. c

17. Minerals serve as catalysts in biochemical reactions.

18. Refer to Chapter 33, Tables 33-1, 33-2, 33-3, and 33-4 (pp. 886-887, 888, 889, and 890).

19. a. 3
b. 1
c. 2
d. 1
e. 3
f. 2

20. c

21. It is easily remembered and can be used as a buying and food preparation guide for individuals on a regular diet.

22. Refer to table at bottom of page.

23. True

24. Any five:
- Eat a variety of foods.
- Maintain reasonable body weight.
- Avoid too much fat, saturated fat, and cholesterol.
- Eat foods with adequate starch and fiber.
- Avoid too much sugar.
- Avoid too much sodium.
- Drink alcoholic beverages in moderation.

25. a. 4
b. 1
c. 3
d. 2

26. a

27. Any three:
- Vitamin C
- Vitamin D
- Fluoride
- Iron

28. 4 to 6 months

29. d

30. b

31. c

32. a. 4 or more
b. 4 or more
c. 5 to 7
d. 2 to 4 or more
e. 1 to 2 tablespoons
f. 6 to 8 glasses

33. d

34. Any four:
- Income (most important)
- State of health
- Living arrangements (living alone)
- Diminished taste acuity
- Less efficient digestion (because of decreased gastric secretions)

35. a. Nursing history
b. Observation (assessment)
c. Anthropometry
d. Laboratory data

36. a. Health status
b. Culture and religion
c. Socioeconomic status
d. Personal preference
e. Psychological factors

Food group	Nutrients supplied	Dietary sources	Daily amounts
Milk	Calcium, protein, riboflavin	Milk, cheese, ice cream, and foods made with whole or skimmed milk	Children < 9 yr: 2-3 cups Children 9-12 yr: 3 or more cups Teenagers: 4 or more cups Adults: 2 or more cups Pregnant women: 3 or more cups Nursing mothers: 4 or more cups
Meats	Protein, iron, thiamine	Beef, veal, lamb, pork, fish, eggs (alternates: dry beans, dry peas, nuts, peanut butter)	2 or more servings
Vegetables and fruits	Niacin, riboflavin, vitamin A, vitamin C, smaller amounts of other vitamins and minerals		4 or more servings
Bread and cereals	Thiamine, niacin, riboflavin, iron, protein		4 or more servings

f. Alcohol and drugs
g. Misinformation and food fads

37. Any three:
- Money is spent on alcohol rather than more nutritional foods.
- Alcohol may replace part of the diet, reducing intake of nutrients.
- Alcohol can depress the appetite.
- Alcohol reduces the efficiency of digestion and nutrient absorption.

38. Refer to Chapter 33, Table 33-10, p. 906.
39. **a.** Weight
b. Height
c. Wrist circumference
d. Mid-upper arm circumference (MAC)
e. Triceps skinfold (TSF)
40. c
41. **a.** Anorexia nervosa
b. Bulimia
42. Any seven:
- Congenital anomalies
- Surgical revision of the gastrointestinal tract
- Intravenous therapy for more than 10 days
- Infancy
- Pregnancy
- Poor dietary habits
- Obesity
- Underweight
- Anorexia
- Bulimia
- Surgery
- Immobility
- Cancer and cancer therapies

43. **a.** Glucose
b. Amino acids
c. Lipids
d. Minerals
e. Vitamins
44. Any three:
- Remove any reminders of treatments (completed or anticipated).
- Control odors.
- Provide mouth care.
- Position comfortably.
- Provide suitable alternative when foods are refused.

45. d
46. **a.** Clear liquid
b. Soft
c. Low residue
d. Regular
e. Bland
f. Full liquid
g. Light
47. **a.** Oral
b. Tube feedings
48. a
49. c
50. **a.** Measure the total distance from the client's nose to ear to xiphoid.
b. Add an additional 20 to 30 cm to the distance determined above.
51. **a.** Aspirate gastric secretions and check gastric residual.
b. Inject 20 to 30 ml of air into the end of the tube while auscultating over the epigastrium for a gurgling, bubbling sound.
52. False
53. The amount of an enteral feeding remaining in the stomach
54. c
55. It is difficult to aspirate even small volumes of fluid through small-bore feeding tubes, making accurate determination of gastric residual impossible. Abdominal distention, nausea, and vomiting may indicate gastric retention and alert the nurse to the risk of regurgitation and possible aspiration of gastric contents.
56. b
57. High Fowler's
58. **a.** Dilates the central veins, reduces the risk of air embolism
b. Increases venous filling of the vein and reduces the risk of air embolism
c. Confirms correct placement, identifies complications such as accidental puncture of the lung or parietal pleura (pneumothorax)
d. Reduces risk of infection
e. Maintains infusion at prescribed rate to avoid too rapid administration (hyperglycemia, osmotic diuresis, hypoglycemia, fluid overload)
f. Evaluates presence of hyperglycemia or hypoglycemia
59. c
60. False

CHAPTER 34

1. Freedom from physical or mental exertion
2. State of rest occurring for sustained periods of time during which consciousness is reduced
3. **a.** Physical comfort
b. Freedom from worry
c. Sufficient sleep
4. c
5. True
6. b
7.

	Sleep mechanisms	Arousal mechanisms
Name	Bulbar synchronizing region (BSR); raphe sleep system	Reticular activating system (RAS)
Anatomical location	Pons and medial forebrain	Upper brainstem
Neurotransmitter	Serotonin	Catecholamines

8. **a.** 3
b. 1
c. 5
d. 2
e. 4
9. d
10. a
11. False
12. Any five:
- Physical illness: any pain, physical discomfort, anxiety, or depression associated with illness can cause sleep difficulties.
- Drugs and substances: prescribed and over-the-counter medications can disrupt rest and sleep. Although some medications are used to induce sleep, these provide only a temporary effect and potentially create problems.

- Life-style: routine patterns of daily living may influence sleep patterns, for example, rotation of shifts, performing unaccustomed work, late night social activities, changing evening mealtimes.
- Sleep patterns: duration of sleep and the time sleep begins influence succeeding attempts to fall asleep. Problems with sleep patterns in turn influence an individual's performance of daily functions.
- Emotional stress: stress, tension, and worry may alter sleep patterns and reduce the benefits of rest derived from time spent sleeping.
- Environment: conditions in which the individual attempts to rest or sleep impact these patterns. Factors in the environment include ventilation, position and condition of the bed, presence or absence of a bed partner, noise levels, light levels, and room temperature.
- Exercise and fatigue: moderate fatigue promotes restful sleep, excessive fatigue may make falling asleep difficult. Optimal time for exercise that promotes rest and sleep is at least 2 hours before bedtime.
- Caloric intake: weight loss and gain influence sleep patterns. Weight gain tends to lengthen sleep periods and reduce the frequency of cycle interruptions; weight loss tends to shorten and fragment sleep.

13. L-tryptophan

14. **a.** 6
b. 3
c. 7
d. 1
e. 5
f. 8
g. 4
h. 2

15. Condition in which the individual experiences a decrease in the amount, quality, and consistency of sleep; results in changes in the normal sequence of sleep stages accompanied by alterations in the individual's behavior

16. Any four symptoms for each category:

Physiological symptoms

Hand tremors
Decreased reflexes
Slowed response time
Reduction in word memory
Decreased reasoning, judgment
Cardiac dysrhythmias

Psychological symptoms

Changes in mood
Disorientation
Irritability
Decreased motivation
Fatigue
Sleepiness
Hyperactivity

17. d

18. Any seven:
- Description of client's sleeping problem
- Severity of sleep problem
- Daytime symptoms
- Normal sleep pattern
- Medical history
- Current life events
- Emotional and mental status
- Bedtime rituals and environment
- Report from bed partner
- Sleep/wake log
- Behaviors of sleep deprivation

19. Any three:
- Obtaining a sense of restfulness following sleep
- Experiencing fewer symptoms of sleep deprivation
- Identifying factors that promote or disrupt sleep
- Establishing an adequate sleep pattern

20. Any six:
- Environmental control
- Promoting bedtime rituals
- Establishing periods of rest and sleep
- Controlling physiological disturbances
- Stress reduction
- Bedtime snacks
- Administration of sleeping medications
- Client teaching

21. a

22. d

23. b

24. Any four:
- Avoid physical and mental stimulation before bedtime.
- Exercise 2 hours before bedtime.
- Engage in a relaxing activity before bedtime, for example, reading, watching television, or listening to music.
- Use bedroom only as bedroom, not as a work area.
- Maintain a consistent bedtime.
- Eat a light snack before bedtime.
- Void before going to bed.
- Practice relaxation techniques at bedtime.

25. Any five:
- Administer analgesics and sedatives about 30 minutes before bedtime.
- Encourage clients to wear loose-fitting nightwear.
- Remove any irritants against the client's skin (moist or wrinkled sheets, drainage tubes, and so on).
- Position and support body parts to protect pressure points and aid muscle relaxation.
- Offer a massage just before bedtime.
- Administer necessary hygiene measures.
- Keep bed linen clean and dry.
- Provide a comfortable mattress.
- Encourage client to void before hour of sleep.

26. False

27. c

28. d

29. b

30. Any three:
- Drugs may provide only temporary (1 week) increase in the quantity and quality of sleep.
- "Daytime hangover" may occur.
- Risk of sleep apnea increases in the elderly.
- Hypnotics should not be taken with alcoholic beverages.
- Activities requiring motor coordination should be avoided.

CHAPTER 35

1. d

2. True

3. c

4. **a.** Reception
   b. Perception
   c. Reaction
5. The point at which the pain stimulus is intense enough to create a nerve impulse and be perceived by the individual
6.

	A fibers	C fibers
Fiber size	Large	Small
Myelination status	Myelinated	Unmyelinated
Transmission speed	Rapid	Slow
Nature of pain message	Localize source; detect pain intensity	Diffuse response

7. A naturally occurring, morphinelike substance in the brain, spinal cord, and gastrointestinal tract
8. c
9. True
10. **a.** S
    b. P
    c. P
    d. S
    e. S
    f. P
11. **a.** Anticipation phase: awareness that pain will occur; most important because if can affect the other phases; allows person to learn about pain and its relief
    b. Sensation phase: phase when pain is felt; involves physical and behavioral responses to the pain
    c. Aftermath phase: occurs when pain is reduced or stopped; does not terminate client's need for nursing care; may involve physical or behavioral responses requiring nursing intervention
12. The point at which there is an unwillingness to accept pain of greater severity or duration
13. Pain impulses can be regulated or blocked by gating mechanisms located along the central nervous system. When gates are open, pain impulses flow freely. When gates are closed, pain impulses are blocked. Partial opening of the gates may also occur. The opening or closing of a gate depends on large and small fiber transmission, reticular formation activity, and cerebral cortex and thalamic mechanisms.
14. b
15. Any four:
    - Rapid onset
    - Variable intensity
    - Brief duration (less than 6 months)
    - Warns of impending injury or disease
    - Self-limiting
16. c
17. Any four:
    - Absence of overt "pain" symptoms
    - Fatigue
    - Insomnia
    - Anorexia
    - Weight loss
    - Depression
    - Hopelessness
    - Anger
18. b
19. c
20. c
21. True
22. Any five:
    - Position change
    - Analgesics
    - Ice bag
    - Massage
    - Heating pad
    - Eating
    - Rest
23. A symptom that often accompanies pain (such as nausea, headache, dizziness, urination, constipation, restlessness)
24. Two examples for each behavioral indicator:
    a. Vocalizations
    - Moaning
    - Crying
    - Screaming
    - Gasping

    b. Facial expressions
    - Grimace
    - Clenched teeth
    - Open, alert eyes
    - Biting the lips
    - Tightened jaw

    c. Body movement
    - Restlessness
    - Immobilization
    - Muscle tension
    - Rhythmical or rubbing motions
    - Protective movement of body parts

    d. Social interaction
    - Avoidance of conversation
    - Focus only on activities for pain relief
    - Avoidance of social contacts
    - Reduced attention span
25. Any three:
    - Specific pain relief methods or techniques
    - Emotional support of others
    - Religious beliefs
    - Involvement in household activities
    - Involvement at work
26. **a.** Meaning of pain
    b. Knowledge and understanding
    c. Level of consciousness
    d. Presence and attitudes of others
27. Any three:
    - Obtain a sense of well-being and comfort.
    - Maintain the ability to perform self-care.
    - Maintain existing physical and psychosocial function.
    - Understand the pain experience.
28. b
29. Any six:
    - Use different types of pain relief measures.
    - Provide pain relief measures before pain becomes severe.
    - Use measures the client believes are effective.
    - Consider the client's ability or willingness to participate in pain relief measures.
    - Choose pain relief measures on the basis of the client's behavior reflecting the severity of pain.
    - If a therapy is ineffective at first, encourage the client to try it again before abandoning it.
    - Keep an open mind about what may relieve pain.
    - Keep trying.
    - Protect the client.
30. **a.** 3

b. 2
c. 1
d. 2
e. 1
f. 2
g. 3

31. Transcutaneous electric nerve stimulation: stimulates cutaneous skin over or near the pain site; believed to either release endorphins or activate large-diameter sensory fibers to block transmission of painful impulses from small-diameter fibers
32. c
33. a
34. True
35. d
36. Any four:
    - Occurrence, onset, and expected duration of pain
    - Quality, severity, and location of pain
    - Information on how the client's safety is assured
    - Cause of pain
    - Methods nurse and client take for pain relief
    - Expectations of the client during a procedure
37. Any six:
    - Rapid onset
    - Effective over a prolonged time
    - Effective for all ages
    - Used orally and parenterally
    - Free of severe side effects
    - Nonaddicting
    - Inexpensive
38. a. Know the client's previous response to analgesics.
    b. Select the proper medication when more than one is ordered.
    c. Know the accurate dosage.
    d. Assess the right time and interval for administration.
39. d
40. Patient-controlled analgesia: portable computerized pump with a chamber for a syringe that allows clients to administer pain medications when they want or need them
41. Any three:
    - Clients have control over their pain.
    - Pain relief does not depend on nurse availability.
    - Clients tend to take less medication.
    - Small doses of analgesics delivered at short intervals stabilize serum drug concentrations for more sustained pain relief.
42. b
43. Any treatment that produces an effect because of its intent rather than its physical or chemical properties
44. False
45. d
46. Epidural
47. Posterior rhizotomy
48. c
49. b
50. a

CHAPTER 36

1. The process by which gases are moved into and out of the lungs
2. Phrenic nerve
3. b
4. a. 2
   b. 3
   c. 1
   d. 4
5. Spirometer
6. Blood flow, the movement of blood to the tissues
7. c
8. Movement of molecules from an area of high concentration to an area of lower concentration
9. a. Ventilation (oxygen entering the lungs)
   b. Perfusion (blood flow to the lungs and tissues)
   c. Diffusion (exchange of carbon dioxide and oxygen between alveoli and capillary)
   d. Capacity of blood to carry oxygen
10. a. Neural regulation: influence of the central nervous system in controlling respiratory rate, depth, and rhythm through cerebral cortex (intermittent voluntary control) and medulla oblongata (continuous automatic control)
    b. Chemical regulation: influence of chemicals such as carbon dioxide and hydrogen ions on the rate and depth of respiration through chemoreceptors in the medulla and aortic and carotid bodies
11. a. 3
    b. 2
    c. 1
    d. 5
    e. 4
    f. 2
    g. 3 or 4
    h. 4
    i. 4
    j. 1
12. a. Decreased hemoglobin production
    b. Increased red cell destruction
    c. Blood loss
13. d
14. Polycythemia
15. b
16. Hypostatic bronchopneumonia
17. One for each developmental level:
    a. Surfactant deficiency
    b. Frequent exposure to other children; teething process, which increases nasal congestion; airway obstruction from foreign objects or airway infections
    c. Exposure to other children, respiratory risk factors (for example, smoking [active or passive])
    d. Decreased lung elasticity, alveolar enlargement, bronchodilation, osteoporotic changes in the thoracic cage
18. True
19. a. Nutrition: obesity decreases lung expansion; malnutrition and associated muscle wasting diminishes respiratory excursion and ability to effectively cough; obese and malnourished clients are at risk for anemia.
    b. Exercise: exercise increases metabolism and therefore oxygen requirements: exercise and physical conditioning can enhance oxygen consumption and utilization.
    c. Cigarette smoking: associated with several disease states, including recurrent respiratory infections, emphysema, chronic bronchitis, chronic obstructive pulmonary disease, lung cancer, peripheral vascular disease, and coronary artery disease.
    d. Substance abuse: chronic substance abuse is often associated with poor nutritional intake and anemia; some

substances can depress respiratory center in the central nervous system.

e. Anxiety: severe anxiety increases oxygen requirements; although tolerated in normal individuals, those with certain illnesses cannot tolerate the additional oxygen demand created by anxiety states.

20. State of ventilation in excess of that required to maintain normal carbon dioxide levels; excreting excess carbon dioxide

21. False

22. Any three:
- Anxiety
- Infection
- Fever
- Drugs (for example, aspirin, amphetamines)
- Acid-base imbalance (acidosis)

23. Any six:
- Tachycardia
- Shortness of breath
- Chest pain
- Dizziness
- Light-headedness
- Decreased concentration
- Paresthesia
- Numbness (extremities, circumoral)
- Tinnitus
- Blurred vision
- Disorientation
- Tetany (carpopedal spasm)

24. c

25. Any three:
- Central nervous system or brainstem trauma
- Drug overdose (for example, barbiturates, hypnotics, tranquilizers)
- Atelectasis
- Inappropriate administration of oxygen

26. Because clients with chronic obstructive pulmonary disease have adapted to a high carbon dioxide level, their respiratory drive is hypoxia. Administration of high concentration of oxygen (greater than 24% to 28% [1 to 3 liters]) will eliminate the hypoxic drive, depress breathing, and in some cases precipitate respiratory arrest.

27. Any five:
- Dizziness
- Headache
- Lethargy
- Disorientation
- Decreased ability to follow instructions
- Cardiac dysrhythmias (arrhythmias)
- Electrolyte imbalances
- Convulsions
- Coma
- Cardiac arrest

28. Inadequate cellular oxygenation that results from a deficiency in oxygen delivery at the cellular level

29. Any four:
- Decreased hemoglobin level
- Diminished oxygen concentration in inspired air
- Inability of the tissues to extract oxygen from the blood
- Decreased diffusion of oxygen from the alveoli to the blood
- Poor tissue perfusion

30. Any seven:
- Restlessness
- Apprehension, anxiety
- Decreased ability to concentrate
- Decreased level of consciousness
- Increased fatigue
- Dizziness
- Behavioral changes
- Increased pulse rate
- Increased rate and depth of respiration
- Elevated blood pressure
- Cardiac arrhythmias
- Pallor
- Cyanosis
- Clubbing
- Dyspnea

31. d

32. Shortness of breath or difficulty breathing (pathological when it is not associated with short-term response to exercise or excitement)

33.
a. Cough
b. Shortness of breath
c. Wheezing
d. Pain
e. Environmental exposures
f. Frequency of respiratory tract infections
g. Pulmonary risk factors
h. Past respiratory problems
i. Medications

34.
a. Color
b. Consistency
c. Taste
d. Odor
e. Blood

35. d

36. Orthopnea

37. A form of rhonchus characterized by a high-pitched, musical quality that does not clear with coughing

38. d

39.
a. Vasoconstriction and diminished peripheral blood flow
b. Heart failure (right sided and left sided)
c. Heart failure (right sided)
d. Increased work of breathing, dyspnea
e. Anemia
f. In young and middle adults: hyperlipidemia; in older adults: normal
g. Decreased oxygenation (hypoxia)
h. Chronic hypoxemia
i. Hyperlipidemia

40.
a. 3
b. 6
c. 2
d. 5
e. 4
f. 1

41. Asynchronous breathing in which the chest contracts during inspiration and expands during expiration

42. a

43.
a. Collapse of a lung region
b. Fluid in the lung field
c. Airway obstruction

44. a

45. Oximetry

46. Refer to table at top of p. 292.

47. Information about diffusion of gases across the alveolar capillary membrane and adequacy of tissue oxygenation (hydrogen ion concentration, partial pressure of carbon dioxide, oxygen concentration, oxyhemoglobin saturation)

Diagnostic test	Test purpose	Nursing implications
Pulmonary function test (PFT)	Determine ability of lungs to exchange oxygen and carbon dioxide	Providing information about test Instruction on deep inhalation and exhalation Ensure that client does not eat a large meal before the test
Complete blood count (CBC)	Determine number and type of RBC and WBC, amount of hemoglobin	Providing information about test Monitor values and changes
Chest x-ray film	Observe lung fields for abnormal processes	Providing information about test Instructions on holding breath on deep inspiration
Bronchoscopy	Direct visualization of trachea and bronchial tree; obtain biopsy, fluid, or sputum; remove mucus plugs or foreign bodies	Provide information about test Keep client NPO before procedure Administration of preprocedure medications (if ordered) Assess vital signs, signs of respiratory distress or hypoxia after procedure Assess gag/swallow reflex before initiating oral fluids
Throat culture	Determine presence of pathogenic microorganisms and antibiotics to which they are sensitive	Pass swab along reddened areas and exudate in the pharyngeal region Position client upright and leaning slightly forward to minimize gag reflex Provide information about test
Sputum specimen	Identify microorganisms and their sensitivity to antibiotics Determine presence of abnormal cells	Provide information about test Obtain early-morning specimens If client unable to cough, obtain order to suction, using sputum trap

48. **a.** 14 to 18 g/100 ml
b. 12 to 16 g/100 ml
c. 14 to 20 g/100 ml
d. 11 to 14 g/100 ml
e. 11 to 13 g/100 ml

49. The importance of holding breath, not coughing, not moving

50. **a.** Ineffective airway clearance
b. Impaired gas exchange
c. Ineffective breathing pattern

51. Any five:
- Improved activity tolerance
- Maintenance and promotion of lung expansion
- Mobilization of pulmonary secretions
- Maintenance of a patent airway
- Maintenance or promotion of tissue oxygenation
- Restoration of cardiopulmonary function

52. Refer to table at top of p. 293.

53. b

54. Assist lung hyperinflation by applying positive pressure to airways

55. Pneumothorax

56. d

57. d

58. True

59. **a.** Percussion: striking the chest wall over the area being drained using a cupped hand position
b. Vibration: fine, shaking pressure applied to the chest wall during exhalation
c. Postural drainage: use of positioning techniques that draw secretions from specific segments of the lungs and bronchi into the trachea

60. d

61. a

62. b

63. c

64. b

65. **a.** Coughing techniques
b. Suctioning
c. Artificial airway

66. Refer to table at center of p. 293.

67. Any two:
- Sputum expectoration
- Client's report of swallowed sputum
- Clearing of adventitious sounds on auscultation

68. c

69. Approximate the distance between the client's earlobe and tip of the nose and place the thumb and forefinger of the gloved hand at that point of the suction catheter; do not advance the catheter beyond that point.

70. b

71. False

72. **a.** Right client
b. Right drug (oxygen)
c. Right dose (liter flow/percentage)
d. Right route (delivery method)
e. Right time (continuous, p.r.n. basis)

73. Any three:
- Post "no smoking" signs on client door and over the bed.
- Inform clients, visitors, and roommates that smoking is prohibited in the area where oxygen is in use.
- Ensure that electrical equipment is functioning correctly and properly grounded.
- Know the institution's fire procedures.
- Know the location of the closest fire extinguisher.

74. **a.** Absence of respirations
b. Absence of pulse
c. Dilated pupils

75. **a.** Establish an airway (A)

Nursing interventions	Purpose	Procedure summary
Positioning the client	Increase chest wall expansion Prevent stasis of pulmonary secretions	Change position at least every 2 hr Increase ambulation
Pursed-lip breathing	Decrease work of breathing Slow respiratory rate Increase tidal volume Decrease dead space ventilation	Deep inspiration with slow exhalation through pursed lips while counting to 4 (increase to 8 when perfecting technique)
Abdominal-diaphragmatic breathing	Decrease work of breathing Decrease air trapping Promote relaxation Control pain	Deep inspiration while watching abdomen move outward Exhalation while forcefully contracting abdominal muscles and observing inward movement Initially performed in supine position, then sitting and standing
Flow-oriented incentive spirometer	Encourage voluntary deep breathing Prevent or treat atelectasis	Controlled inhalation to elevate balls, sustained to keep them floating as long as possible
Blow bottles	Encourage voluntary deep breathing	Hyperinflation of lungs with exhalation into bottle system Small, frequent breaths or use of Valsalva maneuver inappropriate (only effective if hyperinflation of lungs occurs before blowing into bottles)
Maintaining hydration	Maintain normal mucociliary action	1500-2000 ml fluid/day (unless contraindicated)
Inserting an oral airway	Prevent obstruction of trachea by displacement of tongue Facilitate orotracheal suctioning	Insert by turning curve of airway toward cheek and placing it over tongue into oropharynx When airway is in oropharynx, turn it so opening points downward

Cough	Technique	Action/Benefits
Controlled cough	Take two slow, deep breaths (inhaling through nose, exhaling through mouth) Inhale deeply the third time and hold breath to count of 3 Cough fully for two to three consecutive coughs without inhaling between coughs Instruct to "push all air out of lungs" Splint any painful areas while coughing	Clears secretions from upper and lower airways
Cascade cough	Take a slow deep breath and hold it for 2 sec while contracting expiratory muscles Open mouth and perform a series of coughs throughout the breath	Promotes airway clearance and patent airway in clients with large volumes of sputum
Huff cough	While exhaling, say the word "huff"	Stimulates natural cough Generally only effective in clearing central airways Useful as initial technique in clients unable to perform cascade cough
Quad cough	Client or nurse pushes in and up on abdominal muscles toward diaphragm while client breathes with maximal expiratory effort	Used for clients without abdominal muscle control (for example, spinal cord injuries)

b. Initiate breathing (B)
c. Maintain circulation (C)

CHAPTER 37

1. b
2. An element or compound that, when dissolved in water or another solvent, dissociates into ions and is able to carry an electric current
3. **a.** Diffusion: process in which solid, particulate matter in a fluid moves from an area of higher concentration to an area of lower concentration, resulting in an even distribution of the particles in the fluid
   b. Osmosis: movement of a pure solvent, such as water, through a semipermeable membrane from a solution that has a lower solute concentration to one that has a higher solute concentration

c. Active transport: movement of materials across the cell membrane by chemical activity that allows the cell to admit larger molecules than it would otherwise be able to admit
d. Fluid pressures: pressure exerted by fluids that direct the movement of fluid between extracellular and intracellular fluid compartments (includes osmotic and hydrostatic pressure)
(1) Osmotic pressure: the "drawing power" for water, dependent on the activity of the solutes separated by a semipermeable membrane causing water to be pulled through the membrane
(2) Hydrostatic pressure: the pressure exerted by a liquid, pushing it from one compartment to another

4. c
5. a
6. **a.** Isotonic
b. Hypotonic
c. Hypertonic
7. Increased plasma osmolarity or decreased blood volume stimulates the thirst center located within the hypothalamus. Osmoreceptors are receptor cells that continually monitor osmotic pressure, so that when too much fluid is lost, the osmoreceptors detect the loss and activate the thirst center.
8. **a.** Kidneys
b. Skin
c. Lungs
d. Gastrointestinal tract
9. 55 ml [1 ml/kg/hr: 1 × 55 (kg)]
10. Water loss that is continuous and is not perceived by the person or measurable in usual clinical situations
11. Refer to table at bottom of page.
12. c
13. **a.** Sodium (136 to 144 mEq/L)
(1) Function: maintains water balance, transmits nerve impulses, facilitates muscle contraction
(2) Regulatory mechanisms: salt intake, aldosterone, urinary output
b. Potassium (3.5 to 5.0 mEq/L)
(1) Function: regulates neuromuscular excitability and muscle contraction, assists in maintaining acid-base balance
(2) Regulatory mechanisms: kidney is primary regulatory mechanism, aldosterone stimulates K^+ excretion, also exchanges with sodium ion in the tubule (Na^{++} excreted, K^+ retained; Na^{++} retained, K^+ excreted)
c. Calcium (ionized: 4.5 mg/100 ml; nonionized: 5 mg/100 ml)
(1) Function: cell membrane integrity and structure, cardiac conduction, blood coagulation, bone growth and formation, muscle relaxation
(2) Regulatory mechanisms: PTH (parathyroid hormone) controls balance among bone Ca^{++}, gastrointestinal absorption, and kidney excretion; thyrocalcitonin from the thyroid inhibits bone resorption of Ca^{++}
d. Magnesium (1.5 to 2.5 mEq/L)
(1) Function: enzyme activities, neurochemical activities, muscular excitability
(2) Regulatory mechanisms: renal excretion and selected action of the parathyroid hormone
e. Chlorine (95 to 105 mEq/L)
(1) Function: balances cations within the extracellular fluid to maintain electroneutrality in extracellular fluid
(2) Regulatory mechanisms: renal excretion in relation to dietary intake
f. Bicarbonate (22 to 26 mEq/L)
(1) Function: major chemical base buffer
(2) Regulatory mechanisms: renal regulation in response to pH of extracellular fluid
g. Phosphate (3 to 12 mg/100 ml)
(1) Function: development and maintenance of bones and teeth, promotes normal neuromuscular action, participates in carbohydrate metabolism, assists in acid-base regulation
(2) Regulatory mechanisms: regulated by parathyroid hormone, activated by vitamin D, absorbed through GI tract, serum levels inversely proportional to Ca^{++}
14. d
15. 7.36 to 7.44
16. **a.** Primarily involves the carbonic and bicarbonate buffer system, which is the first buffering system to react to changes in the pH. Buffering reaction can accept or donate hydrogen ions to maintain a relatively constant pH. Secondary chemical buffering, which is limited, involves plasma proteins that can bind with or release hydrogen ions.
b. Involves cellular release or absorption of hydrogen ions. The positively charged ion must be exchanged with another positively charged ion, frequently potas-

Hormone	Stimuli	Action
ADH	Increased blood osmolarity reflecting water deficit	Increases reabsorption of water by kidney tubules, decreasing production of urine
Aldosterone	Fluid deficits	Causes kidney tubules to excrete potassium and reabsorb sodium Sodium reabsorption causes water reabsorption
Glucocorticoids	Normally present without significant influence on fluid or electrolytes, but when other conditions cause increased or decreased release, imbalances may occur	Sodium and water retention Potassium loss (exchanged for sodium in tubule)

sium. Hyperkalemia (with acidosis) and hypokalemia (with alkalosis) may result. Another biological buffer is in the hemoglobin-oxyhemoglobin system, in which chloride and bicarbonate may exchange between the blood cell and the plasma.

c. Involves lungs and kidneys. Lungs provide rapid response through changes in respiratory rate and depth (influencing retention or release of carbon dioxide, which combines with water to create carbonic acid for chemical regulation). Kidneys are the slowest to respond, influencing hydrogen ion concentration through bicarbonate regulation, combining phosphate ions with hydrogen to form phosphoric acid, and converting ammonia to ammonium by attaching a hydrogen ion to ammonia.

17. d

18. Refer to no. 16c (above)

19. An excessive loss of water from body tissues

20. **a.** 5
b. 1
c. 4
d. 2
e. 3

21. Any six:
- Hypotension
- Tachycardia
- Cardiac dysrhythmias
- Dry skin
- Poor skin turgor
- Dry mucous membranes
- Pallor
- Lethargy
- Weakness
- Oliguria
- Decreased weight

22. Any three:
- Hypervolemia
- Edema
- Weight gain
- With normal kidney function: transient increase in blood pressure, increased urinary output
- With abnormal kidney function: jugular venous distention, liver enlargement, increased venous pressure, pulmonary edema

23. Edema

24. Refer to Chapter 37, Tables 37-3 and 37-4 (pp. 1031 to 1033).

25. d

26. c

27. b

28. **a.** Age
b. Body size
c. Environmental temperature
d. Life-style
e. Level of health

29. **a.** Inadequate nutritional intake can cause breakdown of protein stores; if serum protein levels fall and hypoalbuminemia occurs, serum colloid osmotic pressure decreases and fluids shift from circulation to interstitial spaces creating edema. Generally, electrolyte status may also be influenced by normal diet.

b. Stress increases release of aldosterone and glucocorticoids and ADH, all causing sodium and water retention.

c. Exercise increases sensible water loss from the skin through sweat.

30. **a.** Stress response causes postoperative fluid imbalance from increased secretion of aldosterone, glucocorticoids, and ADH. Response typically occurs during the second to fifth postoperative day and helps maintain circulating blood volume and blood pressure after surgery. When hormone levels return to normal, excess sodium and water are excreted.

b. Loss of water by one of five routes: plasma-to-interstitial shift, loss of serum proteins from extracellular fluids, plasma and interstitial fluids lost as burn exudate, water vapor and heat loss because there is no skin barrier, and blood leakage from damaged capillaries. Sodium and water also shift into the cells, further depleting extracellular fluid volume.

c. Decreased cardiac output associated with a failing heart results in decreased renal perfusion and decreased urinary output. In an effort to increase perfusion, sodium and water are retained, contributing to circulatory overload (producing more peripheral and pulmonary edema).

d. Renal failure produces an abnormal buildup of sodium, chloride, potassium, and toxic extracellular fluid from waste products of cellular metabolism.

e. Cancer causes a variety of imbalances depending on the type, progression, and therapies for the cancer. Third-space fluid accumulations, which decrease extracellular fluid volume but which may lead to increased total body water through compensatory mechanisms, frequently develop.

31. Any six:
- Chronic diseases
- Trauma
- Burns
- Drug therapy
- Gastroenteritis
- Nasogastric suctioning
- Fistulas
- IV therapy
- Total parenteral nutrition

32. **a.** Dehydration
b. Metabolic or respiratory alkalosis
c. Metabolic adidosis or alkalosis, respiratory acidosis
d. Fluid volume deficit in the infant
e. Fluid volume overload
f. Fluid volume deficit
g. Hypocalcemia, hypomagnesemia
h. Fluid volume overload
i. Metabolic acidosis, respiratory alkalosis and acidosis, hypokalemia
j. Fluid volume deficit
k. Fluid volume deficit
l. Fluid volume excess (in the adult)
m. Fluid volume overload or deficit, respiratory alkalosis
n. Fluid volume overload
o. Metabolic acidosis
p. Metabolic acidosis or alkalosis
q. Fluid volume deficit
r. Fluid volume deficit or overload
s. Fluid volume deficit
t. Hypocalcemia, metabolic or respiratory alkalosis
u. Hypernatremia, metabolic alkalosis
v. Hypercalcemia, hypermagnesemia
w. Hypernatremia

x. Hypernatremia
y. Hyponatremia
z. Fluid volume overload or slow venous return

33. d

34. False

35. **a.** D
b. D
c. D
d. U

36. Refer to table at bottom of page.

37. b

38. 1.010 to 1.025

39. Any two:
- Restore and maintain fluid, electrolyte, and acid-base balance
- Identify and correct the causes of the imbalance
- Prevent complications from therapies needed to restore balance

40. **a.** 120 ml
b. 0
c. 0
d. 240 ml
e. 240 ml
f. 600 ml

41. a

42. c

43. **a.** 500 ml
b. 400 ml
c. 100 ml

44. To correct or prevent fluid and electrolyte disturbances in clients who are or may become acutely ill

45. c

46. b

47. Any three:
- Very young
- Elderly
- Obese
- Thin, emaciated
- Severely dehydrated or with decreased circulatory volume

48. Peripheral lines are located in the hands, arms, feet, or legs; catheter size is small; peripheral lines are used for any fluid replacement except delivery of extremely large volumes or total parenteral nutrition. Central lines are located in large, central veins, such as the subclavian vein; catheter size is large; central lines are used to monitor central venous pressures (CVP) and to deliver large volumes of fluids or total parenteral nutrition.

49. **a.** 83 $\frac{1000}{12} = 83$

b. 21 $\frac{1000 \times 10}{480} = 21$

c. 21 $\frac{500 \times 15}{360} = 21$

d. 100 $\frac{50 \times 60}{30} = 100$

e. 14 $\frac{1000 \times 10}{720} = 14$

50. Any four:
- Patency of the IV needle or catheter
- Infiltration
- Knot or kink in the tubing
- Height of the solution
- Position of the client's extremity
- Viscosity of solution
- Lumen of cannula

51. **a.** Deliver a measured amount of fluid over a specific period of time.
b. Monitor IV fluids based on flow rate or drops per minute.

52. c

53. a

54. **a.** 4
b. 1
c. 6
d. 3
e. 5
f. 2

55. Place the pole next to the involved arm. Hold the pole with the involved hand. Push the pole with the involved hand. Report any blood in the tubing, stoppage in flow, or increased discomfort.

56. b

57.

Complication	Assessment finding	Nursing action
Infiltration	Swelling, pallor at site, decreased or stopped flow, pain	Discontinue infusion, elevate extremity, wrap extremity in warm towel for 20 min
Phlebitis	Pain, increased skin temperature over vein, may have red line along path of vein	Discontinue infusion; apply warm, moist heat
Fluid overload	Signs of fluid volume overload	Slow infusion rate, notify physician, prepare for additional treatment (for example, diuretics)

Laboratory value	Metabolic alkalosis	Metabolic acidosis	Respiratory alkalosis	Respiratory acidosis
pH	Increased	Decreased	Increased	Decreased
P_{CO_2}	Unchanged (increased with compensation)	Unchanged (decreased with compensation)	Decreased	Increased
HCO_3	Increased	Decreased	Unchanged	Unchanged (early)
K^+	Decreased	Increased	Decreased	Increased

- Do not open the drainage system at connection points to obtain specimens or measure urine.
- If the drainage tubing becomes disconnected, do not touch the ends of the catheter or tubing. Wipe the ends of the tubes with antiseptic solution before reconnecting.
- Use a separate receptable for measuring urine for each client.
- Prevent pooling of urine and reflux of urine into the bladder.
- Avoid prolonged clamping or kinking of the tubing (except during conditioning).
- Empty the drainage bag at least every 8 hours.
- Remove the catheter as soon as possible (after conferring with the physician).

58. a
59. True
60. d
61. Washing with mild soap and water

CHAPTER 39

1. **a.** Absorption: absorbs large amounts of water, sodium, and chloride via haustral contractions
b. Protection: releases supply of mucus to lubricate the colon, preventing trauma to the inner walls (particularly important near the distal end of the colon where contents become drier and harder)
c. Secretion: aids in electrolyte balance; bicarbonate secreted in exchange for chloride; potassium released
d. Elimination: removes waste products and gas
2. Flatus
3. Feces
4. Hemorrhoids
5. **a.** 4
b. 3
c. 2
d. 5
e. 1
6. Voluntary contraction of abdominal muscles during forced expiration with a closed glottis (holding one's breath while straining)
7. Any six:
- Loss of teeth, inability to chew
- Decreased digestive enzymes in saliva
- Decreased volume of gastric acid
- Decreased lipase
- Decreased peristalsis
- Slowed esophageal emptying
- Changes in absorptive properties of intestinal mucosa
- Decreased muscle tone of perineal floor and anal sphincter
- Decreased awareness of the need to defecate

8. Fiber provides bulk in fecal material. Bulk-forming foods stretch the bowel walls, creating peristalsis and initiating the defecation reflex.
9. Any four:
- Raw fruits
- Cooked fruits
- Greens
- Raw vegetables
- Whole grains

10. False
11. **a.** Lubricant; decreases fat-soluble vitamin absorption
b. Suppresses peristalsis; common treatment of diarrhea
c. Decrease peristalsis
d. Decrease acid secretion; depress gastric motility; constipation
e. Diarrhea
12. True
13. Increased fluids (if not contraindicated), laxatives (if ordered), enemas (if unresponsive to fluids and laxatives)
14. d
15. Any four:
- Irregular bowel habits: when normal defecation reflexes are ignored, they tend to become weakened; changes in routine can disrupt normal defecation patterns.
- Inadequate diet: low-fiber diet that is high in animal fats and refined sugars can cause constipation; loss of teeth may cause eating soft, processed food with low fiber; low fluid intake impairs peristalsis and fecal lubrication.
- Lack of exercise: decreased mobility and lack of regular exercise cause constipation.
- Medications: frequent use of laxatives causes loss of intestinal muscle tone with loss of normal defecation reflexes; tranquilizers, opiates, anticholinergics, and iron cause constipation.
- Age: slowed peristalsis and loss of abdominal muscle elasticity associated with aging increase frequency of constipation; decreased intestinal secretion of mucus reduces lubrication; many older adults live alone and eat improper diets that are low in fiber.
- Diseases: abnormalities of the GI tract may cause constipation; spinal cord injury or tumor may also cause altered GI function.

16. Any three:
- Following recent abdominal or rectal surgery
- Cardiovascular disease
- Increased intraocular pressure (glaucoma)
- Increased intracranial pressure

17. Exhaling through the mouth during straining
18. A collection of hardened feces, wedged in the rectum, that cannot be expelled
19. Any four:
- Inability to pass a stool for several days despite a repeated urge to defecate
- Continuous oozing of diarrheal stool that develops suddenly
- Anorexia
- Abdominal distention
- Cramping
- Rectal pain
- Palpable rectal mass

20. An increase in the number of stools and the passage of liquid, unformed feces
21. **a.** Fluid and electrolyte imbalance
b. Skin breakdown
22. b
23. Ostomy
24. Ileostomy
25. Colostomy
26. b
27. b
28. Any eight:
- Determination of the usual elimination pattern

- Identification of routines followed to promote normal elimination
- Description of any recent change in elimination pattern
- Client's description of usual characteristics of stool
- Diet history
- Description of daily fluid intake
- History of exercise
- Assessment of the use of artificial aids at home
- History of surgery or illnesses affecting the gastrointestinal tract
- Presence and status of artificial orifices
- Medication history
- Emotional state
- Social history

29. c
30. **a.** Abdominal distention
b. Hypoactive or absent bowel sounds
c. Small intestine obstruction and inflammatory disorders
d. Gas or flatulence
e. Masses, tumors, and fluid
31. a
32. **a.** Absence of bile
b. Iron ingestion or upper GI bleeding
c. Lower GI bleeding, hemorrhoids
d. Diarrhea, reduced absorption
e. Obstruction, rapid peristalsis
33. True
34. b
35. **a.** Any three:
- Age greater than 50 years
- Family history of colon polyps
- History of inflammatory bowel disease
- Living in an urban area
- Diet high in fats, low in fiber

b. Change in bowel habits and rectal bleeding
36. c
37. Any four:
- Instruct client to avoid eating or drinking until the gag reflex returns (2 to 4 hours).
- Check the gag reflex before providing food or fluids.
- Explain that hoarseness and a sore throat are normal for several days.
- Provide cool fluids and normal saline gargling to relieve soreness.
- Observe for bleeding, fever, abdominal pain, difficulty swallowing, and difficulty breathing.

38. Any five:
- Understand normal elimination
- Attain regular defecation habits
- Understand and maintain proper fluid and food intake
- Achieve a regular exercise program
- Achieve comfort
- Maintain skin integrity
- Maintain self-concept

39. Any three:
- Take time for defecation
- Begin establishing a routine during a time when defecation is most likely to occur
- Make certain that treatment routines do not interfere with the client's schedule
- Provide privacy

40. a
41. Shortly before the client's usual time to defecate or immediately after a meal
42. **a.** 4
b. 3
c. 1
d. 5
e. 2
43. b
44. a
45. a
46. Enema is repeated until the client passes fluid that is clear and contains no fecal material.
47. False
48. c
49. True
50. Vagal stimulation from rectal pressure could cause reflex slowing of the heart.
51. Any five:
- Type of ostomy
- Size and contour of the abdomen
- Condition of the skin around the stoma
- Physical activities of the client
- Client's personal preference
- Cost of equipment

52. ET (enterostomal therapist)
53. d
54. Any six:
- Ascending colostomies
- Temporary colostomies
- Disease in remaining colon
- Infant or child
- Physical limitations
- Mental limitations
- Inadequate sanitary facilities
- Stomal abnormalities
- Client lack of interest or motivation

55. **a.** While lying supine, tighten the abdominal muscles as though they were being pushed to the floor; hold the muscles tight to a count of three and then relax (repeat 5 to 10 times as tolerated).
b. Flex and contract the thigh muscles by raising the knees one at a time slowly toward the chest (repeat each leg at least five times; increase as tolerated).
56. b
57. d
58. False
59. Any four:
- Give client an opportunity to discuss concerns or fears about elimination problems.
- Provide clients and families with information to understand and manage the elimination problems.
- Give positive feedback when the client attempts self-care measures.
- Help clients with ostomies to manage their condition, but do not expect them to like it.
- Provide clients privacy during care.
- Show clients acceptance and understanding.

60. c

CHAPTER 40

1. **a.** Basic needs are achievable.
b. Physical hazards are reduced.
c. Transmission of pathogens and parasites is reduced.

d. Sanitation is maintained.
e. Pollution is controlled.

2. a
3. a. Adequate lighting
   b. Decreased clutter
   c. Securing the home
4. Any microorganism capable of producing an illness
5. An organism living in or on another organism and obtaining nourishment from it
6. Immunization
7. d
8. Any four:
   - Disruption of processing ability and problem solving
   - Increased anxiety
   - Paranoia
   - Hallucinations
   - Depression
   - Unrealistic feelings
9. Any five:
   - Developmental stage
   - Life-style habits
   - Mobility state
   - Sensory impairments
   - Safety awareness
10. a
11. True
12. True
13. True
14. Any eight:
   - Decreased circulation in the brain causing dizziness and fainting
   - Mechanical obstruction of vertebral arteries to the brain caused by crushed osteoporotic vertebrae
   - Decreased auditory acuity
   - Decreased night vision, color vision, or visual acuity
   - Arteriosclerosis
   - Orthostatic hypotension
   - Loss of sense of position
   - Diminished space perception
   - Decreased muscle mass, strength, coordination
   - Decreased ability to balance
   - Osteoporosis and increased stress on weight-bearing areas resulting in an unsteady gait and susceptibility to fractures
   - Decreased muscle activity necessary for adequate venous return
   - Decreased capacity of blood vessels
   - Slowed nervous system response
15. a. Falls
   b. Client-inherent accidents
   c. Procedure-related accidents
   d. Equipment-related accidents
16. d
17. d
18. b
19. Any six:
   - Ungrounded equipment
   - Frayed cords
   - Circuits overloaded by too many appliances in one area
   - Improperly functioning equipment
   - Use of extension cords
   - Tangled or cluttered cords
   - Use of electrical appliances near sink, bathtub, shower, or damp areas
   - Electrical cords or appliances within reach of young children
   - Noninsulated wiring in basement or crawl space
20. d
21. Any three:
   - Maintaining an environment that is adapted to the motor, sensory, and cognitive developmental needs of the client
   - Promoting knowledge related to potential threats to the client's safety
   - Reducing the potential for injury
   - Reducing the risk of accidental poisonings
22. a. Change in appetite
   b. Change in sleeping
   c. Change in activity levels
   d. Apathy
23. d
24. Any five:
   - Enroll in a driver's education course.
   - Wear seat belts.
   - Do not drive after using a psychoactive substance, drugs, or alcohol (or ride when the driver has used such substances).
   - Contract to drive any teenager who has been drinking, with no questions asked.
   - Develop safe eating, sleeping, and relaxation habits.
   - Develop awareness of safe-sex decisions and practices.
   - Recognize changes in behavior and mood.
   - Maintain open lines of communication.
   - If a parent, do not try to be a buddy.
25. a. Falls
   b. Automobile accidents
   c. Burns
26. Any eight:
   - Identify clients at risk for falls.
   - Assign clients at risk rooms near the nurse's station.
   - Alert all health care personnel to the client's increased risk of falling.
   - Use night light in room.
   - Reinforce to client or family the need for assistance when ambulating or getting up.
   - Keep side rails up.
   - Have call light easily accessible; promptly answer call light.
   - Keep client's personal and diversional items within easy reach.
   - Follow a scheduled toileting routine.
   - Reassess client's risk of falling each shift.
   - Frequently observe client.
   - Properly use restraints or sitters.
27. b
28. a. To reduce the risk of falling out of bed or from chair or wheelchair
   b. To prevent interruption of therapy such as traction, intravenous infusions, nasogastric tube feeding, or Foley catheter
   c. To prevent the confused or combative client from removing life-support equipment
   d. To reduce the risk of injury to others by the client
29. c
30. d
31. c
32. b

33. d
34. Side rails up and application of a jacket restraint
35. Any six:
    - Know the phone number for reporting a fire, and be sure the number is attached to all telephones.
    - Know the agency's or unit's fire drill or fire evacuation routine.
    - Post accurate, easy-to-follow routes to fire exits.
    - Know the location of fire extinguishers, how to use them, and which type of extinguishers to use for a specific fire.
    - Report a fire before attempting to extinguish it, regardless of its size.
    - Keep hallways free of unnecessary equipment or furniture.
    - Keep fire hoses clear at all times.
    - Periodically check the efficiency of fire extinguishers.
    - Post signs on the outside of elevators warning people to take the stairs in the event of fire.
36. **a.** To protect clients from injury (highest priority)
    b. To report the location of the fire
    c. To contain the fire
37. d
38. Syrup of ipecac
39. c
40. a

CHAPTER 41

1. The coordinated effort of the musculoskeletal and nervous systems to maintain balance, posture, and body alignment during lifting, bending, moving, and performing activities of daily living
2. A force that occurs in a direction to oppose movement
3. Any three:
    - Place client's arms across chest when moving up in bed.
    - Elicit the client's assistance in moving.
    - Lift rather than push a client.
    - Use pull sheets.
4. **a.** Skeletal system
    b. Muscle system (skeletal muscle)
    c. Nervous system
5. **a.** Support of structures of the body
    b. Movement
    c. Protection of vital organs
    d. Regulation of calcium balance
    e. Production and storage of RBCs
6. True
7. **a.** 4
    b. 3
    c. 7
    d. 6
    e. 2
    f. 5
    g. 1
8. Isotonic
9. Isometric
10. True
11. c
12. b
13. Proprioception
14. d
15. True
16. c
17. **a.** 4
    b. 5
    c. 6
    d. 1
    e. 2
    f. 3
18. **a.** Foot-drop
    b. Congenital hip dysplasia
    c. Kyphosis
    d. Clubfoot
    e. Lordosis
    f. Scoliosis
19. b
20. **a.** Inflammation
    b. Degeneration
    c. Articular disruption
21. **a.** 3
    b. 1
    c. 5
    d. 4
    e. 2
    f. 6
22. a
23. False
24. Any five:
    - Determine normal physiological changes in body alignment resulting from growth and development.
    - Identify deviations in body alignment caused by poor posture.
    - Provide an opportunity for the client to observe his or her posture.
    - Identify learning needs of the client for maintaining correct body alignment.
    - Identify the presence of trauma, muscle damage, or nerve dysfunction.
    - Obtain information concerning other factors that contribute to poor alignment, such as fatigue, malnutrition, and psychological problems.
25. **a.** ROM: the maximal amount of movement possible at a joint in one of the three planes of the body (sagittal, frontal, or transverse)
    b. Gait: the manner or style of walking, including rhythm, cadence, and speed
    c. Exercise: physical activity for conditioning the body, improving health, and maintaining fitness
26. **a.** 3
    b. 1
    c. 4
    d. 2
27. a
28. The kind and amount of exercise or work that a person is able to perform
29. Any three for each domain:
    a.
    - Frequency of illness or surgery during past 12 months
    - Types of illness or surgery during past 12 months
    - Cardiopulmonary status
    - Musculoskeletal status
    - Sleep patterns
    - Presence of pain, pain control
    - Vital signs, range
    - Exercise activity and pattern

- Abnormality in laboratory studies (decreased O_2, decreased Hgb, abnormal electrolytes)

b.
- Mood: depression, anxiety
- Motivation
- Chemical addictions
- Self-image

c.
- Age
- Sex
- Pregnancy
- Changes in muscle mass caused by developmental changes
- Changes in skeletal system caused by developmental changes

30. Any four:
- Maintain proper body alignment.
- Restore proper body alignment or optimal level of body alignment.
- Reduce injuries to the skin and musculoskeletal systems resulting from improper body mechanics or alignment.
- Promote full or optimal range of joint motion.
- Prevent contractures.

31. **a.** Position of weight
b. Height of the object
c. Body position
d. Maximal weight

32. 45 pounds (35% of 130 pounds)

33. a

34.

Device	Uses
Pillow	Support body or extremity; elevates a body part; splints incisional area to reduce postoperative pain during activity or coughing and deep breathing
Footboard	Maintains feet in dorsal flexion
Trochanter roll	Prevents external rotation of legs in supine position
Sandbag	Provides support and shape to body contours; immobilizes an extremity; maintains specific body alignment
Hand-wrist splint	Maintains proper functional alignment of thumb and fingers; maintains wrist in slight dorsal flexion
Trapeze bar	Enables client to raise trunk from bed; enables client to transfer from bed to wheelchair; allows client to perform exercises to strengthen upper arms
Side rail	Allows weak client to roll from side to side or to sit up in bed
Bed board	Provides additional support to the mattress and improves vertebral alignment

35. False

36. **a.** Joints should be supported.
b. Position of the joints should be slightly flexed.
c. Pressure points should be removed or minimized.

37. Any five:
- Raising the side rail on the side of the bed opposite the nurse to prevent the client from falling out of bed
- Elevating the level of the bed to a comfortable height
- Assessing the client's mobility and strength to determine what assistance he or she can offer during transfer
- Determining the need for assistance
- Explaining the procedure and describing what is expected of the client
- Assessing for correct body alignment and pressure areas following each transfer

38. a

39. Any four:
- If the client's illness prohibits exertion
- If the client understands what is expected
- The level of the client's comfort
- The nurse's own strength and knowledge of the procedure
- Determination if the client is too heavy or immobile for the nurse to work unassisted

40. b

41. True

42. The permanent shortening of a muscle and eventual shortening of the associated ligaments and tendons within a joint

43. d

44. c

45. **a.** Assess the client's activity tolerance, strength, presence of pain, coordination, and balance to determine assistance needed.
b. Explain how far the client should try to walk, who is going to help, when the walk will take place, and why walking is important.
c. Check the environment to be sure there are no obstacles in the client's path.
d. Establish rest points in case the activity tolerance is less than estimated or the client becomes dizzy.
e. Assist the client to a position of sitting, followed by stationary standing before attempting to walk.

46. d

47. b

48. b

49. Measurement includes three areas:
- Client height: 3 to 4 finger widths from axilla to point 6 inches (15 cm) lateral to client's heel will determine crutch length
- Angle of elbow flexion: 20 to 25 degrees
- Distance between the crutch pad and axilla: 3 to 4 finger widths

50. Any four:
- Clients must not use crutches that fit improperly nor lean on crutches to support their weight.
- Crutch tips should be inspected routinely; worn tips should be replaced.
- Crutch tips should remain dry and should be dried off immediately if they become wet.
- Inspect the structure of the crutches routinely.
- Provide client with a list of medical suppliers in the community to obtain any repairs or replacement parts for crutches.
- Spare crutches and tips should always be on hand.

51. a

52. **a.** 1
b. 3
c. 5
d. 4
e. 2

53. a. 3
 b. 2
 c. 4
 d. 1
54. False
55. a

CHAPTER 42

1. a. Physical inactivity
 b. Physical restriction or limitation of movement
 c. Restriction in changes in body position and posture
 d. Sensory deprivation
 e. Regional paralysis
2. Any three:
 - Decreased physical activity and reduced oxygen tissue requirements
 - Pain reduction and decreased need for analgesics
 - Rest to regain strength
 - Uninterrupted sleep, rest, relaxation
3. True
4. c
5. a. Immobility alters metabolism and decreases the number of RBCs; anemia reduces the amount of oxygen available to the tissues; to compensate the body attempts to increase the respiratory and heart rate, thus increasing work load.
 b. Bed mattresses limit space for lung expansion, causing decreased exchange of respiratory gases, and increased pooling of respiratory secretions occurs.
 c. Muscle weakness diminishes lung expansion and the muscles needed to effectively cough.
 d. Increased distribution of mucus in the bronchi creates a medium for bacterial growth (hypostatic bronchopneumonia).
6. a. Orthostatic hypotension
 b. Increased cardiac work load
 c. Thrombus formation
7. b
8. There is an increased blood return to the heart from lower extremities. This, coupled with the frequent use of the Valsalva maneuver by clients on bed rest, further increases the volume of blood returning to the heart when the held breath is released. The more blood the heart receives to pump, the greater the work load.
9. a. Injury to the vessel lumen
 b. Decreased venous return
 c. Hypercoagulability
10. a. Loss of endurance
 b. Decreased muscle mass
 c. Atrophy
 d. Decreased stability
11. a. Joint contractures
 b. Osteoporosis
12. b
13. c
14. a
15. An inflammation, sore, or ulcer in the skin over a bony prominence
16. a. Pressure
 b. Shearing force
17. True
18. Decreased blood supply to a body part
19. Reactive hyperemia
20. a. Stage 3
 b. Stage 2
 c. Stage 4
 d. Stage 1
21. The pressure exerted when a client is moved or repositioned in bed by being pulled, or when allowed to slide down in bed
22. a. Moisture reduces the skin's resistance to other physical factors, such as pressure or shearing force.
 b. Poor nutrition often leads to weight loss, muscle atrophy, and decreased subcutaneous tissue and muscle mass; protein loss can cause hypoalbuminemia, which shifts fluid to the tissue, resulting in edema; poor nutrition impairs wound healing.
 c. Decreased hemoglobin reduces the amount of oxygen carried by the blood and available to the tissues; decreased oxygen alters cellular metabolism and impairs wound healing.
 d. Infection increases metabolic demands and therefore oxygen and nutritional tissue requirements; diaphoresis associated with infection increases skin moisture and further predisposes to skin breakdown.
23. a. Urine retention
 b. Renal calculi
 c. Urinary tract infections
24. a. Depression
 b. Behavioral changes
 c. Changes in sleep-wake cycles
 d. Decreased coping mechanisms
25. True
26.

System	Abnormal findings
Metabolic	Slowed wound healing Muscle atrophy Decreased subcutaneous fat Generalized edema (hypoalbuminemia)
Respiratory	Asymmetrical chest wall movement Presence of adventitious sounds Increased rate
Cardiovascular	Orthostatic hypotention Increased heart rate S_3 Weak peripheral pulses
Musculoskeletal	Increased diameter in calf or thigh (thrombus) Decreased joint motion Decreased strength
Skin	Break in skin integrity (decubitus ulcer)
Elimination	Decreased urine output Cloudy or concentrated urine Decreased frequency of bowel movements

27. c
28. Any three:
 - Localized redness
 - Localized warmth
 - Localized tenderness
 - Increased circumference (calf or thigh)
29. Any eight:

- Restoring proper body alignment or client's optimal level of body alignment
- Reducing and preventing injuries to the skin and musculoskeletal systems resulting from improper body mechanics, improper body alignment, or immobility
- Maintaining a patent airway
- Promoting optimal lung expansion
- Mobilizing airway secretions
- Increasing activity tolerance
- Promoting normal elimination patterns
- Maintaining normal sleep-wake patterns
- Promoting socialization
- Promoting independent completion of self-care activities
- Promoting physical and mental stimulation

30. Three interventions for each system identified:
Metabolic: high-protein diet, high-calorie diet, B and C vitamins, supplemental nutritional feedings, alternative nutritional routes (if indicated)
Respiratory: position changes every 2 hours, cough and deep breathe every 1 to 2 hours, judicious use of pain medications, chest PT, suctioning (if client unable to cough effectively)
Cardiovascular: leg exercises, out of bed as soon as possible, gradual position changes, use of pursed-lip breathing with position changes, preventing constipation, position to promote venous return, use of elastic hose (if ordered)
Musculoskeletal: active ROM, passive ROM, progressive exercise programs
Skin: meticulous skin care, position changes at least every 2 hours, maintain clean and smooth bed linens, keep skin dry, use mechanical devices to minimize pressure
Elimination: provide adequate hydration, increase dietary fiber (fruits, vegetables, bran), obtain orders for stool laxatives, cathartics, or enemas (as indicated)
Psychological: provide routine and informal socialization, provide stimuli to maintain orientation and entertain; promote body image maintenance activities; involve client in care; promote normal rest and sleep cycles; incorporate other consultants as indicated
Developmental: provide stimuli appropriate to the client's age and developmental stage; provide orientation information; encourage ADL within the client's capabilities

31. False
32. c
33. d
34. c

CHAPTER 43

1. An invasion of the body by pathogens or microorganisms capable of producing disease
2. **a.** Infectious agent or pathogen
b. Reservoir for pathogen growth
c. Portal of exit from reservoir
d. Means of transmission or vehicle
e. Portal of entry to host
f. Susceptible host
3. **a.** 4
b. 5
c. 6
d. 2
e. 7
f. 1
g. 3
4. True
5. **a.** Contact: direct physical transfer, indirect contact with contaminated inanimate object, droplet (coming in contact within 3 feet through sneezing or coughing)
b. Air: droplet nuclei suspended in air or dust
c. Vehicle: contaminated items such as liquids, food
d. Vectors: insects, animals
6. d
7. **a.** 2
b. 1
c. 4
d. 3
8. **a.** Normal flora
b. Body systems
c. Inflammatory response
d. Immune system
9. b
10. Refer to Chapter 43, Table 43-4 (p. 1269).
11. Body's cellular response to injury or infection; a protective vascular reaction that delivers fluid, blood products, and nutrients to interstitial tissues in an area of injury; process neutralizes and eliminates pathogens or necrotic tissues and establishes a means of repairing body cells and tissues
12. True
13. **a.** Redness
b. Localized warmth
c. Swelling
d. Pain or tenderness
e. Loss of function
14. **a.** Vascular and cellular responses
b. Formation of inflammatory exudate
c. Tissue repair
15. **a.** Fever
b. Leukocytosis
c. Malaise
d. Anorexia
e. Nausea
f. Vomiting
g. Lymph node enlargement
16. **a.** 3
b. 4
c. 2
d. 5
e. 1
f. 7
g. 6
17. **a.** 2
b. 4
c. 1
d. 3
e. 5
18. c
19. **a.** Nosocomial
b. Iatrogenic
c. Exogenous
d. Endogenous
20. Any three:
- Number of health care employees having direct contact with the client
- Number of invasive procedures
- Type of invasive procedures
- Medications

- Treatments
- Length of hospital stay

21. a

22. **a.** Age
b. Nutritional status
c. Stress
d. Heredity
e. Disease process
f. Medical therapies

23. b

24. b

25. Any three:
- Preventing exposure to infectious organisms
- Controlling or reducing the extent of infection
- Understanding of infection control techniques
- Maintaining a sense of comfort and self-esteem

26. **a.** Preventing the onset and spread of infection
b. Promoting measures for treatment of infection

27. **a.** 4
b. 8
c. 6
d. 3
e. 1
f. 7
g. 2
h. 9
i. 5

28. **a.** Waterproof gloves
b. Stiff brush
c. Detergent or soap
d. Running water (cool to rinse, warm to wash)

29. c

30. **a.** 6
b. 5
c. 2
d. 4
e. 1
f. 3
g. 2
h. 3
i. 4

31. Hand washing

32. Any six:
- Before contact with clients who are susceptible to infection
- After caring for an infected client
- After touching organic material
- Before performing invasive procedures
- Before and after handling dressings or touching open wounds
- After handling contaminated equipment
- Between contact with different clients in high-risk units

33. c

34. **a.** Disease-specific system: practices followed for each disease. System less costly and time consuming because certain diseases require only minimal protection.
b. Category-specific system: used in most hospitals. Diseases requiring similar isolation precautions, based on methods of organism transmission, are grouped together.

35. **a.** Prevents transmission of highly contagious or virulent infections spread by air and contact
b. Prevents transmission of highly transmissible infections spread by close or direct contact (which do not warrant strict precautions)
c. Prevents transmission of infectious diseases over short distances via air droplets
d. Prevent infections transmitted by direct or indirect contact with feces
e. Special category for clients with pulmonary tuberculosis who have positive results on sputum or chest x-ray film indicating active disease
f. Prevent infections transmitted by direct or indirect contact with purulent material or drainage from an infected body site
g. Prevent infections transmitted by direct or indirect contact with infective blood or body fluids
h. Protects an uninfected client with lowered immunity and resistance from acquiring infectious organisms

36.

Type of isolation	Room	Gown	Gloves	Mask
Strict	X	X	X	X
Contact	X	X	X	X
Respiratory	X			X
Enteric precautions	If poor hygiene	X	X	
Tuberculosis isolation	X			X
Drainage and secretion precautions		X	X	
Universal blood and body fluid precautions	If poor hygiene	X	X	If droplet splattering likely
Care of the severely compromised client	X	X	X	X

37. True

38. **a.** Gloves should be worn for touching blood and body fluids, mucous membranes, or nonintact skin of all clients.
b. Gloves should be worn for handling items or surfaces soiled with blood or body fluids and for performing venipuncture and other vascular access procedures.
c. Gloves should be changed after contact with each client.
d. Masks and protective eyewear or face shields should be worn during procedures that are likely to generate droplets of blood or other body fluids.
e. Gowns should be worn during procedures that are likely to generate splashes of blood or other body fluids.
f. Hands and other skin surfaces should be washed immediately and thoroughly if contaminated with blood or other body fluids.
g. To prevent needle-stick injuries, needles should not be recapped, purposely bent, broken, or removed from disposable syringes; they should be disposed of in puncture-resistant containers near the work area.
h. To reduce the need for mouth-to-mouth resuscitation, mouthpieces, resuscitator bags, or other ventilation devices should be used.
i. Health care workers who have exudative lesions should refrain from all direct client care and from handling client care equipment.

39. Any four:
   - Hands should be washed thoroughly before entering and leaving the room of a client receiving protective asepsis.
   - Contaminated supplies and equipment should be disposed of in a manner that prevents spread of microorganisms to other persons.
   - Knowledge of the disease process and the means of infection transmission should be applied when using protective barriers.
   - Measures should be implemented to protect other people who might be exposed during transport of the client to locations outside the isolated room.
   - Equipment required in the care of the client and in establishing protective asepsis precautions should be organized and easily accessible.
40. **a.** Family education about the client condition, need for isolation, and how to perform needed precautions
   b. Provision of meaningful stimuli
41. a
42. d
43. True
44. a
45. b
46. True
47. **a.** 2
   b. 4
   c. 1
   d. 5
   e. 3
48. Any five:
   - Providing staff education on infection control
   - Reviewing infection control policies and procedures
   - Screening client's laboratory reports for culture results
   - Screening client records for incidence of community-acquired infections
   - Gathering statistics regarding epidemiology of nosocomial infections
   - Notifying community health department of incidence of infections
   - Conferring with support services such as housekeeping and the dietary department
   - Educating clients and their families
49. True
50. False
51. **a.** Avoid sudden movements of body parts covered by sterile drapes.
   b. Refrain from touching sterile supplies, drapes, or the nurse's gloves and gown.
   c. Avoid coughing, sneezing, or talking over a sterile area.
52. **a.** C
   b. S
   c. C
   d. C
   e. S
   f. C
53. d
54. **a.** 2
   b. 4
   c. 1
   d. 3
55. c
56. **a.** Remove all jewelry.
   b. Keep nails short and clean, without nail polish.
   c. Fingertips to elbows
   d. At least 5 minutes (based on institutional policy)
   e. Brush, orange stick or nail file, antiseptic solution, sterile towel
   f. Fingers and hands up, elbows down
   g. Fingers to elbows, rotating motion
57. False
58. True
59. False
60. b
61. b
62. **a.** Grasp the corner of the drape with the dominant hand, touching only the 1-inch margin at the corner.
   b. Lift the drape straight up with one hand, and allow it to gently unfold (do not shake or allow the drape to touch the uniform).
   c. With the nondominant hand, grasp the adjacent corner of the drape and hold it straight.
   d. Approach the area to be draped, being careful not to touch any contaminated surfaces with the drape.
   e. First, position the bottom half of the drape over the area.
   f. Position the top half of the drape last, to avoid reaching over the sterile field.
   g. Grasp the 1-inch border around the drape edge to position as needed.
63. True
64. **a.** Client susceptibility to infection
   b. Chain of infection, with emphasis on the means of organism transmission
   c. Basic hand-washing technique
   d. Hygienic practices to minimize organism growth and spread
   e. Preventive health care (diet, immunization, exercise)
   f. Proper methods for handling and storing food
   g. Family members at risk for acquiring infections

CHAPTER 44

1. **a.** Reception
   b. Perception
   c. Reaction
2. a
3. Any seven:
   - Age
   - Medications
   - Environment
   - Comfort level
   - Preexisting illnesses
   - Smoking
   - Noise levels
   - Endotracheal intubation
4. A defect in the normal function of sensory reception and perception
5. Sensory deprivation
6. **a.** Reduced sensory input (sensory deficit)
   b. Elimination of order or meaning from input (for example, a strange environment)
   c. Restriction of the environment that produces monotony and boredom (for example, bed rest)
7. Sensory overload
8. Two for each category:
   a. Reduced capacity to learn, inability to problem solve, poor task performance
   b. Boredom, restlessness, increased anxiety, emotional la-

bility, increased need for physical stimulation and socialization

c. Reduced attention span, disorganized visual and motor coordination, temporary loss of color perception, disorientation, confusion of sleeping and waking states

9. Any three:
   - Elderly
   - Clients who are immobilized
   - Clients who are isolated (in home or hospital)
   - Clients with a known sensory deficit
10. Refer to Chapter 44, Table 44-2 (p. 1311).
11. Any five:
    - Maintain function of existing senses.
    - Maintain meaningful sensory stimulation.
    - Provide a safe environment.
    - Prevent additional sensory loss.
    - Communicate effectively with existing sensory alterations.
    - Understand the nature and implications of sensory loss.
    - Achieve self-care.
12. **a.** Strengthening visual stimuli
    b. Using other senses
    c. Using sharp visual contrasts
    d. Minimizing glare
13. Any four:
    - Telephone bell amplification
    - Telephone speaker amplification
    - Amplification of other environmental sounds (for example, smoke alarms)
    - Reduction of background noise
    - Proper fit and function of hearing aids
14. d
15. a
16. c
17. d
18. c
19. Any six:
    - Get client's attention.
    - Face client, with face and lips illuminated.
    - If client wears glasses, be sure they are clean.
    - Speak slowly and articulate clearly, using normal tones of voice and inflections.
    - Restate with different words when you are not understood.
    - Do not shout.
    - Talk toward the client's best or normal ear.
    - Use gestures to enhance the spoken word.
20. False

CHAPTER 45

1. Any drug, chemical, or biological entity that can be self-administered
2. True
3. Drug use occurs when a drug is appropriately taken as it is prescribed (for intended psychological or physiological effects). Drug misuse occurs when the drug is taken indiscriminately or taken improperly (whether it is prescribed or over-the-counter). Drug abuse occurs when the drug is regularly taken indiscriminately in excessive quantities that impair the person's physiological, psychological, or social functioning.
4. b
5. Psychological dependence
6. Fetal alcohol syndrome: a permanent disorder characterized by retardation and physical abnormalities, caused by maternal alcoholism
7. d
8. False
9. d
10. True
11.

Substance	Psychological effect produced
Alcohol	Euphoria; followed by depression Decreased inhibitions Impaired judgment
Opiates	Euphoria Relaxation Pain relief Lack of concern Detachment from reality Impaired judgment
Barbiturates	Euphoria, followed by depression Decreased inhibitions Impaired judgment
Antianxiety agents	Relaxation Increased self-confidence Relief of anxiety
Cocaine	Euphoria Elation Agitation Hyperactivity Irritability Grandiosity
Marijuana	Relaxation Mild euphoria Loss of inhibition Decreased motivation
Hallucinogens	Distorted perception Heightened sense of awareness Grandiosity Hallucinations Illusions Distortions of time and space Depersonalization Mystical experiences
Amphetamines	Euphoria Hyperactivity Irritability Hyperalertness Insomnia

12. Any two:
    - Pleasure seeking
    - Curiosity
    - Escape mechanism
13. **a.** Primary disease: situation in which the abuse problem is seen as primary, with other problems (psychological or physical) viewed as secondary to the abuse
    b. Genetic: chemical dependency viewed as predisposed through heredity but influenced through environment
    c. Psychological: variety of theories, including (1) stress as contributing to the onset and continuation of addiction and (2) substance use and continuation associated with a reward or reinforcement
    d. Sociocultural: abuse viewed as part of one's socialization through the values, perceptions, norms, and beliefs passed from one generation to another

14. Individual goes for long periods of time not drinking at all and then drinks continuously for hours (or days), not stopping until forced to by unconsciousness, illness, or accident.
15. False
16. c
17. True
18. **a.** Providing accurate information to the health care system and communities regarding chemical dependency
    b. Nurse works as case finder in assisting parents, educators, and other health care professionals in identifying persons with actual or potential chemical abuse
    c. Nurse cares for clients in chemical dependency treatment centers, acute care hospitals, home care settings, and clinical and long-term care facilities who have other health care problems
19. **a.** Empathetic style: demonstrates an acceptance and understanding of the client's problem
    b. Clarifying style: seeks to sort through the client's perception of his or her problems with specific questions
    c. Giving advice: an intervention strategy that may be appropriate at the early stage of interview since abusers tend to look to outside sources for answers
    d. Confrontation: nurse confronts elements in the interview that are impeding effective interaction
20. b
21. **a.** To determine if a substance abuse problem exists
    b. To explore causative factors and effects in all areas of the client's life
    c. To assess the psychological, behavioral, and physiological impact of the abused substance
    d. To assess the extent of the physiological or psychological dependence
22. Any four:
    - Cessation of substance use
    - Use of stress management techniques
    - Restoration to ideal body weight
    - Balanced nutritional status
    - Beginning return to normal family dynamics
23. **a.** Recognize the disease and how it has affected the person's life.
    b. Learn about chemical dependency.
    c. Provide tools for changing behavior.
24. Detoxification
25. d
26. Any four:
    - Teaching and counseling about substance abuse
    - Values clarification about substance abuse
    - Stress management techniques
    - Interventions for developmental needs of children
    - Development of support systems
    - Referral to agencies or self-help groups
27. c
28. **a.** Acute care interventions
    b. Interventions for abusive behavior
    c. Teaching
    d. Counseling
    e. Support system building
    f. Family interventions
    g. Community resource and referral
29. **a.** Referral to the appropriate community agency or mental health clinic
    b. Education about drugs
    c. Promotion of effective coping mechanisms
    d. Provision of needed physical and psychosocial support

CHAPTER 46

1. The role of the nurse during the preoperative, intraoperative, and postoperative phases of surgery
2. **a.** Seriousness
   b. Urgency
   c. Purpose
3. **a.** 6
   b. 4
   c. 9
   d. 5
   e. 3
   f. 11
   g. 2
   h. 1
   i. 7
   j. 10
   k. 8
4. Any four:
   - Assess the client's physical and emotional well-being.
   - Recognize the degree of surgical risk.
   - Coordinate diagnostic tests.
   - Identify nursing diagnoses reflecting client's and family members' needs.
   - Prepare the client physically and mentally for surgery.
   - Communicate pertinent information to the surgical team.
5. **a.** Increases risk of hemorrhaging during and after surgery
   b. Impairs wound healing and increases risk of infection from altered glucose metabolism and associated circulatory impairment; blood sugar levels may cause CNS malfunction during anesthesia
   c. Stress of surgery increases demands on myocardium to maintain cardiac output; general anesthesia further depresses cardiac function
   d. Increases risk of other respiratory complications during anesthesia
   e. Alters metabolism and elimination of drugs administered during surgery; impairs wound healing because of altered protein metabolism
   f. Predisposes client to fluid and electrolyte imbalances; may indicate underlying infection
   g. Reduces client's ability to compensate for acid-base alterations; anesthetic agents reduce respiratory function, increasing risk for severe hypoventilation
6. False
7. Chronic smoker has increased amounts and thickness of mucous secretions already present in the lungs. General anesthetics stimulate pulmonary secretions, which are retained from reduced ciliary activity during anesthesia. The client who smokes has local irritation to the respiratory mucosa and diminished ciliary action, which are further compromised by anesthetic agents.
8. d
9. Any three:
   - Age: very young and elderly clients are surgical risks as a result of immature or declining physiological status.
   - Nutrition: normal tissue repair and resistance to infection depend on adequate nutrients, and these needs are intensified by surgery. Malnourishment predisposes to improper wound healing, reduced energy, and infection. Obese clients are often malnourished and also have reduced ventilatory and cardiac function; further, the structure of fatty tissues, which contain a poor blood supply, further compromises wound healing.
   - Radiotherapy: used preoperatively to reduce the size of

the cancerous tumor, causes excess thinning of skin layers, destruction of collagen, and impaired vascularization of tissue, which impairs wound healing.
- Fluid-electrolyte balance: surgery is a form of trauma that precipitates the adrenocortical stress response (sodium and water retention and potassium loss); fluid imbalance or electrolyte disturbance poses significant risks during and after surgery.

10. d
11. a
12. c
13. a
14. Any six:
- Understanding physiological and psychological responses to surgery
- Understanding intraoperative and postoperative events
- Acquiring emotional comfort
- Gaining a return of normal physiological function postoperatively
- Maintaining a normal fluid and electrolyte balance intraoperatively and postoperatively
- Achieving comfort and rest
- Remaining free of postoperative surgical wound infection
- Remaining safe from physical harm intraoperatively

15. False
16. c
17. a
18. **a.** Improved ventilatory function
b. Optimal recovery of physical functional capacity
c. Improved sense of well-being
d. Shortened length of hospital stay
19. c
20. Any six:
- Client cites reasons for each of the preoperative instructions provided and exercises explained or practiced.
- Client states the time surgery is scheduled.
- Client states the unit to which he or she will return after surgery and the location of family during the intraoperative and immediate recovery periods.
- Client discusses anticipated monitoring and therapeutic devices or materials likely to be used postoperatively.
- Client describes in general terms the surgical procedures and subsequent treatment plan.
- Client describes anticipated steps in postoperative activity resumption.
- Client verbalizes expectations about pain relief and measures likely to be taken to alleviate pain.
- Client expresses feelings regarding surgical intervention and its expected outcomes.

21. **a.** Improve circulation and prevent stasis, mobilize secretions, promote lung expansion
b. Assist in removing retained mucus in airways
c. Improve lung expansion and oxygen delivery without using excess energy, clears out anesthetic gases remaining in airway
d. Improve blood flow to lower extremities and reduce stasis
22. **a.** Decrease risk of vomiting and aspiration; prevent complications associated with slowing of gastrointestinal peristalsis
b. Decrease incidence of postoperative wound infections
c. Reduce incidence of postoperative constipation
d. Promote effective rest and sleep before surgery
23. False
24. True
25. To provide the nurse with a guideline for ensuring completion of all required nursing interventions before the client's surgery
26. **a.** Check medical record contents and complete required recording.
b. Check vital signs.
c. Provide hygiene.
d. Check hair and cosmetics.
e. Remove prosthetics.
f. Prepare bowel and bladder.
g. Check antiembolic stockings.
h. Promote client dignity.
i. Perform special procedures.
j. Safeguard client valuables.
k. Administer preoperative medications.
27. **a.** 2
b. 3
c. 4
d. 1
28. d
29. a
30. **a.** Sphygmomanometer, stethoscope, and thermometer
b. Emesis basin
c. Clean gown
d. Washcloth, towel, and facial tissues
e. Intravenous pole
f. Suction equipment
g. Oxygen equipment
h. Extra pillows for positioning the client comfortably
i. Bed pads to protect bed linen from drainage
31. **a.** 1,3
b. 1,2
c. 1,2,3
d. 1
e. 1,3
f. 2
32. c
33. b
34. d
35. d
36. c
37. d
38. d
39. **a.** Respiratory rate
b. Respiratory rhythm
c. Depth of ventilation
d. Symmetry of chest wall movement
e. Breath sounds
f. Color of mucous membranes
40. **a.** Aspiration of emesis
b. Accumulation of mucous secretions in the pharynx
c. Swelling or spasm of the larynx
41. c
42. True
43. a
44. **a.** Nail bed and skin color
b. Peripheral pulses
c. Blood pressure

45.

Area of assessment	Characteristic finding
Blood pressure	Decreased
Heart rate	Increased
Respiratory rate	Increased
Pulse volume	Weak, thready

Area of assessment	Characteristic finding
Skin	Cool, clammy, pale
Client behavior	Restless

46. d
47. b
48. False
49. c
50. b
51. By noting the number of saturated gauze sponges; drawing a circle around the outer perimeter of the drainage
52. True
53. c
54. False
55. True
56. d
57. b
58. **a.** Physician's office phone number
b. Surgery center's phone number
c. Follow-up appointment, date, and time
d. Review of prescribed medications
e. Guidelines related to specific surgery (for example, activity restrictions)
f. Warning signs of complications
59. **a.** Vital signs stable
b. Body temperature controlled
c. Good ventilatory function
d. Orientation to surroundings
e. Absence of complications
f. Minimal pain and nausea
g. Controlled wound drainage
h. Adequate urine output
i. Fluid-electrolyte balance
60. Obtain a complete set of vital signs and compare to those obtained in the recovery room
61. False
62. Any four:
- Gaining a return of normal physiological function
- Remaining free of postoperative surgical wound infection
- Achieving rest and comfort
- Maintaining self-concept
- Returning to a functional state of health within limitations posed by surgery

63. c
64. Three interventions for each area:

Area of need	Nursing interventions
Maintaining respiratory function	Encourage diaphragmatic breathing and coughing at least every 2 hr
	Instruct client to use incentive spirometer
	Encourage early ambulation
	Turn every 1-2 hr
	Provide orotracheal or nasotracheal suction if indicated
Preventing circulatory stasis	Encourage performance of leg exercises at least every hour while awake
	Apply elastic antiembolism hose as ordered
	Encourage early ambulation
	Avoid positioning with pressure on popliteal vessels, or sitting with legs crossed
	Elevate legs on footstool when out of bed in chair
	Give anticoagulants as ordered
	Provide adequate fluid intake
Promoting normal bowel elimination	Assess return of peristalsis
	Maintain gradual progression in dietary intake
	Promote ambulation and exercise
	Maintain adequate fluid intake
	Administer cathartics, laxatives, enemas, suppositories, and rectal tubes as ordered
Promoting adequate nutrition	Remove sources of noxious odors
	Assist to a comfortable position during meals
	Provide small servings of food
	Provide frequent oral hygiene
	Provide meals when client is rested and pain free
Promoting normal urinary elimination	Assist to normal positions during voiding
	Check frequently for need to void
	Assess for bladder distention; obtain catheterization order if needed
	Monitor intake and output

65. b
66. c
67. c
68. Any five:
- Provide privacy during dressing changes or inspection of the wound.
- Maintain client's hygiene.
- Prevent drainage sets from overflowing.
- Maintain a pleasant environment.
- Offer opportunities for client to discuss feelings about appearance.
- Provide family with opportunities to discuss ways to promote the client's self-concept.

CHAPTER 47

1. **a.** 3
b. 6
c. 9
d. 2
e. 14
f. 15
g. 4
h. 10
i. 1
j. 8
k. 5
l. 11
m. 7
n. 12
o. 13
i. 1
j. 8
k. 5
l. 11

m. 7
n. 12
o. 13

2. a
3. d
4. **a.** Inflammatory phase
   b. Destructive phase
   c. Proliferative phase
   d. Maturation phase
5. b
6. Any four:
   - Protein: collagen formation
   - Vitamin C: synethesis of collagen
   - Vitamin A: reduces negative effects of steroids
   - Zinc: epithelialization, collagen synthesis
   - Copper: collagen fiber linking
7. Hematoma
8. a
9. b
10. Any four:
    - Fever
    - Tenderness and pain at the wound site
    - Elevated white blood cell count
    - Wound edges inflamed
    - Purulent, odorous drainage
11. b
12. Place sterile towels soaked in sterile saline over the extruding tissues, stay with client, monitor vital signs, and call physician immediately.
13. Fistula
14. c
15. **a.** Bleeding
    b. Contamination or presence of foreign bodies
    c. Size
16. d
17. **a.** If there is a written order to do so
    b. If a serious complication is suspected
18. **a.** Alters all phases of the wound healing process; impaired circulation to wound; reduces synthesis of clotting factors; depresses inflammatory response; reduces formation of antibodies and lymphocytes; collagen tissue less pliable
    b. Lacks adequate blood supply to resist bacterial infection or deliver nutrients and cellular elements for healing
    c. Reduces amount of functional hemoglobin, decreasing tissue oxygenation; may increase platelet aggregation and cause hypercoagulability; interferes with normal cellular mechanisms that promote release of oxygen to tissues
    d. Reduce inflammatory response and slow collagen synthesis; suppress protein synthesis, wound contraction, epithelialization, and inflammation
    e. Increase risk of superinfection
    f. Impairs tissue perfusion; causes hemoglobin to have greater affinity for oxygen so it fails to release oxygen to the tissues; alters phagocytosis of the leukocytes, supports overgrowth of fungal and yeast infection
    g. Tissues become fragile and poorly oxygenated because of fibrosis and vascular scarring in irradiated skin layers
19. **a.** Appearance
    b. Presence of drainage
    c. Presence of drains
    d. Wound closure
    e. Pain
    f. Cultures
20. d
21. **a.** Purulent
    b. Serous
    c. Serosanguineous
    d. Sanguineous
22. True
23. Aerobic: use a sterile swab from a Culturette tube, gently swabbing wound to collect deeper secretions; return swab to Culturette tube and activate inner ampule containing the medium for organism growth.
    Anaerobic: use a syringe without a needle; gently place syringe tip in the inner wound and aspirate; on removal apply a sterile needle, expel air from syringe and needle, and inject into special vacuum container or cork the needle.
24. Any six:
    - Promoting wound hemostasis
    - Preventing infection
    - Preventing further tissue injury
    - Promoting wound healing
    - Maintaining skin integrity
    - Regaining normal function
    - Gaining comfort
25. **a.** Stabilizing cardiopulmonary function
    b. Promoting hemostasis
    c. Cleansing the wound
    d. Protecting the wound from further injury
26. a
27. d
28. Any six:
    - Protect a wound from microorganism contamination
    - Aid in hemostasis
    - Promote healing by absorbing drainage and debriding a wound
    - Support or splint the wound site
    - Protect the client from seeing the wound
    - Promote thermal insulation to the wound surface
    - Provide maintenance of high humidity between the wound and dressing
29. **a.** Contact or primary dressing: covers the incision and part of the adjacent skin
    b. Absorbent dressing: serves as a reservoir for additional secretions
    c. Outer protective layer: helps prevent bacteria and other external contaminants from reaching the wound surface; supports or immobilizes to minimize movement of underlying incision and injured tissues; insulates and keeps wound surface well hydrated
30. c
31. d
32. The nurse may add dressings without removing the original one.
33. **a.** Nurse should perform thorough hand washing before and after wound care.
    b. Personnel should not touch an open or fresh wound directly without wearing sterile gloves.
    c. If a wound is sealed, dressings may be changed without gloves.
    d. Dressings over closed wounds should be removed or changed when they become wet or if the client has signs or symptoms of infection.

34. **a.** Administer required analgesics so that peak effects occur during the dressing change.
b. Describe steps of the procedure to lessen anxiety.
c. Describe normal signs of healing.
d. Answer questions about the procedure or wound.
35. b
36. a
37. d
38. **a.** Clean wound.
b. Apply heat.
c. Apply medications.
39. True
40. d
41. True
42. Sutures
43. A portable unit that connects to tubular drains lying within a wound bed and exerts a safe, constant, low-pressure vacuum to remove and collect drainage (for example, Hemovac, Jackson-Pratt)
44. Any five:
- Create pressure over a body part
- Immobilize a body part
- Support a wound
- Reduce or prevent edema
- Secure a splint
- Secure a dressing

45. **a.** Inspect the skin for abrasions, edema, discoloration, or exposed wound edges
b. Cover exposed wounds or open abrasions with a sterile dressing
c. Assess the condition of underlying dressings and change them if soiled
d. Assess the skin of underlying body parts and parts that will be distal to the bandage for signs of circulatory impairment
46. True
47. b
48 **a.** H
b. C
c. H
d. C
e. H
f. C
49. Any five:
- Very young or very old
- Open wounds, broken skin, stomas
- Areas of edema or scar formation
- Peripheral vascular disease, diabetes, arteriosclerosis
- Confusion or unconsciousness
- Spinal cord injury
- Abscessed tooth or appendix

50. **a.** Duration of application
b. Body part
c. Damage to body surface
d. Prior skin temperature
e. Body surface area
f. Age and physical condition
51. **a.** Presence of any contraindicating conditions
b. Client's response to assessment stimuli
c. Client's level of consciousness
d. Condition of equipment to be used
52. Three for each category:
Do's
- Explain sensations to be felt during the procedure
- Instruct client to report changes in sensation or discomfort immediately
- Provide a timer, clock, or watch so the client can help time the application
- Keep the call light within client reach
- Refer to the institution's policy and procedure manual for safe temperatures

Don't's
- Allow the client to adjust temperature settings
- Allow the client to move an application or place hands on the wound site
- Place the client in a position that prevents movement away from the temperature source
- Leave client unattended who is unable to sense temperature changes or move from the temperature source

53. True
54. c
55. d
56. **a.** Cold compress
b. Warm soak
c. Sitz bath
d. Heat lamp
57. **a.** 59° F (15° C)
b. 110° to 115° F (43° to 46° C)
c. 105° to 110° F (40.5° to 43° C)
d. 110° to 115° F (43° to 46° C)
58. a
59. False

CHAPTER 48

1. The ability to influence others toward accomplishment of a goal
2. Direction, coordination, and supervision of a group's activities
3. **a.** 5
b. 6
c. 2
d. 3
e. 7
f. 1
g. 4
4. **a.** Likert's system 4 management theory
b. Fiedler's leader match theory
c. Ohio State leadership studies
d. McGregor's theory X
e. Taylor's scientific management movement
5. a
6. a
7. c
8. d
9. **a.** Technical skills
b. Human skills
c. Conceptual skills
10. The formal leader is appointed by the organization and therefore is the manager. The informal leader does not have an official appointment within the organization but still influences the behavior of others.
11. b
12. a
13. **a.** Leader provides specific instructions and supervises task accomplishment.

b. Leader directs and closely supervises task accomplishment; leader also explains decisions, seeks suggestions, and supports progress.
c. Leader facilitates and supports the efforts of the subordinates toward task accomplishment; leader shares responsibility for decision making with employees.
d. Leader gives the responsibility for decision making and problem solving to surordinates.

14. All four categories, two behaviors for each category
 a. Skills of personal behavior
  - Sensitive to feelings of the group
  - Identifies self with the needs of the group
  - Listens attentively
  - Does not ridicule or criticize another's suggestions
  - Helps others feel important and needed
  - Does not argue
 b. Skills of communication
  - Makes sure everyone understands what is needed and the reason why
  - Establishes positive communication with the group as a routine part of the job
  - Recognizes that everyone's contributions are important
 c. Skills of organization
  - Develops long-range and short-range objectives
  - Breaks big problems into small ones
  - Shares responsibilities and opportunities
  - Plans, acts, follows up, and evaluates
  - Is attentive to details
 d. Skills of self-examination
  - Is aware of personal motivations
  - Is aware of group member's level of hostility so that appropriate countermeasures are taken
  - Helps the group be aware of their attitudes and values

CHAPTER 49

1. A process by which alterations occur within the behavior and function of an individual, family, group, or community
2. a. 2
 b. 3
 c. 4
 d. 1
3. Any six:
 - Conscious
 - Deliberate
 - Collaborative
 - Goal oriented
 - Improvement
 - Problem solving
 - Uses scientific knowledge
 - Purposeful
4. a. Rogers
 b. Lippitt
 c. Lewin
5.

Model of change	Characteristic concepts
Traditional	Change occurs by exposition, teaching, or promotion of ideas and accumulated knowledge
Confrontational	Change occurs by direct confrontation, challenge, or criticism Change agent must remain calm and objective
Elite corps	Change occurs when the people in charge use knowledge or power maneuvers
Systems	Need for change grows out of structural stress or dysfunction in some part of system Change agent defines or diagnoses dysfunction
Psychoanalytical	Change occurs through use of power and knowledge, but leader uses insight about self, others, and change process to institute change
Scholarly consultation	Change occurs when an expert or consultant uses scientific findings or information as a basis for proposing a solution
Developmental	Change is required to respond to discrepancies between potential growth and actual growth, development, or change Change agent defines and diagnoses conflict areas and strategies to promote growth and development

6. True
7. Any behavior that will inhibit or impede the movement toward change
8. Any seven:
 - Effort, time, or money investment
 - Threat to present values or norms
 - Skewed power relationship, loss of status or power
 - Fear of failure in the new situation
 - Anxiety or stress from loss of routine or security
 - Risk of losing the group's wholeness
 - Loss of the familiar pattern of behavior
 - Loss of familiar roles or status
 - Insufficient consideration to consequent problems
 - Lack of clear communication
9. Three for each step of the nursing process:
 a. Assessment
  - Collect information related to the client or organization.
  - Determine how people involved relate to one another.
  - Identify stressors.
  - Identify positive traits or qualities of the system.
  - Determine centers of resistance.
  - Establish the relationship between change, the change agent, and the client.
 b. Diagnosis
  - Formulate a clear definition of the problem.
 c. Planning (goal establishment)
  - State goals as desired outcomes.
  - Obtain input from all involved in determining short-term and long-term goals.
  - Devise methods for dealing with resistance.
  - Select a change agent to "sell" the change.
  - Plan specific interventions through collaboration with those involved.
 d. Intervention
  - Formulate a written outline of the steps in the change.

- Develop a time frame for the change process.
- If possible, institute a small "pilot" program.
- Open and maintain lines of communication.
- Use effective communication and interpersonal skills.
- Continue collaboration with client, family, or agency during the process.

e. Evaluation
- Examine outcomes to see if goals have been accomplished.
- Modify plan to meet established goals.
- Analyze positive and negative elements in the planned change and report these to the individuals involved in the change.
- Evaluate personal reactions to the change and modify personal behavior accordingly.

10. d

11. b

12. a. Is there a genuine desire to improve something?

b. Does the motivation arise from a personal desire for power or recognition (or is the change simply being done for the sake of change)?

c. Will there be an improvement as a result of the change?

13. Any four:
- How much experience has the change agent had with the particular problem?
- Does the nurse change agent have the credentials of an expert in the situation as defined by the key people involved in the problem?
- Will the personality of the change agent be conducive to promoting effective change? Can this person be the facilitator for change in this situation?
- Is the nurse change agent sensitive to what can or cannot be changed?
- What is the approach or orientation of the change agent? What model of change is used by the change agent?

14. The ability to influence, produce, control, or exert authority

15. a. Expert

b. Appointed

c. Managerial

d. Line

e. Elected

16. Any four:
- The project has support from the administrative level.
- Participants are actively involved in the process.
- Group decisions are reached by consensus.
- Provisions are made for immediate feedback.
- There are open and objective feelings and attitudes about testing revisions and reconsiderations.

17. a. Understand theories of and approaches to change.

b. Use the theory or approach that is most applicable to the situation.

c. Recognize and work with the normal reactions to changes.

d. Acknowledge and work with interference and resistance that are normally found during any change.

e. Use carefully and appropriately the level of power or influence that is personally and professionally available during the change process.

f. Use the principles of communication and interpersonal relationships with patience and skill.